Lecture Notes in Computer Science 15227

Founding Editors

Gerhard Goos
Juris Hartmanis

Editorial Board Members

Elisa Bertino, *Purdue University, West Lafayette, IN, USA*
Wen Gao, *Peking University, Beijing, China*
Bernhard Steffen, *TU Dortmund University, Dortmund, Germany*
Moti Yung, *Columbia University, New York, NY, USA*

The series Lecture Notes in Computer Science (LNCS), including its subseries Lecture Notes in Artificial Intelligence (LNAI) and Lecture Notes in Bioinformatics (LNBI), has established itself as a medium for the publication of new developments in computer science and information technology research, teaching, and education.

LNCS enjoys close cooperation with the computer science R & D community, the series counts many renowned academics among its volume editors and paper authors, and collaborates with prestigious societies. Its mission is to serve this international community by providing an invaluable service, mainly focused on the publication of conference and workshop proceedings and postproceedings. LNCS commenced publication in 1973.

Luigi Carro · Francesco Regazzoni ·
Christian Pilato
Editors

Embedded Computer Systems: Architectures, Modeling, and Simulation

24th International Conference, SAMOS 2024
Samos, Greece, June 29 – July 4, 2024
Proceedings, Part II

Editors
Luigi Carro
Federal University of Rio Grande do Sul
Porto Alegre, Rio Grande do Sul, Brazil

Francesco Regazzoni
University of Amsterdam
Amsterdam, The Netherlands

Christian Pilato
Polytechnic University of Milan
Milan, Italy

ISSN 0302-9743   ISSN 1611-3349 (electronic)
Lecture Notes in Computer Science
ISBN 978-3-031-78379-1   ISBN 978-3-031-78380-7 (eBook)
https://doi.org/10.1007/978-3-031-78380-7

© The Editor(s) (if applicable) and The Author(s), under exclusive license to Springer Nature Switzerland AG 2025

This work is subject to copyright. All rights are solely and exclusively licensed by the Publisher, whether the whole or part of the material is concerned, specifically the rights of translation, reprinting, reuse of illustrations, recitation, broadcasting, reproduction on microfilms or in any other physical way, and transmission or information storage and retrieval, electronic adaptation, computer software, or by similar or dissimilar methodology now known or hereafter developed.
The use of general descriptive names, registered names, trademarks, service marks, etc. in this publication does not imply, even in the absence of a specific statement, that such names are exempt from the relevant protective laws and regulations and therefore free for general use.
The publisher, the authors and the editors are safe to assume that the advice and information in this book are believed to be true and accurate at the date of publication. Neither the publisher nor the authors or the editors give a warranty, expressed or implied, with respect to the material contained herein or for any errors or omissions that may have been made. The publisher remains neutral with regard to jurisdictional claims in published maps and institutional affiliations.

This Springer imprint is published by the registered company Springer Nature Switzerland AG
The registered company address is: Gewerbestrasse 11, 6330 Cham, Switzerland

If disposing of this product, please recycle the paper.

Preface

SAMOS is a conference with a unique format. It brings together every year researchers from both academia and industry on the topic of embedded systems in the perfect setting of Samos island. The SAMOS 2024 keynotes covered a wide range of topics including embedded systems design aspects by Alberto Sangiovanni-Vincentelli (UC Berkeley, USA) and bioinspired techniques for autonomous robots by Theocharis Theocharides (University of Cyprus, Cyprus). A specific focus was been put on security through tutorials by Apostolos Fournaris (Industrial Systems Institute, Greece) and Francesco Regazzoni (Amsterdam University, The Netherlands).

The SAMOS 2024 proceedings comprise a selection of publications targeting either systems themselves - through their applications, architectures, and underlying processors - or methods created to automate their design. A total of 57 papers were submitted to the general track and 24 papers were selected by the program committee to be presented at the conference (42% Acceptance rate). Two special sessions were introduced in the program to respectively gather novel work on security and to report recent results of European projects. Finally, a poster session was organized to provide young researchers a chance to receive high-quality feedback from distinguished researchers from both academia and industry.

The SAMOS 2024 committee wants to acknowledge the generous support of the many reviewers who contributed to the quality of these proceedings. We hope that you enjoy reading them!

July 2024

Luigi Carro
Francesco Regazzoni
Christian Pilato

Organization

General Chair

Luigi Carro — Instituto de Informática UFRGS, Brazil

Program Chairs

Francesco Regazzoni — Università della Svizzera italiana, Switzerland and University of Amsterdam, The Netherlands
Christian Pilato — Politecnico di Milano, Italy

Special Session Chairs

Innovative Architectures and Tools for Security

Apostolos Fournaris — Industrial Systems Institute, Greece

Reports from European Research Projects

Giovanni Agosta — Politecnico di Milano, Italy
Dimitrios Soudris — NTUA, Greece

Poster Session

Carlo Galuzzi — TU Delft, The Netherlands
Georgi N. Gaydadjiev — TU Delft, The Netherlands

Tutorial Chairs

Apostolos Fournaris — Industrial Systems Institute, Greece
Francesco Regazzoni — Università della Svizzera italiana, Switzerland and University of Amsterdam, The Netherlands

Web Chair

Tom Slooff — Università della Svizzera italiana, Switzerland

Proceedings and Finance Chair

Carlo Galuzzi — TU Delft, The Netherlands

Submission Chair

Andy D. Pimentel — University of Amsterdam, The Netherlands

Publicity Chair

Rubén Salvador — CentraleSupélec, IRISA, Inria, France

Steering Committee

Shuvra Bhattacharyya	University of Maryland, College Park, USA and IETR, France
Holger Blume	Leibniz Universität Hannover, Germany
Ed F. Deprettere	Leiden University, The Netherlands
Nikitas Dimopoulos	University of Victoria, Canada
Carlo Galuzzi	Delft University of Technology, The Netherlands
Georgi N. Gaydadjiev	TU Delft, The Netherlands
John Glossner	Optimum Semiconductor Technologies, USA
Walid Najjar	University of California Riverside, USA
Andy D. Pimentel	University of Amsterdam, The Netherlands
Olli Silvén	University of Oulu, Finland
Dimitrios Soudris	NTUA, Greece
Jarmo Takala	Tampere University of Technology, Finland
Stephan Wong	TU Delft, The Netherlands

Program Committee

Giovanni Agosta	Politecnico Di Milano, Italy
Shuvra Bhattacharyya	University of Maryland, USA
Holger Blume	Leibniz Universität Hannover, Germany
Jeronimo Castrillon	TU Dresden, Germany

Ricardo Chaves	INESC-ID, Portugal
Francesco Conti	UniBo, Italy
Serena Curzel	Politecnico Di Milano, Italy
Karol Desnos	INSA Rennes, France
Vassilios V. Dimakopoulos	University of Ioannina, Greece
Giorgos Dimitrakopoulos	Democritus University of Thrace, Greece
Holger Flatt	Fraunhofer IOSB, Germany
Apostolos Fournaris	Industrial Systems Institute, Greece
Carlo Galuzzi	Delft University of Technology, The Netherlands
Georgi N. Gaydadjiev	Delft University of Technology, The Netherlands
Andreas Gerstlauer	University of Texas at Austin, USA
John Glossner	Rivier University, USA
Diana Göhringer	TU Dresden, Germany
Xinfei Guo	Shanghai Jiao Tong University, China
Said Hamdioui	TU Delft, Netherlands
Frank Hannig	Friedrich Alexander University, Germany
Christian Haubelt	University of Rostock, Germany
Jasmin Jahić	University of Cambridge, UK
Matthias Jung	University of Würzburg and Fraunhofer IESE, Germany
Pekka Jääskeläinen	Tampere University of Technology, Finland
Christoforos Kachris	InAccel, Greece
Georgios Keramidas	Aristotle University of Thessaloniki, Greece
Leonidas Kosmidis	BSC, Spain
Angeliki Kritikakou	Inria - Irisa, France
John McAllister	Queen's University Belfast, UK
Paolo Meloni	Università degli Studi di Cagliari, Italy
Alexandre Mercat	Tampere University of Technology, Finland
Chrysostomos Nicopoulos	University of Cyprus, Cyprus
Alex Orailoglu	UC San Diego, USA
Andrés Otero	Universidad Politécnica de Madrid, Spain
Anuj Pathania	University of Amsterdam, The Netherlands
Maxime Pelcat	INSA Rennes, France
Christian Pilato	Politecnico di Milano, Italy
Andy Pimentel	University of Amsterdam, Netherlands
Oscar Plata	University of Málaga, Spain
Dionisios Pnevmatikatos	NTUA, Greece
Francesco Regazzoni	University of Amsterdam, Netherlands
Marc Reichenbach	Universität Rostock, Germany
Ruben Salvador	CentraleSupélec, IETR, France
Cristina Silvano	Politecnico di Milano, Italy
Dimitrios Soudris	NTUA, Greece

Ioannis Sourdis — Chalmers University of Technology, Sweden
Leonel Sousa — Universidade de Lisboa, Portugal
Todor Stefanov — Leiden University, Netherlands
Christos Strydis — Erasmus MC and Delft University of Technology, Netherlands
Jarmo Takala — Tampere University of Technology, Finland
Mottaqiallah Taouil — TU Delft, Netherlands
George Theodoridis — University of Patras, Greece
Pedro Trancoso — Chalmers University of Technology, Sweden
Stavros Tripakis — Northeastern University, USA
Carlos Valderrama — University of Mons, Belgium
Alexander V. Veidenbaum — University of California, Irvine, USA
Stephan Wong — TU Delft, Netherlands
Roger Woods — Queen's University Belfast, UK
Sotirios Xydis — NTUA, Greece
Lilia Zaourar — CEA Saclay, France

Secondary Reviewers

Abdullah Aljuffri
Ahmad Othman
Ahmed Kamaleldin
Andrej Friesen
Anish Govind
Antti Rautakoura
Benjamin Beichler
Christoph Niemann
Cornelia Wulf
Daniel Pacheco
Emanuel Trabes
Ensieh Aliagha
Fabian Kummer
Federico Reghenzani
Florian Grützmacher
Folkert de Ronde
Fouwad Mir
Ilias Papalamprou

J. L. F. Betting
Joonas Multanen
José Brito
Kari Hepola
Leandro Fiorin
Leon (Xuanang) Li
Mahdi Zahedi
Manolis Katsaragakis
Mateo Vázquez Maceiras
Matthew Barondeau
Max Engelen
Mihir Kekkar
Mohammad Ali Maleki
Ruben Afonso
Shrihari Gokulachandran
Sotirios Panagiotou
Tiago Rodrigues

Contents – Part II

Poster Session

A Logic-Based Physical Simulation Framework for Digital Microfluidic Biochips 1
   Joel August Vest Madsen, Carl Alexander Jackson, Alexander Marc Collignon, Jan Madsen, and Luca Pezzarossa

A Parallel Synchronous Execution Engine and Target Language for Digital Microfluidics 17
   Luca Pezzarossa, Georgi Tanev, Winnie Edith Svendsen, and Jan Madsen

QCEDA: Using Quantum Computers for EDA 32
   Matthias Jung, Sven O. Krumke, Christof Schroth, Elisabeth Lobe, and Wolfgang Mauerer

Real-Time Linux on RISC-V: Long-Term Performance Analysis of PREEMPT_RT Patches 47
   Tobias Schaffner, Jan Altenberg, and Stefan Wallentowitz

RV-VP^2: Unlocking the Potential of RISC-V Packed-SIMD for Embedded Processing 59
   Muhammad Ali, Ensieh Aliagha, Mahmoud Elnashar, and Diana Göhringer

A Novel System Simulation Framework for HBM2 FPGA Platforms 72
   Hector Gerardo Muñoz Hernandez, Veronia Iskandar, Lukas Steiner, Philipp Holzinger, Matthias Jung, Diana Göhringer, Michael Hübner, Norbert Wehn, and Marc Reichenbach

ONNX-To-Hardware Design Flow for Adaptive Neural-Network Inference on FPGAs 85
   Federico Manca, Francesco Ratto, and Francesca Palumbo

Efficient Post-training Augmentation for Adaptive Inference in Heterogeneous and Distributed IoT Environments 99
   Max Sponner, Lorenzo Servadei, Bernd Waschneck, Robert Wille, and Akash Kumar

Pooling On-the-Go for NoC-Based Convolutional Neural Network
Accelerator 109
    Wenyao Zhu, Yizhi Chen, and Zhonghai Lu

Vitamin-V: Serverless Cloud Computing Porting on RISC-V 119
    Thrasyvoulos Iliadis, Nikolaos C. Papadopoulos, Kostantinos Nikas,
    and Dionisios Pnevmatikatos

Design and Implementation of an Open Source OpenGL SC 2.0.1
Installable Client Driver and Offline Compiler 127
    Matina Maria Trompouki, Marc Solé Bonet, Josué Pedrajas Pérez,
    and Leonidas Kosmidis

Special Session on Security

Plan Your Defense: A Comparative Analysis of Leakage Detection
Methods on RISC-V Cores 139
    Konstantina Miteloudi, Asmita Adhikary, Niels van Drueten,
    Lejla Batina, and Ileana Buhan

iVault: Architectural Code Concealing Techniques to Protect
Cryptographic Keys 152
    George Christou, Giorgos Vasiliadis, Apostolis Zarras,
    and Sotiris Ioannidis

I2DS: FPGA-Based Deep Learning Industrial Intrusion Detection System 165
    Ioannis Morianos, Konstantinos Georgopoulos, Andreas Brokalakis,
    Thomas Kyriakakis, and Sotiris Ioannidis

**Special Session on European Projects: Actions Towards Security,
Digital Rights, and Crime Investigation in the Cyberspace**

ACRA: A Cutting-Edge Analytics Platform for Advanced Real-Time
Corruption Risk Assessment and Investigation Prioritization 179
    Nikolaos Peppes, Emmanouil Daskalakis, Theodoros Alexakis,
    and Evgenia Adamopoulou

Post Quantum Cryptography Research Lines in the Italian Center
for Security and Rights in Cyberspace 191
    Alessandro Barenghi and Gerardo Pelosi

Advancing Future 5G/B5G Systems: The Int5Gent Approach 203
  *Evrydiki Kyriazi, Panagiotis Toumasis, Alexandros Valadasis,
  Georgios P. Katsikas, Ilias Papalamprou, Ioannis Stratakos,
  George Lentaris, Giannis Giannoulis, Dimitris Apostolopoulos,
  Dimitrios Soudris, and Hercules Avramopoulos*

RISC-V Accelerators, Enablement and Applications for Automotive
and Smart Home in the ISOLDE Project 215
  *Cătălin Bogdan Ciobanu, Honorius Gâlmeanu, Alexandru Puşcaşu,
  Mihai Gologanu, Octavian Buiu, Mihai Antonescu,
  Vlad-Gabriel Serbu, Vasile-Mădălin Moise, Cristian-Tiberius Axinte,
  Alexandru-Tudor Popovici, George-Iulian Uleru, Andrei Stan,
  Mihai Munteanu, Alexandru Drîmbărean, Csaba Nemeti, Dănuţ Rotar,
  Daniel Grosu, Cosmin Moisă, Bogdan Ditu, Petre Cristian Trusca,
  Marius Antache, Simona Costinescu, Mari-Anais Sachian,
  George Suciu, Cristian Gheorghe, Cristina Tudor, and Kejsi Koci*

PMDI: An AI-Enabled Ecosystem for Cooperative Urban Mobility 231
  *William Fornaciari, Giovanni Agosta, Massimo Fioravanti,
  Paolo Giuseppetti, Alessandro Solinas, Luigi Gallo, Manuel Pernigotto,
  Mario Pedol, Francesco Pro, Irene Amerini, Lorenzo Papa,
  Luca Maiano, Giovanni Trovini, Mauro Di Giamberardino,
  and Paolo Satta*

Open Source Software Randomisation Framework for Probabilistic
WCET Prediction on Multicore CPUs, GPUs and Accelerators 247
  *Leonidas Kosmidis, Matina Maria Trompouki, Pau López Castillón,
  Eric Rufart Blasco, Javier Fernandez Salgado, and Andreas Jung*

A Hypervisor Based Platform for the Development and Verification
of Reliable Software Applications 261
  *N. Petrellis, M. Mavropoulos, V. Kelefouras, G. Keramidas,
  K. Radonjic, and N. Voros*

Author Index 277

Contents – Part I

FAA+RTS: Designing Fault-Aware Adaptive Real-Time Systems —From Specification to Execution— 1
   Lukas Miedema, Dolly Sapra, Petr Novobilsky, Sebastian Altmeyer, Clemens Grelck, and Andy D. Pimentel

Experimental Assessment and Biaffine Modeling of the Impact of Ambient Temperature on SoC Power Requirements 18
   Kameswar Rao Vaddina, Florian Brandner, Gérard Memmi, and Pierre Jouvelot

EPIC-Q: Equivalent-Policy Invariant Comparison Enhanced Transfer Q-learning for Run-Time SoC Performance-Power Optimization 34
   Anmol Surhonne, Haitham S. Fawzi, Florian Maurer, Oliver Lenke, Michael Meidinger, Thomas Wild, and Andreas Herkersdorf

Accelerating Depthwise Separable Convolutions on Ultra-Low-Power Devices 46
   Francesco Daghero, Alessio Burrello, Massimo Poncino, Enrico Macii, and Daniele Jahier Pagliari

It's All About PR: Smart Benchmarking AI Accelerators Using Performance Representatives 59
   Alexander Louis-Ferdinand Jung, Jannik Steinmetz, Jonathan Gietz, Konstantin Lübeck, and Oliver Bringmann

Travel Time-Based Task Mapping for NoC-Based DNN Accelerator 76
   Yizhi Chen, Wenyao Zhu, and Zhonghai Lu

HW-EPOLL: Hardware-Assisted User Space Event Notification for Epoll Syscall 93
   Lars Nolte, Tim Twardzik, Camille Jalier, Jiyuan Shi, Thomas Wild, and Andreas Herkersdorf

SIZALIZER: Multilevel Analysis Framework for Object Size Optimization 108
   Andreas Hager-Clukas, Jonathan Schröter, and Stefan Wallentowitz

SafeFloatZone: Identify Safe Domains for Elementary Functions 122
   Markus Krahl, Matthias Güdemann, and Stefan Wallentowitz

Radar Object Detection on a Vector Processor Using Sparse Convolutional
Neural Networks 138
    Daniel Köhler, Frank Meinl, and Holger Blume

Optimizing QAM Demodulation with NEON SIMD and Algorithmic
Approximation Techniques 155
    Ilias Papalamprou, Giorgos Armeniakos, Ioannis Stratakos,
    George Lentaris, and Dimitrios Soudris

A Novel Chaining-Based Indirect Addressing Mode in a Vertical Vector
Processor 167
    Sven Gesper, Daniel Köhler, Gia Bao Thieu, Jasper Homann,
    Frank Meinl, Holger Blume, and Guillermo Payá-Vayá

AutoSync Framework for Expressing Synchronization Intentions
in Multithreaded Programs 183
    Jasmin Jahić and Matheus Bortoloti

HyRPF: Hybrid RRAM Prototyping on FPGA 199
    Daniel Reiser, Johannes Knödtel, Liliia Almeeva, Jianan Wen,
    Andrea Baroni, Miloš Krstić, and Marc Reichenbach

GLoRia: An Energy-Efficient GPU-RRAM System Stack for Large
Neural Networks 216
    Rafael Fão de Moura, Michael Jordan, and Luigi Carro

Evaluating the Impact of Racetrack Memory Misalignment Faults
on BNNs Performance 230
    Leonard David Bereholschi, Mikail Yayla, Jian-Jia Chen,
    Kuan-Hsun Chen, and Asif Ali Khan

NanoSoftController: A Minimal Soft Processor for System State Control
in FPGA Systems 246
    Moritz Weißbrich, Germain Seidlitz, and Guillermo Payá-Vayá

Author Index 263

A Logic-Based Physical Simulation Framework for Digital Microfluidic Biochips

Joel August Vest Madsen, Carl Alexander Jackson, Alexander Marc Collignon, Jan Madsen, and Luca Pezzarossa

Department of Applied Mathematics and Computer Science, Technical University of Denmark, Kgs. Lyngby, Denmark
{s194580,s194585,s194605}@student.dtu.dk, {jama,lpez}@dtu.dk

Abstract. Digital microfluidic biochips provide a controlled and miniaturized environment to carry out biochemical protocols in an automated fashion. Software-based simulators are essential tools that aid the design of such protocols by enabling users to verify correct execution before targeting the physical biochip. To produce a simulation that is faithful to reality, the fluidic behavior of the droplets and their interaction with the driving electrodes must be taken into account. This paper presents a framework for simulating DMF biochips in a resource-constrained web-based environment. The framework is based on a novel droplet model that uses logic-based calculations to capture fluidic behavior. Thus, enabling to faithfully simulate the movement, merging, and splitting of arbitrary-shaped droplets with a low-computational footprint. The simulation framework also includes modular component models to capture the behavior of sensors and actuators, an event-driven simulation engine, and a graphical user interface. The framework is implemented as a client-side web application and runs in a browser. The evaluation carried out using artificial and real-life test cases shows that the framework can deliver real-time simulations with a high level of fidelity.

Keywords: Digital microfluidics biochips · Simulation framework · Logic-based simulation · Web application

1 Introduction

Digital microfluidic (DMF) biochips exploit the electrowetting on dielectric (EWOD) effect [5] to manipulate microliter-sized droplets on a planar surface patterned with driving electrodes. The droplets serve as vehicles and reaction chambers, which can be moved, mixed, merged, and split to carry out the steps of biochemical protocols in an automated fashion without the need for manual pipetting. Sensors (color, pH, impedance, etc.) and actuators (heating, cooling, magnetic field, etc.) can also be integrated into the DMF biochip to measure or modify the physical and biochemical parameters of the liquid analytes contained in the droplets [9]. This technology has the potential to automate and miniaturize the current wet lab processes by providing a controlled environment to execute biochemical protocols.

To test the protocol execution without risks or resource loss before targeting the physical biochip, simulation environments can be used to verify that the control sequences used to drive the movement of the droplets produce the expected results. In simulations, droplets are usually represented as circles located on top of the active electrodes, and predefined animations for merge and split operations are triggered when two droplets come close to each other. However, the physical behavior of real droplets in a DMF biochip is much more complex, and various shaped droplets can be observed. Figure 1 shows a selection of real droplets with complex shapes: round, I-shaped, L-shaped, and deformed droplets during a split operation. To include these complex shapes and produce a simulation that is faithful to the observed reality, the fluidic behavior of the droplets should be taken into account.

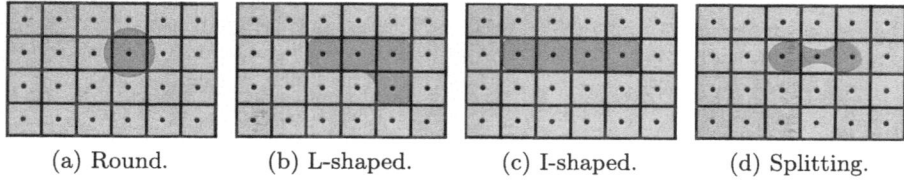

(a) Round.   (b) L-shaped.   (c) I-shaped.   (d) Splitting.

Fig. 1. A selection of macro pictures of droplets with complex shapes taken on a physical DMF biochip.

In general, simulation tools are provided as standalone applications. A web-based solution running in a browser on the client side offers significant advantages by eliminating the need for installation, thereby increasing accessibility and appeal for a large number of researchers and professionals. This approach can simplify deployment and usage, making it easier for users to quickly start simulations without the hassle of software setup, ensuring that more individuals can benefit from the tool's capabilities regardless of their technical background.

However, web-based applications are often resource-constrained since they do not have access to the same computational resources as a standalone application. This introduces a trade-off between simulation fidelity (i.e. the degree to which the simulation replicates reality) and execution time. When aiming for real-time simulations, the realistic fluidic behavior of the droplets is omitted due to the complexity of the fluid dynamic models.

This paper addresses this trade-off challenge by presenting a logic-based framework for simulating the physical behavior of DMF biochips in a resource-constrained web-based environment. The framework consists of a novel lightweight model for capturing the behavior of the liquid droplets, a set of flexible and interchangeable models for the biochip components, a simulation engine, and a graphical user interface (GUI). The droplet model is based upon simple logical calculations to simulate fluidic behavior without utilizing advanced fluid dynamic models and is able to capture the interaction between the controlling electrodes and liquids. Thus, it can precisely simulate the movement, merging, and splitting of arbitrary-shaped droplets. The biochip component models, which capture the behavior of sensors and actuators, are also based on logical calculations and are constructed to be modular allowing for easy modifications and further expansion. The simulation engine is event-driven and uses the models to compute the droplet and component behavior over a set of discrete time steps. Finally, the GUI visually presents the simulation data and offers control options to the user.

The simulation framework is developed to run as a client-side web application in a browser and it is implemented using the Blazor framework. The simulation framework is evaluated using a selection of artificial and real-life experiments. Fidelity is evaluated by comparing the simulated behavior against the one observed on the physical DMF biochip. Results show that the framework is able to run real-time simulations in a web-based resource-constrained environment with a high level of fidelity.

The rest of this paper is structured in 5 sections. Section 2 provides a summary of the most important related works. Section 3 presents the logic-based model developed to capture the physical behavior of the droplets. Section 4 describes the structure of the simulator. Section 5 presents the experimental evaluation of the proposed solution and discusses the results. Finally, Sect. 6 concludes the paper.

2 Related Work

Different approaches can be applied when simulating DMF biochips and droplet behavior, resulting in different specialized tools.

A complete simulator for biochemical reactions and DMF biochips, named Kaemika, is presented in [1]. Kaemika is available as a stand-alone application and is based on deterministic and stochastic simulation for the reactions. It also includes a liquid-handling protocol sub-language that is compiled into a virtual DMF device to allow the simulation of droplets moving on the biochip surface. The tool offers a GUI where the movement, merging, and splitting of the droplets are handled by animations. This is the most similar tool to the one presented in this work.

A simulation framework with similar characteristics to the one presented in this paper, but targeting continuous-flow microfluidics, can be found in [3]. The authors use a one-dimensional model analogous to the one used for electrical circuits to compute the paths of droplets through the channels network, the flow changes caused by the moving droplets, and the droplets' velocity.

A different approach for simulating the fluidic behavior of the droplets can be found in commercial tools such as FLOW-3D[1] and COMSOL[2]. These tools

---
[1] FLOW-3D website: https://www.flow3d.com/.
[2] COSMOL website: https://www.comsol.com/.

apply finite element analysis and partial differential equations solvers to carry out multi-physics simulations. Thus supporting fluid dynamics behavior even including the interaction with the electric field to simulate EWOD effects. These tools are very precise in capturing the fluidic behavior of the droplets when subjected to an electric field but are computationally heavy and they do not support full simulation of a DMF biochip.

A similar approach based upon precise fluid dynamics models is used in the work presented in [4], which is a very specialized simulator for DMF-based manipulation processes of a single micro-particle with a liquid droplet.

The Munich Microfluidics Toolkit (MMFT) is a collection of design automation and simulation tools to aid the design and testing of microfluidic devices. The MMFT Simulator [2] supports various levels of abstraction, providing both rapid simulations for quick validation and detailed simulations for more complex analyses. However, this tool targets continuous-flow microfluidic systems, only enabling precise fluidic simulation in microchannels.

The work presented in [6,7] outlines general techniques for designing DMF biochips as well as the basic principles upon which a simulation can be carried out. The work shows simulations of the presented ideas but does not provide a complete simulation framework.

The works presented in [8,12] investigate and implement preliminary ideas for a simulator consisting of a GUI and an event-driven engine. The simulator runs as a client-side web application, but fluidic droplet behavior is not taken into account, and droplets are only represented as circles on top of the activated electrode.

Our work offers a comprehensive DMF biochip simulation that accurately models the fluidic behavior of droplets in various shapes. Our simulator stands out due to its low computational footprint and modular design, allowing it to efficiently handle complex fluidic behaviors while maintaining flexibility for easy modifications and extensions.

3 The Droplet Model

Droplets are the key elements to be simulated in a DMF biochip. Their behavior can be built upon two basic operations: elongation and contraction. These operations model the physical effects on the droplet fluid generated by the electric potential variation in the underlying electrodes. Figures 2a and 2b show the movement of a droplet consisting of an elongation followed by a contraction. Merging and splitting of droplets can also be decomposed as a sequence of elongations and contractions, as shown in Figs. 2c and 2d. Thus, by capturing these two operations, a model can be used to simulate any droplet behavior.

We developed a non-physical abstraction that captures the fluidic behavior of the droplets using a set of logic-based rules on elongation and contraction. To guarantee a high level of behavioral fidelity, we developed the model on a series of observations carried out on the physical biochip.

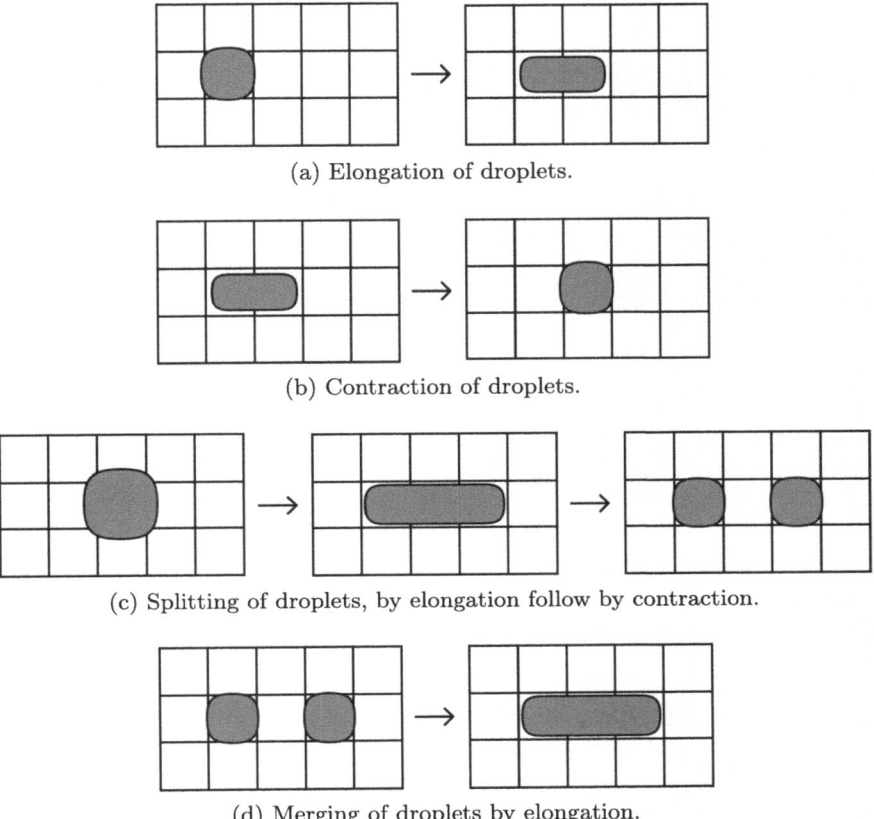

Fig. 2. Droplet behavior based on the elongation and contraction operations.

3.1 Group Abstraction

To capture a droplet behavior, we defined the abstraction to represent it as a group of multiple smaller circular sub-droplets, as shown in Fig. 3. To be considered a group, sub-droplets have to be located next to one another, in such a way, that any one droplet should be reachable by traversing the group from any droplet in that group. This abstraction allows for the creation of droplets in any shape and size since any one droplet is a set of many sub-droplets that can be arranged in any order. This abstraction does not use any complex fluid dynamic calculations, which is essential for execution in a resource-constrained environment.

3.2 Moving Droplets

As previously mentioned, the movement of a droplet consists of an elongation followed by a contraction. Since a droplet is represented by a group of smaller sub-droplets, elongation can be achieved by simply creating a new droplet within the existing group, while contraction can be achieved by removing an existing sub-droplet from the group. By first elongating and then contracting, the grouping of sub-droplets moves across the surface as observed in the physical DMF biochip. When creating or removing a sub-droplet, the total volume of the group is kept constant.

The elongation and contraction depend upon the state (electric potential) of the electrodes underlying the sub-droplets group. To ensure that the movement is realistic we have defined a set of rules for elongation and contraction. An elongation can only happen if:

1. The state of the electrode directly underneath a sub-droplet is on, *AND*
2. An electrode that is located as a direct (non-diagonal) neighbor to the sub-droplet changes state from off to on, *AND*
3. The volume of the individual sub-droplets in the droplet group is above a certain threshold, minimal volume.

A contraction can only happen if:

1. The droplet grouping is already elongated and every electrode directly underneath the surface area of the droplet grouping is in the state of on, *AND*
2. The state of one or multiple of said electrodes then changes state from on to off.

Besides modeling the movement of droplets, the elongation and contraction abstraction also supports shape-deformation into complex shapes, such as the ones shown in Fig. 3.

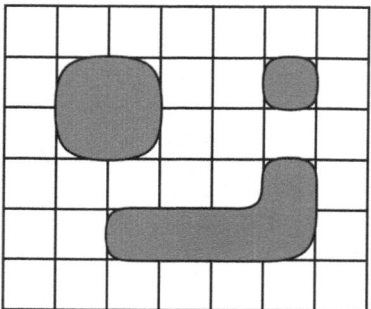
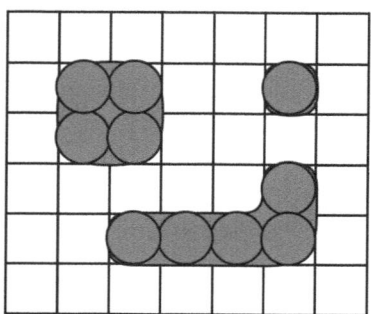

(a) Droplets as seen by the user.   (b) Sub-droplets displayed on top of the droplets.

Fig. 3. Droplets modeled as a group of sub-droplets.

3.3 Merging and Splitting Droplets

Modeling the merging and splitting of droplets using our group abstraction amounts to a specific resulting state while applying the elongation and contraction operations. A merge happens when an elongation results in the state where separate droplet groups are located directly beside one another. Thus, resulting in the unification of the groups which becomes a larger group with a combined volume. A split happens when an elongation followed by a contraction results in the state where part of the group is no longer reachable from any sub-droplet. Thus, becoming a separate group. The volume of the new group is based on the EWOD pull, the sizes of the electrodes, and the original droplet volume. This definition allows droplets to split into an arbitrary amount of droplets, as long as they follow the base principles of elongation and contraction.

Model Accuracy. The droplet model employed in our simulation framework is sufficient for capturing the essential droplet behaviors such as movement, merging, and splitting with a low computational footprint, which is particularly advantageous for fast simulations in resource-constrained web-based environments. More detailed models may be required for applications demanding higher accuracy in fluid dynamics interactions, such as simulation targeting continuous-flow devices or involving complex biochemical reactions. The trade-off between simulation accuracy and computational workload is a critical consideration, and while our model achieves a balance suitable for many practical scenarios (as demonstrated in Sect. 5), specific high-fidelity requirements might necessitate more complex models.

4 The Simulation Framework

The simulation framework covers the whole software-based simulation and it consists of three parts: the models, the simulation engine, and the GUI. These parts align with the model-view-controller pattern. The framework is constructed to be modular by segregating the three components, allowing each one to be replaced with a different implementation, as long as the communication interfaces are respected. The framework runs as a client-side web application using the Blazor framework and is implemented using a combination of C# and JavaScript. The simulation engine and the models are implemented using C#, while the GUI also uses JavaScript. The biochip layout is provided in JSON format, enabling the framework to support any biochip typology.

4.1 The Models

Models are the base of the simulation framework and are based on logical approximations of physical observations from the DMF biochip. Models are responsible for providing the rules and mathematical relations that capture the behavior of the droplets (as described in Sect. 3) and all the components of the DMF biochip. There are two types of components: actuators and sensors. Actuators include physical devices that are able to alter properties in the DMF biochip. For example, a heating module that can increase the temperature of droplets located on it, or the electrodes that can produce elongation and contraction of droplets. Sensors include devices that are able to measure specific properties of droplets. For example, a sensor measuring the droplet color and a sensor measuring the droplet temperature. The measurements from the sensors provide the ability to gather information from the simulation in real-time. The information can then be used to control the execution of the platform based on measurements of the physical parameters of the DMF biochip.

Models are used by the simulation engine, which determines their execution priority. All the models have a well-defined interface toward the simulation engine, enabling modularity and flexibility. Thus, enabling easy modification or addition of new models. The addition of new models only requires the implementation of the pre-defined model interface, which includes the core rules the model has to follow. These rules are executed by the simulation engine along with the other models.

4.2 The Simulation Engine

The core part of the framework is the simulation engine, which keeps track of the time and coordinates all model calls. The engine takes external commands as a primary input. A command is, for example, the act of turning on or off an electrode. These inputs are the same commands given to the real board. Based on the commands received in input, the engine chooses which models to execute and their execution order.

To improve the computation time of the simulator, we use an event-driven implementation. Thus, the models of components are only called when necessary. This means, for instance, that a command producing a change in one side of the biochip does not necessarily require models of components on the opposite side to be executed. Thus, reducing unnecessary computations. To implement this execution mechanism, all components can subscribe to specific commands or other components, and only be alerted when necessary. For example, droplets subscribe to electrodes. This means that if an electrode is turned on or off, nearby droplets are notified and their model is executed.

The order in which the models are executed may lead to different results of the simulation. Tests showed that the simulation is more faithful to reality if the models are executed breadth-first. For example, in the case where multiple droplets are present on the biochip and multiple models are subscribed to changes in each droplet, a breadth-first approach executes the first model of every droplet, followed by the second model of every droplet, and so on, until every model of every droplet has been executed. The breadth-first approach works by having a command activate the models of subscribed components, which then start executing their models. This creates a breadth-first cascade. When there are no more models to be executed, it means that all droplets and components that had a dependency on the command have been updated. The simulator is then ready to process the next command.

The simulation engine also manages time progression for those models that are dependent on time, such as models describing the temperature of droplets. The commands given as input to the simulator hold a timestamp at which they must be executed. If multiple commands hold the same time stamp, the breadth-first approach is used to allow to ensure correct execution. When executing a specific protocol on the DMF biochip, it is possible to have long time intervals without new commands. This can be, for example, a droplet increasing its temperature by positioning itself on top of a heating region. In this case, we do not want large gaps in the time by only executing the simulation engine when the next command occurs. To achieve this, the simulation engine executes time-dependent models at regular time intervals. This means that even if no action is occurring within a 10 s time interval, the time-dependent models are still executed every 0.1 s to simulate real behavior. This 0.1 s time interval is referred to as delta-time. The delta-time allows for high simulation granularity and it is configurable.

4.3 The GUI

The main purpose of the GUI is to provide a visual representation of the actions executed by the simulation engine and models. The GUI also provides information about the current state of the simulation and customization options. It also offers the ability to alter the state of the simulation while running and to extract simulation data.

The GUI consists of four components: sketch, control, information, and selection, as presented in Fig. 4. The sketch component contains the main view, and is where the actual representation of the simulation is displayed, The control component presents inputs for the user, which can alter the running simulation. The information component presents information about the state of selected elements in the simulation. The user can click on simulation elements to get specific information. The selection component provides togglable feature selection allowing for customization of properties in the simulation, such as the ability to enable real-time execution, droplet animations, and visibility of simulation components. Each GUI component consists of a frontend panel and a backend manager. The manager controls the data manipulation and sends visual updates to the respective panel for display.

As previously mentioned, the GUI is mainly written in JavaScript using the p5js framework[3], while the simulation engine and models are written in C#. Since the two languages do not directly interact, a broker module for transferring simulation data is needed. The broker acts as a two-way data transfer pipeline allowing the GUI to send and receive data from, and to, the simulation engine. This two-way data transfer allows for updating properties of the simulation elements at run-time. Thus, affecting the continuation of simulation engine

---

[3] p5js website: https://p5js.org/.

execution. By utilizing the selection component the user is presented with options to edit certain properties of elements, making it possible to conduct experiments at run-time.

A key part of the simulation framework is the ability to execute protocols in real-time, making them directly comparable to protocols running on the physical DMF biochip. The real-time execution is controlled by the GUI, by applying back-pressure on the simulation engine. This effect is achieved by having the GUI call for the next simulation step when the correct amount of time has passed. In the data passed by the simulation engine to the GUI, a value for the current time, and the time to the next execution step, are included. By utilizing these values, a time difference (delta time) is calculated. When delta time has passed, the GUI requests the engine to execute the next simulation step. The delta time is utilized to control the droplet animations. Thereby producing real-time behavior that mimics the observed reality. In addition, we use interpolation models to interpolate between the droplet shapes over delta time. Thus, producing smooth shape transitions.

Data extraction is essential for the simulation framework and provides the users with the means to analyze the behavior of the running protocol. The GUI allows to define the duration of simulated time for which to extract data, as well as the time interval for which the data points should be gathered. Raw simulation data are then produced, enabling users to use their own means of data analysis.

5 Evaluation

To evaluate the capabilities and the fidelity of the simulation framework, we carried out a series of artificial and real-life experiments and tests. For the simulation fidelity, the simulated behavior is compared against the one observed on a physical DMF biochip. The target DMF platform used for the test is our Bioware DMF system [10,11].

5.1 Basic Fluidic Behavior of Droplets

To demonstrate the ability of the simulator and the droplet model to capture the basic fluidic behavior of droplets, we present a static and a dynamic experiment.

The static experiment consists of replicating the complex shapes of the droplets seen in Fig. 1. In the simulation, droplets of the same volume as the real ones have been positioned on the electrodes activated with the same pattern as the physical biochip. Figure 5 shows the result of the simulation, where the electrodes' color and opacity of the droplets have been configured to match the real biochip pictures shown in Fig. 1. The comparisons show that our simulation framework can replicate the complex shapes observed in the physical biochip very closely. A minor difference is noticeable in Fig. 5d for the splitting operation, where the splitting 'tails' are not visible in the simulated version. However,

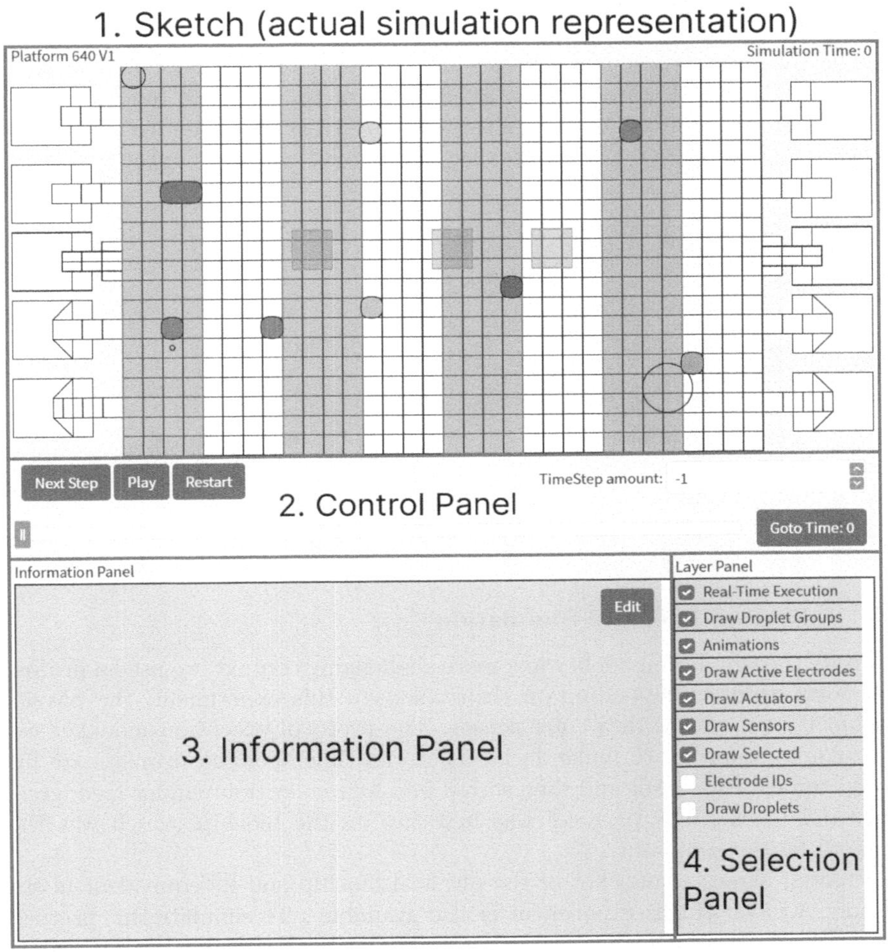

Fig. 4. 1. The sketch panel, where the actual simulation data is passed and represented; 2. The control panel, contains various controls allowing the user to traverse the simulation; 3. The information panel, presenting the user with information about selected elements; 4. The selection panel, allowing the user to select specific properties of the simulation.

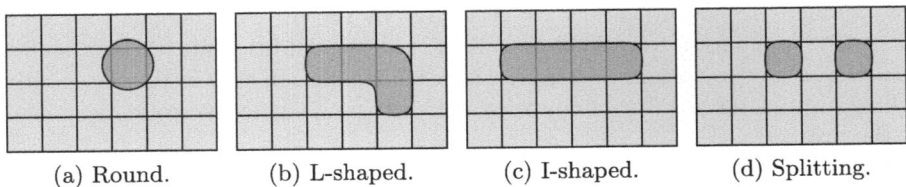

(a) Round.   (b) L-shaped.   (c) I-shaped.   (d) Splitting.

Fig. 5. The simulated version of the complex droplet shapes from Fig. 1.

this does not represent an issue since those 'tails' are immediately re-absorbed into the droplet after the splitting operation.

The dynamic experiment consists of moving a droplet back and forth on a horizontal path. Figure 6 shows a snapshot of the physical biochip and its equivalent in simulation. A video of this experiment is also available[4]. The figure and the video show that, also in this case, the simulation is very faithful to reality.

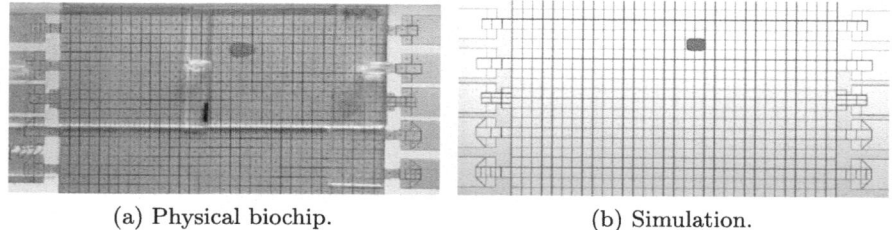

(a) Physical biochip. (b) Simulation.

Fig. 6. Snapshots of the test moving a droplet back and forth on a horizontal path.

5.2 Advanced Protocol Simulation

To verify the simulation fidelity in a more challenging context, we used a protocol that sorts droplets depending on their color. In this experiment, the physical biochip is equipped with a color sensor. The protocol execution manager uses the color information to make decisions at run-time. Colored droplets are first moved toward the sensor and then sorted into four collection regions (red, green, blue, and black). The protocol was first run on the biochip, which was then replaced by the simulator.

Figure 7 shows a snapshot of the physical biochip and its equivalent in simulation. A video of this experiment is also available[5]. To simulate this protocol, we extended the droplet model to capture the color of a droplet and developed a model for the color sensor component. The simulated sensor can be accessed by the protocol manager as the physical one. This test aims to demonstrate the ability of our framework to model sensing components. It should be noted that the physical experiment on the biochip was performed using an open system configuration (no top glass) to enable easy access to the operator. Thus, the shape of the simulated droplets is not completely faithful. The test successfully shows that simulated sensor readings are accessible by the protocol manager and can be used in simulation to make decisions at runtime. Additionally, the test shows that the simulator runs in real-time, with each simulation step in this case study taking around 100 ms (i.e. computing and showing a single electrode movement of the droplets).

---

[4] Video showing the physical vs. simulated equivalence: https://tinyurl.com/anxnzb28.
[5] Video of the color sort experiment: https://tinyurl.com/mpf6ksu2.

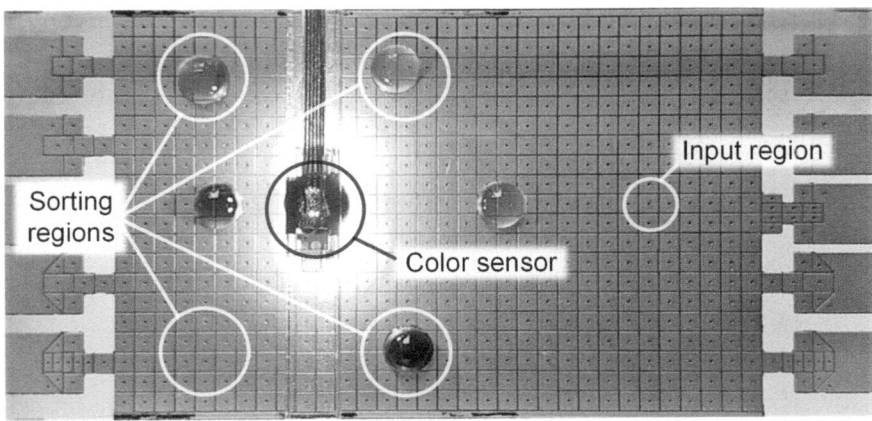
(a) Physical biochip.

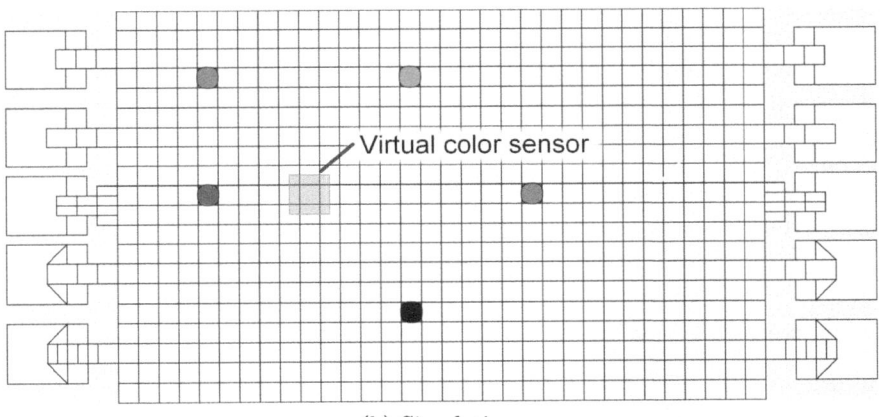
(b) Simulation.

Fig. 7. Snapshots of the test that sorts droplets depending on their color.

5.3 Actuators and Data Extraction

To demonstrate the functionality of the actuator component models, we simulated four droplets of equal volume moving in and out of two heating regions. To achieve this, we extended the droplet model with a temperature model and we developed a component model for the heaters on the biochip. After running the simulation, we used the data extraction feature and plotted the graph shown in Fig. 8. The experiment uses two heaters, which are kept at a constant temperature of 90 °C and 60 °C, respectively. The ambient temperature is set at 20 °C.

In the experiment, four droplets of equal volume are used. Droplet D1 is initially in contact with the 60 °C heater, resulting in a temperature rise. At time T = 20 s, D1 is moved outside the heated zone, leading to a temperature

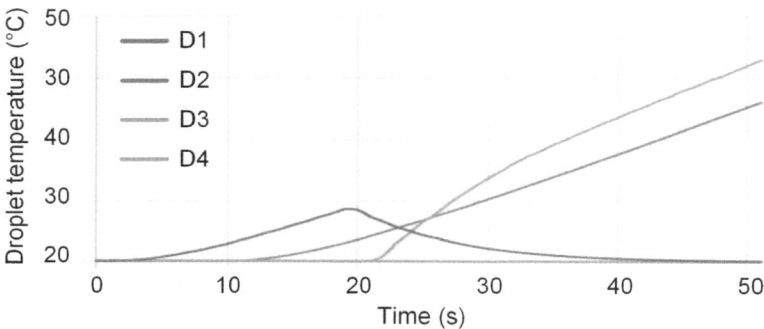

Fig. 8. Temperature of four droplets of equal volume moving in and out two heating zones.

decrease. D2 is moved on the same heater at T = 10 s. Here, it is possible to observe the same rate of temperature increase between D1 and D2. Droplet D3 is placed on the 90 °C heater at T = 20 s. This produces a faster temperature slope compared to the D1 and D2. Droplet D4 is always kept outside of the heaters.

This simple experiment gives insight into how the simulation framework can provide valuable and detailed data that can be effectively used during the design phase of a biochemical protocol to verify its correct execution.

5.4 Automated Testing

In addition to the simulation fidelity, unit testing was carried out using the unit-testing framework NUnit for C#. We constructed tests for different core functionalities such as initialization and droplet behavior. The initialization tests ensure that the droplets are subscribed to the correct electrodes and that their sub-droplets are assigned to the correct groups. The movement tests simulate a series of actions and use the position of the droplets after they have been split, merged, and moved on the biochip as a testing metric. The testing allowed us to confirm that the simulation engine and the models were behaving as expected after implementing new functionalities and can be used in the future after modifying existing models or adding new ones.

6 Conclusion

This paper presented a software-based simulation framework for DMF biochips. The simulation framework is able to execute in real-time within a resource-constrained web-based environment, due to the use of logic-based approximation of physical observations for the droplets' fluidic behavior. The web-based aspect ensures that the simulator is highly accessible and user-friendly, as it can run directly in a browser without the need for installation, making it attractive to a broader audience of researchers and professionals.

The simulation framework is built to be modular. It supports the base elements of DMF biochips but allows for easy modifications and additions, ensuring scalability as the development of DMF biochips continues. Artificial and real-life test experiments show that the simulation framework is able to simulate the observed reality with high fidelity. Therefore, the simulation framework can be used to test protocols before targeting the physical biochip and to conduct experiments without risk or resource losses.

Source, Tool, and Video Access

The simulator is released as open-source under the MIT License. The source code is available at https://github.com/DracusC/Development-of-a-simulation-framework-for-digital-microfluidic-biochips. The web-based simulator is available at https://microfluidicsimulator.azurewebsites.net/. A playlist containing a collection of videos for the tests and experiments used for evaluation and testing is available at https://tinyurl.com/36zk59pp.

References

1. Cardelli, L.: Kaemika app: Integrating protocols and chemical simulation. In: Abate, A., Petrov, T., Wolf, V. (eds.) Computational Methods in Systems Biology, pp. 373–379. Springer International Publishing, Cham (2020). https://doi.org/10.1007/978-3-030-60327-4_22
2. Fink, G., Costamoling, F., Wille, R.: MMFT droplet simulator: efficient simulation of droplet-based microfluidic devices. Softw. Impacts (2022). https://doi.org/10.1016/j.simpa.2022.100440
3. Grimmer, A., Hamidović, M., Haselmayr, W., Wille, R.: Advanced simulation of droplet microfluidics. J. Emerging Technol. Comput. Syst. **15**(3), 26 (2019). https://doi.org/10.1145/3313867
4. Lan, C., Pal, S., Li, Z., Ma, Y.: Numerical simulations of the digital microfluidic manipulation of single microparticles. Langmuir **31**(35), 9636–9645 (2015). https://doi.org/10.1021/acs.langmuir.5b02011
5. Mugele, F., Baret, J.C.: Electrowetting: from basics to applications. J. Phys.: Condens. Matter **17**(28), R705 (2005). https://doi.org/10.1088/0953-8984/17/28/R01
6. Pop, P., Alistar, M., Stuart, E., Madsen, J.: Fault-Tolerant Digital Microfluidic Biochips: Compilation and Synthesis. Springer (2015). https://doi.org/10.1007/978-3-319-23072-6
7. Pop, P., Minhass, W.H., Madsen, J.: Microfluidic Very Large Scale Integration (VLSI). Springer, Cham (2016). https://doi.org/10.1007/978-3-319-29599-2
8. Schibelfeldt, F.E.: A model-based simulation engine for digital microfluidic biochips. B.Sc. thesis, Technical University of Denmark (2021)
9. Tanev, G.P.: A Modular Design Approach For Programmable Cyber-Fluidic Systems. Ph.D. thesis, Technical University of Denmark (2021)
10. Tanev, G.P., Pezzarossa, L., Madsen, J.: The bioware cyber-fluidic platform: a holistic approach to digital microfluidics. In: Proceedings of the 13th International Workshop on Bio-Design Automation. ACM (2021)

11. Tanev, G.P., Pezzarossa, L., Svendsen, W.E., Madsen, J.: A reconfigurable digital microfluidics platform. In: Proceedings of the 11th International Workshop on Bio-Design Automation. ACM (2019)
12. Tsanev, V.A.: Front end for a digital microfluidic biochips simulator. B.Sc. thesis, Technical University of Denmark (2021)

A Parallel Synchronous Execution Engine and Target Language for Digital Microfluidics

Luca Pezzarossa[1]([✉]), Georgi Tanev[1], Winnie Edith Svendsen[2], and Jan Madsen[1]

[1] Department of Applied Mathematics and Computer Science, Technical University of Denmark, Kgs. Lyngby, Denmark
{lpez,geta,jama}@dtu.dk
[2] Department of Biotechnology and Biomedicine, Technical University of Denmark, Kgs. Lyngby, Denmark
wisv@dtu.dk

Abstract. Digital microfluidic biochips allow the execution of biochemical protocols on a chip-scaled device delivering cost and performance advantages over the traditional benchtop wet-laboratory processes. Several microfluidic high-level programming languages have been proposed, but none is currently adopted as a standard since their compilers and execution engines often target specific platforms. To address this issue and favor standardization, we propose a biochip-independent execution engine and low-level target language. The execution engine supports the execution of parallel synchronized tasks allowing each droplet or process to be controlled by an independent task. The target language run by the engine is inspired by traditional computer instruction set architectures and offers instructions covering the full range of low-level functionalities offered by digital biochips. The versatility of the proposed solution and its ability to support the selection and iteration control structures commonly used in programs is demonstrated with a real-life case study that sorts droplets based on real-time measurements of their color.

Keywords: Digital microfluidic biochips · Domain-specific languages · Digital microfluidic programming · Execution engine · BioAssembly

1 Introduction

Digital microfluidic (DMF) biochips are devices that integrate precise fluidic handling and a range of sensors and actuators in order to automate and miniaturize traditional wet-laboratory processes. Microliter-sized discrete droplets can be programmatically moved on a planar substrate patterned with individually addressable insulated electrodes. The movement is directed by applying an electric potential to the electrodes along the droplet actuation path. This actuation technique is known as electrowetting on dielectric [6], and it provides an elegant first-order digital control over liquid droplets. Droplets serve the function of fluidic vehicles and reaction chambers, and they can be moved, mixed, merged, split, dispensed, and disposed, as shown in Fig. 1.

To provide the full sample-to-answer functionality of a traditional wet lab, digital biochips often implement on-chip measuring capabilities such as biosensing and temperature monitoring. For reagent long-term storage or for ensuring proper reaction conditions, on-chip cooling and heating are also possible, as also shown in Fig. 1. This high level of integration enables biochemical analysis to be performed with reduced reagent volumes yielding shorter reaction times and reduced cost. Nevertheless, the simple operation and performance advantages of the DMF biochips come at the cost of increased complexity in their control since automated control of hundreds of electrodes and a variety of sensor and actuator interfaces should be provided.

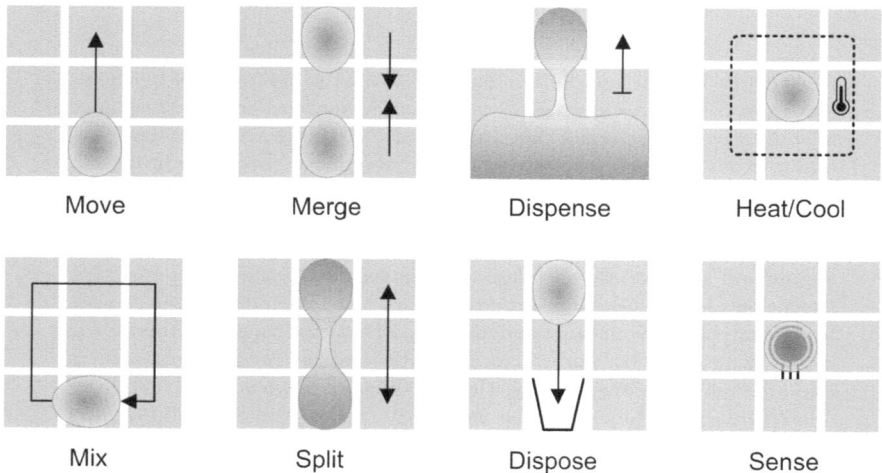

Fig. 1. A selection of operations on droplets that can be performed on a DMF biochip. Move, mix, merge, split dispense, and dispose involve moving the droplets. Heat/cool and sense are static operations.

Building reconfigurable and programmable digital biochips that can be used for a broad range of laboratory protocols inevitably shows the need for an easy and structured process to capture a protocol and translate it into a sequence of steps that can be run on a DMF biochip. In fact, this process can be captured with the classical software tool-chain consisting of a programming language, a compiler, and an execution platform. All of these three elements have been already researched in isolation, and domain-specific languages, a variety of compilation techniques [8], and several execution platforms have been developed.

A comprehensive review of domain-specific languages for programmable biochemistry, including DMF, can be found in [9]. Different approaches have been used in the development of these languages. For instance, BioCoder [3] extends the existing C++ language with a library enabling biologists to express the steps of a lab protocol. AquaCore [2] proposes an instruction set offering instructions that implement complete functionalities of DMF biochips, such as merge, split, heat, etc. BioScript [7] is a standalone language characterized by an intuitive syntax optimized for human readability, as well as a type system ensuring that unsafe compound interaction does not happen. State-of-the art execution platforms for these domain specific-languages include DropBot [5], OpenDrop [1], Puddle [13], and our Bioware platform [10–12].

Regardless of the decades of development and the numerous programming paradigms explored, integration between these tools is virtually non-existent, and DMF biochips and instrumentation platforms remain with limited programming capabilities. None of the languages is currently adopted as a standard since their compilers and execution engines typically target specific platforms. Programming is often done with primitive scripting routines or custom application programming interfaces mainly due to the lack of a common compiler target. In addition, a more versatile solution supporting the selection and iteration control structures commonly used in programs would enable controlling the flow of the biochemical protocols upon on-the-fly sensing results from the processes occurring on the biochip. Thus, enabling true programmability.

To address these issues and favor the full adoption of a common toolchain, this paper proposes a biochip-independent execution engine and low-level language. The execution engine supports running parallel synchronized tasks allowing each droplet or process to be controlled by an independent task. The target language, named BioAssembly, is inspired by classic computer ISAs and offers a platform-independent programming interface for DMF and aims to be used as a target for DMF compilers. BioAssembly runs on the execution engine and offers a set of core instructions dedicated to DMF, as well as classic arithmetic, flow control, and memory access instructions upon which complex operations can be built. In other words, the execution engine abstracts the functionality of the physical biochip and offers a well-defined interface for DMF programming, which can be considered the missing link in the full adoption of a modern programming model in the DMF context. Throughout the paper, we use an example where two droplets are moved, merged, and mixed to explain the used parallel synchronized execution model. The proposed solution and its versatility are demonstrated with a real-life application that sorts droplets based on real-time measurements of their color.

The rest of this paper is divided into five sections. The following section presents the synchronous parallel execution model we adapted for DMF programming. Sections 3 and 4 respectively present the execution engine and the BioAssembly language, which are the main contributions of this work. Section 5 presents the color sorting case study. Finally, Sect. 6 concludes the paper.

2 The Synchronous Parallel Execution Model

When dealing with the execution of a protocol on a DMF platform, we can identify two different time scales: the biochemical and actuation scale and the computing scale. The biochemical and actuation scale is in the order of tens of milliseconds (e.g., moving a droplet from one electrode to a nearby one) to minutes or even hours (e.g., keeping a sample to a specific temperature for a DNA amplification reaction). In contrast, the computing scale is typically in the order of nanoseconds per instruction, and it is related to the clock period of the computing unit. In general, computation is very fast compared to the response time of the physical platform.

During the execution of a protocol, multiple droplets are moved simultaneously to resemble the liquid handling operations currently done with pipetting. Therefore, it is natural to employ a programming model where parallel tasks manage individual droplets, in a similar way as threads are used in modern computers. The movement of a droplet on a path is produced by step-by-step activation and deactivation of electrodes. Performing these operations synchronously for all the droplets greatly simplifies the scheduling and place-and-route operations during compilation since the biochip droplet configuration evolves in discreet uniform steps.

Based on these observations, we adapted the synchronous parallel execution model for DMF protocol execution. The idea is to consider time as divided into synchronization periods. A synchronization tick marks the boundary between two periods. At the beginning of a synchronization period, all the active tasks are executed in parallel. At the end of a synchronization period, when all tasks have completed execution, changes are applied to the platform in an atomic manner. Tasks are, therefore, implicitly synchronized and execution proceeds step-by-step at each tick.

This execution model is suitable for DMF platforms since the movement of each droplet managed by an independent task is synchronized. Besides moving droplets, additional tasks can be used to control other aspects of the program (e.g., DMF platform status, interaction with sensors and actuators, etc.). Explicit synchronization barriers are also supported to synchronize specific parallel tasks.

To illustrate the parallel synchronous execution model, let us consider the example shown in Fig. 2. Tasks τ_1 and τ_2 are two independent tasks moving two droplets (D_1 and D_2) toward a region where a merge and mix operation is performed by tasks τ_3, as shown in Fig. 2a. Figure 2b shows the timing diagram and synchronization for the three tasks. Tasks execution is started at the beginning of each synchronization period and carried out in parallel (implicit synchronization). Changes to the DMF platform are applied at the end of each synchronization period, corresponding to a droplet step toward the merge and mix region. Only when both tasks τ_1 and τ_2 complete their execution (regardless of which one finishes first) and the droplets are in position for merging and mixing, task τ_3 can be started in order to perform the merge and mix. This is achieved using an explicit synchronization barrier.

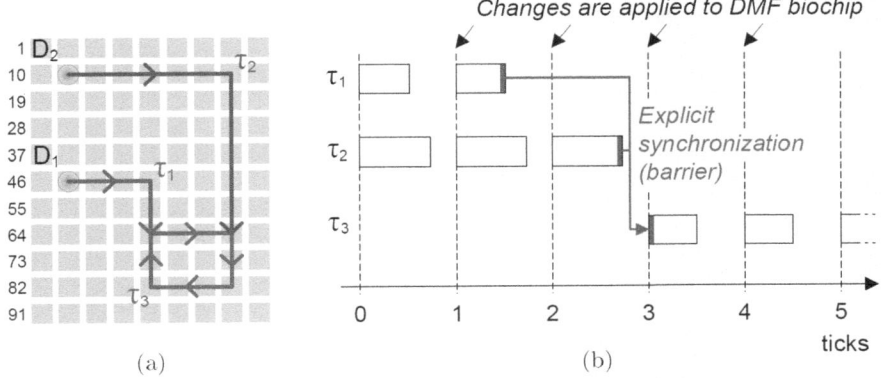

Fig. 2. Application example where tasks τ_1 and τ_2 move two droplets (D_1 and D_2) toward a region where a merge and mix operation is performed by tasks τ_3. (a) Paths for moving, merging, and mixing on the biochip. (b) Timing diagram and synchronization for the three tasks.

The synchronization period should be chosen long enough to allow the required computation, but still fine-grain in comparison to the chemistry/biology and actuation processes. Due to the different time scales, a considerable amount of computation can be performed between ticks. For example, continuous sensing to monitor protocol execution, re-computation of routes, sensor data analysis, etc. It is important to remark that, if a task execution does not finish before the tick, the tick period gets stretched to match the execution time of the longest task. In other words, the next tick is delayed until all tasks finish execution. Due to the large time scale of chemistry/biology processes relative to the tick period, an occasional tick stretch is not expected to affect the outcome of the protocol. The BioAssembly implementation of the example shown in Fig. 2 are presented later in Sect. 4.

3 The Execution Engine

The role of the execution engine and the BioAssembly language in the DMF compilation and execution toolchain is shown in Fig. 3. Starting from the top of the figure, we have the biochemistry protocol defining the list of steps and the required conditions for the experiment to be executed. The protocol is then expressed using a high-level language (e.g., BioGo [4], BioScript [7]). This can be done in a programming environment where the user has the option of a text-based or graphical interface to represent the protocol (for users who are less acquainted with programming). The high-level language protocol is then compiled, linked, and assembled [4,8] into the BioAssembly low-level language. Information regarding the DMF platform architecture, such as electrode and chip topology, availability and placement of actuators, sensors, etc. is provided as input to the compiler. This information is used by the compiler for scheduling and routing the droplets.

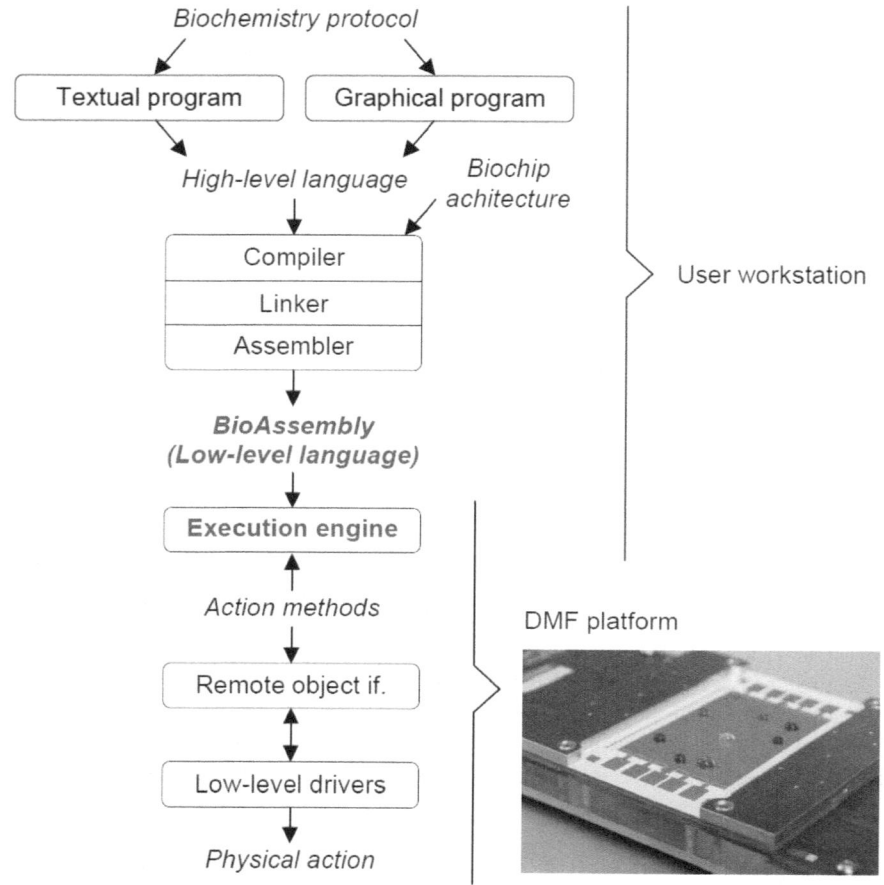

Fig. 3. Diagram of the compilation and execution tool-chain integrating the execution engine and the BioAssembly language (highlighted in red). (Color figure online)

The compiled protocol is then executed by our execution engine, which virtualizes the DMF platform and emulates a processor-based system able to execute BioAssembly code according to the synchronous parallel execution model presented in Sect. 2. The interface to the DMF platform is based on an object-oriented approach. The execution engine perceives the platform as a remote object and can interact with it by calling its action methods.

The use of the execution engine aims to decouple the BioAssembly execution and the functionality offered by the underlying DMF platform. BioAssembly instructions that do not produce a physical action in the platform (e.g., arithmetic and logic, memory access, branches, etc.) are resolved and executed locally by the engine, while the instructions that interact with the DMF platform trigger the execution of action methods. The prototypes of these action methods are standardized, but their implementation can be adapted to the functionalities offered by the DMF platform. This makes the execution of BioAssembly code independent of the low-level interaction with the physical platform, which needs to be resolved during the implementation of the action methods.

In other words, the execution engine can be seen as an environment that virtualizes and abstracts the physical DMF platform, as shown in Fig. 4. The figure also outlines the memory architecture used in the engine, where the execution unit is the equivalent of a CPU supporting BioAssembly execution. The program memory holds the BioAssembly program and the data memory holds the variables used in the computation. Each parallel task has assigned a private data memory segment and can access a shared global segment. The electrodes/device memory implements the interface toward the DMF platform. Electrodes and devices (e.g., heaters, sensors, etc.) are mapped into their address space, in a similar way as peripherals are mapped in a traditional computing system. Writing into this memory produces a physical change in the state of the DMF platform at the end of a synchronization period. The possibility to produce an immediate asynchronous change is also provided, as described later.

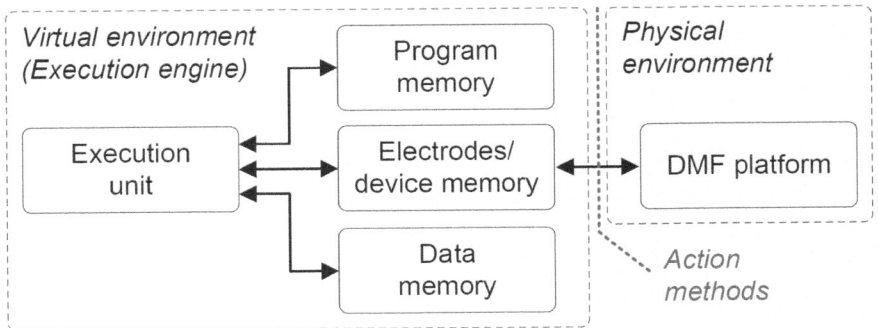

Fig. 4. Relation between virtual and physical environment through action methods and memory architecture of the execution engine.

The execution engine is implemented in C# and can run on the user workstation or directly on the DMF platform (see Fig. 3), depending on the computational capacity integrated into the platform itself and on the use case. Running the execution engine is not computationally intensive, and a modern microcontroller is a suitable target.

4 The BioAssembly Target Language

This section presents and describes the BioAssembly target language and provides a code example for a simple artificial application.

4.1 The Instructions

The BioAssembly target language is inspired by, but not the same as, ISAs commonly found in RISC-based processors (e.g., RISC-V, ARM, MIPS). Our goal is to offer a clear programming interface between the experimental protocol representation and the DMF platform. The idea is to provide a set of fundamental instructions which can be used to build complex functionality. For example, we do not include specific instructions to route a droplet from one point to another or to perform a mix operation, but only instructions to activate and deactivate electrodes. Classic computing instructions including memory access, arithmetic, logic, flow control, and real numbers support are therefore used to build complex functionalities.

Table 1 presents the BioAssembly core instructions dedicated to DMF, divided into three groups. For reasons of space, the table reports only the opcode of the instructions and a brief description. Also, the classic computing instructions are omitted. The full list of instructions, operands, and detailed descriptions can be found in the additional material repository[1]. In the following, we describe and motivate the three instruction groups of Table 1.

DMF Electrode Control Instructions. This group includes dedicated instructions for activating (set) and deactivating (clear) the electrodes of the DMF platform. The group contains both immediate and variable instructions. Immediate instructions (SETELI and CLRELI) specify the electrode ID as an immediate in the program, while variable ones (SETEL and CLREL) specify the memory location in which the electrode ID is stored. The latter can be useful when setting and clearing electrodes in a sequence in which the next electrode has a mathematical relationship with the previous one (e.g., a straight line). Since these instructions interact with the physical system, their action is only applied at the end of a synchronization period as an atomic event.

DMF Device Access Instructions. The instructions in this group allow interaction with the platform devices (e.g., heaters, coolers, sensors, etc.). Devices are seen as mapped to the electrodes/device memory (see Fig. 4), which can be accessed with read and write instructions. The ISA offers two types of device access instructions: asynchronous and synchronous. Similar to the electrode control instructions, the synchronous instructions take effect only at the end of a synchronization period as an atomic event. On the contrary, the asynchronous

---

[1] Additional material repository: https://github.com/blind-review-developer/dmf_eetl_files.

Table 1. BioAssembly core instructions dedicated to DMF.

Instruction	Description
DMF electrode control instructions	
SETEL	Set electrode
CLREL	Clear electrode
SETELI	Set electrode immediate
CLRELI	Clear electrode immediate
CLRALL	Clear all electrodes
DMF device access instructions	
DEVWR	Device write
ADEVRD	Asynchronous device read
ADEVWR	Asynchronous device write
ADEVEX	Execute asynchronous device reads and writes
ADEVCL	Clear queued asynchronous device reads and writes
Task management and synchronization instructions	
TSTART	Start a task
TSTOP	Stop the current task
TICK	Apply changes and wait next tick (implicit synch.)
BARR	Synchronization barrier (explicit synch.)

ones do not need to wait for a tick to be executed. During execution, asynchronous read and write operations (ADEVRD and ADEVWR) are queued and carried out immediately as a block (queue order is maintained) when the instruction ADEVEX is executed, without waiting for the end of the synchronization period.

Synchronous device access instructions are meant to be used when the read and write operation causes a physical change in the state of the DMF platform (e.g., turning on a heater), according to the synchronous execution model. Asynchronous instructions are meant for configuring the device parameters that do not cause a physical change in the state (e.g., initializing a device), and to acquire status and sensing information needed before the end of a synchronization period. For example, reading a measurement from a sensor and using it for program flow control. In general, electrodes could be considered as devices, making the previous instruction group redundant. However, we decided to have dedicated instructions since electrodes are the fundamental actuation unit of a DMF platform, and we expect frequent use of these in the control program.

Task Management and Synchronization Instructions. This group contains the instructions related to the synchronous parallel execution model presented above. The task management instructions TSTART and TSTOP are respectively used to start and stop the execution of a task. New tasks are started after the next tick and executed in parallel to the existing tasks.

The instructions TICK and BARR implement synchronization barriers. This means that, for each active parallel task, the sequential execution of instructions continues until one of these two instructions is executed. When all the active tasks (executed in parallel) have executed this instruction, no more computing has to be carried out in the current synchronization period. Thus, changes are applied to the DMF biochip as an atomic event, and execution is resumed after the next tick.

TICK implements an implicit synchronization barrier: the changes are applied, and execution is resumed from the instruction following the TICK one. BARR implements an explicit synchronization barrier between tasks. The instruction BARR represents a barrier characterized by a unique ID and by the number of tasks that need to be synchronized by the same barrier. When BARR is executed by a task, changes are applied, but the execution is resumed from the following instruction only when all the tasks have reached the barrier associated with the same ID. For example, BARR is used in Fig. 2 for explicit synchronization.

4.2 Code Example

To provide a better understating of BioAssembly code, Fig. 5 shows an example of the BioAssembly code for the protocol that moves, merges, and mixies two droplets D_1 and D_2 presented in Sect. 2 and shown in Fig. 2. Due to space limitations, some code segments are omitted (indicated with [...]), but line numbers are kept consistent with the full program. The full code is available in the additional material repository(see footnote 1).

At first, the program starts the task τ_1 and τ_2 (lines 9 and 10), respectively controlling the movement of droplet D_1 and D_2 from their initial position to the merge and mix region. Then, the program encounters a synchronization barrier (BARR) characterized by an ID of 0 and by a task count of 3 (line 11). This means that only when two other tasks execute a BARR instruction with the same ID, the barrier is released and the tasks can continue execution.

The code segments from line 17 to 36 and from line 38 to 78 respectively implement tasks τ_1 and τ_2. Here, we can observe that for each tick (TICK instruction), SETELI and CLRELI instructions are used to move the droplet one step at a time. When both tasks τ_1 and τ_2 are completed, all the barrier instructions are executed (lines 11, 34, and 76). As a consequence, τ_1 and τ_2 are terminated (TSTOP) and task τ_3 is released (line 12).

The code segment from line 80 to line 119 implements τ_3, which merges the two droplets and mixes the product of the merging by moving it in a squared path five times. Here, the squared path is only stored once (from lines 85 to 113) and executed five times in a loop using branching and testing instructions. The variables *cnt* and *max_cnt* are used to keep track of the loop execution.

```
 8: start:                                  43:    TICK;           ⎤
 9:    TSTART move_D1;                             [...]            |
10:    TSTART move_D2;                      74:    CLRELI 62;       |
11:    BARR 0 3;                            75:    SETELI 71;       ⎦
12:    TSTART merge_mix_D1_D2;              76:    BARR 0 3;
13:    TICK;                                77:    TSTOP;
14:    TSTOP;                               78:    TICK;
15:    TICK;                                79:
16:                                         80: merge_mix_D1_D2:
17: move_D1:                                81:    LI cnt 0;
18:    SETELI 47;       ⎤                   82:    LI max_cnt 5;
19:    TICK;             |                  83: loop:
20:    CLRELI 47;        |                  84:    BEQ loop_end cnt max_cnt;
21:    SETELI 48;        | τ₁ path          85:    CLRELI 68;      ⎤
22:    TICK;             |                  86:    SETELI 69;       |
       [...]             |                  87:    TICK;            | τ₃ path
32:    CLRELI 59;        |                         [...]            |
33:    SETELI 68;       ⎦                  112:    CLRELI 77;       |
34:    BARR 0 3;                           113:    SETELI 68;       ⎦
35:    TSTOP;                              114:    TICK;
36:    TICK;                               115:    ADDI cnt cnt 1;
37:                                        116:    JI loop;
38: move_D2:                               117: loop_end:
39:    SETELI 11;       ⎤                  118:    TSTOP;
40:    TICK;             | τ₂ path         119:    TICK;
41:    CLRELI 11;        |
42:    SETELI 12;       ⎦
```

Fig. 5. BioAssembly implementation of the example presented in Sect. 2 and shown in Fig. 2 where two droplets D_1 and D_2 are moved, merged, and mixed.

For clarity, in the example, we have used immediate electrode numbers (SETELI and CLRELI) for moving droplets. An alternative, more complex, and versatile approach offered by BioAssembly consists of storing the electrode IDs of the droplet path in an array in memory and using the SETEL and CLREL instructions pointing to an array entry at a time. The pointer is then incremented in a loop to walk through the array, producing the desired movement. This approach is used in the study case explained in Sect. 5.

5 Case Study

The case study consists of an application that sorts droplets depending on their current color and aims to demonstrate the capabilities of the execution engine and the BioAssembly language in a real-life context. The application is developed in BioAssembly and runs on the execution engine, which sends commands to the DMF platform to control the movement of the droplets. The case study targets and is executed on our Bioware platform [10–12]. To achieve this, action methods have been implemented to support communication between the execution engine and the DMF platform.

Figure 6 shows a picture of the experimental setup and highlights the relevant regions of the biochip as well as the possible paths of the droplets (dashed red line). At first, the user places a droplet of any color in the input region using a pipette. Then, the program moves the droplet under the TCS34725 color sensor, which is perceived by the execution engine as a remote object. The red, green, and blue value readings are mapped to the device memory of the execution engine by a dedicated action method (see Fig. 4) and are used by the program to decide the path for the droplet. Depending on the detected color, a red, green, or blue droplet is then moved on a path toward the respective sorting region. If the droplet color is not recognized as red, green, or blue, it is moved to the unknown region. In Fig. 6, it is possible to observe the four regions collecting the droplets, a green droplet traveling towards the sensor region, and a green droplet being placed using a pipette. A video of the experiment is also available[2].

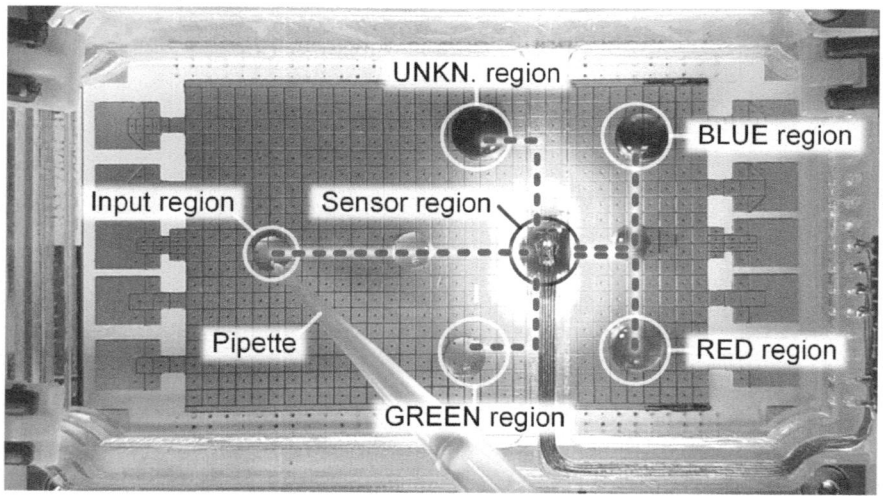

Fig. 6. The experimental setup based on our Bioware platform [10–12] used in the study case. Relevant regions, components, and possible droplet paths (dashed line) of the droplets are highlighted. (Color figure online)

The control flow graphs of the tasks used in the program are shown in Fig. 7. The *main()* task runs on a loop and dispatches a *sense()* task every 2.5 s. The *sense()* task moves the droplet potentially placed in the input region towards the sensor. Dispatching a *sense()* task every 2.5 s creates a 'conveyor belt' effect from the input region to the sensor. Since not every sense task receives a droplet in the input region, if the background color is detected when a droplet is expected under

---

[2] Video of the color sorting case study: https://tinyurl.com/2zcz7ptu.

the sensor, the task is terminated. Otherwise, a *sort(region)* task is dispatched and the argument containing the color information is passed to the task through shared data memory (see Fig. 4). The *sort(region)* task then continues the droplet path toward the correct region. The full BioAssembly code for this experiment is available in the additional material repository (see footnote 1).

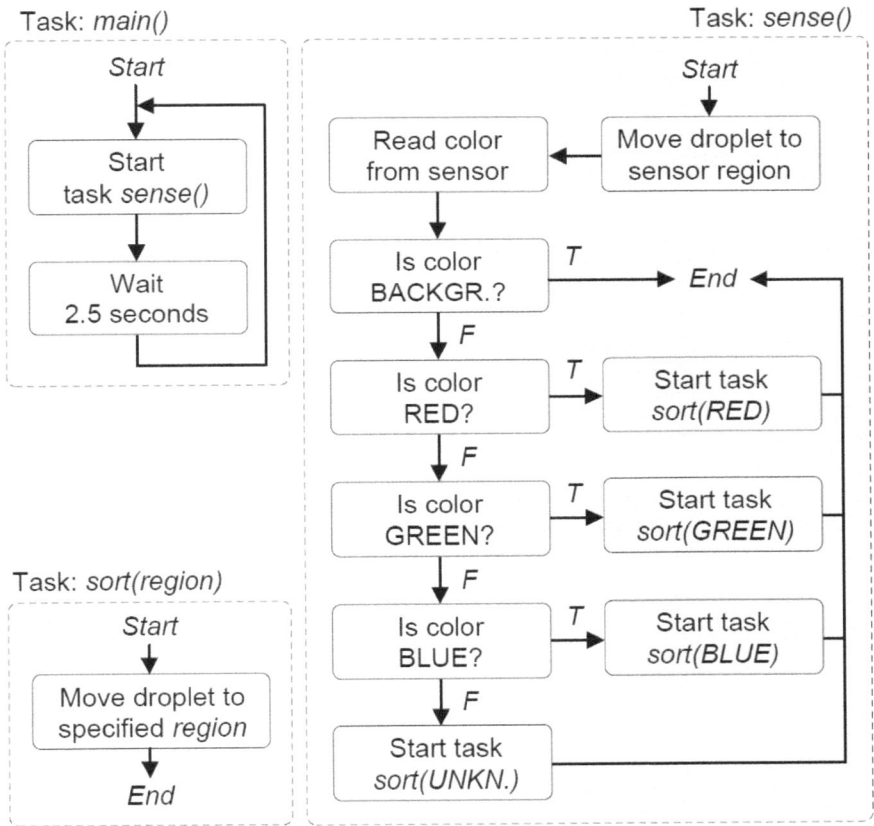

Fig. 7. Control flow graphs of the BioAssembly program tasks for the case study.

The case study demonstrates:

1. The potential of the synchronous parallel execution model supported by our solution for controlling multiple droplets and different phases in a droplet lifetime as separate tasks.
2. The ability to easily map physical devices, such as sensors and actuators, to the device memory of the execution engine using action methods. Thus, virtualizing and abstracting the physical DMF platform.

3. The ability to support true programmability in the protocol execution by allowing the use of selection and control structures that can depend on data produced at run-time by the processes happening on the DMF biochip.

In contrast to existing scripting languages for DMF that execute commands sequentially, the parallel execution of the tasks carried out by the execution engine simplifies program generation. This approach allows for scalability since more droplets can be controlled with additional parallel tasks without interference. Other parallel tasks can also be added to manage other aspects of the DMF biochip (e.g., voltages, user I/O, etc.) without affecting the protocol execution.

6 Conclusion

In this paper, we presented an execution engine and the related BioAssembly low-level language. The engine and the language are biochip-independent and are meant to be used as targets for digital microfluidics compilers. They support the synchronous parallel execution model to allow each droplet or process to be controlled by an independent task. A real-life study case running on a physical platform and a smaller artificial example demonstrated the versatility and true programmability offered by our solution. In summary, the contributions of this paper are: (1) the adaptation of the parallel synchronous execution model for DMF, (2) the execution engine, and (3) the BioAssembly low-level target language. Future work include the development of the compilation from a high-level language into BioAssembly. Initial efforts in developing the language, named BioGo, and its compiler are presented in [4].

References

1. Alistar, M., Gaudenz, U.: OpenDrop: an integrated do-it-yourself platform for personal use of biochips. J. Bioeng. **4**(4), 45 (2017)
2. Amin, A.M., Thottethodi, M., Vijaykumar, T.N., Wereley, S., Jacobson, S.C.: AquaCore: a programmable architecture for microfluidics. In: Proceedings of the 34th Annual International Symposium on Computer Architecture, pp. 254–265. ACM (2007)
3. Ananthanarayanan, V., Thies, W.: BioCoder: a programming language for standardizing and automating biology protocols. J. Biol. Eng. **4**(1), 13 (2010)
4. Fan, W.: Programming biochemistry on digital microfluidics biochips, MSc thesis, Technical University of Denmark (2023)
5. Fobel, R., Fobel, C., Wheeler, A.R.: DropBot: an open-source digital microfluidic control system with precise control of electrostatic driving force and instantaneous drop velocity measurement. Appl. Phys. Lett. **102**(19), 1129–1132 (2013). https://doi.org/10.1063/1.4807118
6. Mugele, F., Baret, J.C.: Electrowetting: from basics to applications. J. Phys.: Condens. Matter **17**(28), 705–774 (2005)
7. Ott, J., Loveless, T., Curtis, C., Lesani, M., Brisk, P.: BioScript: programming safe chemistry on laboratories-on-a-chip. Proc. ACM Program. Lang. **2**, 1–31 (2018)

8. Pop, P., Alistar, M., Stuart, E., Madsen, J.: Fault-Tolerant Digital Microfluidic Biochips. Springer, Cham (2016). https://doi.org/10.1007/978-3-319-23072-6
9. Sadowski, M.I., Grant, C., Fell, T.S.: Harnessing QbD, programming languages, and automation for reproducible biology. Trends Biotechnol. **34**(3), 214–227 (2016)
10. Tanev, G.P.: A Modular Design Approach For Programmable Cyber-Fluidic Systems. Ph.D. thesis, Technical University of Denmark (2021)
11. Tanev, G.P., Pezzarossa, L., Madsen, J.: The bioware cyber-fluidic platform: a holistic approach to digital microfluidics. In: Proceedings of the 13th International Workshop on Bio-Design Automation. ACM (2021)
12. Tanev, G.P., Pezzarossa, L., Svendsen, W.E., Madsen, J.: A reconfigurable digital microfluidics platform. In: Proceedings of the 11th International Workshop on Bio-Design Automation. ACM (2019)
13. Willsey, M., et al.: Puddle: a dynamic, error-correcting, full-stack microfluidics platform. In: Proceedings of the 24th International Conference on Architectural Support for Programming Languages and Operating Systems, pp. 183–197 (2019)

QCEDA: Using Quantum Computers for EDA

Matthias Jung[1,3](✉), Sven O. Krumke[2], Christof Schroth[1], Elisabeth Lobe[4], and Wolfgang Mauerer[5]

[1] Fraunhofer IESE, Kaiserslautern, Germany
`matthias.jung@iese.fraunhofer.de, m.jung@uni-wuerzburg.de`
[2] RPTU Kaiserslautern-Landau, Kaiserslautern, Germany
`sven.krumke@math.rptu.de`
[3] JMU Würzburg, Würzburg, Germany
[4] German Aerospace Center (DLR), Institute of Software Technology, Cologne, Germany
`Elisabeth.Lobe@dlr.de`
[5] OTH Regensburg, Regensburg, Germany
`wolfgang.mauerer@othr.de`

Abstract. The field of *Electronic Design Automation* (EDA) is crucial for microelectronics, but the increasing complexity of *Integrated Circuits* (ICs) poses challenges for conventional EDA: Corresponding problems are often NP-hard and are therefore in general solved by heuristics, not guaranteeing optimal solutions. Quantum computers may offer better solutions due to their potential for optimization through entanglement, superposition, and interference. Most of the works in the area of EDA and quantum computers focus on how to use EDA for building quantum circuits. However, almost no research focuses on exploiting quantum computers for solving EDA problems. Therefore, this paper investigates the feasibility and potential of quantum computing for a typical EDA optimization problem broken down to the Min-k-Union problem. The problem is mathematically transformed into a *Quadratic Unconstrained Binary Optimization* (QUBO) problem, which was successfully solved on an IBM quantum computer and a D-Wave quantum annealer.

1 Introduction

As one of the most important areas of microelectronics, *Electronic Design Automation* (EDA) has a long history, dating back to the mid-1960s. Nevertheless, EDA methods are still being intensively developed with the inclusion of the latest algorithms and technologies. In recent years, with the development of semiconductor technology, the complexity of *Integrated Circuits* (IC) has increased exponentially, posing challenges to the scalability and reliability of circuit design. Therefore, EDA algorithms and software need to be more effective and efficient to handle an extremely large search space with low runtime. However, a large number of the problems in EDA, such as placement and wiring or scheduling, are NP-hard. Therefore, there is no algorithm for conventional computers that can solve these problems efficiently, i.e., in polynomial time depending on the problem size. Rather, the processing time grows exponentially. This means in the worst case that, for large but still reasonable problem sizes, a classical computer might have to compute millions of years to find an optimal solution, and that this situation cannot be relaxed by simply improving the performance of classical computers. Thus, in practice, these problems can only be solved with the help of approximation algorithms or heuristics, which find feasible solutions but in general do not provide the mathematically optimal result. Quantum computers can take advantage of entanglement, superposition, and interference to speed up optimization algorithms through massive parallelism. Thus, for the EDA problems, there is the potential to achieve a significant speedup compared to a classical computer.

Most of the works in the area of EDA and quantum computers focus on how to use EDA for building quantum circuits. However, almost no research focuses on exploiting quantum computers for EDA problems. A typical EDA optimization problem is presented by the authors of [1,2]. The objective is to discover an optimal address mapping of a specific application for a *Dynamic Random Access Memory* (DRAM), which is composed of banks, rows, and columns. This mapping is typically achieved through a hardware scrambler in the memory controller. The aim of the EDA problem is to determine an optimal configuration for this hardware scrambler, reducing the number of row misses, thereby increasing bandwidth and reducing latency. It has been shown by [1,2] that this problem is NP-hard and that the core of the problem can be reduced to the so-called Min-k-Union problem.

In this paper we investigate the feasibility and discuss potential of quantum computing for this specific EDA optimization problem. In order to speedup the calculation, the goal of this paper is to formulate the Min-k-Union problem for the quantum computer. While we find that currently available quantum computer prototypes do not scale to realistically sized problem instances, we quantitatively estimate required machine sizes, and verify general feasibility of our approach on an IBM quantum computer and a D-Wave quantum annealer, and discuss paths towards quantum advantage on EDA. In summary this paper makes the following contributions:

- We show, how a very specific EDA problem can be formulated to be executed on a quantum computer.
- We present, for the first time, a *Quadratic Unconstrained Binary Optimization* (QUBO) formulation of the Min-k-Union problem, to achieve that.
- We execute this EDA problem on real quantum computers and prove the feasibility of this approach.
- We show how this problems scales for real world problem instances and point out limitations for the future.

The paper is structured as follows: Sect. 2 discusses the related work. The mathematical description and the transformation for the quantum computers of the Min-k-Union problem is discussed in Sect. 3. The results on the execution on two real quantum machines is presented in Sect. 4. Finally, the paper is concluded in Sect. 5.

2 Related Work

Most of the works in the area of EDA and quantum computers focus on how to use EDA for building quantum circuits [3]. For instance, the authors of [4] present a logic synthesis for reversible circuits. Hillmich *et al.* present new approaches for quantum circuit simulations based on decision diagrams [5]. The synthesis and mapping of quantum circuits to specific hardware is presented in [3,6–8]. There exists also some work in the field of quantum circuit verification [9,10]. However, to the best of our knowledge, so far, there exists only two works with focus on exploiting quantum computers for specific EDA problems, although the potential for the other direction of this symbolic relationship of quantum computing and EDA has been highlighted by Raghunathan and Stok [11] In [12] the authors analyze a quantum annealing approach to solve SAT problems. Like a lot of combinatorial optimization problems, the Min-k-Union problem could also be transferred to SAT and then further processed with the existing approaches. This transformation however introduces overhead in terms of variables and quadratic terms, which is why direct approaches are preferable. The authors of [13] present a very similar study based on the Max-Cut problem. We did our experiments at the same time (2021), however our paper was several times rejected on the major EDA conferences, leading to this overlap.

Quantum computing in general and quantum optimization in particular have seen a large body of work come into existence during the last years, yet many aspects are not yet fully understood. In particular, any quantum processing units (QPUs) that are available either commercially or in research labs today suffer from considerable imperfections and resource constraints, and are therefore termed *noisy, intermediate-scale quantum* (NISQ) machines. This influences both, the choice of the optimization algorithm and the approach to evaluation.

Variational quantum algorithms, that are particularly tailored to the capabilities NISQ-era machines, include the *Quantum Approximate Optimization Algorithm* (QAOA) family of algorithms (see, e.g., Refs. [14,15]). These algorithms aim at solving optimization problems and are hypothesized to achieve computational gains over classical approaches, albeit a practical advantage has not yet been observed to the best of our knowledge in any field. Nonetheless, it has been shown that it is impossible for any generic classical algorithm to efficiently sample the output distribution of QAOA algorithms, even in very restricted scenarios (i.e., with the level parameter $p = 1$, which we elaborate in Sect. 3.1), at least when generally accepted complexity-theoretic assumptions are true [16]. While this indicates quantum advantage in a certain sense, further experimental progress is required to explore the capabilities of the approach in relevant scenarios, in particular when executed on noisy devices. Leymann *et* al. [17] discuss the (considerable) impact of imperfections in NISQ machines on quantum algorithms; Greiwe et al. [18] show illustratively the performance degradation of typical quantum algorithms under the influence of noise. How to benchmark quantum algorithms is considered, amongst others, by Becker et al. [19], Tomesh et al. [20] and Resch et al. [21].

3 Formulation for Quantum-Based Optimization

In this section, we present the details of our quantum formulation of the EDA problem. Given that QC is a relatively new paradigm, it behooves to first recall some fundamentals on how QPUs operate algorithmically, as this differs substantially from the patterns known from classical computing. We also discuss the primitives available for our formulation and provide a rationale for our choice of empirical evaluation approach.

3.1 Quantum Optimization

Multiple quantum approaches allow us to solve our subject problem; two are particularly common for currently available machines:

(1) The *Quantum Approximate Optimization Algorithm* (QAOA) [22] is an iterative, hybrid quantum-classical algorithm for *gate-based* QPUs that can be used to seek minimal solutions to QUBO problems. Roughly speaking, QAOA applies a set of parameterized quantum operations including an evaluation of the target function to an initial state, samples the resulting probability distribution of possible outcomes caused by quantum superposition, and then uses classical optimization to update parameters for the quantum operations that lead to improved measurement results in the next iteration. Additionally, the core quantum part of the algorithm can be performed p times in each iteration, correspondingly increasing the number of parameters. For perfect QPUs, it can be shown that results improve with increasing p and thus increased computational effort, whereas NISQ machines will experience a trade-off between a more expressive computation and increasing amounts of noise with increasing p.

Possibilities to improve the performance of QAOA on NISQ machines are plentiful: Noise mitigation techniques (*e.g.*, [23,24]); choosing good initial parameters (often referred to as warm-starting) by classical (*e.g.*, [25]) and machine learning approaches (*e.g.*, [26]); by reducing classical optimization to lower-dimensional, nearly equivalent spaces (see, *e.g.*, Ref. [27]). Note that recent insights on variational quantum circuits in general and QAOA in particular (for instance, using large Fourier series [28]) give criteria for the feasibility of classically approximating quantum variational algorithms, which limit the potential of quantum approaches. Likewise, the detrimental impact of noise on QAOA has been characterised experimentally (*e.g.*, [29], based on a sound theoretical understanding (*e.g.*, [30,31]), which further limits the merit of evaluations on current-generation hardware.

(2) *Quantum annealing*[1] (respectively adiabatic quantum computation [32]) is – depending on the point of view – a particular transformation executed on a quantum computer using global operations [33], or is performed by a special class of machines purpose-built [34] to solve, respectively, approximate [35] QUBO problems. The scheme operates similar to classical annealing procedures, yet it can benefit from quantum effects to speed up the underlying optimization problem [36]. For the physical and algorithmic details of these base patterns, and other algorithmic possibilities, we refer to the available introductory texts on quantum computing [37], or recent reviews [38].

We emphasize that the focus of our paper is to introduce the required reformulation of the EDA problem, which can be used as starting point for all aforementioned approaches. Since there is no unified theoretical understanding behind all variants of quantum optimization discussed above, it is challenging to predict which variant is best suited to a given combination of machine and problem, and an comprehensive empirical evaluation is mandated. However, for realistic settings, this necessitates a comparison with classical heuristics and probabilistic approaches, especially regarding to their average-case performance. The complexity of this task is universally appreciated, independent of quantum computing, and considered at textbook level (see, *e.g.*, [39]). Furthermore, quantum performance evaluation itself is highly non-trivial [40]. Since NISQ machines fail to provide the required qubit resources for realistic instances of our problem by a wide margin (cf. Table 2), we deliberately refrain from conducting an empirical performance evaluation beyond the scale of toy problems in this paper. Finally, note that it would be possible to derive runtime bounds for a given task for the mechanism underlying QAOA and annealing, which unfortunately requires knowledge of the so-called *minimal spectral gap*, which is as hard to compute as solving the problem itself.

3.2 Problem Extraction

DRAMs consist of memory cells organized into memory arrays composed of columns, rows, and banks. The amalgamation of primary and secondary sense amplifiers within a bank's memory arrays is commonly termed a *row buffer*. Typically, the row buffer possesses a capacity ranging from 1 KB to 8 KB, which is known as the DRAM page size. It operates as a compact cache, storing the most recently accessed row within the bank. The latency of a memory access to a bank is heavily influenced by the state of this row buffer. A memory access targeting the same row as the one currently cached in the buffer (referred to as a *row hit*) results in minimal latency and energy consumption. Conversely, if a memory access targets a different row than the one stored in the buffer (referred to as a

---

[1] Quantum annealing is a restricted variant of the more general adiabatic evolution of a quantum system. In turn, QAOA can be seen as a finite approximation to an adiabatic evolution, which is recovered in the limit $p \to \infty$. Consequently, most of the remarks on the need for empirical evaluation of the performance of NISQ machines on our subject problem apply in equal measure to both approaches.

row miss), it leads to heightened latency and energy consumption. Meanwhile, the concurrent access of activated rows in distinct banks without penalty, known as *Bank Parallelism*, can be harnessed to enhance overall performance. Thus, the achieved DRAM bandwidth and latency strongly depends on the access patterns of the applications. Therefore, memory controllers have configurable address scramblers, which permute the address bits by means of simple lookup tables or a network of multiplexers, in order to maximize the sustainable DRAM bandwidth.

The EDA problem in focus is to find an optimal configuration for the scrambler such that row misses are minimized and the bank parallelism is maximised. The work presented in [2] demonstrated that a multi-bank DRAM can be effectively simplified into a single-bank DRAM, given the independent operation of all DRAM banks. Consequently, we will exclusively focus on DRAMs with a single bank for the remainder of this paper. It has been shown by [1,2] that this problem is NP-hard and that the core of the problem can be reduced to the so-called Min-k-Union problem. As the solution to this problem holds the highest time-criticality, our primary focus lies in accelerating its resolution.

Roughly summarizing the deductions of [2], the problem can be extracted as follows: We are given a memory address sequence for an arbitrary application. These addresses should be mapped to a DRAM memory, where the goal is to find an assignment of the address bits to new row and column bits – and in the general case also to bank bits – such that the number of row misses is minimized. A row miss appears wherever we have at least one bit flip from one address to the following in the assigned row bits. Due to the resulting overhead, this should happen as few as possible. Therefore, each column of the stacked addresses defines a set containing the row numbers where a bit change appears and the goal is to select a specified number of these sets where we have the least row misses, i.e., the least number of elements.

The resulting problem is the Min-k-Union problem, which is defined mathematically as this: Given a finite ground set V, a collection $\mathcal{S} \subseteq 2^V$ of subsets of the ground set (where 2^V denotes the power set of V) and $k \in \mathbb{N}$, the goal is to choose exactly k sets $M_1, \ldots, M_k \in \mathcal{S}$ such that the cardinality of the union $T = \bigcup_{i=1}^{k} M_i$ of the chosen sets is as small as possible. As shown in Theorem 1 of [2], finding an optimal permutation, i.e., an optimal assignment from address bits to row bits, is equivalent in solving an instance of the Min-k-Union problem where k denotes the number of row bits that have to be assigned. The deduction to this problem will also become more clear with the concrete example explained in Sect. 4.1.

3.3 QUBO Formulation

The Min-k-Union problem is known to be NP-hard to solve and even NP-hard to approximate [41]. Thus, it seems unlikely that one is able to find an algorithm which solves all instances efficiently in polynomial time (since this would imply that the complexity classes P and NP coincide). Moreover, essentially all known formulations of the Min-k-Union problem as *linear* integer programs suffer from the weakness that the corresponding linear relaxation is rather weak, meaning that integer linear programming solvers tend to explore many nodes in the branch-and-bound tree which in turn means a rather inefficient solution procedure.

Thus, the approach taken in this paper is different: Instead of using a *linear* formulation for the Min-k-Union problem, we use a *quadratic* formulation, which is suitable for quantum computing. As mentioned before, one type of optimization problems which have proven to be appropriate in this respect are *Quadratic Unconstrained Binary Optimization* problems (QUBOs). A QUBO is an optimization problem of the form

$$\min \sum_{i=1}^{n}\sum_{j=1}^{n} q_{ij}x_i x_j = x^T Q x = H(x)$$
$$\text{s.t.} \quad x \in \{0,1\}^n,$$

where $Q = (q_{ij})_{i,j=1,\ldots,n}$ is a given matrix. In the following, we will show how to transform the Min-k-Union problem to a QUBO.

In order to formulate the Min-k-Union problem as a QUBO, we define binary variables with the following meaning: For $M \in \mathcal{S}$ we set the binary variable

$$x_M = \begin{cases} 1, & \text{if } M \in \mathcal{S} \text{ is chosen,} \\ 0, & \text{otherwise.} \end{cases}$$

We also have binary variables $y_v \in \{0,1\}$ with the following meaning:

$$y_v = \begin{cases} 1, & \text{if } v \text{ is contained the union} \\ & \text{of the chosen } k \text{ sets,} \\ 0, & \text{otherwise.} \end{cases}$$

We now construct the objective H of the QUBO, which is is composed of three parts, i.e., $H = H_A + H_B + H_C$, each of which is non-negative, and which we describe now.

We first have

$$H_A(x) := A \left(k - \sum_{M \in \mathcal{S}} x_M \right)^2 \geq 0, \tag{1}$$

where $A > 0$ is a constant to be chosen later. Obviously $H_A(x) = 0$ if and only if the selection of sets described by x contains exactly k sets. The term H_A is intended as a "penalty term" and we will show at the end of this section how to determine the penalty parameter $A > 0$, such that any optimal solution x^* of the QUBO fulfils $H_A(x^*) = 0$, i.e., forms a feasible solution of the original problem.

In order to properly count the number of elements in the union $\bigcup_{M \in \mathcal{S}: x_M = 1} M$ of the chosen sets, we need to ensure the activation of an element

v once a set is activated in which contains the element. This can be done with the inequality constraint $y_v \geq x_M$ for each $v \in V$ and each $M \in \mathcal{S}$ with $v \in S$. For the QUBO reformulation, consider the term $t_{M,v} = (1 - y_v)x_M \geq 0$ for $M \in \mathcal{S}$ and $v \in M$. If $x_M = 1$, then the only way to achieve $t_{M,v} = 0$ is to set $y_v = 1$. If in turn $x_M = 0$, then $t_{v,M} = 0$ no matter what the value of y_v is. These considerations lead us to our new part H_B, where $B > 0$ is again a suitable penalty parameter to be determined later:

$$H_B(x,y) := B \sum_{v \in V} \sum_{M \in \mathcal{S}: v \in M} (1 - y_v) x_M. \quad (2)$$

The third term H_C is the actual objective function of the Min-k-Union problem:

$$H_C(y) := C \sum_{v \in V} y_v. \quad (3)$$

We now address the choice of the constants A, B and C in the above formulation. Recall that $H_A \geq A$ if our choice of sets does not contain exactly k sets. If we have set $x_M = 1$ and $y_v = 0$ for some element $v \in M$, then $H_B \geq B$. Furthermore, we always have $0 \leq H_C \leq C|V|$. Thus, if we choose $A = B > C|V|$, then any solution that minimizes $H = H_A + H_B + H_C$ will have $H_A = H_B = 0$ and thus form a feasible solution to the Min-k-Union problem, where H_C correctly counts the number of chosen elements. In particular $C = 1$, $A = B = |V| + 1$ satisfy this condition.

This means, in the end, the formulation given above integrates all constraints of the Min-k-Union problem via (1) and (2) into the objective in an *exact* formulation: Any optimal solution of the QUBO is in fact an optimal solution for the given instance of the Min-k-Union problem and one does not need to vary penalty parameters. The QUBO then is an *unconstrained* problem which can be given to a quantum computer without any further manipulations.

Furthermore, this QUBO formulation has a number of advantages. First, it uses only a number of variables, which is linear in the number of elements and sets. Due to their structure, the constraints of the original Min-k-Union problem formulation do not introduce any additional variables in the QUBO formulation. This is important since the number of variables translates directly into the number of quantum bits needed. Additionally, the coefficients of the resulting QUBO, i.e., the values $q_{i,j}$, have a simple structure; they are integer and only dependent on the parameter k and the constants A, B and C. This might support finding the solution using NISQ devices.

4 Case Study

To demonstrate the feasibility of our approach, we transform the example of [2] into a QUBO problem, employing the formalism presented in Sect. 3. First, we describe the artificial example. Second, we describe the execution on the IBM quantum computer and the D-Wave quantum annealer, and third, we discuss the results with respect to scalability of the approach.

Table 1. Sequence of Memory Addresses with Highlighted Bit-Toggling

a	$a_{i,0}$	$a_{i,1}$	$a_{i,2}$	$a_{i,3}$	$a_{i,4}$
a_0	1	0	0	0	1
a_1	**0**	0	0	**1**	1
a_2	0	0	**1**	1	**0**
a_3	0	**1**	1	**0**	**1**
a_4	0	1	1	**1**	1
a_5	0	1	1	**0**	1
a_6	**1**	1	**0**	0	**0**
a_7	1	1	0	0	**1**
a_8	1	**0**	**1**	0	1

4.1 Example Problem

Table 1 shows the memory address sequence a for an artificial application. The addresses of this application shall be mapped in an artificial DRAM with 8 rows (3 row address bits) and 4 columns per row (2 column address bits). The goal is to find a selection of the address bits to serve as the row bits, such that the number of row misses is minimized. As mentioned before, the reduction to a single bank is suitable and we therefore assign no bank address bits here.

The bold numbers in Table 1 represent the address bits that toggle between consecutive accesses. This toggling behavior is observed column-wise. Consequently, for each column $a_{*,j}$, $j \in 0,\ldots,4$, we define a set M_j, which contains row indices $i \in 0,\ldots,8$ corresponding to bit changes from $a_{i,j-1}$ to $a_{i,j}$, i.e., the highlighted numbers in the table. In this specific case, we have $M_0 = \{1,6\}$, $M_1 = \{3,8\}$, $M_2 = \{2,6,8\}$, $M_3 = \{1,3,4,5\}$, and $M_4 = \{2,3,6,7\}$. The size of set M_j reflects the number of bit changes for the j-th address bit.

Figure 1a shows the sets which are formed. Since our artificial DRAM has 8 rows, we want to choose 3 of these sets. A valid optimal solution of this small artificial example is easy to find: consider the union of the sets M_0, M_1 and M_2 given by $T := M_0 \cup M_1 \cup M_2 = \{1,2,3,6,8\}$, as shown in Fig. 1b. The elements of T are exactly the positions of bit changes happening combined in columns 0, 1 and 2 and the size $|T| = 5$ equals the minimal number of row misses.

4.2 Execution on IBM Quantum Computer

In this study, we have utilized Qiskit, an open-source python based SDK developed by IBM. Qiskit allows users to work with quantum computers at the circuit, pulse, and algorithm level. We formulated the example above as QUBO with Qiskit and executed it on the ibmq_ehningen quantum computer, which is one of the IBM Quantum Canary Processors. Qiskit compiles the formulation in python in an according quantum circuit consisting of quantum gates. To ascertain reproducibility of our results [42], we will upload our code on Github once

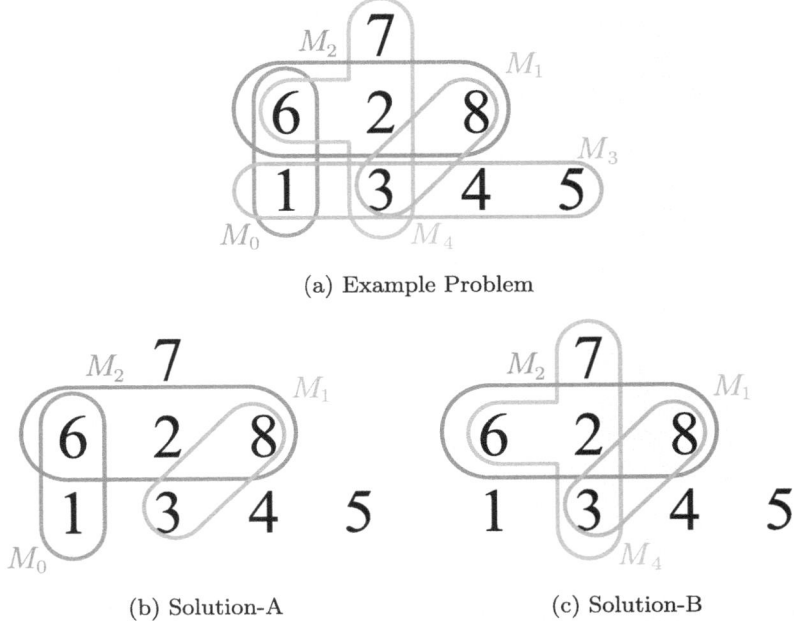

Fig. 1. Hypergraphs and Solutions for Example Problem Corresponding to Table 1

the publication is accepted. The `ibmq_ehningen` quantum computer has a total number of 27 qubits, where for our example only 13 qubits are required (8 nodes and 5 sets). It has a coherence time around 150 us.

The solution that the `ibmq_ehningen` quantum computer found is shown in Fig. 1c. In contrary to our example solution in Fig. 1b, the quantum computer decided to pick the sets M_1, M_2 and M_4. However, this is a valid optimal solution as well, because the number of row misses (the number of Elements in the set $T = M_1 \cup M_2 \cup M_4$) is also 5. This proves that the execution of the EDA problem is feasible on a real quantum computer.

4.3 Execution on D-Wave Quantum Annealer

Over D-Wave's cloud platform *Leap*[2], using the trial access, and their python library `dwave-ocean-sdk`[3], one can easily send problems to the connected quantum annealers of the current *Advantage* generation with about 5000 qubits. Using the internally implemented embedding and de-embedding strategy, we were able to submit the above test instance in our QUBO formulation directly. The size of the annealing sample was set to 100 and besides that we used the default

---

[2] https://cloud.dwavesys.com/leap/.
[3] https://github.com/dwavesystems/dwave-ocean-sdk.

solver parameters, such as 20 μs annealing time. The full sample set for a single run is shown in Fig. 2. The different parts of the bars indicate different solutions yielding the same objective value. We obtained both optimal solutions at once, where Solution A was found in 6 of the 100 cases and Solution B in 5 cases. The other cases are sub-optimal solutions with varying objective values. Note that the values differ slightly in subsequent runs, due to the heuristic nature of the machines. The implementation of the corresponding test script was supported by the tool quark[4].

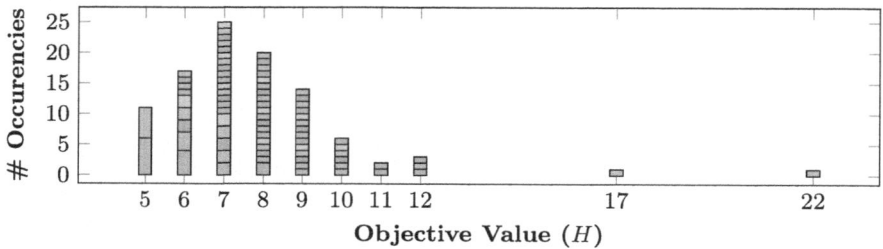

Fig. 2. Histogram of solutions from D-Wave run

4.4 Discussion

Table 2. Required Number of Qubits, Benchmarks from [43]

Benchmark	Elements	Sets	Qubits
filter7	524288	19	524307
rot6	65536	16	65552
rot3d7	2097152	21	2097173
NN8	356400	22	356422

Having demonstrated the feasibility of executing the formulation on two quantum machines, the question that arises is how well the formulation scales for real-world applications that store their data in real DRAM-Chips like DDR5 oder LPDDR5. As previously mentioned, the number of required qubits depends on the sum of elements and sets, thus scaling linearly. Table 2 illustrates the necessary number of qubits for various real-world FPGA benchmark applications [43]. The primary factor influencing the qubit requirement is the number of elements. Since the number of elements corresponds to the number of unique

---
[4] https://gitlab.com/quantum-computing-software/.

DRAM addresses present in a benchmark, it serves as a reasonable approximation for the required number of qubits. Let us highlight that the problem size only grows linearly with the number of elements and sets, compared to other approaches that exhibit non-linear growth in problem size. Given this favorable property, we believe that solving the EDA problem using quantum computers or quantum accelerators in the future holds promise.

Of course, the scope of our empirical feasibility evaluation remains far from touching practical utility. While today's quantum computers lack a sufficient number of qubits to solve real-world instances, we are currently witnessing exponential growth in qubit availability, backed by ambitious roadmaps of commercial vendors. Additionally, quantum-inspired computational accelerators like Fujitsu's digital annealer will allow us, pursuing a slightly different route, to explore considerably larger instances in future work. We therefore believe our approach to contribute an important milestone towards using quantum computers for EDA workloads, as it establishes a solid foundation for entirely new viewpoints that have not been considered before by the community for addressing an important and crucial problem in EDA.

5 Conclusion and Future Work

The field of EDA has to solve complex problems for IC design, often relying on heuristics. Quantum computers offer potential solutions through their optimization capabilities, yet research on leveraging them for EDA problems is limited. This paper explores the feasibility and potential of quantum computing for a typical EDA optimization problem, successfully executed on an IBM quantum computer and D-Wave's quantum annealing machines. Despite current qubit limitations, the presumably ongoing exponential growth in qubit availability suggests that quantum computing holds promise for EDA challenges. With problem size scaling linearly, quantum optimization techniques could provide effective solutions in the future.

Moving forward, our future endeavors encompass conducting additional analyses of this specific EDA problem, involving multiple executions on a quantum computer. Additionally, we aim to explore and analyze various other EDA problems like scheduling, placement and routing.

Acknowledgement. We acknowledge the use of IBM Quantum services through the Fraunhofer Quantum Programme. The views expressed are those of the authors and do not reflect the official policy or position of IBM or the IBM Quantum team.

References

1. Jung, M., et al.: ConGen: an application specific DRAM memory controller generator. In: Proceedings of the Second International Symposium on Memory Systems, ser. MEMSYS 2016, pp. 257–267. ACM, New York (2016). https://doi.org/10.1145/2989081.2989131

2. Natale, M.V.: Efficient generation of application specific memory controllers. In: International Symposium on Memory Systems (MEMSYS 2020). ACM/IEEE (October 2020)
3. Soeken, M., Meuli, G., Schmitt, B., Mozafari, F., Riener, H., De Micheli, G.: Boolean satisfiability in quantum compilation. Philos. Trans. Royal Soc. Mathe. Phys. Eng. Sci. **378**(2164), 20190161 (2020). https://royalsocietypublishing.org/doi/abs/10.1098/rsta.2019.0161
4. Zulehner, A., Wille, R.: Exploiting coding techniques for logic synthesis of reversible circuits. In: 2018 23rd Asia and South Pacific Design Automation Conference (ASP-DAC), pp. 670–675 (2018)
5. Hillmich, S., Zulehner, A., Kueng, R., Markov, I.L., Wille, R.: Approximating decision diagrams for quantum circuit simulation. ACM Trans. Quantum Comput. **3**(4) (2022). https://doi.org/10.1145/3530776
6. Zulehner, A., Paler, A., Wille, R.: Efficient mapping of quantum circuits to the ibm qx architectures. In: 2018 Design, Automation & Test in Europe Conference & Exhibition (DATE), pp. 1135–1138 (2018)
7. Niemann, P., Datta, R., Wille, R.: Logic synthesis for quantum state generation. In: 2016 IEEE 46th International Symposium on Multiple-Valued Logic (ISMVL), pp. 247–252 (2016)
8. Shende, V., Bullock, S., Markov, I.: Synthesis of quantum logic circuits. In: Proceedings of the ASP-DAC 2005. Asia and South Pacific Design Automation Conference, vol. 1, pp. 272–275 (2005)
9. Burgholzer, L., Wille, R.: Advanced equivalence checking for quantum circuits (2021)
10. Burgholzer, L., Raymond, R., Wille, R.: Verifying results of the IBM Qiskit quantum circuit compilation flow. In: International Conference on Quantum Computing and Engineering (2020)
11. Raghunathan, S., Stok, L.: Eda and quantum computing: a symbiotic relationship? IEEE Design & Test **37**(6), 71–78 (2020)
12. Su, J., Tu, T., He, L.: A quantum annealing approach for boolean satisfiability problem. In: Proceedings of the 53rd Annual Design Automation Conference, ser. DAC 2016. Association for Computing Machinery, New York (2016). https://doi.org/10.1145/2897937.2897973
13. Verghese, A., Byron, D., Amann, A., Popovici, E.: Max-cut problem implementation and analysis on a quantum computer. In: 2022 33rd Irish Signals and Systems Conference (ISSC), pp. 1–6 (2022)
14. Alam, M., Ash-Saki, A., Ghosh, S.: Design-space exploration of quantum approximate optimization algorithm under noise. In: 2020 IEEE Custom Integrated Circuits Conference (CICC), pp. 1–4 (2020)
15. Wang, S., Fontana, E., Cerezo, M., Sharma, K., Sone, A., Cincio, L., Coles, P.J.: Noise-induced barren plateaus in variational quantum algorithms. Nat. Commun. **12**(1), 6961 (2021). https://doi.org/10.1038/s41467-021-27045-6
16. Farhi, E., Harrow, A.W.: Quantum supremacy through the quantum approximate optimization algorithm, arXiv:1602.07674 (2016)
17. Leymann, F., Barzen, J.: The bitter truth about gate-based quantum algorithms in the nisq era. Quantum Sci. Technol. **5**(4), 044007 (2020)
18. Greiwe, F., Krueger, T., Mauerer, W.: Effects of imperfections on quantum algorithms: a software engineering perspective. In: Proceedings of the IEEE Quantum Software Week (2023)

19. Kai-Uwe Becker, C., Tcholtchev, N., Gheorghe-Pop, I.-D., Bock, S., Seidel, R., Hauswirth, M.: Towards a quantum benchmark suite with standardized kpis. In: 2022 IEEE 19th International Conference on Software Architecture Companion (ICSA-C), pp. 160–163 (2022)
20. Teague Tomesh, P.G.: Supermarq: a scalable quantum benchmark suite. In: 28th IEEE International Symposium on High-Performance Computer Architecture (2022). https://par.nsf.gov/biblio/10339323
21. Resch, S., Karpuzcu, U.R.: Benchmarking quantum computers and the impact of quantum noise. ACM Comput. Surv. (CSUR) **54**(7), 1–35 (2021)
22. Farhi, E., Goldstone, J., Gutmann, S.: A quantum approximate optimization algorithm (Nov. 2014)
23. van den Berg, E., Minev, Z.K., Kandala, A., Temme, K.: Probabilistic error cancellation with sparse pauli-lindblad models on noisy quantum processors (2022)
24. Lao, L., Korotkov, A., Jiang, Z., Mruczkiewicz, W., O'Brien, T.E., Browne, D.E.: Software mitigation of coherent two-qubit gate errors. Quantum Sci. Technol. **7**(2), 025021 (2022). https://doi.org/10.1088/2058-9565/ac57f1
25. Egger, D.J., Mareček, J., Woerner, S.: Warm-starting quantum optimization. Quantum **5**, 479 (2021). https://doi.org/10.22331/q-2021-06-17-479
26. Khairy, S., Shaydulin, R., Cincio, L., Alexeev, Y., Balaprakash, P.: Learning to optimize variational quantum circuits to solve combinatorial problems. In: Proceedings of the AAAI Conference on Artificial Intelligence, vol. 34(03), pp. 2367–2375 (Apr. 2020). https://ojs.aaai.org/index.php/AAAI/article/view/5616
27. Zhou, L., Wang, S.-T., Choi, S., Pichler, H., Lukin, M.D.: Quantum approximate optimization algorithm: Performance, mechanism, and implementation on nearterm devices. Phys. Rev. X **10**, 021067 (2020). https://doi.org/10.1103/PhysRevX.10.021067
28. Landman, J., Thabet, S., Dalyac, C., Mhiri, H., Kashefi, E.: Classically approximating variational quantum machine learning with random fourier features (2022)
29. Harrigan, M.P., Sung, K.J., Neeley, M., et al.: Quantum approximate optimization of non-planar graph problems on a planar superconducting processor. Nat. Phys. **17**(3), 332–336 (2021). https://doi.org/10.1038/s41567-020-01105-y
30. Marshall, J., Wudarski, F., Hadfield, S., Hogg, T.: Characterizing local noise in qaoa circuits. IOP SciNotes **1**(2), 025208 (2020). https://doi.org/10.1088/2633-1357/abb0d7
31. Xue, C., Chen, Z.-Y., Wu, Y.-C., Guo, G.-P.: Effects of quantum noise on quantum approximate optimization algorithm. Chin. Phys. Lett. **38**(3), 030302 (2021). https://doi.org/10.1088/0256-307X/38/3/030302
32. Albash, T., Lidar, D.A.: Adiabatic quantum computation. Rev. Mod. Phys. **90**, 015002 (2018). https://doi.org/10.1103/RevModPhys.90.015002
33. Wintersperger, K., et al.: Neutral atom quantum computing hardware: Performance and end-user perspective (2023)
34. McGeoch, C., Farré, P.: The D-Wave Advantage system: An overview, D-Wave Systems Inc, Tech. Rep. 14-1049A-A (2020)
35. Sax, I., Feld, S., Zielinski, S., Gabor, T., Linnhoff-Popien, C., Mauerer, W.: Approximate approximation on a quantum annealer. In: Proceedings of the 17th ACM International Conference on Computing Frontiers, pp. 108–117 (2020). https://arxiv.org/pdf/2004.09267
36. McGeoch, C.C.: Adiabatic Quantum Computation and Quantum Annealing: Theory and Practice, ser. Synthesis Lectures on Quantum Computing. Morgan & Claypool Publishers (2014). https://doi.org/10.2200/S00585ED1V01Y201407QMC008

37. Nielsen, M.A., Chuang, I.L.: Quantum Computation and Quantum Information. Cambridge University Press (2000)
38. Bharti, K., et al.: Noisy intermediate-scale quantum algorithms. Rev. Mod. Phys. **94**, 015004 (2022). https://link.aps.org/doi/10.1103/RevModPhys.94.015004
39. Arora, S., Barak, B.: Computational Complexity: A Modern Approach. Cambridge University Press (2006). https://theory.cs.princeton.edu/complexity/book.pdf
40. McGeoch, C.C.: Principles and guidelines for quantum performance analysis. In: Feld, S., Linnhoff-Popien, C. (eds.) QTOP 2019. LNCS, vol. 11413, pp. 36–48. Springer, Cham (2019). https://doi.org/10.1007/978-3-030-14082-3_4
41. E. Chlamtáč, M. Dinitz, and Y. Makarychev, "Minimizing the Union: Tight Approximations for Small Set Bipartite Vertex Expansion," in *SODA '17 Proceedings of the Twenty-Eighth Annual ACM-SIAM Symposium on Discrete Algorithms*, 2017, pp. 881–899
42. Mauerer, W., Scherzinger, S.: 1-2-3 reproducibility for quantum software experiments. In: Q-SANER@IEEE International Conference on Software Analysis, Evolution and Reengineering (2022)
43. Natale, M.V.: On Packing and Partitioning Problems with Applications to DRAM Allocation

Real-Time Linux on RISC-V: Long-Term Performance Analysis of PREEMPT_RT Patches

Tobias Schaffner[1]((✉)) [iD], Jan Altenberg[2] [iD], and Stefan Wallentowitz[3] [iD]

[1] Siemens AG, Otto-Hahn-Ring, 81739 Munich, Germany
tobias.schaffner@siemens.com
[2] Open Source Automation Development Lab (OSADL) eG, Im Neuenheimer Feld 583, 69120 Heidelberg, Germany
jan.altenberg@osadl.org
[3] Munich University of Applied Sciences, Lothstraße 34, 80335 Munich, Germany
stefan.wallentowitz@hm.edu
https://www.siemens.com/ , https://www.osadl.org/ , https://www.hm.edu/

Abstract. Currently, the market is witnessing the introduction of the first RISC-V development boards capable of running Linux. In the embedded sector, these boards could serve as alternatives to the commonly used ARM or x86-based platforms.

Ongoing efforts are being made to enhance the real-time capabilities of the Linux kernel, allowing it to handle both time-critical and non-time-critical tasks with complex software stacks in so called Mixed-Criticality Systems (MCS).

One project that may merge into the Linux kernel soon is PREEMPT_RT. PREEMPT_RT is a patch for the Linux kernel source code that enables low-latency real-time execution directly within the kernel. At the time of writing, RISC-V support has just been merged into the PREEMPT_RT patch series.

The paper presents a comprehensive analysis of this new release on a RISC-V platform, utilizing an extensive collection of long-term measurement data generated for this study. It compares the Worst Case Latencies (WCL) to the results on a common ARM platform having the same configuration. The measurement environment is thoroughly described, providing a detailed explanation of all the necessary information for replicating the results, including tuning procedures.

Keywords: RISC-V · PREEMPT_RT · real-time · MCS

1 Introduction

1.1 Linux for Hard Real-Time

In industries such as automotive and avionics, the rising demand for software features necessitates the management of an expanding array of tasks, encompassing both time-critical and non-time-critical functionalities [1–3].

Traditionally, these tasks were executed on separate hardware platforms using different operating systems. General-purpose operating systems (GPOS), such as Linux, were used for running complex software stacks related to user interaction or multimedia display, while real-time operating systems (RTOS) ensured deterministic execution of time-critical tasks.

However, a recent trend has emerged towards MCS, where both safety-critical and non-critical tasks are consolidated on a single embedded system [4]. This shift is motivated by the desire to integrate the functionalities of both systems onto one cost-effective, often off-the-shelf hardware platform [3].

But while RTOS systems do not provide the features needed to run complex applications, Linux initially was not designed to be a real-time system [5]. To overcome the limitation of the latter, several real-time Linux solutions have been developed.

One approach, is the employ of a co-kernel like Xenomai [6] that handles the decision-making process of whether a real-time task or the Linux kernel should be executed when an interrupt occurs. But currently, there is no co-kernel approach available that supports the RISC-V architecture.

On the other hand, PREEMPT_RT is a kernel patch that can be applied to the Linux kernel source code. It enables low-latency real-time execution within the Linux kernel itself, allowing the use of existing Linux APIs and drivers. RISC-V support was added to PREEMPT_RT at the end of 2023 [7].

1.2 RISC-V

RISC-V [8] is an open standard Instruction Set Architecture (ISA) that is available free of charge.

The openness of the ISA has led to a growing interest in open processors within academia [9]. Adopting an open design not only eliminates licensing costs but also enables peer reviewing to identify potential security vulnerabilities [10] and customize the processor according to user-specific requirements [11].

The idea of having a custom processor for Linux with real-time capabilities is appealing, as it would allow the creation of processors with features such as deterministic caching or deterministic pipelines.

A thriving ecosystem is evolving around RISC-V, with significant developments in progress. Recently, the introduction of more powerful hardware platforms, albeit with closed source designs, has made RISC-V a feasible choice for (real-time) Linux-based products and allows for initial testing.

1.3 Organization of the Paper

This paper evaluates the performance of Linux with the PREEMPT_RT patches, running on one of the first RISC-V processors, specifically the JH7110 on a StarFive VisionFive2 board. It primarily focuses on the time-critical aspect of MCS in terms of WCL, while leaving other considerations like fault tolerance and certification aside.

Initially, the paper provides an overview of the test configuration, including all the essential details required for result replication. It describes the hardware used, as well as the generated testing images and tuning procedures. Test tools, stress tools and the used parameters are included.

Further, it shows a large dataset of 3.5 billion samples that was generated over three months under different load scenarios. The results are compared to a well known ARM platform with the same test setup to be able to set the numbers into perspective.

2 Methods

To ensure the comparability of results, we have to select hardware with similar specifications. Additionally, it is crucial to ensure that the software used, which encompasses the Linux kernel, the Linux root file system, and all the necessary test tooling, is as closely matched as possible.

2.1 Hardware

We chose the RISC-V based StarFive VisionFive V2 Board as device under test and the Raspberry Pi 4 as comparative platform.

StarFive VisionFive V2 Board. The StarFive VisionFive V2 board is based on the JH7110 quad-core, 64-bit RISC-V CPU, with clock frequencies up to 1.5GHz and 2 MB L2 cache [12]. It is one of the first multicore RISC-V processors publicly available. To achieve latency reduction, a minimum of two cores is required. Allocating dedicated cores for Linux housekeeping tasks becomes crucial in order to effectively separate them. This separation becomes necessary due to the potential disruptions caused by IRQs, timers, and kernel threads when scheduled on the same core as real-time tasks.

Raspberry Pi 4 as Comparison Target. The Raspberry Pi 4 is based on the BCM2711 SOC, which is a quad-core, ARM Cortex-A72 CPU, clocked at up to 1.5 GHz and equipped with 1MB of L2 Cache [13]. We will use this for comparison with the VisionFive2 board, as it is a common ARM platform with a comparable processor.

2.2 Test Images

To ensure consistent results, it is necessary to utilize identical software on both targets.

Isar. We used Isar [14] to build similar Debian based Linux images for both the StarFive VisionFive V2 (DT) and the Raspberry Pi 4 that can be directly flashed to an SD card. It allows us to create reproducible images with custom Linux kernel and a custom bootloader while depending on prebuilt Debian packages for the base system as well as the real-time tooling. By leveraging this capability, we can effortlessly generate a consistent and replicable test image with all the prepackaged test tooling from upstream Debian while diverting our attention towards customizations and fine-tuning aspects of a PREEMPT_RT kernel that is build from source. The created Isar layer [15] can be used to reproduce the testing images and the results of this paper. Prebuild images for both platforms can be downloaded in the actions tab [16].

Kernel. At the time of writing, the PREEMPT_RT enablement patches just got merged [7]. We used the upstream kernel version 6.6-rc6 and applied the PREEMPT_RT 6.6-rt14 patch [17] to this base. Some add-on patches [18] provided by the Open Source Automation Development Lab [19] (OSADL) have been added on top. These patches allow further diagnostics but have no impact on the measured WCL.

2.3 Test Tooling

To determine the WCL we used a test tool called cyclictest while running different load scenarios in the background.

Cyclictest. Cyclictest is a tool of the real-time test suite [20], used to evaluate the real-time latency of a system. It runs a given number of real-time threads with the scheduling class SCHED_FIFO and a high priority. The time it takes for the thread to wake up and start is periodically measured.

Best-case, this is just the minimal latency introduced by the interrupt and the scheduling of the real-time thread and some hardware jitter. But there are events that can prolong it, e.g. when IRQs have been temporarily masked, when a higher IRQ is running or when kernel threads, which are non-preemptive, cause blocking. Architecture specific implementations in the Linux kernel and in the preempt_rt patch series, the selection of drivers and different bootloaders can lead to different results on both platforms.

The most important value measured by cyclictest therefore is the maximum latency, which is equal to the WCL. The maximum latency value indicates the longest time it took for the thread to wake up, which is critical for assessing the real-time performance of a system.

Figure 1 illustrates a single measurement cycle, where the thread is sent to sleep for a specified interval. The latency refers to the time gap between the scheduled wake-up time of the thread and the actual time it awakens.

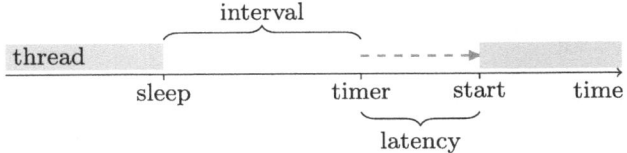

Fig. 1. real-time latency

Stress Generation. Running cyclictest in different load scenarios ensures that the results are valid for workloads typical in MCS. Latencies can be caused by a number of different factors, such as heavy CPU load or power management functions. Figure 2 shows an overview of the different load scenarios. All measurements are done twice a day (repeating every 12 h).

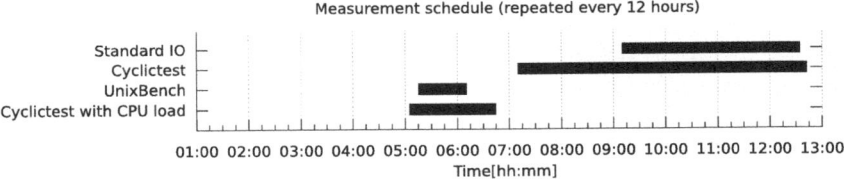

Fig. 2. Measurement Schedule in the OSADL QA farm

For all runs, the cyclictest threads are set up to run at a frequency of 5kHz. One test run with 100,000,000 cycles is done in an idle system (partly combined with additional IO load, caused by copying files over network). This measurement is supposed to catch latencies introduced by power management functions or by IO. Another measurement with 30,000,000 cycles is scheduled with UnixBench [21] running in the background. This emulates different heavy load scenarios like high CPU load or numerous system calls.

3 Results

3.1 Tuning

To minimize delays of the real-time task by low level system activities like kernel threads or unexpected IRQs the system should be optimized. We can do this by optimizing the kernel configuration and by running the kernel with some advanced options given to the kernel command line.

Kernel Configuration. The PREEMPT_RT specific kernel configurations [22] are applied to the board-specific kernel configurations before starting the build process.

Disable lock correctness checks as they can lead to additional latencies:

```
CONFIG_PROVE_LOCKING=n
CONFIG_LOCKDEP=n
```

Make sure that the CPU does not scale down:

```
CONFIG_CPU_FREQ=n
CONFIG_CPU_IDLE=n
```

The scheduling ticks have to be deterministic:

```
CONFIG_NO_HZ=n
CONFIG_HZ_PERIODIC=y
```

Disable all power management features:

```
CONFIG_SUSPEND=n
CONFIG_HIBERNATION=n
CONFIG_PM=n
```

We use the SLUB memory allocator for its deterministic allocation and freeing algorithm. For the time being, SLUB is the only allocator that can be selected with PREEMPT_RT enabled. At the same time, we disable its debug capabilities like cache validation as these can have a significant impact on the latencies.:

```
CONFIG_SLUB=y
CONFIG_SLUB_DEBUG=n
```

Kernel Command Line. As recommended by the CERN [23], the following tuning parameters were applied on the kernel command line, mainly to isolate the real-time tasks from the Linux housekeeping:

- isolcpus: Isolate certain cores from the CPU scheduling in order to keep the kernel housekeeping workloads on separate cores;
- rcu_nocbs: Disable call backs upon preemption in order to reduce latency;
- nohz_full: Select nohz_full mode in order to reduce timer interrupts;
- irqaffinity: Pin IRQs to specific CPUs in order to optimize performance;
- tsc=nowatchdog: Disable TSC watchdog, which is not suitable for real-time applications [24].

This resulted in the following kernel command line additions:

```
isolcpus=2-3 rcu_nocbs=2-3 nohz_full=2-3 irqaffinity=0-1 \
tsc=nowatchdog
```

3.2 Measurements

To gauge the performance of the PREEMPT_RT patch series on RISC-V, we ran cyclictest on both the VisionFive V2 (DT) and the Raspberry Pi 4, with the kernel command line parameters specified above while stressing the system in different scenarios. For this purpose, the boards have been integrated into the OSADL QA Farm [25].

UnixBench was started using the included Run script without any option. This will run the following tests on all unisolated cores:

- Dhrystone 2
- Double-Precision Whetstone
- Execl Throughput
- File Copy 1024 bufsize 2000 maxblocks
- File Copy 256 bufsize 500 maxblocks
- File Copy 4096 bufsize 8000 maxblocks
- Pipe Throughput
- Pipe-based Context Switching
- Process Creation
- System Call Overhead
- Shell Scripts
- Shell Scripts (8 concurrent)

Cyclictest was run with the following parameters on both platforms:

```
cyclictest --affinity 0-3 --threads 4 --prio 99 --distance 0 \
    --quiet --loops=30000000 --interval=200 --histogram=400
```

In SMP mode, cyclictest by default runs one thread per CPU. The number of CPUs is derived from the default affinity mask. Therefore, isolated CPUs are ignored. In our scenario, we want to use all CPU cores to spot differences in the latencies of isolated and non-isolated cores. For this purpose, we start four threads using the option –threads and set the affinity to 0-3 to force cyclictest to create one thread per online core. This allows us to monitor all four cores, the first two system cores as well as the two isolated ones designated for our real-time load. The priority has to be set to a value higher than any thread on the system to avoid that other threads get favored. The distance between the thread intervals was set to zero. We use the quiet and histogram options to disable output while running but create a histogram in the end. The detailed description of the used options can be looked up in the Debian manual page [26].

Single test runs are displayed in the Figs. 3, 5, 4 and 6.

The plots show the WCL per core in the legend in the top right. The distribution of latencies can be seen in the plot, with the measured latency on the x-axis and the number of times the value was measured logarithmic on the y-axis. Only the isolated core #2 and #3 in green and red are object to the comparison, as the first two unisolated cores may be interrupted by system tasks. We can see that the isolation works as expected, as the latencies are much higher on the first two cores.

In idle, the VisionFive 2 board shows a WCL of 40 and 43us on the isolated cores, while the Pi4 shows values of 57 and 33us.

While stressed, The VisionFive 2 board shows a WCL of 40 and 43us, while the Pi4 shows values of 41 and 39us in this run.

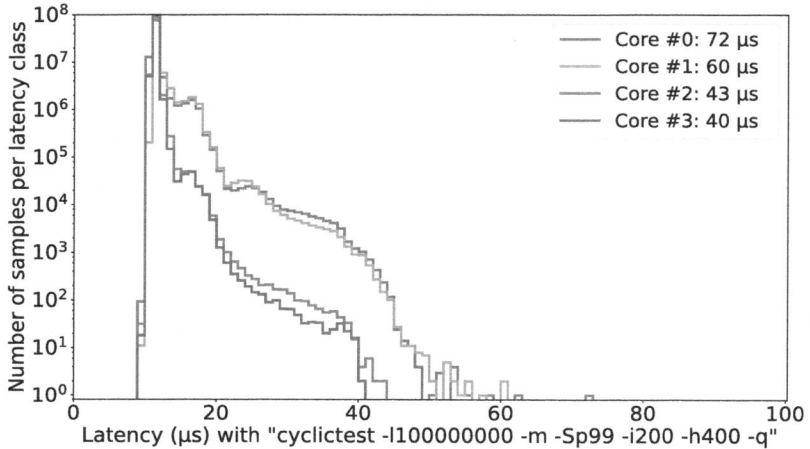

Fig. 3. Latency histogram on Starfive VisionFive 2 in idle

The Figs. 7 and 8 show combined long term latency plots of the two systems. Only the real-time cores are presented this time. It shows 236 graphs with 30,000,000 samples for both platforms. 118 graphs show the system in idle with some network IO and 118 graphs show the system under stress with UnixBench.

The black graph shows the median number of samples per latency class. The red graph shows the maximum value. The WCL is 92us for the Starfive Visionfive 2 and 94us for the Raspberry Pi 4.

4 Discussion

The results show that with PREEMPT_RT the real-time performance in terms of worst time latencies is comparable on both architectures. Even if the mean latency is a bit higher on the VisionFive 2 the PREEMPT_RT patches offer similar performance on both platforms in terms of WCL.

The measurements presented in this paper focus solely on the wake-up time of the thread and do not account for potential delays that may occur during runtime in a real-time thread. Analyzing and evaluating unexpected delays during runtime is beyond the scope of this study.

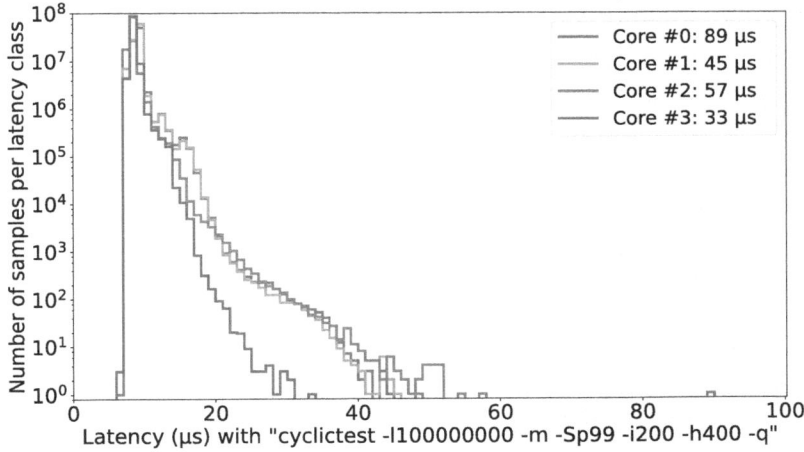

Fig. 4. Latency histogram on Raspberry Pi 4 in idle

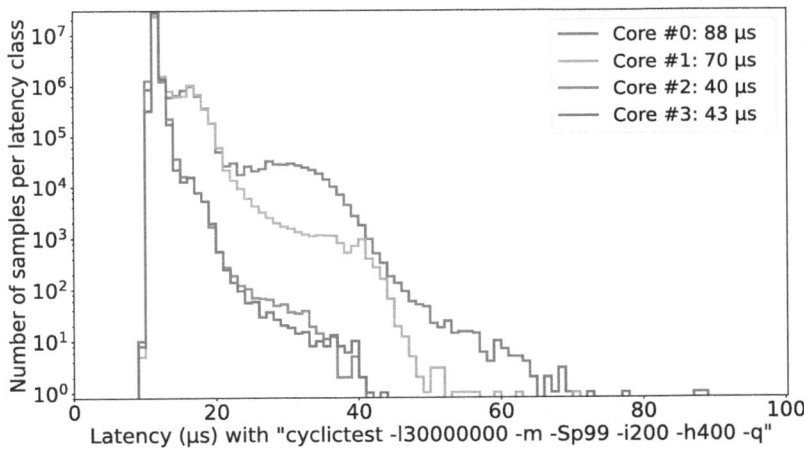

Fig. 5. Latency histogram on Starfive Visionfive 2 while stressed

At present, support for the PREEMPT_RT patch series on RISC-V is still in its early stages. Moreover, the results presented are specific to the hardware and configuration tested. Different hardware may yield different results, possibly even better performance, depending on the architecture and features of the processor and any additional hardware it may be connected to.

5 Related Work

Although there are different papers about real-time performance on other architectures, there are only a few regarding real-time performance on RISC-V plat-

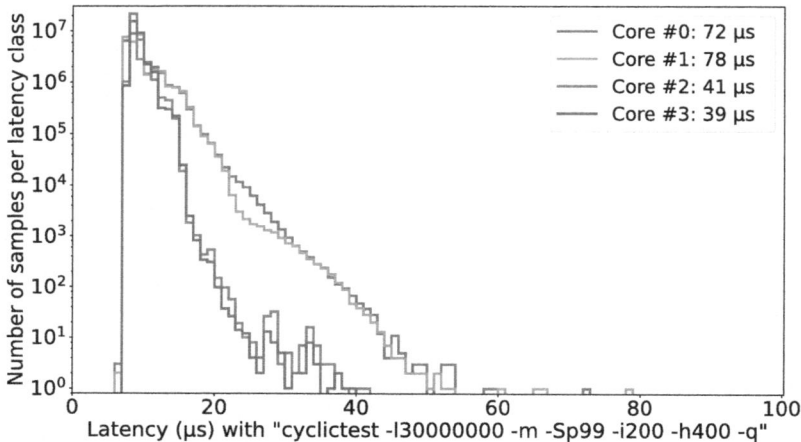

Fig. 6. Latency histogram on Raspberry Pi 4 while stressed

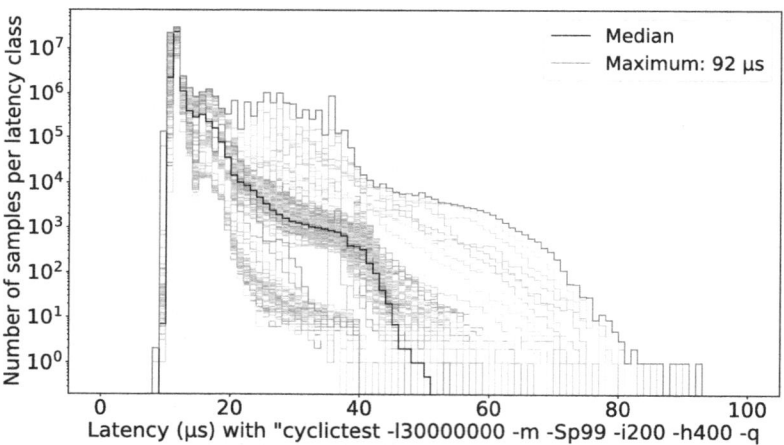

Fig. 7. Longterm histogram on Starfive Visionfive 2

forms. While some of them are in depth [27], this paper focused on a tuned and reproducible test setup for two comparable platforms, one being RISC-V based.

StarFive published some real-time measurement results [28] of the Visionfive2. The tests were done prior to the merge of the RISC_V enablement to the PREEMPT_RT patches and are based on a custom Linux kernel with version 5.15.

Markus Jämbäck also developed some custom patches in his master's thesis to make the PREEMPT_RT patches run on a 5.12 kernel [29].

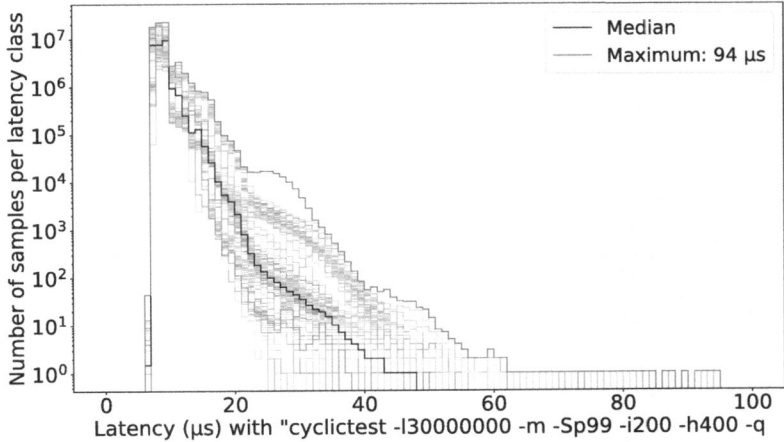

Fig. 8. Longterm histogram cores on Raspberry PI 4

6 Conclusion

This paper discussed the performance of Linux with the PREEMPT_RT patches running on a RISC-V processor, specifically the StarFive VisionFive V2 board. The results were then measured against a similar ARM platform, the Raspberry Pi 4.

The large dataset shows that the PREEMPT_RT patch series can archive similar results in terms of worst case latencies on a RISC-V platform compared to other architectures.

References

1. Reghenzani, F., Massari, G., Fornaciari, W.: The real-time linux kernel: A survey on preempt_rt. https://doi.org/10.1145/3297714
2. Burkacky, O., Deichmann, J., Jan, S., Stein, P.: Automotive software and electronics 2030 mapping the sector's future landscape
3. Jiang, Z., et al.: Bridging the pragmatic gaps for mixed-criticality systems in the automotive industry. IEEE Trans. Comput.-Aided Design Integrated Circ. Syst., 1116–1129 (2022). https://doi.org/10.1109/TCAD.2021.3075422
4. Reghenzani, F., Massari, G., Fornaciari, W.: Mixed time-criticality process interferences characterization on a multicore linux system. In: Proceedings - 20th Euromicro Conference on Digital System Design, DSD 2017, pp. 427–434 (Sep 2017). https://doi.org/10.1109/DSD.2017.18
5. Linux in mixed-criticality systems [lwn.net]. https://lwn.net/Articles/774217/
6. Xenomai. https://xenomai.org/, Accessed 18 Jan 2024
7. Preempt rt v6.6-rt14 announcement. https://lore.kernel.org/lkml/20231110153229.9CLWVN0E@linutronix.de/, Accessed 18 Jan 2024
8. Risc-v international – risc-v: The open standard risc instruction set architecture. https://riscv.org/

9. Meng, Z., Zhang, Y., Zhou, J., Guo, Z.: Design of 64-bit high-performance embedded processor supporting risc-v b-extension. Proceedings of the International Conference on Anti-Counterfeiting, Security and Identification, ASID, pp. 28–32 (2022). https://doi.org/10.1109/ASID56930.2022.9995771
10. Lu, T.: A survey on risc-v security: Hardware and architecture (uly 2021), 2107.04175
11. Gonzalez-Gomez, J., et al.: Tailoredcore: generating application-specific risc-v-based cores. In: 2021 IEEE 12th Latin American Symposium on Circuits and Systems, LASCAS 2021 (Feb 2021). https://doi.org/10.1109/LASCAS51355.2021.9459152
12. Visionfive 2 datasheet. https://doc-en.rvspace.org/VisionFive2/PDF/VisionFive2_Datasheet.pdf, Accessed 18 Jan 2024
13. Bcm2711 arm peripherals. https://datasheets.raspberrypi.com/bcm2711/bcm2711-peripherals.pdf, Accessed 18 Jan 2024
14. isar - integration system for automated root filesystem generation. https://github.com/ilbers/isar, Accessed 18 Jan 2024
15. A debian based isar layer with preempt rt kernel 5.15 and osadl test tooling. https://github.com/TobiasSchaffner/isar-osadl-rt-testing-images, Accessed 18 Jan 2024
16. Prebuild rt testing images. https://github.com/TobiasSchaffner/isar-osadl-rt-testing-images/actions, Accessed 18 Jan 2024
17. Preempt rt patch 6.6 rt14. https://mirrors.edge.kernel.org/pub/linux/kernel/projects/rt/6.6/older/patch-6.6-rt14.patch.gz, Accessed 18 Jan 2024
18. Osadl linux add-on patches. https://www.osadl.org/OSADL-Linux-Add-on-Patches.kernelpatches.0.html, Accessed 18 Jan 2024
19. Osadl: Osadl - open source automation development lab eg. https://www.osadl.org/
20. rt-tests/rt-tests.git - suite of real-time tests. https://git.kernel.org/pub/scm/utils/rt-tests/rt-tests.git
21. byte-unixbench. https://github.com/kdlucas/byte-unixbench
22. Preempt rt specific configurations. https://github.com/TobiasSchaffner/isar-osadl-rt-testing-images/blob/master/recipes-kernel/linux/files/preempt-rt.cfg, Accessed 18 Jan 2024
23. Realtime tuning guide. https://linux.web.cern.ch/mrg/2/Realtime_Tuning_Guide/, Accessed 18 Jan 2024
24. Linux @ cern. https://linuxsoft.cern.ch/cern/centos/7/rt/x86_64/repoview/tuned-profiles-realtime.html, Accessed 18 Jan 2024
25. Osadl qa farm. https://www.osadl.org/?id=850, Accessed 18 Jan 2024
26. cyclictest - high resolution test program. https://manpages.debian.org/jessie/rt-tests/cyclictest.8, Accessed 18 Jan 2024
27. Adam, G.K., Petrellis, N., Doulos, L.T.: Performance assessment of linux kernels with preempt_rt on arm-based embedded devices. Electronics (Switzerland) (2021)
28. Analysis of running real-time linux on visionfive 2. https://doc-en.rvspace.org/VisionFive2/RTLinux/, Accessed 18 Jan 2024
29. Jämbäck, M.: Evaluation of real-time linux on risc-v processor architecture (March 2022). https://trepo.tuni.fi/bitstream/handle/10024/138547/J

RV-VP²: Unlocking the Potential of RISC-V Packed-SIMD for Embedded Processing

Muhammad Ali[✉][iD], Ensieh Aliagha[iD], Mahmoud Elnashar[iD], and Diana Göhringer[iD]

Technische Universität Dresden, Chair of Adaptive Dynamic Systems, Dresden, Germany
{Muhammad.Ali,Ensieh.Aliagha,Mahmoud.Hatem_Elnasher, Diana.Goehringer}@tu-dresden.de

Abstract. The RISC-V instruction set architecture (ISA) is increasingly gaining traction as an open-source standard, enabling the development of a variety of processor designs. These designs are capable of addressing a broad spectrum of application needs, spanning from embedded systems to high-performance computing. The RISC-V ISA features a modular structure, offering a selection of base ISAs and standardized extensions for customization. In this work, we present the first and open-source extension of a SystemC TLM-based RISC-V *Virtual Prototype* (VP) which supports the *RISC-V "P" Packed-SIMD* Version 0.9.11-draft-20211209 called `RV-VP`². The RISC-V VP is an open-source simulation platform in SystemC TLM that supports RV32GC and RV64GC. The RISC-V VP is extended for the P-extension of the RISC-V for RV32 specification to focus on simulating embedded application scenarios. A total of 243 instructions are added in the RISC-V VP simulator, which belongs to the mandatory specification of P-extension for RV32. The extended RISC-V VP simulator is evaluated for different test cases; matrix multiplication, convolution, max-pooling, and fully connected layer, to demonstrate the efficiency of P-extension in comparison to base ISA. A convolution neural network called Lenet-5 is also used as a test case to compare performance with the base RV32IM. The results show a maximum speed-up of 5.87× and 2.97× when using P-extension for a 4-way (8-bit) SIMD and a 2-way (16-bit) SIMD for matrix multiplication respectively. For Lenet-5 a speed-up of 4.08× when using P-extension (4-way (8-bit) SIMD) was observed.

Keywords: RISC-V VP · Instruction Set Architecture · SystemC TLM · Simulator · Machine Learning · Deep Learning

1 Introduction

As RISC-V emerges as an open-source Instruction-Set Architecture (ISA), there is a notable surge in both academic and industrial adoption of processor design implementations. Various application domains are being targeted for computer architecture leveraging the RISC-V ISA, ranging from low-power Internet-of-Things (IoT) devices to High Performance Computing (HPC) systems. A diverse array of processors is now available, with ongoing efforts to further optimize the architectures [10]. The modular nature of the RISC-V architecture facilitates its utilization across a wide spectrum of application domains. Hennessy et al. underscore the importance of domain-specific processor designs in enhancing system efficiency [3]. With the diminishing pace of general computer performance improvements, attention has shifted towards domain-specific processor architectures. The RISC-V P-extension [11] provides an ISA specification for Packed-Single Instruction Multiple Data (SIMD) for 32-bit and 64-bit base specifications. Packed-SIMD allows data-level parallelism for RV32I and RV64I without adding additional general-purpose registers or variable bit-width registers like in the V-extension which focuses on vector operations.

Various simulation tools such as Spike [9], RISC-V VP [4], emulation platforms [6], and traditional synthesized simulation platforms offer valuable insights into performance, power consumption, and resource utilization. Except for Spike, which is an official Instruction Set Simulator (ISS) from RISC-V, other tools do not provide support for simulating the P-extension.

The main contribution of this work can be summarized as follows:

- RV-VP^2: a free and open-source [1] RISC-V VP simulator based on SystemC TLM which supports the RISC-V "P" Packed-SIMD extension Version 0.9.11-draft-20211209 for RV32 specification.
- A total of 243 instructions from P-extension for RV32 specification are implemented in SystemC TLM.
- The extended version of RISC-V VP is evaluated for different test cases: matrix multiplication, convolution, max-pooling, and fully connected. A Convolutional Neural Network (CNN) algorithm called Lenet-5 [7] is also used as a test case to compare P-extension with base RV32IM specification.
- Design Space Exploration (DSE) of the P-extension is also presented using different SIMD instructions to maximize data-level parallelism in the test cases and to demonstrate the efficiency of P-extension.

The following parts of the paper are structured as follows: Sect. 2 presents the background and related work. Section 3 provides an overview of the tool and describes the components in detail. Section 4 discusses the evaluation of the tool flow with different test cases. DSE of P-extension is also presented in the test cases. Finally, Sect. 5 presents a conclusion and an outlook for future work.

2 Background and Related Work

RISC-V, as presented in [14], is an open-source ISA initially developed at the University of California, Berkeley. Characterized by its modularity, the RISC-V ISA architecture comprises of foundational base ISAs, such as RV32I and RV64I, alongside a wide range of standard extensions like the M-extension and

F-extension. Importantly, these extensions are optional, which allows developers the flexibility to select the specifications that align with their application requirements. One of the standard extensions of RISC-V is the P-extension [11] which focuses on Packed-SIMD operations with respect to base RV32I and RV64I. Currently, the P-extension is not frozen and it is in a draft version 0.9.11-draft-20211209. Figure 1 shows an overview of how a simple operation takes place in base ISA specification of RISC-V, P-extension, and V-extension. In base ISA specification, the element width is fixed as 32 (RV32I) or 64 (RV64I), and arithmetic operations are performed on the whole element (element width = base register width). Even for a smaller data type e.g. int8, the element width is considered 32 or 64-bit wide. For P-extension, the element width can be set to 32-, 16-, and 8-, irrespective of base ISA and an arithmetic operation can be performed on all elements in parallel. This allows data-level parallelism and improves performance while maintaining the data width with respect to the base ISA specification. In contrast, V-extension which focuses on vector operations has parameterized vector registers and element width. Since the element width and the register width are flexible, it provides further possibilities of data-level parallelism although the ISA specification is more complicated as compared to the base and P-extension specification. Figure 1 shows the difference between the three cases mentioned above and how the register width and element width are perceived in each case. In the following section, different works related to the simulation of RISC-V architectures are mentioned for an overview.

The Spike simulator, as referenced in [9], is an official ISS from RISC-V. Currently, the Spike simulator supports version v0.9.2 of the P-extension specification. This simulator allows exploration and analysis of RISC-V processors. It offers a detailed functional model of one or multiple RISC-V hardware threads (harts). Spike supports a wide range of RISC-V ISA specifications, both base ISAs and standard extensions. It also allows simulation of new or custom instructions thus providing a platform to evaluate the feasibility of new instructions.

Petersen in [8] presents an open-source computer architecture simulator designed for the RISC-V ISA called Ripes. The presented work supports RV32IMC and RV64IMC-based processor architectures. The work combines an assembler, compiler support, and cache simulation. For the mentioned specification a visual microarchitecture simulator is presented which allows users to explore different processor pipeline models, from single-cycle to a classic five-stage pipeline. Ripes is actively maintained and can be used in university teaching and research.

Silveira et al. in [13] presents Prof5, which is a profiling tool for RISC-V ISA. Prof5 helps in understanding how different design choices affect performance and energy usage for RISC-V specification. This tool provides detailed information on timing and energy at the function level, which helps in making design decisions quickly. It is based on the Spike simulator [9] and can even create new models for custom designs. Compared to traditional methods, Prof5 is faster as compared to synthesis-based tools and still maintains high accuracy (95%). Although this

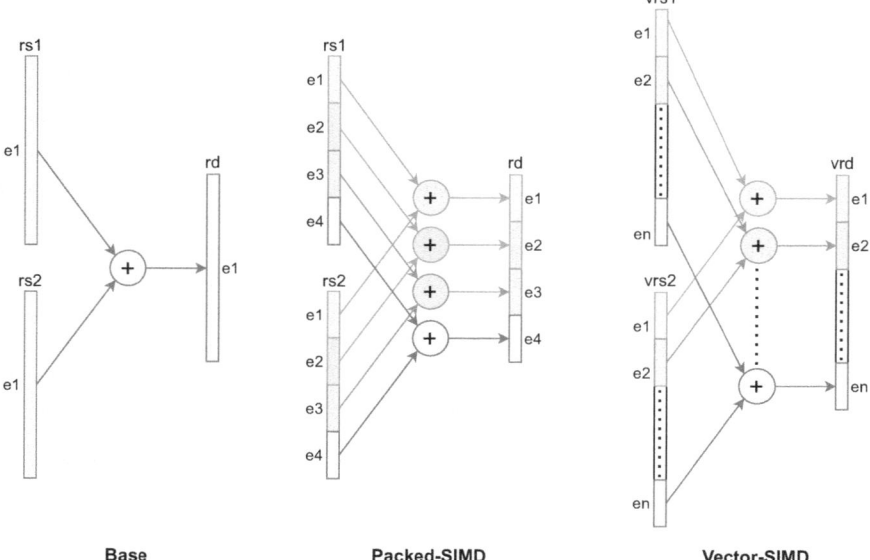

Fig. 1. Overview of RISC-V base, Packed-SIMD, and Vector operations. *(e= element, rs= source register, rd= destination register, vrs= vector source register, vrd= vector destination register)*

work does not mention P-extension, however since it is based on Spike [9], it should be able to support P-extension.

Zhang et al. in [15] discuss using Machine Learning (ML) to estimate the performance of RISC-V processors across different microarchitectures. ML can speed up the exploration of different processor designs and software optimization. Traditional performance estimation based only on clock cycles is insufficient for modern, complex microarchitectures. The paper proposes a new ML-based approach that combines a fast functional simulator, detailed Register Transfer Level (RTL) implementations, and ML techniques to create Predictive Models (PMs) for accurate performance estimation with quick simulation times. Along with clock cycles, the approach also estimates cache hits/misses, branch prediction behavior, and memory dependencies to provide deeper insights into microarchitectural behavior. Experimental results on real-world RISC-V implementations show significant performance improvements using this approach, up to 2261.4 times faster compared to traditional methods.

Herdt et al. in [4] presents a RISC-V Virtual Prototype (VP): `RISCV-VP` implemented in SystemC TLM to address the limitations of existing ISS. The `RISCV-VP` includes a 32-bit (RV32GC) and 64-bit (RV64GC) support with various privilege levels, interrupt controllers, and essential peripherals. Multi-core platform simulation is also possible, and it supports software debugging and works with FreeRTOS and Zephyr operating systems. The `RISCV-VP` is highly configurable and implemented in standard-compliant SystemC. It offers faster simulation than RTL and more accuracy than existing ISS. The presented simulator is open-source to encourage further development and expand the RISC-V ecosystem.

Schlägl et al. in [12] introduce the free and open-source SystemC TLM-based RISC-V VP with native support for the RISC-V "V" Vector Extension (RVV) Version 1.0. Over 600+ instructions from the RISC-V V-extension instructions are added to the RISCV-VP [4]. Furthermore, the work describes the validation process of the resultant VP through the utilization of the Instruction Sequence Generator (ISG) FORCE-RISCV and the ISS riscvOVPsim [5]. The advantages of the extended RVV-VP for system-level evaluation are presented using different test cases. Evaluation of this work presents both non-vectorized and vectorized iterations of two prevalent algorithms, executed on the VP with varying parameters.

Haase et al. in [2] presents a simulation environment that combines the PANACA simulation platform with the RISC-V VP [4]. The proposed simulator is a highly efficient and flexible platform for simulating Multiprocessor System-on-Chip (MPSoC) designs with Network-on-Chip (NoC) architectures. This allows for early evaluation of complex designs and application mapping before physical implementation. The simulation platform supports real-time operating systems like FreeRTOS and can run various applications, including machine learning. Memory-mapped network adapters are used for communication between RISC-V processors and the NoC, to enhance efficiency.

In contrast to the above-mentioned related work, this work focuses on extending the RISC-V VP [4] for P-extension for RV32-related specification to exploit Packed-SIMD operations. The details of the tool and evaluation are discussed in detail in the following sections.

3 Simulation Platform: RV-VP^2

As mentioned before, RISC-V VP [4] is a RISC-V ISS implemented in SystemC TLM. The current implementation of RISC-V VP supports RV32GC and RV64GC specifications. Additional V-extension support is provided in [12]. RISC-V VP overall provides a lot of features e.g. software debugging and virtual breadboard Graphical User Interface (GUI). Additionally, RISC-V VP also provides support for Operating System (OS) e.g. FreeRTOS, RIOT, Zephyr, and Linux. The unique feature of this ISS is that it implements a generic bus-based system. This allows the addition of memory-mapped peripherals e.g. display, and ethernet, and the overall system forms a System-on-Chip (SoC). Further, the timing of instruction calls can be estimated through simulation. The proposed ISS also supports simulation for multi-core architectures. An overview of the RISC-V VP [4] is shown in Fig. 2. Figure 2 also highlights the modified extended parts of the simulator in red dotted lines.

In this work, the RISC-V VP [4] was extended by adding the 32-bit P-extension [11] instructions. The extended VP is called the RV-VP^2 and it is the

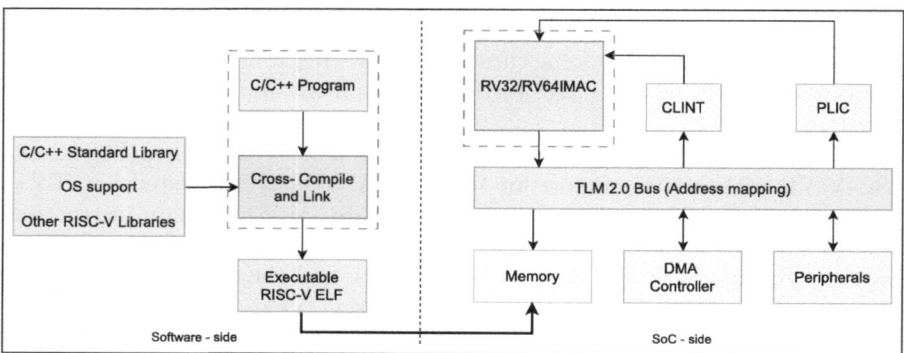

Fig. 2. RISC-V VP architecture overview. Figure adopted from [4]. Red dotted lines present the extended parts of the simulation environment. (Color figure online)

first and open-source implementation of P-extension [11]. Currently, the latest version of P-extension is V0.9.11-draft-20211209 [11]. A total of 243 instructions of the mandatory P-extension instructions for the base ISA RV32I were implemented in the 32-bit ISS module. In contrast to RISC-V V-extension, the P-extension does not add new registers in the processor architecture. P-extension specification reinterprets the data residing in the general-purpose integer registers and treats them as vectors. For extending the RISC-V VP the decoding logic for the P-extension instructions was implemented in the corresponding decoding submodule (core/rv32/instr.cpp). Furthermore, the execution logic for each P-extension instruction was included in the corresponding submodule (core/rv32/iss.cpp). Since the P-extension also introduces some new general-purpose register access patterns, namely 64-bit access patterns, the corresponding logic for these new access patterns had to be implemented. The register read and write patterns for SIMD-8 elements and SIMD-16 elements were also added to the RISC-V VP. The P-extension also introduces a new CSR register, namely the *vxsat* CSR register that contains the saturation flag. The available CSR register addresses were therefore extended to include the *vxsat* CSR register. For programming, the RISC-V toolchain with P-extension support was used. An example of matrix multiplication of for standard RV32IM, 16-bit elements (2-way SIMD for 32-bit), and 8-bit elements (4-way SIMD for 32-bit) is presented in Fig. 3. The example uses `kmada` instruction from the P-extension, which performs two signed 16-bit multiplications from two chunks of 32-bit registers and then adds the two 32-bit results and the corresponding 32-bit register together, thus performing a two-way SIMD. Similarly, `smaqa` instruction performs four signed 8-bit multiplications from two chunks of 32-bit registers and then adds the four 16-bit results and the corresponding 32-bit register together, thus performing a four-way SIMD. For programming, the intrinsic function library from RISC-V is used, which is named `rvp_intrinsic.h`. This library allows the use of P-extension instructions as intrinsic functions. Without this library, programmers would need to write in-line assembly code in order to execute P-extension instructions. In the next section, the evaluation of the extended RISC-V VP is presented.

```
1  for (int i=0; i < MATMUL_SIZE; i += 1){
2    for (int j=0; j < MATMUL_SIZE; j += 1){
3      int32_t sum = 0;
4      for (int k = 0; k < MATMUL_SIZE; k += INC){
5        sum += in1[i][k] * in2[j][k];                                           // Scalar
6        sum = __rv_kmada(sum,*(int32_t*)&in1[i][k],*(int32_t*)&in2[j][k]);      // SIMD-16
7        sum = __rv_smaqa(sum,*(int32_t*)&in1[i][k],*(int32_t*)&in2[j][k]);      // SIMD-8
8      }
9      out[i][j] = sum;
10   }
11 }
```

Fig. 3. Example C-code program for matrix multiplication for base, SIMD16, and SIMD8.

4 Evaluating RISC-V ISA

This section describes the different test cases used to evaluate the RV-VP^2 ISS. Since this work is the first in the implementation of a simulator for P-extension, the evaluation focuses on the benefits of RISC-V P-extension and how it can be perceived for different application scenarios. For evaluation and to show the coverage of DSE for P-extension of RISC-V ISA, the target specifications used are RV32IM as the base, and RV32IMP (SIMD8 and SIMD16). For Packed-SIMD, SIMD8 refers to an element size of 8-bit and a total of 4 elements for 32-bit wide registers while SIMD16 refers to an element size of 16-bit and a total of 2 elements for 32-bit wide registers For test cases, matrix multiplication, convolution, maxpooling, and fully connected functions of various sizes were used. For an application test case, a CNN algorithm called Lenet-5 [7] is used. Each test case is implemented and tested for the base (RV32IM), for P-extension; SIMD-8 (4-way SIMD), and SIMD16 (2-way SIMD). The compiler optimization is set to -O2 in general since it is the most predictable and stable state. For comparison, the memory access cycles and multiplication cycles are set to 1. The data type for the P-extension is set as int8 and int16 for SIMD8 and SIMD16 test cases respectively, while for the base (RV32IM) as int32. The results are verified for P- by comparing them with the results of base implementation. In the following sections, the evaluation from each test case is presented.

4.1 Matrix Multiplication

The first test case used to evaluate the RV-VP^2 is the matrix multiplication. In this test case, the matrix sizes used are 256×256, 128×128, 64×64, and 32×32.

A summary of the results is presented in Fig. 4. The results show a comparison of SIMD8 and SIMD16 of P-extension compared to base RV32IM. smaqa and kmada instruction from P-extension is used as presented in Fig. 3. A maximum speed up of 5.87× and 2.97× is observed for SIMD8 and SIMD16 respectively as compared to RV32IM.

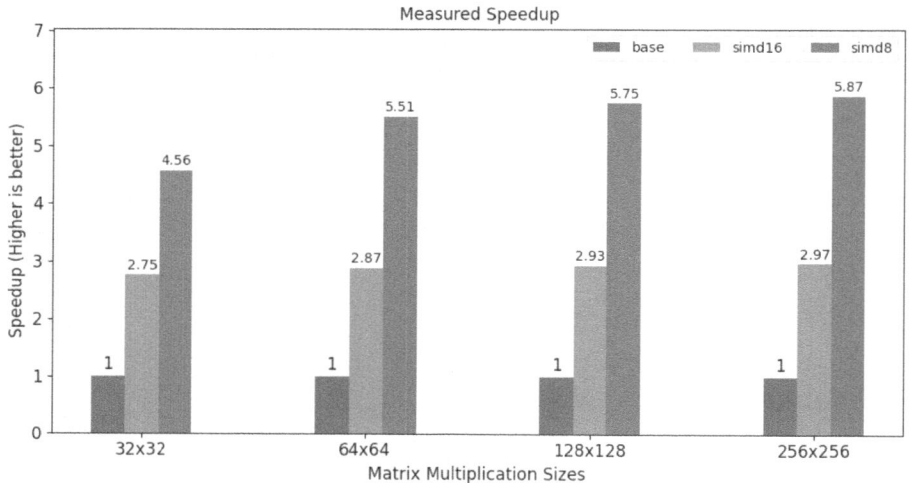

Fig. 4. Matrix multiplication test case speed up summary (-O2 compiler optimization)

Compiler optimization results are presented in Fig. 5 for the matrix multiplication of size 256×256. It can be observed that -O0 performs slightly worse as compared to other optimizations. Usually, -O0 performs the worst, and –O1, –O2, and –O3 have similar or slight differences. But for the P-extension that is not the case, and it is expected since the extension is not finalized yet, the compiler is not optimized yet.

4.2 Convolution

The second test case used is the convolution function. Different input sizes were used for evaluation; 256 × 256, 128 × 128, 64 × 64, and 32 × 32. The kernel size was set as 4 ×4 ×4. Although it is not a conventional kernel size in CNN algorithms, however, this size has a benefit for P-extension, where the parallelism is focused for even sizes. The results are summarized in Fig. 6. A maximum speed up of 4.24× and 3.08 × is observed for SIMD8 and SIMD16 respectively for the maximum data-level parallelism approach. Similar to the matrix multiplication test case, smaqa instruction was used to parallel the computation of convolution multiplication and accumulation. It can observed that the convolution speed-up was less as compared to the matrix multiplication. This is because the for-loops

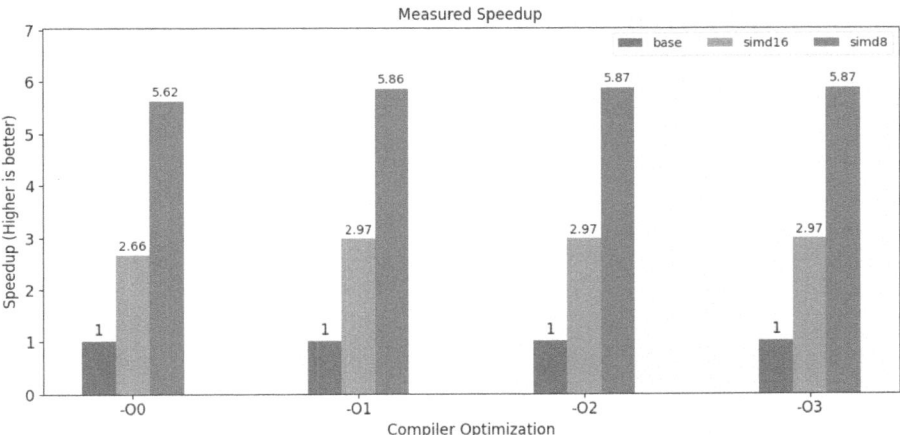

Fig. 5. Compiler optimization evaluation for matrix multiplication size of 256×256

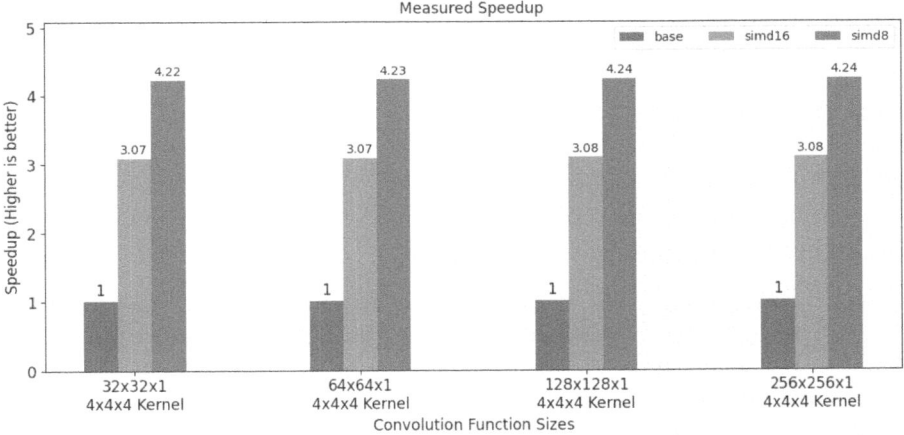

Fig. 6. Convolution function test case speed up summary (-O2 compiler optimization)

of the sliding kernel over the input add a lot of load and store instructions. The compiler optimization results were similar to matrix multiplication and thus not included.

4.3 Max Pooling

For evaluating the max-pooling function the following input sizes were used; 256×256, 128×128, 64×64, and 32×32. The feature size was fixed to 8. The results are summarized in Fig. 7. A maximum speed up of 8.33× and 4.82× is observed for SIMD8 and SIMD16 respectively. For maxpooling `smax` instruction is used from P-extension. It can observed that the speed-up is significantly higher in max-pooling functions as compared to matrix multiplication and convolution functions. This is because the base ISA RV32IM does not have a direct instruction for calculating the maximum value. The compiler generates conditional branching and direct assignment which reduces the overall efficiency as compared to P-extension.

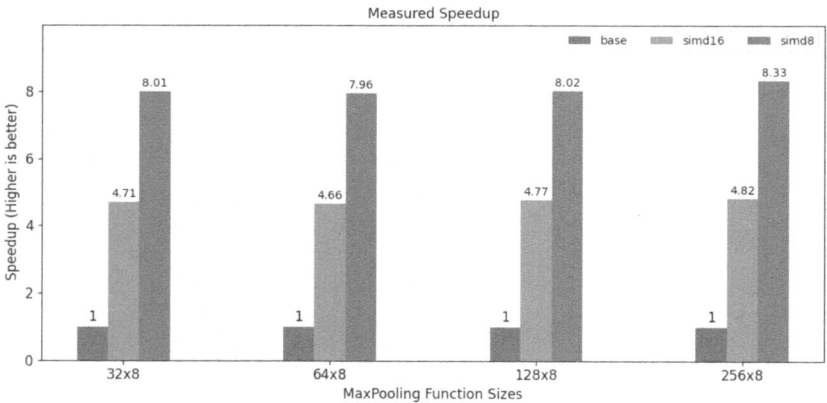

Fig. 7. MaxPooling function test case speed up summary (-O2 compiler optimization)

4.4 Fully Connected

For the next test case, the fully connected function is used. The following sizes were used for fully connected functions; 128×128, 256×256, 512×512, and 1024×1024. The results are summarized in Fig. 8. A maximum speed up of 4.64× and 2.33× is observed for SIMD8 and SIMD16 respectively. It can observed that the speed-up is significant in a fully connected function since the function can easily benefit from SIMD. Similar to matrix multiplication and convolution, smaqa instruction is used for fully connected functions.

4.5 Lenet-5

As mentioned earlier, a real CNN example algorithm is also tested for the simulation tool. For this purpose, the Lenet-5 [7] algorithm is used which can detect handwritten digits using the MNIST dataset. The algorithm configuration and number of integer operations in each layer are mentioned in Table 1. Lenet-5 consists of two convolution layers, two max-pooling layers, and three fully connected layers. Similar to previous test cases, the Lenet-5 algorithm was adapted for P-extension (SIMD8 and SIMD16) for all layers. The evaluation results for Lenet-5 and an overall summary of results are presented in Fig. 9. Similar to the previous evaluation, the comparison is made between base ISA and SIMD8 and

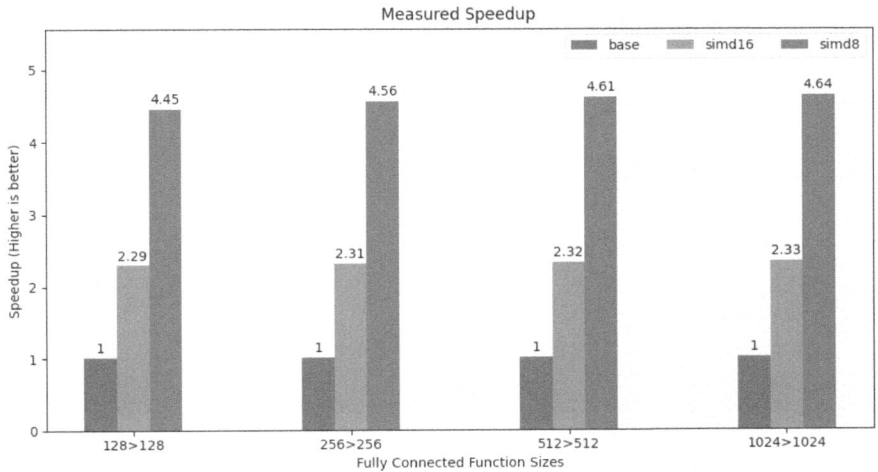

Fig. 8. Fully connected function test case speed up summary (-O2 compiler optimization)

Table 1. Lenet-5 algorithm overview

Lenet-5 layers (input size)	kernel size	Integer Operations
Convolution (28×28)	5×5×6	176256
MaxPooling (24×24×6)	2×2	3456
Convolution (12×12×6)	5×5×16×6	308224
MaxPooling (8×8×16)	2×2	1024
Fully Connected (256)	120	61680
Fully Connected (120)	84	20328
Fully Connected (84)	10	1700

SIMD16. It can be observed from Fig. 9, that a maximum speed-up for SIMD8 is 4.08× and for SIMD16 a speed-up of 1.97× is observed for Lenet-5.

From the evaluation, the advantage of SIMD approach of RISC-V P-extension as compared to base specification RV32IM can be observed. Figure 9, shows a summary of the results of all test cases and the speed-up achieved. Although there are a few works that focus on profiling and simulation based on RISC-V [2,4,8]. However, they do not focus on P-extension specification and ISA behavior. So a direct comparison with other simulator environments does not make sense.

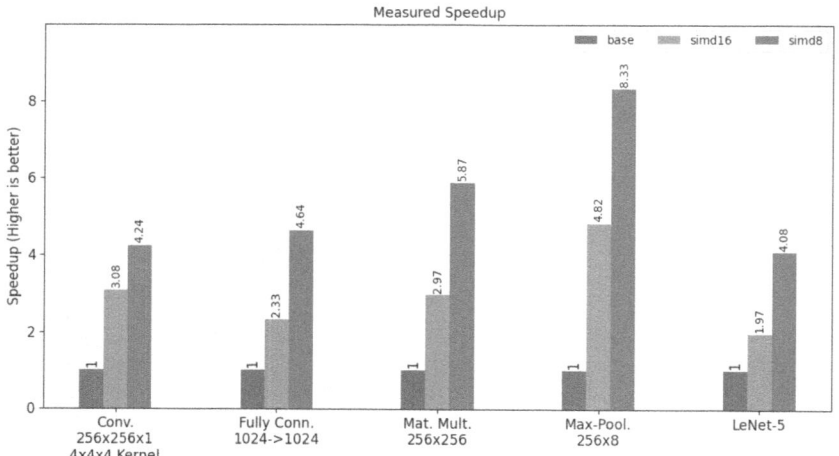

Fig. 9. Lenet-5 test case speed up and overall summary of evaluation (using -O2).

5 Conclusion

As a summary, a first and open-source RISC-V VP simulating environment for RISC-V P-extension is presented called the RV-VP^2 [1]. The RISC-V VP is an ISS which implements 243 instructions from the RISC-V "P" Packed-SIMD Version 0.9.11-draft-20211209 specification. The implemented instructions are mandatory instructions for base RV32I ISA. For P-extension DSE is also possible for 8-bit and 16-bit elements. To demonstrate the feasibility of the ISS different functions are used; matrix multiplication, convolution, max-pooling and fully connected. The results show a speed-up of 5.87×, 4.24×, 8.33×, and 4.64× for SIMD8 for matrix multiplication, convolution, max-pooling, and fully connected functions respectively. For SIMD16, a speed-up of 2.97×, 3.08×, 4.82×, and 2.33× for matrix multiplication, convolution, max-pooling, and fully connected functions respectively. A CNN algorithm called Lenet-5 [7] is also used as a test case to evaluate RISC-V P-extension. A speed-up of 4.08× and 1.97× is observed for SIMD8 and SIMD16 of P-extension respectively. For future work, we would like to extend the work for the RV64 specification of the P-extension. Also, broaden the test cases of applications and functions other than CNNs. This will further demonstrate the importance of Packed-SIMD for data-level parallelism.

Acknowledgment. This work has been partially funded by the German Federal Ministry of Education and Research BMBF as part of the DAKORE (Datenfunknetz mit Adaptivhardware und KI-Optimierung zur Reduktion des Energieverbrauchs) project under grant agreement number 16ME0433K and by the German Research Foundation ("Deutsche Forschungsgemeinschaft") (DFG) under Project-ID 287022738 TRR 196 for Project S05.

References

1. Ali, M., Aliagha, E., Elnashar, M., Göhringer, D.: RISC-V VP^2. https://github.com/TUD-ADS/RV-VP2
2. Haase, J., Ali, M., Göhringer, D.: Unlocking the potential of RISC-V heterogeneous MPSoC: a PANACA-based approach to simulation and modeling. In: International Conference on Embedded Computer Systems. pp. 269–282. Springer (2023). https://doi.org/10.1007/978-3-031-46077-7_18
3. Hennessy, J.L., Patterson, D.A.: A new golden age for computer architecture. Commun. ACM **62**(2), 48–60 (2019). https://doi.org/10.1145/3282307
4. Herdt, V., Große, D., Pieper, P., Drechsler, R.: RISC-V based virtual prototype: an extensible and configurable platform for the system-level. J. Syst. Architect. **109**, 101756 (2020). https://doi.org/10.1016/j.sysarc.2020.101756
5. Imperas: RISC-V OVPsim: Free Imperas RISC-V Instruction Set Simulator. https://www.imperas.com/riscvovpsim-free-imperas-risc-v-instruction-set-simulator (Accessed 2024)
6. Khamis, M., El-Ashry, S., Shalaby, A., AbdElsalam, M., El-Kharashi, M.W.: A configurable RISC-V for NoC-Based MPSoCs: a framework for hardware emulation. In: 2018 11th International Workshop on Network on Chip Architectures (NoCArc), pp. 1–6 (2018). https://doi.org/10.1109/NOCARC.2018.8541158
7. LeCun, Y., Bottou, L., Bengio, Y., Haffner, P.: Gradient-based learning applied to document recognition. Proc. IEEE **86**(11), 2278–2324 (1998)
8. Petersen, M.B.: Ripes: a visual computer architecture simulator. In: 2021 ACM/IEEE Workshop on Computer Architecture Education (WCAE), pp. 1–8 (2021). https://doi.org/10.1109/WCAE53984.2021.9707149
9. RISC-V: Spike RISC-V ISA simulator. https://github.com/riscv-software-src/riscv-isa-sim
10. RISC-V Archive: RISC-V Cores List. https://github.com/riscvarchive/riscv-cores-list (2021)
11. RISC-V Foundation: RISC-V "P" Extension Proposal. https://github.com/riscv/riscv-p-spec (Accessed 2024)
12. Schlägl, M., Stockinger, M., Große, D.: A RISC-V "V" VP: Unlocking Vector Processing for Evaluation at the System Level
13. Silveira, J., et al.: Prof5: a RISC-V profiler tool. In: 2022 IEEE 34th International Symposium on Computer Architecture and High Performance Computing (SBAC-PAD), pp. 201–210 (2022). https://doi.org/10.1109/SBAC-PAD55451.2022.00031
14. Waterman, A., Asanović, K., Hauser, J.: The RISC-V Instruction Set Manual Volume II: Privileged Architecture. SiFive Inc. and CS Division, EECS Department, University of California, Berkeley, document version 20211203 edn. (December 2021). https://github.com/riscv/riscv-isa-manual/releases/download/Priv-v1.12/riscv-privileged-20211203.pdf
15. Zhang, W., Goli, M., Hassan, M., Drechsler, R.: Efficient ML-based performance estimation approach across different microarchitectures for RISC-V processors. In: Euromicro Conference Series on Digital System Design (DSD) (2023)

A Novel System Simulation Framework for HBM2 FPGA Platforms

Hector Gerardo Muñoz Hernandez[1](✉)[iD], Veronia Iskandar[2][iD],
Lukas Steiner[3][iD], Philipp Holzinger[4][iD], Matthias Jung[5,6][iD],
Diana Göhringer[2][iD], Michael Hübner[1][iD], Norbert Wehn[3][iD],
and Marc Reichenbach[7][iD]

[1] Chair of Computer Engineering, Brandenburg University of Technology Cottbus-Senftenberg, Cottbus, Germany
{munozher,michael.huebner}@b-tu.de

[2] Chair of Adaptive Dynamic Systems, Dresden University of Technology, Dresden, Germany
{veronia.iskandar,diana.goehringer}@tu-dresden.de

[3] Microelectronic Systems Design, University of Kaiserslautern-Landau, Kaiserslautern, Germany
{lukas.steiner,norbert.wehn}@rptu.de

[4] Chair of Computer Architecture, Friedrich-Alexander University, Erlangen, Germany
philipp.holzinger@fau.de

[5] Fraunhofer IESE, Kaiserslautern, Germany
matthias.jung@iese.fraunhofer.de

[6] University of Würzburg, Würzburg, Germany
m.jung@uni-wuerzburg.de

[7] Chair of Integrated Systems, University of Rostock, Rostock, Germany
marc.reichenbach@uni-rostock.de

Abstract. Every year, the disparity between processing power and memory bandwidth continues to expand. This well-established trend has been recognized for several years. Recently, innovative concepts have emerged to address and narrow this growing gap. One notable example of such technology is High Bandwidth Memory (HBM), which is specifically designed to tackle this challenge. HBM has a much higher throughput thanks to their wider data buses, making it an innovative solution for this problem. Due to its configurability and timing requirements, HBM and Field-Programmable Gate Arrays (FPGAs) offer a great combination for prototyping, and the hardware that includes both is slowly gaining popularity and accessibility. In this work, we introduce an open-source simulator capable of accurately predicting and modeling HBM based FPGA systems in a fast-prototyping manner. This design not only simulates an HBM but also a memory controller and a memory interconnect, like the one used by AMD/Xilinx. To prove accuracy, this work shows side-by-side comparison between the real hardware and simulated benchmarks of different specific types of memory access patterns, where we measure an overall error of *9.91%*. Finally, we compare the performance of some real-life applications where we report an average error of *2.72%*.

Keywords: High Bandwidth Memory · Memory system simulation · Approximately timed simulation

1 Introduction

Many modern applications, including artificial neural networks, image processing or real-time signal processing, require powerful embedded computer architectures. In addition to an optimized parallel processor architecture, this also requires a fast memory connection in order to supply computing cores with corresponding inputs. Traditional DRAM is not sufficient for this purpose because the throughput is too low [11].

Accordingly, new 3D stacked-based memory technologies such as High Bandwidth Memory (HBM) have become established in recent years. By stacking different dies in conjunction with through-silicon vias (TSVs), it is possible to access the memory in a highly parallel manner and thus also with a high throughput. This memory technology is now also finding its way into modern FPGAs for High Performance Computing (HPC). HBM and FPGA are combined on an interposer and thus allow a theoretical bandwidth of up to 460 GB/s [2].

However, these new technological developments regarding memory also lead to a paradigm shift in the data processing computer architecture. This must cope with highly parallel data access. Moreover, certain side effects occur due to the memory structure, making both latency and throughput dependent on the physical address of the memory location. Furthermore, HBM is only the memory physical basis, many of these previously mentioned effects are massively influenced by the memory controller [7].

HBM technology in FPGAs is slowly getting more accessibility. One example is the Heterogeneous Accelerated Compute Cluster (HACC) from AMD/Xilinx [3]. Options like this make it easier to get access to HBM technology while using FPGAs. One of the main drawbacks of such solutions are the FPGA synthesis/implementation times which can take up to several hours for big designs.

According to these observations, it is necessary to create a fast-prototyping **simulation framework** for the use of HBM memory on FPGAs. Although simulators for HBM already exist, some of them work on the technology basis and do not include the system view or the memory interconnect [15,16]. Others do include a memory interconnect, but it is too generic to accurately simulate the AMD/Xilinx model [4,12]. The proposed simulation framework allows fast exploration of the design space at system level early in the development process, being able to reliably simulate AMD/Xilinx HBM devices.

Therefore, the goal of this paper is to provide and evaluate such an open-source simulation framework[1] and use real-world applications to verify its accuracy. In summary, the contributions of this paper are:

- We address current state-of-art of design space exploration for HBM2 technology.

---
[1] https://github.com/CEatBTU/HBM_sim.git

- An introduction of our novel HBM2 simulator tool is made, which accurately models the AMD/Xilinx Interconnect module.
- We prove the efficacy of our tool using benchmarks of various memory access patterns in real hardware to provide comparisons.
- Further evaluation of the simulator with real-life applications, recording a *2.72%* error with respect to hardware.

The structure of the paper is as follows: Sect. 2 discusses the latest steps that have been made towards modeling HBM2 systems. The description of the model is done in Sect. 3. Later, we provide the experimental setup in Sect. 4, where the comparisons between the hardware and the simulation are made. Afterwards, we present the results of said experiments in Sect. 5 along with a brief analysis. Finally, we conclude the work and address our plans to continue with this research.

2 Related Work

FPGA-HBM architectures have been recently used in numerous works to accelerate applications, such as sparse matrix operations [10,19] and data analytics [13]. From the analysis of such works, we note that careful design is required to leverage the full bandwidth of the HBM memory, especially in terms of controlling the access of processing elements to the HBM channels, and data placement to ensure parallel computation. In addition, several works [5,7] analyse the performance of AMD/Xilinx's built-in switch network when there are memory accesses that are global across HBM channels. They observe that the network cannot efficiently execute such accesses, which causes significantly low performance for the system.

Some studies have estimated application performance on systems integrating high-performance memories. Ghose et al. [6] use Ramulator [16] to investigate the performance of applications having different characteristics in several memory systems such as HBM and HMC. NAPEL [18] and NDP-RANK [9] use machine learning to predict the performance of kernels on platforms integrating 3D-stacked memories. However, most previous works offer high-level models for simulating or predicting the performance of CPUs connected to high-bandwidth memories.

The most known open-source cycle-accurate DRAM simulators that support HBM technology are *DRAMSys, gem5, Ramulator2,* and *DRAMSim3* [1,15,16,20]. These simulators are suitable for modeling a DRAM subsystem consisting of at least one DRAM device and a DRAM controller, but are too generic to accurately simulate an AMD/Xilinx HBM module. This work therefore adds appropriate models for the crossbar switches and bus fabrics to this DRAM subsystem.

In terms of accuracy and easiness to modify the source code, all these simulators are a suitable candidate for us. It is at run-time where the first differences are noticeable. *DRAMSim3* [15] and *Ramulator2* [16] are loop-based models, meaning that they evaluate every clock cycle with a simple loop, even if the system has recorded no changes. *Gem5* and *DRAMSys* on the other hand omit unnecessary clock cycles, making them faster at run-time than their counterparts [20].

DRAMSys is implemented using the SystemC TLM library, which gives it a very flexible nature. This is the main reason we decided to use *DRAMSys* as the DRAM subsystem to incorporate into our model. The simulator presented in this work is to the author's knowledge the first that is able to simulate an approximately-timed HBM2 memory as well as the AMD/Xilinx Interconnect module. On top of this, the performance of the simulation is validated against actual hardware.

3   Simulation Model Architecture

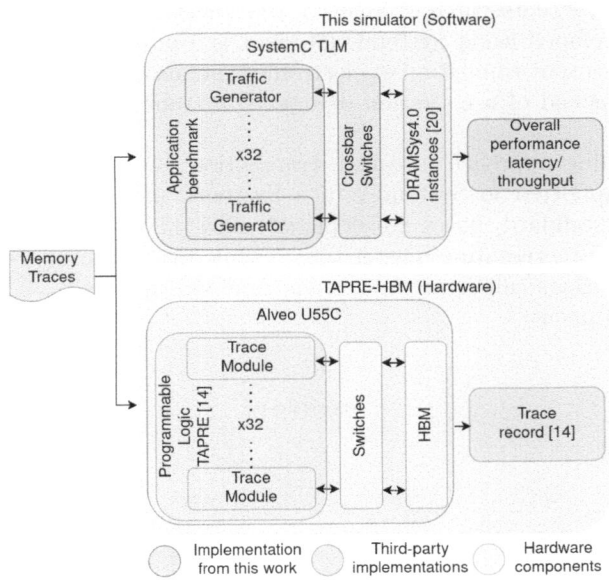

Fig. 1. Complete model overview.

Figure 1 shows the architecture of the overall model. This model can use memory traces from an application as an input. A custom SystemC benchmark creates instances of traffic generators according to the memory traces of the application. The traffic generators then create reads or writes commands that are fed into the Crossbar Switches. The Crossbar Switches redirect and pass the transactions to the *DRAMSys* instances accordingly. At the end of the simulation, a report is generated where some metrics like the overall latencies and throughputs of the memory instances are shown. For a more in-depth description of the model, see Subsect. 3.1.

In order to be able to compare these results with actual hardware, a similar process is done using *TAPRE-HBM* [14]. After the model has been implemented, the memory traces are fed at run-time using a JTAG to AXI module. *TAPRE-HBM* then forwards the corresponding memory accesses to the AMD/Xilinx Interconnect module, which is directly connected to the HBM module. As an output, *TAPRE-HBM* provides a record of every transaction from which latency and throughput can be calculated. For more information about *TAPRE-HBM*, see Subsect. 4.2.

3.1 SystemC TLM Model

Reading or writing on a bus in real hardware is done via the transmission of numerous signals. When modeling this behaviour with a discrete-event simulation, each signal is represented by an event that must be processed. The proposed model was developed using SystemC [8], as it is a powerful modeling language for the discrete-event simulation of electronic systems and offers various degrees of accuracy. Instead of a collection of signals, a transaction is considered as a single entity.

This modeling approach is called Transaction Level Modelling (TLM) [8] and is well supported in SystemC. In a SystemC model compliant with the new TLM-2.0 standard, buses are depicted using TLM socket interfaces, with initiator sockets representing master buses, while target sockets represent slave buses. These sockets can communicate via function calls, with a *TLM Generic Payload* as argument.

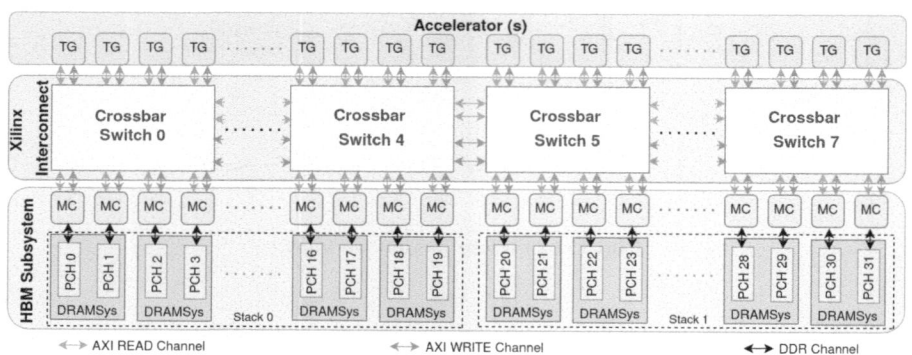

Fig. 2. Structure of two-stack AMD/Xilinx HBM model.

A TLM model can be implemented either as loosely-timed (LT) or as the approximately-timed (AT). Unlike the LT modeling, AT uses a non-blocking transport interface and requires much more synchronisation points for better accuracy. The simulator presented in this work is realised as an AT model, which splits transactions using a four-phase handshake protocol.

Figure 2 illustrates the model of a complete two-stack HBM system consisting of three main modules. First, a total of 32 application-specific traffic generators (TGs) represent the accelerator cores implemented in the programmable logic area of an FPGA board. The TGs are connected to the implementation that simulates the interconnect switch from AMD/Xilinx, which consists of eight instances of 4×4 switching elements. This module can also be seen in Fig. 1, which is depicted by a red box under the name of *Crossbar Switches*. The third module is the HBM subsystem, which consists of memory controllers and pseudo channels (PCHs). Every pair of PCHs is modelled using a *DRAMSys* instance. Our Memory Controller (MC) implements only one master and one slave bus per PCH, meaning that we require 32 MCs. The following subsections give an overview of the modules of the model.

Bus Communication. The Advanced eXtensible Interface 3 (AXI3) protocol requires five channels. It is worth mentioning that while AXI4 protocol is already available, the HBM-IP from Vivado/AMD is using AXI3 as the default protocol. Read transactions use a data and an address channel. Write transactions have an additional response channel. Figure 3a shows how transactions are sent over the AXI3 channels. A transaction is issued when its address *Addr* is sent from the master to the slave bus via the address channel. In the case of write transactions, the data *Data* must also be sent from the master to the slave bus via the data channel. Read transactions end when the data has been sent from the slave to the master and write transactions end when the master receives a response *Resp* from its slave. The AXI3 protocol enables parallel transmission of read and write transactions, since the read and write channels are independent of each other.

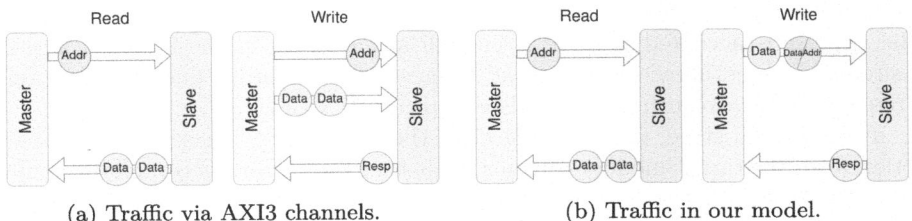

(a) Traffic via AXI3 channels. (b) Traffic in our model.

Fig. 3. Traffic description model.

Instead of three channels for write transactions, our SystemC model uses two channels as shown in Fig. 3b. Our model sends the address and data together in the first beat as a single entity for the write transaction. For read transactions, our model uses two channels according to the AXI3 protocol, thus we require one beat to send the address and two beats to receive the data, totalling three beats.

The AMD/Xilinx Interconnect Module. This module generates the vertical interconnect, the memory controllers, and binds them together. The memory size, clock rates, and number of crossbar switches, among other parameters, can be configured using a JSON configuration file. Every crossbar switch instantiated is connected to each other, while the first and last element are connected to end elements in accordance with the SystemC standard.

The AMD/Xilinx Switch Module. This module is used to model an AXI crossbar switch. Figure 4 shows an example switch assembly having two bilateral connections (L0 and L1) to other switches and connected to four TGs on the upper part and four MCs on the bottom. The bilateral connections are divided equally between the bus masters. Bilateral connection L0 is shared amongst BM0 and BM1, depicted in orange, and connection L1 is shared amongst BM2 and BM3, depicted in blue.

During the simulation, all incoming traffic is forwarded to a Payload Event Queue (PEQ) instance. Once a transaction has been submitted to the PEQ along with its delay and phase, it is scheduled for processing via a callback function. The phase corresponds to the SystemC TLM base protocol used in AT models: The beginning and end of a request *BEGIN_REQ, END_REQ* and the beginning and end of a response *BEGIN_RESP, END_RESP*. The switch module uses a callback function which manages the transaction traffic by forwarding requests over the corresponding slave channel and sending responses back to the corresponding master. Thereby, the callback function has four states that correspond to the phases of the TLM base protocol.

In the first state, transactions in the *BEGIN_REQ* phase, i.e., requests sent by an initiator, are processed. At first, the target channel is determined based on the target address of the request and whether it is a read or write transaction. The request is accepted if there is enough space in the request queue of the desired channel, otherwise the request is placed in the pending queue. Accepting a request means executing the handshake protocol.

In the second state, the model receives the *END_REQ* phase for the transaction from the target module, which signals that the request is complete. Thus, the occupied channel becomes available for new transactions. If there is enough space in the request queue, requests from the pending queue are accepted, then the next request is sent over the channel.

The last two states, the *BEGIN_RESP* and *END_RESP* phases, are implemented similarly to their request counterpart, but there are some important differences. First, the transactions are routed from the target module back to the initiator. Second, instead of the request queue, a response queue is used to store the accepted transactions, which may have a different size than the request queue. Third, the delay is only dependent on the number of beats required for transmission.

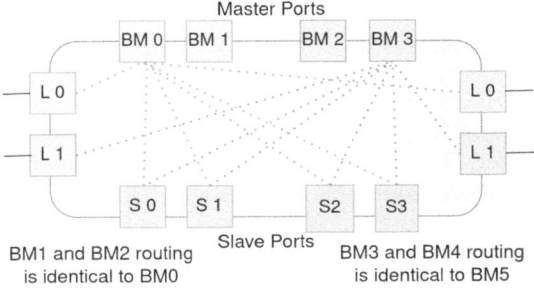

Fig. 4. Example of a crossbar switch routing setup.

The AMD/Xilinx Memory Controller Module. This module was designed as an extension for the MC implementation included in DRAMSys, which by itself is not accurate enough. During simulation, all incoming traffic is forwarded to a PEQ instance, which schedules transactions for processing via a callback function. One major difference with the switch module is that here whenever requests are sent to the target module, the delay is always set to zero, since the MC included in *DRAMSys* already takes care of this timing. To simulate the DDR protocol, the requests are sent over only one channel, which is shared by read and write transactions. Although the *DRAMSys* MC is able to convert between AXI and DDR, our simulator performs the conversion in this module, as this leads to better results.

4 Experiment Setup

In this section, the two main evaluations of the simulator are presented. For the hardware measurements, we used the Alveo U55C board [2] which has a *128 Gb* two-stacked HBM. The operating frequency for every evaluation was set to *300 MHz* for the complete design, including the HBM AXI interfaces. The reference clock for the HBM was set to *100 MHz*, and the memory controller frequency inside the HBM IP was set to *900MHz*.

4.1 Hardware Profiler

For the first evaluation, we decided to employ the benchmarking convention used on [7], where there are four test cases based on the access locality to memory channels. Single Channel (SC) forces every Bus Master (BM) to communicate with the directly connected PCH in a 1:1 fashion. Cross Channel (CC) removes this restriction, making every PCH available from any BM in a N:M manner. Both memory locality test cases can be either in a strided or a random memory access pattern. Stride (S) linearly increases the addresses every time a new bus transaction is made. Random (RA) has no defined pattern and the next bus transaction is calculated randomly.

The hardware model includes a modified version of the hardware profiler used in [7], which can be used to control the pattern, size, command type, and other parameters of the memory accesses. This hardware profiler is connected on the master side to a JTAG to AXI block that can be used to interface at run-time with the design, and on the slave side to the HBM IP. The simulation works in a very similar manner. A C++ benchmark is needed to use the design, and all the parameters are easily modifiable as attributes of an object.

4.2 Real-Life Applications

For the second section of the evaluation, we used real-life applications to measure the effectiveness of the simulator. The selected applications were a simple matrix-vector multiplication, an insert sort algorithm, a small implementation of a Yolo lite network [17], and a basic application of the Kruskal's Minimum Spanning Tree (KMST) algorithm. The applications where chosen to represent different type of memory intensive applications, ranging from CPU-bound to more memory-bound applications. For the hardware setup, we used gem5 [4] to simulate a custom basic microarchitecture running an application. This custom microarchitecture had to have an option to simulate more than one memory channel, and a burst mode. From our gem5 model, we obtained the memory traces of the application, which then later was fed into *TAPRE-HBM* [14].

TAPRE-HBM is a trace-based processor for Rapid Emulation using HBM on FPGAs. A sequence of memory accesses is fed into *TAPRE-HBM*, which emulates them in real hardware using the AXI protocol to manage the communication with the HBM module. The output of *TAPRE-HBM* are the latencies of the memory accesses from the AR/AW handshake to the last beat of the R/W channel. With these values, we calculated the overall latency of the application and compared it to the simulation. The simulator once again only needs a C++ benchmark to accommodate the memory traces of the application and run them.

5 Discussion

The results of the first evaluation can be found in Fig. 5, where the simulation result is next to the Hardware baseline for each benchmark. Every point of every memory access and every transaction type were compared against the hardware to obtain the error percentage. The error of Read transactions was of *10.53%*, with a standard deviation of *12.37*. Write transactions had an average error of *6.48%*, with a standard deviation of *8.61*, and finally for the combined cases, the error and standard deviation were *12.73%* and *14.07* accordingly. This leads to an overall average error was of *9.91%*. As seen in these results, the random cases (SCRA and CCRA respectively) are less accurate in relation to the hardware than the strided benchmarks. The AMD/Xilinx Interconnect Module was treated as a 'black box' due to its proprietary nature. As such, we have no way of knowing exactly how the traffic gets queued and re-directed in the actual hardware, making it harder to fine-tune the random access patterns.

A Novel System Simulation Framework for HBM2 FPGA Platforms   81

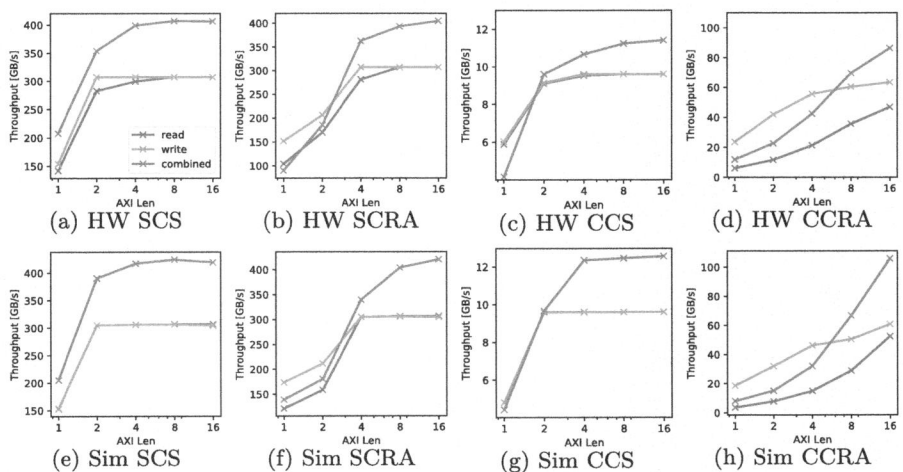

Fig. 5. Comparison between hardware and simulation benchmarks.

The second evaluation was done with real-life applications, as discussed in Subsect. 4.2, and the comparison of latency and throughput between the hardware and the simulation is reported in Fig. 6. In this figure, the biggest difference was seen in the KMST benchmark, where the throughput of the simulation has an error of 5.45% with respect to the hardware. It is worth noting that the reported throughput is per PCH. Also, as the sizes and parameters of each benchmark are relative, the objective of these results is not to compare the latency among different benchmarks, but only to compare the performance of the simulation and hardware for each benchmark.

The error percentages of every benchmark's latency can be seen in Table 1, as well as the total elapsed time which shows the time required by the simulation to complete, which is in the *ms* order, as opposed to designing a hardware specific application which can take hours. Both the simulation results and the baseline hardware were tuned to have the same number of memory traces as inputs, the same operating frequency, and same HBM parameters for every benchmark. As Table 1 suggests, more repetitive memory accesses reported higher error than spaced accesses. This can be due to the AMD/Xilinx proprietary Switch when it comes to re-ordering memory transactions, and how it handles cases where one pseudo-channel gets saturated by multiple consecutive accesses, as opposed to more spaced requests. Also, as seen in Table 1, the more memory-bound applications like KMST have more discrepancy between the simulation and the hardware. In these cases the fine tuning can become incrementally complex, which is why we compromised with the errors reported. When calculating the average of all error rates in Table 1, we obtain 2.72% as the overall error percentage for the real-life applications.

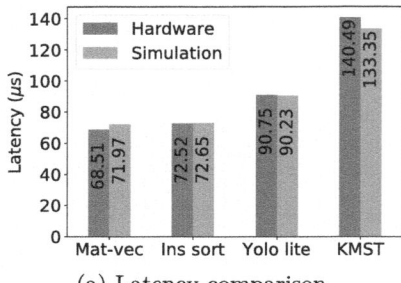
(a) Latency comparison.

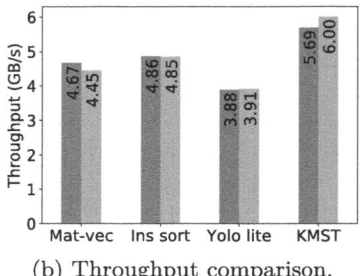
(b) Throughput comparison.

Fig. 6. Performance comparison between Hardware and our simulator.

Table 1. Error percentages and elapsed time of real-life applications

Application	Error (latency)	Simulation Elapsed Time [ms]
Matrix-vector multiplication	5.06%	5.91
Insert sort	0.17%	6.11
Yolo lite	0.57%	6.54
KMST	5.08%	7.00
Total average	2.72%	

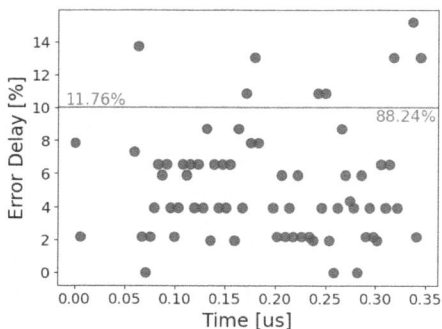

Fig. 7. Individual transactions delays comparison in Yolo Lite.

Finally, a more detailed comparison of individual transactions is shown in Fig. 7. In this figure, the first transactions from the benchmark of *Yolo Lite* were analyzed. Using TAPRE to emulate the hardware, the delay of each transaction is measured from the AR/AW handshake, until the last R/W handshake. Equivalently, in the simulator the delay from the *END_REQUEST* to *END_RESPONSE* phase was recorded. Figure 7 shows the error rate when comparing said delays from each independent transaction. As Fig. 7 shows, *88.24%*

of the analyzed simulated transactions had less than *10%* error with respect of the hardware.

6 Conclusion and Future Work

This work presents a unique complete open-source HBM2 simulator, which accurately simulates the AMD/Xilinx Interconnect and the HBM module. The simulator is tested by comparing the results with an Alveo U55C board, which has HBM2 incorporated. Our simulator had an average error of *9.91%* when using different very specific memory access patterns, in contrast to real hardware. Also, when testing real-life applications, we recorded an average of *2.72%* error against real hardware. The high accuracy and reduced run-time compared to real hardware, make our simulator a great candidate for predicting real hardware behavior.

Our simulator was more accurate when the memory accesses were deterministic, because of the black-box nature of the hardware we simulate. It can be challenging to model exactly how the proprietary hardware is re-ordering transactions in more random cases. Therefore, for future work, and although showing an acceptable error rate with respect to actual hardware, our simulator can be fine-tuned further to obtain even more accurate results. As this tuning can become quickly overwhelming, machine learning techniques have been contemplated to train these parameters.

References

1. Akram, A., Babaie, M., Wlsasser, W., Lowe-Power, J.: Modeling HBM2 Memory Controller. In: gem5 Users' Workshop ISCA 2022 (2022)
2. AMD / Xilinx. Alveo U55C High Performance Compute Card (2023). https://www.xilinx.com/products/boards-and-kits/alveo/u55c.html
3. AMD-Xilinx. HACC cluster 2024. https://xilinx-center.csl.illinois.edu/xacc-cluster/
4. Binkert, N., et al.: The Gem5 simulator. SIGARCH **39**, 1-7 (2011) issn: 0163-5964
5. Choi, Y.-k., Chi, Y., Qiao, W., Samardzic, N., Cong, J.: HBM Connect: High-Performance HLS Interconnect for FPGA HBM in ACM/SIGDA, New York, USA, pp. 116-126 (Feb. 2021) (2022). isbn: 978-1-4503-8218-2
6. Ghose, S., Li, T., Hajinazar, N., Cali, D.S,. Mutlu, O.: Demystifying complex workload-dram interactions: an experimental study. Proc. ACM **3** (Dec 2019). https://doi.org/10.1145/3366708
7. Holzinger, P., Reiser, D., Hahn, T., Reichenbach, M.: Fast HBM Access with FPGAs: Analysis, Architectures, and Applications in IEEE (IPDPSW), Portland, OR, USA, June 2021, pp. 152-159 (2022). isbn: 978-1-66543-577-2
8. IEEE Standard for Standard SystemC Language Reference Manual. IEEE Std 1666-2011 (Revision of IEEE Std 1666-2005), 1-638 (2012)
9. Iskandar, V., Abd El Ghany, M. A., Goehringer, D.: NDP-RANK: prediction and ranking of ndp systems performance using machine learning. Microprocess. Microsyst. **96**, 104707 (2023), issn: 0141-9331

10. Jain, A.K., et al.: Modular and Lean Architecture with Elasticity for Sparse Matrix Vector Multiplication on FPGAs in FCCM, pp. 133-143 (2023)
11. Jun, H., et al.: HBM (high bandwidth memory) DRAM technology and architecture en. In: 2017 IEEE (IMW), pp. 1-4. IEEE, Monterey, CA, USA (May 2017), isbn: 978-1-5090-3274-7 (2022)
12. Jung, M., Weis, C., Wehn, N.: DRAMSys: a flexible DRAM subsystem design space exploration framework. IPSJ Trans. **8**, 63–74 (2015)
13. Kara, K., Hagleitner, C., Diamantopoulos, D., Syrivelis, D., Alonso, G.: High Bandwidth Memory on FPGAs: A Data Analytics Perspective in FPL, pp. 1–8 (Aug 2020), ISSN: 1946–1488
14. Knödtel, J. et al.: TAPRE-HBM: Trace-based processor rapid emulation using HBM on FPGAs. In: Palumbo, F., Keramidas, G., Voros, N., Diniz, P.C. (eds.) Applied Reconfigurable Computing. Architectures, Tools, and Applications. ARC 2023. LNCS, vol. 14251. Springer, Cham (2023). https://doi.org/10.1007/978-3-031-42921-7_21
15. Li, S., Yang, Z., Reddy, D., Srivastava, A., Jacob, B.: DRAMsim3: a cycle-accurate, thermal-capable DRAM simulator. IEEE Comput. Architect. Lett. **19**, 106–109 (2020), ISSN: 1556-6064
16. Luo, H., et al.: Ramulator 2.0: a modern, modular, and extensible DRAM simulator. IEEE Comput. Architect. Lett. **23**, 112–116 (2023)
17. Pedoeem, J., Huang, R.: YOLO-LITE: A Real-Time Object Detection Algorithm Optimized for Non-GPU Computers. CoRR. arXiv: 1811.05588 (2018)
18. Singh, G. et al.: NAPEL: Near-Memory Computing Application Performance Prediction via Ensemble Learning in 56th ACM/IEEE (DAC), pp. 1-6 (2019),
19. Song, L. et al.: Sextans: A Streaming Accelerator for General-Purpose Sparse-Matrix Dense-Matrix Multiplication in the 2022 ACM/SIGDA (2022)
20. Steiner, L., Jung, M., Prado, F.S., Bykov, K., Wehn, N.: DRAMSys4.0: **A Fast and Cycle-Accurate** SystemC/TLM-Based DRAM simulator. In: Orailoglu, A., Jung, M., Reichenbach, M. (eds.) SAMOS 2020. LNCS, vol. 12471, pp. 110–126. Springer, Cham (2020). https://doi.org/10.1007/978-3-030-60939-9_8

ONNX-To-Hardware Design Flow for Adaptive Neural-Network Inference on FPGAs

Federico Manca[1], Francesco Ratto[1(✉)], and Francesca Palumbo[2]

[1] University of Sassari, Piazza Università 21, 07100 Sassari, Italy
{fmanca2,fratto}@uniss.it
[2] University of Cagliari, via Marengo 2, 09123 Cagliari, Italy
francesca.palumbo@unica.it

Abstract. The challenges involved in executin Neural Networks (NNs) at the edge include providing diversity, flexibility, and sustainability. That implies, for instance, supporting evolving applications and algorithms energy-efficiently. Using hardware (hw) or software accelerators can deliver fast and efficient computation of the NNs, while flexibility can be exploited to support long-term adaptivity. Nonetheless, handcrafting a NN for a specific device, despite the possibility of leading to an optimal solution, takes time and experience, and that's why frameworks for hw accelerators are being developed. This work, starting from a preliminary semi-integrated ONNX-to-hardware toolchain [23], focuses on enabling Approximate Computing (AC) leveraging the distinctive ability of the original toolchain to favor adaptivity. The goal is to allow lightweight adaptable NN inference on FPGAs at the edge.

Keyword: Convolutional Neural Networks, Approximate Computing, FPGAs, Cyber-Physical Systems

1 Introduction

Cyber-Physical System (CPS) integrate *"computation with physical processes whose behavior is defined by both the computational and the physical parts of the system"*[1]. These systems are characterized by significant information exchange with the environment and dynamic, reactive behaviors. In modern systems, whether CPS or not, NN-assisted decision-making can be directly deployed at the edge on embedded platforms. This approach reduces latency, energy consumption, and often ensures higher privacy levels [25]. Nonetheless, executing AI

This work is supported by MYRTUS that is funded by the European Union (GA No. 101135183). Views and opinions expressed are however those of the author(s) only and do not necessarily reflect those of the European Union. Neither the European Union nor the granting authority can be held responsible for them.

[1] https://csrc.nist.gov/glossary/term/cyber_physical_systems.

models on resource-constrained edge devices presents several challenges, including limited computing and memory capacities. Balancing model accuracy and execution efficiency exposes a crucial design trade-off.

In response to these challenges, Field Programmable Gate Arrays (FPGAs) emerge as a valuable choice for NN inference at the edge [13]. They can guarantee hw acceleration, execution flexibility, and energy efficiency thanks to the possibility of tailoring the hw architecture to the specific application. Despite existing solutions, there remains a lack of support for advanced features, particularly the adaptivity naturally supported over these kinds of platforms. Computing adaptivity empowers CPS to thrive in complex, ever-changing environments.

This paper aims to take steps towards filling that gap. The goal is to feature adaptivity targeting Convolutional Neural Network (CNN) models as applications and edge FPGAs as computing platforms. CNN models have proven to be positively affected by the application of AC methodologies [3]. State-of-the-art approaches [1,7,9] apply it in a data-oriented manner, as discussed in Sect. 2.1. This paper presents the combination of data-oriented and computation-oriented strategies targeting runtime adaptivity, through reconfiguration. Different execution profiles are operated at runtime by an adaptive inference engine developed with the proposed design flow. In summary, the contributions of this work are:

- A novel design flow that enables the inference of Quantized ONNX models on FPGAs (Sect. 3) featuring, for the first time to the best of our knowledge, both data-approximation and computation-approximation.
- The analysis of the effect of data-approximation in a mixed-precision tiny CNN model for MNIST classification (Sects. 4.2 and 4.3).
- The assessment of the benefits of computation-approximation through the deployment of an adaptive CNN inference engine for the data-approximated models (Sect. 4.4).

2 Related Work

To execute NN at the edge, three main types of architectures can be found in literature [29]: the Single Computational Engine architecture, based on a single computation engine, typically in the form of a systolic array of processing elements or a matrix multiplication unit, that executes the CNN layers sequentially [12]; Vector Processor architecture, with instructions specific for accelerating operations related to convolutions [8]; the Streaming architecture consists of one distinct hw block for each layer of the target CNN, where each block is optimized separately [1,9], as depicted in Fig. 1. In this study, we adopted the latter for two main reasons:

- a distinct hw processing element for each layer of the CNN model allows for higher customization, thus favoring adaptivity;
- the streaming architecture is the most natural implementation of a dataflow application, such CNNs, thus easing the High Level Synthesis (HLS) design.

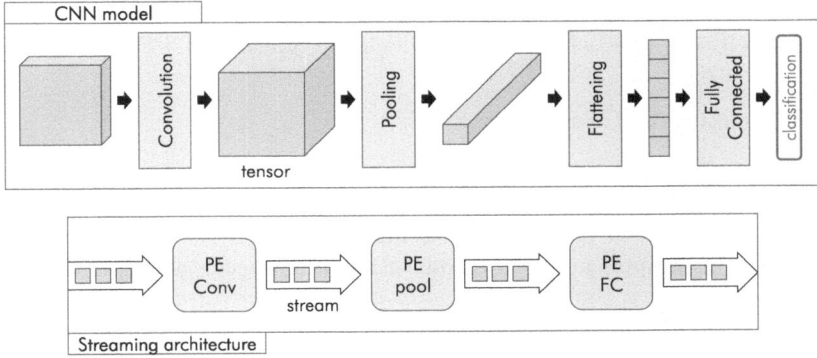

Fig. 1. Representation on a simple CNN and its mapping to a streaming architecture.

2.1 Streaming Architectures

In our previous work [23], a toolchain for porting CNNs on FPGAs was proposed. The resulting hw is a streaming architecture that uses on-chip memory, guaranteeing low-latency and low-energy computing. Solutions that exploit a similar streaming architecture are FINN [9], a framework from AMD Research Labs; HLS4ML [1], an open-source software designed to facilitate the deployment of machine learning models on FPGAs, targeting low-latency and low-power edge applications. FINN enables building scalable and fast NN, with a focus on the support of Quantized Neural Network (QNN) inference on FPGAs. A given model, trained through Brevitas [21], is compiled by the FINN compiler, producing a synthesizable C++ description of a heterogeneous streaming architecture. All QNN parameters are kept stored in the on-chip memory, which greatly reduces the power consumed and simplifies the design. The computing engines communicate via the on-chip data stream. Avoiding the "one-size-fits-all", an ad-hoc topology is built for the network. The resulting accelerator is deployed on the target board using the AMD Pynq framework. The main operation of the HLS4ML library is to translate the model of the network into an HLS Project. The focus in [18] was centered on reducing the computational complexity and resource usage on a fully connected network for MNIST dataset classification: the data is fed to a multi-layer perceptron with an input layer of 784 nodes, three hidden layers with 128 nodes each, and an output layer with 10 nodes. The work exploits the potential of Pruning and Quantization-aware Training (QAT) to reduce the model size with limited impact on its accuracy.

This Work Positioning: To the best of our knowledge, neither FINN nor HLS4ML, despite targeting FPGA-based streaming architecture and supporting AC features, have ever proposed an adaptive solution. These existing frameworks primarily focus on data-oriented approximation. However, there remains an untapped opportunity for computation-oriented approaches, which can be achieved through reconfigurable systems design [17]. Such computation-oriented strategies could naturally be harnessed by runtime management infrastructures aiming at self-adaptive behaviors [19], which are typical of CPSs.

2.2 Approximate Computing

The AC paradigm is founded on *"the idea that computer systems can let applications trade-off accuracy for efficiency"*. Indeed, AC has been established as a design paradigm for energy-efficient circuits. It exploits the inherent ability of a large number of applications to produce results of acceptable quality despite being run on systems that *"intentionally exposes incorrectness to the application layer in return for conserving some resource"*[2]. This trade-off ultimately balances computation accuracy with efficiency. According to textbook definitions [2], AC provides three degrees of freedom by acting on *data, hardware*, and *computation*. Approximating *data* means processing either less up-to-date data (temporal decimation), fewer input data (spatial decimation), less accurate data (word-length optimization), or corrupted data. *Hardware* approximation leverages inexact operators or voltage scaling. *Computation* approximation corresponds to model modifications to expose different implementations, aiming to enable different execution profiles, over the same substrate.

AC is particularly relevant in applications like NNs that have demonstrated remarkable resilience to errors [16]. For NNs employed in the classification task, resilience to approximation can be evaluated by referring to the resulting accuracy of the model, i.e. the ratio of samples correctly classified. Within this specific application domain, NN approximation can be broadly categorized into three main approaches: *Computation Reduction, Approximate Arithmetic Units*, and *Precision Scaling* [3]. The *Computation Reduction* approximation category aims at systematically avoiding certain computation at the hw level, thereby significantly reducing the overall workload. An example of this is pruning: biases, weights, or entire neurons can be evicted to lighten the workload [26]. By employing *Approximate Units* that replace more accurate units, such as the Multiply-and-Accumulate (MAC) unit, energy consumption and latency in NN accelerators can be improved [4]. The most used *Precision Scaling* practice is quantization: quantized hw implementations feature reduced bit-width dataflow and arithmetic units attaining substantial energy, latency, and bandwidth gains compared to 32-bit floating-point implementations. Instead of executing all the required mathematical operations with ordinary 32-bit floating point, quantization allows the exploitation of lighter operations by mapping real numbers to integers within a specified range [10,14].

This Work: NN *Precision scaling* is exploited by implementing quantization to feature *data* approximation. We combine different data-approximate profiles to enable *computation* approximation and to deliver adaptivity. Our proposed flow utilizes Vitis HLS, which provides an arbitrary precision data types library, that

---

[2] http://approximate.computer/approxbib/.

goes beyond the standard C++. This library also supports customizable fixed-point data types[3], easing the data precision control among layers. Additionally, we introduce another tool called MDC, explained further below, to enable adaptivity and *computation* approximation.

3 Proposed Design Flow

The utilization of a CNN model involves two distinct phases: training and inference. The training phase aims at setting the model parameters to execute a given classification task. This phase typically occurs on powerful platforms, often in the cloud. The inference phase executes the trained model to perform the classification task. It is usually performed on a different platform, in our case an FPGA edge device. The two phases can be decoupled by adopting an intermediate representation to exchange the model between the respective frameworks. The de facto standard for this purpose is the ONNX format.

The proposed design flow automates the design and deployment of an FPGA processor for the inference of a given Quantized CNN model. The model must be provided in the QONNX format [22], which extends the ONNX[4] format by allowing the specification of layers with arbitrary-precision data types. The adopted tools are described in Sect. 3.1 and their integration and usage in Sect. 3.2.

3.1 Tools

Various commercial and open-source academic tools are utilized throughout the design flow:

- the ONNXParser[5], a Python application, is designed to parse the ONNX models and create the code for a target device. The tool consists of a Reader and multiple Writers, each tailored for different target platforms supported within the ALOHA framework [15]. For this work, we developed a Writer targeting HLS.
- The Vitis HLS tool[6] synthesizes a C or C++ function into RTL code for implementation on AMD FPGAs. The resulting hw can be optimized and customized by inserting directives in the code.
- The Multi-Dataflow Composer (MDC) tool[7] is an open-source tool that can offer Coarse-Grained reconfigurability support for hw acceleration [24]. It takes as input the applications specified as dataflow, together with the library of the HDL files of the actors. These dataflows are then combined, and the resulting multi-dataflow topology is filled with the actors taken from the HDL library.

---

[3] https://jiafulow.github.io/blog/2020/08/02/hls-arbitrary-precision-data-types.
[4] https://onnx.ai/.
[5] https://gitlab.com/aloha.eu/onnxparser.
[6] https://www.AMD.com/support/documentation-navigation/design-hubs/dh0012-vivado-high-level-synthesis-hub.html.
[7] https://mdc-suite.github.io/.

3.2 Design Flow

The proposed flow, as depicted in Fig. 2, starts from the QONNX representation of the NN and produces a streaming architecture that executes the input model. The QONNX file acts as a bridge between the training and the inference frameworks. Two distinct paths are present in the design flow: the actor-related path and the network-related path. They can be carried out once, to obtain a non-adaptive data-approximate solution, or multiple times, to derive a computation-approximate adaptive engine of data-approximate solutions.

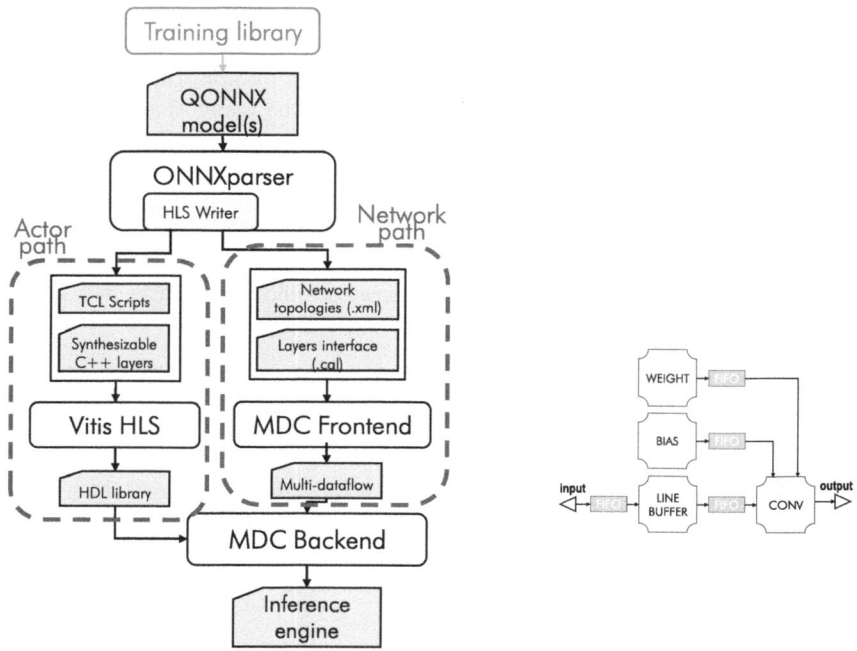

Fig. 2. On the left, is the ONNX-to-Hardware design flow for generating adaptive neural-network inference engines on FPGAs. The training library could be any library able to export to QONNX. On the right, is the streaming-based template architecture for a convolutional layer.

The QONNX file serves as input to the extended ONNX Parser, which is capable of processing the additional quantization layers included in the QONNX format. Initially, the Reader reads the QONNX file and produces an intermediate format with a list of objects describing the layers' hyperparameters (e.g. kernel size, data precision, etc.) and connections within the QONNX model. Subsequently, the HLS Writer creates the target-dependent files.

The ONNX Parser extracts the network topology from the QONNX and the data precision in each layer. This information is used by the Front End of the MDC tool to derive the datapath of the accelerator. When designing an adaptive engine, multiple data-approximate profiles of the same CNN model are processed. The tool automates the merging process by sharing layers of different profiles that use the same data precision.

The HLS Writer produces the C++ files that implement the layers, and the TCL scripts to automate the synthesis by Vitis HLS. The C++ description of the layers is based on a template architecture: for the convolutional layers, the core of a CNN, the template is composed of a Line Buffer actor that stores the input stream to provide data reuse; the Convolutional actor, that executes the actual computation; and the Weight and Bias actors that store the kernel parameters needed for the convolution. The resulting template, depicted in Fig. 2, ensures streaming dataflow between layers, eliminating the need to store full tensors. Each actor is developed to be customizable with the hyperparameter, e.g. input and kernel size, extracted from the QONNX model. The HDL library produced by Vitis HLS and the reconfigurable datapath (Multi-dataflow) serve as input to the MDC Backend to generate the HDL description of the inference engine.

4 Evaluation

The proposed design flow was evaluated on a tiny CNN model trained for MNIST classification. The model comprises two convolutional blocks and a final fully connected layer. Each block consists of a convolutional layer with a 3x3 kernel, 64 filters, and ReLU activation, followed by a batch normalization and a maxpooling layer. The inference engines that execute this model have been designed with the proposed flow targeting the FPGA available on an AMD KRIA board.

First, we describe how the quantized models have been trained in Sect. 4.1. Then, to evaluate the proposed flow, we carried out an initial exploration, described in Sect. 4.2, on *data* approximated designs. This exploration is meaningful to assess the impact of quantization on both accuracy and inference performance. Then, in Sect. 4.3, different execution profiles are selected and, then, merged to generate an adaptive inference engine, as described in 4.4.

4.1 Quantization-Aware Training

The model previously described has been designed and trained using QKeras [6]. QKeras is an extension of the Keras framework that offers several features, including the ability to specify a custom fixed-point precision for each layer of a NN and perform QAT, which has demonstrated significant advantages over post-training quantization in terms of resulting model accuracy [11]

Through its APIs, QKeras allows to specify the number of bits used to represent the activations and the weights of the NN model. The activations are the outputs of an NN layer, while the weights are the trainable parameters of the kernel used either for convolution, in convolutional layers, or matrix multiplication in fully connected layers. In the exploration of Sect. 4.2 we varied both these bit-widths, thus implementing a mixed-precision quantization strategy.

For the QAT, we selected an optimizer that implements the *Adam algorithm* and *Categorical Crossentropy* as the loss function to be minimized during regression. The trained CNN models have been exported to QONNX format and implemented with the proposed design flow.

It is worth underlying that other frameworks, e.g. Brevitas [21], offer QAT and export to QONNX, so that the proposed design flow is interoperable with any QONNX-compliant framework.

4.2 Data Approximation Analysis

In this section, we report the results of the analysis using mixed-precision fixed-point quantization. A string identifies a profile as Ax-Wy, where x represents the number of bits used to represent activations and y the number of bits used for weights. For each mixed-precision configuration, a non-adaptive inference engine has been realized with the proposed design flow. We report accuracy, latency for a classification, resource utilization, and power consumption for each engine in Table 1.

Table 1. Results of the analysis with data mixed-precision approximation. In the string Ax-Wy, x represents the number of bits for the activations, and y is the number of bits used for the weights.

Datatype	Accuracy [%]	Latency [us]	LUT [%]	BRAM [%]	Power [mW]
A16-W8	98.9	329	12	18	160
A16-W4	95.3	329	7	18	134
A8-W8	98.8	329	11	17	142
A8-W4	95.3	329	6	17	132
A4-W4	95.8	329	6	17	141

It can be noticed that the execution latency for a classification remains constant independently of the data precision. This behavior can be explained by considering how the HLS compilation flow works: the HLS compiler schedules the operations depending on data dependencies and user directives. After that, the operations are bound to the physical resources. Therefore, a larger precision increases resource utilization rather than slowing down the system. Indeed, we can see that adopting a reduced bit precision for activations and weights leads to a reduction in Look-Up Tables (LUTs) and Block RAMs (BRAMs) utilization.

The two metrics where we see an exploitable trade-off at runtime are model accuracy and power consumption. The model's accuracy decreases with reduced bit precisions. From a baseline 99.8% which can be obtained with floating point operations, not feasible to be ported to an FPGA, the quantized model A16-W8 achieves a classification accuracy of 98.9%. This accuracy drops down to 95.3%

with A8-W4. We can notice that with 4-bit precision in the weights, the final accuracy is around 95%. Small variations are due to the intrinsic randomness of the training process rather than to the activations' precision.

On the other hand, this drop in accuracy is compensated by reduced dynamic power consumption. A general trend shows that power consumption decreases with reduced precision. A graphical description of the resulting execution profiles that consider only accuracy and power consumption is reported in Fig. 3. The variability in the power consumption, which is not directly proportional to the data precision, shows the advantage of having a fast design flow that goes from the high-level description in QONNX to the FPGA implementation. This allows us to consider the joint effects of the resource utilization, which is affected by the FPGA backend and the HLS compiler, and switching activity, which depends on the actual values of weights and the data being processed.

4.3 Execution Profiles Selection

From Fig. 3, we observe that the non-adaptive inference engines obtained with the initial exploration offer valuable trade-offs. However, these engines lack some common layers necessary to achieve some degree of resource sharing. To address this limitation, we started from the A8-W8 profile and trained an additional profile that further exploits mixed precision. This new profile generally uses the same precision as A8-W8, but in the inner convolutional layer, where instead it uses the A4-W4 one. The resulting non-adaptive engine (named Mixed) performance is reported with a green dot in Fig. 3. This demonstrates the additional level of *data* approximation that can be achieved with the proposed methodology.

Finally, the Mixed and A8-W8 profiles are good candidates for merging using the proposed methodology. This will allow us to design an adaptive inference engine that enables *computation* approximation, as shown in the following section.

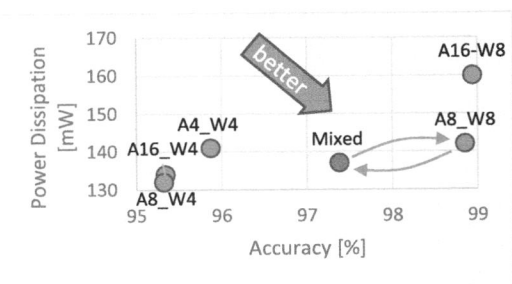

Fig. 3. Accuracy VS power chart of the obtained profiles. In green the Mixed design. The yellow arrows point to the two configurations selected for adaptivity. (Color figure online)

4.4 Adaptive Inference Engine

In the previous designs, we partially used the functionality of the proposed methodology, resulting in non-adaptive inference engines. To achieve adaptivity we need to design a *computation* approximate inference engine that allows selecting different profiles at runtime. For this purpose, we leverage the merging capabilities of MDC. As anticipated, Mixed and A8-W8 profiles are selected as entry points, since they share the same layers, but the inner convolutional one. The characteristics of the resulting adaptive inference engine are summarized on top of Fig. 4. The resulting inference engine has a limited overhead with respect to the non-adaptive ones. Indeed, MDC guarantees lightweight reconfiguration by inserting routing elements in the datapath. These routing elements address tokens depending on the configuration, which sets the values of the routing table. Thus, reconfiguration happens in a few clock cycles (the time required to update the configuration register) and with no additional energy cost.

The switch among profiles can guarantee a 5% power saving with a 1.5% accuracy drop. Given the low accuracy penalty, we can suppose that in a real CPS application, the inference engine would run most of the time in the Profile 1 and switch to the more accurate only under critical circumstances, when higher accuracy is necessary. This further motivates the proposed methodology that is going to be adopted as part of a recently started EU project [20].

Indeed, a CPS is meant to react and dynamically adjust to mutable constraints and system conditions. This can be achieved, as shown on the left-hand side in Fig. 4, by an infrastructure composed of two main parts: the *Adaptive Inference Engine* and the *Profile Manager*. The former is responsible for implementing the adaptive solution that, in this case, can alternatively execute one of the two profiles. The latter, following the self-adaptive management approach presented in [19], monitors the energy status and the given constraints

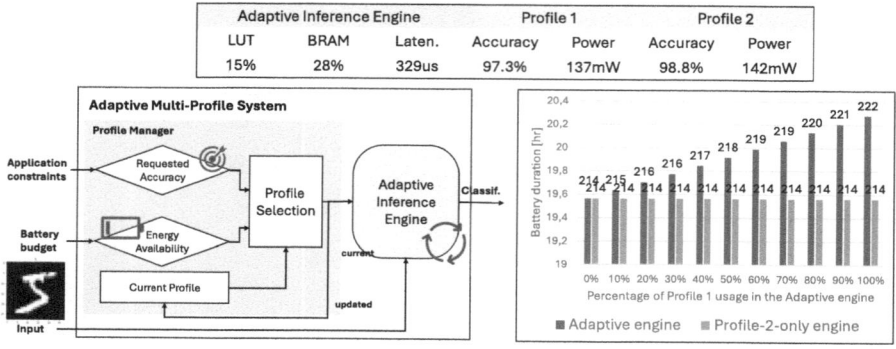

Fig. 4. On top, the resource utilization of the adaptive engine and its performance metrics. On the left, is a system architecture that exploits the proposed adaptive engine. On the right, a comparison of the resulting battery duration (supposing a 10Ah budget) and number of classifications executable by the adaptive engine and a non-adaptive one supporting the higher accuracy profile only.

and decides which is the most suitable profile. The profile selected at runtime must be capable of meeting the accuracy requirements while minimizing power dissipation. As an example, if the remaining battery budget is lower than a pre-defined threshold the *Profile Manager* might select a less energy-consuming profile, if the user-/application-defined constraints are still met or if they can be negotiated. On the right-hand side in Fig. 4, the potentials of the implemented adaptive engine are presented. Even considering this preliminary implementation, it is shown how the adaptive engine (in blue) extends the battery duration, and in turn increases the number of executable classifications, with respect to the non-adaptive (in orange) counterpart, which is running at full performance.

5 Conclusion

CPS integrate computation with physical processes, characterized by information exchange with the environment and dynamic behaviors. FPGAs offer hw acceleration, flexibility, and energy efficiency, but challenges persist in achieving full adaptivity for dealing with complex environments.

The utilization of a CNN model involves two distinct phases: training and inference. These phases can be decoupled using an intermediate representation like the ONNX format. The proposed design flow automates FPGA inference for quantized CNN models, specified in the QONNX format, which allows data approximation through arbitrary-precision data types. At the same time, the flow also features adaptivity, implementing computation approximation.

A data approximation analysis on a tiny CNN model for MNIST classification has been conducted to select valuable profiles. These latter have been combined in an adaptive inference engine, which can adapt its accuracy and power consumption at runtime by switching among the selected profiles.

Future work will aim at validating the proposed approach on more complex CNN models and datasets, allowing for quantitative state-of-the-art comparison, besides the already provided qualitative discussion.

References

1. Aarrestad, T., et al.: Fast convolutional neural networks on FPGAs with hls4ml. Mach. Learn. Sci. Technol. **2**(4) (2021)
2. Agrawal, A., et al.: Approximate computing: Challenges and opportunities. In: ICRC Conference (2016)
3. Armeniakos, G., et al.: Hardware approximate techniques for deep neural network accelerators: a survey. ACM CSUR **55**(4), 1–36 (2022)
4. Bhardwaj, K., et al.: Power-and area-efficient approximate wallace tree multiplier for error-resilient systems. In: ISQED symposium (2014)
5. Canis, A., et al.: LegUp: an open-source high-level synthesis tool for FPGA-based processor/accelerator systems. ACM TECS **13**(2), 1–27 (2013)
6. Coelho, C.N., et al.: Automatic heterogeneous quantization of deep neural networks for low-latency inference on the edge for particle detectors. Nat. Mach. Intell. (2021)

7. Ducasse, Q., et al.: Benchmarking quantized neural networks on FPGAs with FINN. arXiv preprint arXiv:2102.01341 (2021)
8. Farabet C., et al.: An FPGA-based processor for convolutional networks. In: FPL Conference (2009)
9. Fraser, N.J., et al.: Scaling binarized neural networks on reconfigurable logic. In: PARMA-DITAM Workshop (2017)
10. Fuengfusin, N., Tamukoh, H.: Mixed-precision weights network for field-programmable gate array. PLoS ONE **16**(5), e0251329 (2021)
11. Gholami, A., et al.: A survey of quantization methods for efficient neural network inference. Low-Power Computer Vision Book (2021)
12. Guan, Y., et al.: FP-DNN: An automated framework for mapping deep neural networks onto FPGAs with RTL-HLS hybrid templates. In: FCCM Symposium (2017)
13. Guo, K., et al.: [DL] A survey of FPGA-based neural network inference accelerators. ACM TRETS **12**(1), 1–26 (2019)
14. Jungwook, C., et al.: Accurate and Efficient 2-bit Quantized Neural Networks. In: MLSys Proceedings (2019)
15. Meloni, P., et al.: Optimization and deployment of CNNs at the edge: the ALOHA experience. In: CF Conference (2019)
16. Mittal, S.: A survey of techniques for approximate computing. ACM CSUR **48**(4), 1–33 (2016)
17. Nezan, J.-F., et al. Multi-purpose systems: A novel dataflow-based generation and mapping strategy. In: ISCAS Symposium (2012)
18. Ngadiuba, J., et al.: Compressing deep neural networks on FPGAs to binary and ternary precision with hls4ml. Mach. Learn. Sci. Technol. (2020)
19. Palumbo, F., et al.: Hardware/Software Self-adaptation in CPS: The CERBERO Project Approach. In: SAMOS Conference (2019)
20. Palumbo, F., et al.: MYRTUS: Multi-layer 360° dYnamic orchestration and inter-opeRable design environmenT for compute-continUum Systems. In: 21th ACM International Conference on Computing Frontiers (2024)
21. Pappalardo, A.: Xilinx/brevitas. Zenodo (2023). https://doi.org/10.5281/zenodo.3333552
22. Pappalardo, A., et al.: Qonnx: Representing arbitrary-precision quantized neural networks. In: AccML Workshop (2022)
23. Ratto, F., et al.: An automated design flow for adaptive neural network hardware accelerators. J. Signal Process. Syst., 1-23 (2023)
24. Sau, C., et al.: The multi-dataflow composer tool: an open-source tool suite for optimized coarse-grain reconfigurable hardware accelerators and platform design. MICPRO J. **80** (2021)
25. Shafique, M., et al.: TinyML: current progress, research challenges, and future roadmap. In: DAC Conference (2021)
26. Han, S., et al.: EIE: efficient inference engine on compressed deep neural network. ACM SIGARCH Comput. Architect. News 44(3) (2016)
27. Summers, S., et al.: Using MaxCompiler for the high level synthesis of trigger algorithms. J. Instrument. **12**(02) (2017)
28. Umuroglu, Y., et al.: Finn: A framework for fast, scalable binarized neural network inference. In: FPGA Symposium (2017)
29. Venieris, S., et al.: Toolflows for mapping convolutional neural networks on FPGAs: a survey and future directions. ACM CSUR **51**(3), 1–39 (2018)

Poster Session

Efficient Post-training Augmentation for Adaptive Inference in Heterogeneous and Distributed IoT Environments

Max Sponner[1,4](✉), Lorenzo Servadei[2], Bernd Waschneck[3], Robert Wille[2], and Akash Kumar[4]

[1] Infineon Technologies Dresden GmbH & Co. KG, Dresden 01099, Germany
[2] Chair for Design Automation - TU Munich, Munich 80333, Germany
[3] Infineon Technologies AG, Neubiberg 85579, Germany
[4] Chair of Processor Design, CfAED - TU Dresden, Dresden01069, Germany
max.sponner@infineon.com

Abstract. Early Exit Neural Networks (EENNs) achieve enhanced efficiency compared to traditional models, but creating them is challenging due to the many additional design choices required. To address this, we propose an automated augmentation flow that converts existing models into EENNs, making all necessary design decisions for deployment on heterogeneous or distributed embedded targets. Our framework is the first to perform all these steps, including EENN architecture construction, subgraph mapping, and decision mechanism configuration.

We evaluated our approach on embedded Deep Learning scenarios, achieving significant performance improvements. Our solution reduced latency by 65.95% on a speech command detection problem and mean operations per inference by 78.3% on an ECG classification task. This showcases the potential for EENNs in embedded applications.

Keywords: Deep Learning · Early Exit Neural Networks · Network Architecture Search

1 Introduction

Early Exit Neural Networks (EENNs) offer a promising solution to reduce the mean inference cost of Neural Networks (NNs). By inserting additional classifier branches between the network's hidden layers, EENNs enable dynamic termination of inference at intermediate layers, reducing computational cost and latency. This makes them ideal for improving the energy efficiency of Deep Learning (DL) applications, particularly in resource-constrained Internet of Things (IoT) scenarios.

The project "RadarSkin" has received funding from the German Federal Ministry of Education and Research (BMBF) under the call "Electronic Systems for Edge Computing" (grant number 16ME0543). The responsibility for the content of this publication lies with the author.

© The Author(s), under exclusive license to Springer Nature Switzerland AG 2025
L. Carro et al. (Eds.): SAMOS 2024, LNCS 15227, pp. 99–108, 2025.
https://doi.org/10.1007/978-3-031-78380-7_8

However, designing and implementing an EENN for a specific scenario requires expertise in configuring the network architecture and at-runtime termination decision mechanism. Moreover, an incorrect configuration can increase inference costs or degrade prediction quality. This expertise barrier and risk of suboptimal design limit the adoption of EENNs. Network Architecture Search (NAS) frameworks can automate EENN design, but they often rely on expensive algorithms, resulting in long search times and high computational resource demands. This makes such frameworks inaccessible to many developers.

To democratize EENNs, we propose a novel Network Augmentation (NA) flow that converts an existing, trained traditional NN into an EENN. Our flow automates the deployment process, mapping the EENN's subgraphs to heterogeneous or distributed devices and configuring its decision mechanism. By leveraging existing models and automating the deployment process, we aim to make EENNs more accessible to developers, reducing the barriers to entry and enabling their adoption in a wider range of IoT applications. To the best of our knowledge, our framework is the first to offer this range of functionality, making it an important step towards widespread EENN adoption in IoT. The paper is organized as follows: we review related work on EENNs in the Related Work section, describe the proposed NA framework in the Methodology section, present the results and analysis of the framework's performance in the Evaluation section, and finally, summarize our findings and discuss the implications of our work in the Conclusion.

2 Related Work

Early Exit Neural Networks (EENNs) and automated NAS for EENNs have been the subject of a growing body of research in recent years.

2.1 Early Exit Neural Networks

EENNs are a class of NNs that adapt the inference process at runtime based on the current circumstances. Building upon the concept of Big/Little neural networks, which combine a small and a larger model [13], EENNs extend this approach by sharing backbone layers between models and enabling the incorporation of more than two models. This reduces the storage, memory, and compute footprint compared to using multiple individual models. EENNs were first introduced with BranchyNet [14]. The at-runtime decision mechanism, which selects between classifiers, can be implemented in various ways. Common approaches include utilizing the confidence of already evaluated classifiers to decide on the current inference's termination [14], considering the available resource budget [7], or using an additional agent model trained to perform this decision [12].

EENNs offer faster inference times, reduced energy consumption, and improved accuracy on certain tasks. However, designing effective decision mechanisms and configuring architectures for early exits remain significant challenges.

2.2 Network Architecture Search for Early Exit Neural Networks

Designing an EENN requires careful consideration of additional hyperparameters and design decisions, including the locations, count, and architectures of the early exits; the decision mechanism and its thresholds; as well as the training strategy. To assist developers, NAS solutions automate these configurations, covering a range of functionalities such as optimal branch location [3], output confidence score calibration [11], and mapping to heterogeneous platforms [2].

Current NAS solutions primarily utilize genetic search algorithms [1,2,4,5], although multi-objective Bayesian search [11] and dynamic programming [3] have also been used. However, a key limitation of these solutions is the high search cost. Our NA flow addresses this limitation by providing a fast and efficient solution that reuses existing models and enables developers to easily convert their standard models after training. Table 1 provides a comparison of our novel contribution in terms of features covered by other solutions.

Table 1. A comparison of features within the state-of-the-art solutions for EENN-NAS frameworks and our NA flow.

Work	EE location	EE architecture	Decision Thresholds	MPSoC Mapping
Optimal Location [3]	✓	✗	✗	✗
EExNAS [11]	✓	?	✗[a]	✗
HADAS [1]	✓	✓[b]	✗	✗
Map-and-Conquer [2]	✓	?	✗	✓
EDANAS [5]	✓	✗	✓	✗
NACHOS [4]	✓	✓	✗	✗
Our NA flow	✓	✓	✓	✓

[a] EExNAS calibrates the output confidence of the classifiers, but does not define a threshold value.
[b] HADAS utilizes the same EE structure across all branches and backbone models.

Our approach is distinct from traditional NAS solutions, which focus on designing EENNs from scratch. Instead, our flow augments an existing model with additional branches and a decision mechanism to select the most suitable classifier at runtime.

3 Methodology

Our framework addresses the high search cost of traditional NAS approaches by leveraging a pretrained base model and reducing the search space. The input requirements include the base model, training and validation sets, and hardware descriptions. Optionally, a worst-case latency constraint can be set that the found solution needs to satisfy. The hardware description includes high-level information such as computational speed, memory and storage size, as well as an interface to describe unsupported layers and layer configurations for the processors and the interconnects between them. This simple representation is intended to keep the user interface simple, while being sufficient to describe the hardware targets.

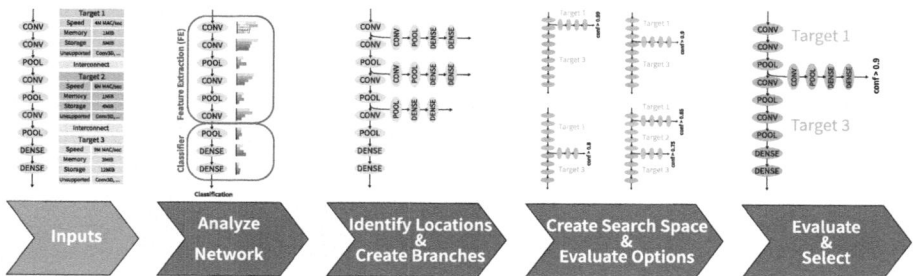

Fig. 1. Overview of the steps that are performed by the NA toolkit to transform the submitted model into an EE-version that is tailored for the hardware target and application requirements.

We use worst-case latency as a constraint because it is critical for many embedded applications, especially in control loops, where delays in processing can have severe consequences.

We assume the EEs of an EENN are independent, similar to IDK classifier cascades [15]. This assumption is based on the fact that EEs share weights through the feature extraction layers of the backbone, but do not operate on the same representation as their classifiers are attached at different locations of the backbone and use exclusive weights within their branches. This enables us to treat the predictions produced by the classifiers of an EENN as uncorrelated.

This assumption allows us to individually evaluate the EEs and treat architectures within the search space as cascades of their contained classifiers. This enables the flow to reuse the costly training steps across architectures, reducing the overall search cost. A joint-training step can be applied to the found solution to fine-tune shared backbone layers.

The steps of the automated flow are summarized in Fig. 1 and are detailed in the following subsections.

3.1 Analysis Step

In this step, the framework extracts relevant information from the input model, including the computational, latency, memory, and storage footprint of each layer on each processor. Additionally, it determines whether each layer is supported by the processor. The analysis step also employs a rule-based system to identify the feature extraction and classifier subgraphs within the model. Furthermore, it determines the task of the model, such as (binary) classification or regression.

The extracted information is used in the following steps of the framework to guide the search for the optimal EENN architecture.

3.2 Identifying Viable Locations and Creating Branches

Firstly, the framework identifies locations within the feature extraction subgraph where EEs can be attached. The viable locations for attaching EEs are identified as the edges after the post-processing layers (such as pooling, activation functions, or normalization) of trainable layers.

When creating branch architectures, the framework considers the varying input sizes at different locations due to the different shapes of intermediate feature maps within the feature extraction subgraph. This poses two risks: (1) the early exit classifiers may have a large resource footprint, or (2) they may perform poorly, if not properly designed.

To mitigate these risks, the framework leverages the extracted classifier subgraph from the submitted model as a template for the EEs at the attachment locations. A rule-based system inserts downsampling layers, such as pooling or convolutional layers, to adapt the classifier to the new input sizes. This may involve inserting additional layers or modifying the hyperparameters of existing layers from the template. By doing so, the framework designs classifiers that achieve good prediction quality while maintaining a small footprint.

3.3 Creation of the Search Space

The framework creates a search space of EENN architectures by recombining the untrained EE options with the final classifier and backbone. All possible architectures are created, as long as they satisfy the latency and hardware constraint, and limit the number of classifiers per target to not more than one. This limitation reduces the memory and storage footprint of the evaluated solutions, while also minimizing the worst-case overhead and the search cost.

Each classifier is assigned to one of the available targets, with the order of targets specified in the hardware description to enable targeting of hierarchical power domains. Targets can be skipped as long as an interconnect allows for passing the intermediate results to the next target. An example of this mapping is shown in Fig. 2a.

3.4 Evaluation of Options and Selection of Solution

During this step, the created architectures are evaluated and the best is picked. For this, the contained EEs are trained and evaluated in isolation on a frozen backbone. This approach reduces the backpropagation cost and enables the reuse of already trained classifiers across architecture options, resulting in a drastic reduction in search cost.

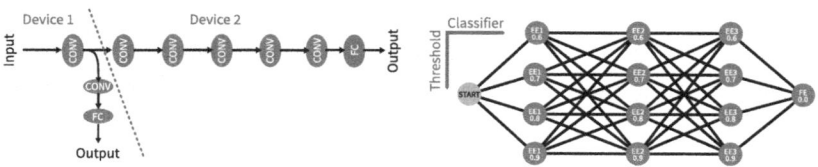

(a) An EENN that has been mapped to a platform that contains two processing targets.

(b) Illustration of the graph structure used to search for exit-wise confidence thresholds in a 3-EE EENN, with a limited threshold range for readability.

Fig. 2. EENN Architecture and Decision Search Space

After training an EENN option, the framework configures the exit-wise confidence thresholds. To do this, it converts the threshold search space into a directed graph, where nodes represent tuples of classifiers and confidence thresholds, and edges between nodes are associated with changes in accuracy and inference cost. The accuracy and cost values are evaluated on the validation set, or the training set if no validation set is available.

The graph resembles a fully connected network, with each classifier adding a layer, and nodes in each layer representing different thresholds evaluated for that classifier. The edges are associated with the change in cost and prediction quality. An example search graph can be found in Fig. 2b. The optimal threshold configuration is found by computing the shortest path through the graph.

The framework then evaluates the performance of EENN architectures on the validation set, collecting early termination rates, prediction quality, and efficiency gains. A scalar score is assigned to each architecture using the cost function, and the option with the best score is returned as the solution.

Optionally, the framework can perform joint training of all classifiers, followed by another round of decision mechanism configuration with higher resolution in threshold parameters.

4 Evaluation

We evaluate the performance of our framework on typical embedded Deep Learning workloads, including speech command recognition and ECG classification.

Additionally, we evaluate the conversion of ResNet-152 for a distributed system consisting of a local Cortex-A and Mali GPU, with remote processing to simulate a smartphone-based application. Although this is outside the intended scope of our framework, we use it as an extreme case to demonstrate the scalability of our approach, as the depth of the network creates a very large search space.

All network augmentations were performed on a consumer-grade mobile Core-i5 CPU (i5-1240P) without any GPU acceleration, rather than using high-performance clusters. A comparison of our experimental results with the reported performance from related work can be found in Fig. 3.

Table 2. The performance of the created EENNs compared to placing the entire original network on a single processor of the target platform (either the M4F core of the PSoC6 and NXP i.MX RT1160, or the Mali GPU). The difference in relevant performance metrics to the original model are marked in bold.

Model	ARM-DS (L)	1D-CNN	ResNet-152							
Calibration	val.	val.	1	2/3	1/2	val.	1	2/3	1/2	val.
Dataset	GSC	MIT-BIH	CIFAR-10				CIFAR-100			
Target	RT1166: CM4F, CM7	PSoC6: CM0P, CM4F	Cortex-A55+A76, Mali G610, LTE Uplink (50Mbps), RTX 3090 Ti							
Training	89 min	17 min	pretrained			1,1119 min	pretrained			1,076 min
Search	18 min	7 min	504 min			270 min	561 min			266 min
Acc.	87.67% **-5.48**	96.5% **-3.1**	92.81% **-1.18**	86% **-7.99**	72.72% **-21.25**	92.66% **-0.32**	72.56% **+0.02**	72.49% **-0.05**	71.85% **-0.69**	70.48% **+0.65**
Prec.	92.13% **-2.11**	99.4% **-0.2**	92.84% **-1.25**	86.2% **-8.09**	73% **-21.08**	92.68% **-0.31**	73.04% **-2.31**	72.92% **-2.43**	72.29% **-3.06**	70.72% **+0.52**
Recall	87.67% **-5.27**	98.6% **-1.0**	92.81% **-1.11**	86% **-7.89**	72.74% **-21.15**	92.66% **-0.32**	72.56% **+1.11**	72.49% **+1.04**	71.85% **+0.4**	70.48% **+0.65**
Mean MACs	16.39M **-44.35%**	0.33M **-78.3%**	318.12M **-11.3%**	226.04M **-36.99%**	147.99M **-58.75%**	330.97M **-7.75%**	357.24M **-0.43%**	349.4M **-2.61%**	342.73M **-4.47%**	358.28M **-0.13%**
Mean Latency	225.06 ms **-65.95%**	0.62 sec **-58.9%**	16.2 ms **-9.18%**	12.35 ms **-30.79%**	8.6 ms **-51.79%**	16.28 ms **-8.77%**	21.05 ms **+19.72%**	19.57 ms **+11.33%**	18.94 ms **+7.76%**	17.19 ms **-2.2%**
Mean Energy	31.17 mJ **-61.62%**	11.83 mJ **-74.9%**	–	–	–	–	–	–	–	–
Early Term.	62.04%	100%	36.99%	86.97%	95.4%	31.16%	13.69%	61.65%	74.39%	0.33%

4.1 Speech Command Detection

We evaluate the performance of our proposed method on a speech command detection task, where the goal is to detect a limited set of speech commands from audio data. This use case is relevant for voice-controlled appliances or wake word detection for smart speakers. We use the Google Speech Commands dataset [16] and a Depthwise-Separable CNN from ARM in its largest configuration [17] as the base model. The hardware platform used is the NXP i.MX RT1160, which features a Cortex-M4F core at 240 MHz and a Cortex-M7 core at 600 MHz[1].

The reference model achieves an accuracy of 93.15% on the test set, with a latency of 661 ms on the M4F core. We set a worst-case latency constraint of 300 ms to ensure timely processing while handling overlapping input windows. The search process resulted in an EENN that introduces an EE for the M4F core after the second convolutional block in the backbone, with a configured confidence threshold of 0.8. The performance of the solution is shown in Table 2.

The M4F subgraph requires 204 ms and 25.06 mJ energy, while the M7 subgraph requires 55.47 ms and 16.08 mJ energy. The found solution reduces power consumption compared to executing the model solely on the M4F core, and eliminates the need to keep the M7 core active at all times, resulting in

---

[1] https://www.nxp.com/docs/en/data-sheet/IMXRT1160CEC.pdf

further power savings. This enables constant monitoring of properties at lower power consumption with faster reaction times.

4.2 ECG Classification on Wearable Devices

We evaluate our method on a single-lead ECG signal classification task using a convolutional NN. We use the MIT-BIH dataset [10] and a fully convolutional NN as the backbone model [8]. The model achieves 99.29% accuracy, 99.33% precision, and 99.25% recall on the test set. A possible application is deploying the model to wearable devices like smartwatches for constant monitoring.

The experiment was conducted on an Infineon PSoC6 MCU[2]. The resulting EENN contains an early exit after the first convolutional block with a threshold of 0.6. The execution times are 618 ms on the M0 and 1.376 s on the M4F. The high termination rate suggests that the backbone model might be over-parameterized. However, the ability to execute the entire EENN ensures high accuracy beneficial for healthcare applications.

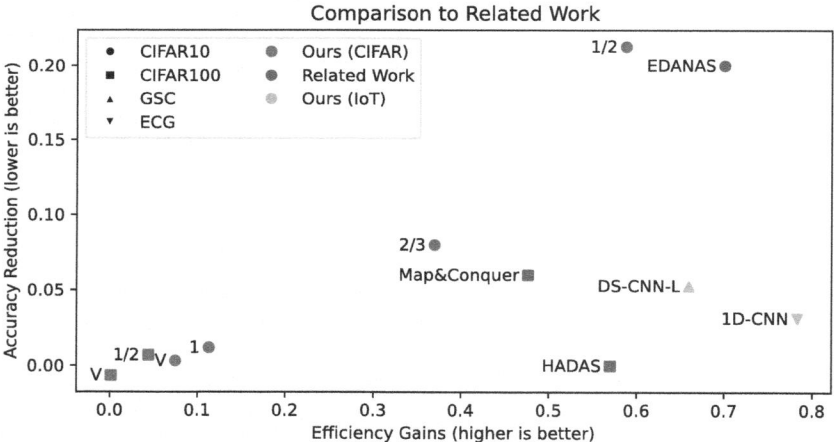

Fig. 3. Performance comparison of our framework to previous work using different base models on the same datasets.

4.3 Image Classification

We evaluate our method on image classification tasks using the CIFAR-10 and -100 datasets [9] and converted ResNet-152 [6] accordingly. We use a distributed system consisting of a Rockchip RK3588-based platform, and a Nvidia RTX 3090 Ti workstation, to simulate a smartphone with cloud-based offloading.

---

[2] https://www.infineon.com/dgdl/Infineon-PSOC_6_MCU_CY8C62X8_CY8C62XA-DataSheet-v16_00-EN.pdf?fileId=8ac78c8c7d0d8da4017d0ee7d03a70b1.

We use ResNet-152 as a challenging test case, resulting in a search space of approximately 450,000 configurations. We performed two evaluations: one with a dedicated calibration/validation set and another without it. If no calibration data is used, the thresholds are configured on the training data and a correction factors needs to be applied to them. Our results show that using a correction factor and only the training set can be a viable alternative.

This experiment demonstrates the scalability of our approach, with search times under 9.35 h. Although our current framework is primarily designed for the embedded/MCU field, it was able to achieve efficiency gains across all CIFAR-10 solutions. The efficiency gains on CIFAR-100 were more limited. The design decisions limiting performance include the rule-based system to adapt EEs to the backbone, which aims to minimize overhead and was designed for embedded-sized NNs.

5 Conclusion

Our framework efficiently converts models into EENNs for distributed or heterogeneous IoT devices, achieving substantial gains in latency and power efficiency. We demonstrate good results in embedded scenarios, showcasing the framework's effectiveness in this domain.

The search process is efficient and scalable. Moreover, its efficiency eliminates the need for high-performance hardware, as the search can be performed on consumer-grade hardware. Notably, the NA is faster than the training of the original model, making it a practical solution for real-world applications.

Using a traditional model as the starting point for the search improves the accessibility of our NA over related work that relies on Once-For-All models, as traditional models are easier to acquire. Furthermore, our framework is the first to perform all necessary design decisions automatically, making it a unique and valuable contribution to the field.

Future work could explore the extension of the framework for more-performant target devices and deeper models, enabling even more efficient and effective EENNs for a wider range of applications.

References

1. Bouzidi, H., Odema, M., Ouarnoughi, H., Faruque, M.A.A., Niar, S.: HADAS: hardware-aware dynamic neural architecture search for edge performance scaling. In: Design, Automation & Test in Europe Conference & Exhibition, DATE 2023, pp. 1–6. IEEE (2023). https://doi.org/10.23919/DATE56975.2023.10137095
2. Bouzidi, H., Odema, M., Ouarnoughi, H., Niar, S., Faruque, M.A.A.: Map-and-conquer: energy-efficient mapping of dynamic neural nets onto heterogeneous mpsocs. In: 60th ACM/IEEE Design Automation Conference, DAC 2023, pp. 1–6. IEEE (2023). https://doi.org/10.1109/DAC56929.2023.10247722
3. Chiang, C., Liu, P., Wang, D., Hong, D., Wu, J.: Optimal branch location for cost-effective inference on branchynet. In: 2021 IEEE International Conference on Big Data (Big Data), pp. 5071–5080. IEEE (2021). https://doi.org/10.1109/BIGDATA52589.2021.9671948

4. Gambella, M., Pomponi, J., Scardapane, S., Roveri, M.: Nachos: Neural architecture search for hardware constrained early exit neural networks. arXiv preprint arXiv:2401.13330 (2024)
5. Gambella, M., Roveri, M.: EDANAS: adaptive neural architecture search for early exit neural networks. In: International Joint Conference on Neural Networks, IJCNN 2023, pp. 1–8. IEEE (2023). https://doi.org/10.1109/IJCNN54540.2023.10191876
6. He, K., Zhang, X., Ren, S., Sun, J.: Deep residual learning for image recognition. In: 2016 IEEE Conference on Computer Vision and Pattern Recognition, CVPR 2016, pp. 770–778. IEEE Computer Society (2016). https://doi.org/10.1109/CVPR.2016.90
7. Hu, H., Dey, D., Hebert, M., Bagnell, J.A.: Learning anytime predictions in neural networks via adaptive loss balancing. In: The Thirty-Third AAAI Conference on Artificial Intelligence, AAAI, pp. 3812–3821. AAAI Press (2019). https://doi.org/10.1609/AAAI.V33I01.33013812
8. Issa, M.F., Yousry, A., Tuboly, G., Juhasz, Z., AbuEl-Atta, A.H., Selim, M.M.: Heartbeat classification based on single lead-ii ecg using deep learning. Heliyon **9**(7), e17974 (2023). https://doi.org/10.1016/j.heliyon.2023.e17974
9. Krizhevsky, A., Hinton, G., et al.: Learning multiple layers of features from tiny images (2009)
10. Moody, G.B., Mark, R.G.: The impact of the mit-bih arrhythmia database. IEEE Eng. Med. Biol. Mag. **20**(3), 45–50 (2001)
11. Odema, M., Rashid, N., Faruque, M.A.A.: EExNAS: early-exit neural architecture search solutions for low-power wearable devices. In: IEEE/ACM International Symposium on Low Power Electronics and Design, ISLPED 2021, pp. 1–6. IEEE (2021). https://doi.org/10.1109/ISLPED52811.2021.9502503
12. Odena, A., Lawson, D., Olah, C.: Changing model behavior at test-time using reinforcement learning. In: 5th International Conference on Learning Representations, ICLR 2017 (2017)
13. Park, E., et al.: Big/little deep neural network for ultra low power inference. In: 2015 International Conference on Hardware/Software Codesign and System Synthesis, CODES+ISSS 2015, pp. 124–132. IEEE (2015). https://doi.org/10.1109/CODESISSS.2015.7331375
14. Teerapittayanon, S., McDanel, B., Kung, H.T.: Branchynet: fast inference via early exiting from deep neural networks. In: 23rd International Conference on Pattern Recognition, ICPR 2016, pp. 2464–2469. IEEE (2016). https://doi.org/10.1109/ICPR.2016.7900006
15. Wang, X., Luo, Y., Crankshaw, D., Tumanov, A., Yu, F., Gonzalez, J.E.: IDK cascades: fast deep learning by learning not to overthink. In: Proceedings of the Thirty-Fourth Conference on Uncertainty in Artificial Intelligence, UAI 2018, pp. 580–590. AUAI Press (2018)
16. Warden, P.: Speech commands: A dataset for limited-vocabulary speech recognition. arXiv abs/ arXiv: 1804.03209 (2018)
17. Zhang, Y., Suda, N., Lai, L., Chandra, V.: Hello edge: Keyword spotting on microcontrollers. arXiv abs/ arXiv: 1711.07128 (2017)

Pooling On-the-Go for NoC-Based Convolutional Neural Network Accelerator

Wenyao Zhu, Yizhi Chen, and Zhonghai Lu

KTH Royal Institute of Technology, Kistagången 16, Stockholm, Sweden
{wenyao,yizhic,zhonghai}@kth.se

Abstract. Due to the complexity and diversity of deep convolutional neural networks (CNNs), Network-on-chip (NoC) based CNN accelerators have grown in popularity to improve inference efficiency and flexibility. Current optimization approaches focus on computational-heavy layers. Therefore, pooling layers are often ignored and processed individually using general processing units. In this work, we explore the acceleration of pooling layers by in-network processing. We propose a pooling on-the-go method to do the pooling operations while transmitting its prior layer outputs. Consequently, we combine the pooling layer with its prior convolution layer to remove unnecessary data movements. We demonstrate our method on a cycle-accurate NoC-CNN accelerator simulator on two CNN models, LeNet and VGG16. The results show that the processing time of individual pooling layers is almost eliminated by around 99%. Compared with the pooling standalone baseline, we can achieve 1.09x speedup in the full LeNet model, and up to 1.16x speedup in the combined layers that our approach applies.

Keywords: CNN Accelerator · In-network Processing · Network-on-Chip · Pooling

1 Introduction

Network-on-chip-based convolutional neural network accelerators (NoC-CNNs) have gained significant interest since their structure is flexible and enables large-scale parallelism for running myriad CNN models on the same chip [3,13]. In current NoC-CNN designs, CNN models undergo layer-by-layer processing, with intermediate feature maps stored in memory [4,8]. Pooling layers are processed like convolutional layers and handled by PEs in NoC-CNNs [5,14].

Reducing pooling layer latency doesn't attract much attention as their computational cost is less significant than other layers. However, since pooling layers are treated independently, the memory access and communication latency are

---

The research has been supported in part by Vetenskapsrådet (Swedish Research Council) through the LearnPower project (2020-03494).

not negligible. This work is motivated by the in-network processing concept and explores the possibility of offloading the pooling operation to network devices. We propose the pooling on-the-go approach for NoC-CNN to seamlessly integrate the pooling layer operations while transmitting the adjacent convolution layer outputs. In this case, we can remove the pooling layer latency with little overhead. We summarize our contributions as follows.

- We propose a new optimization method that combines the pooling layer with its prior layer for NoC-CNN to eliminate pooling layer latency.
- We design the pooling on-the-go structure in the network interface of NoC to offload pooling operations from PE.
- We validate our approach in a cycle-accurate NoC-CNN simulator on two CNN models and discuss the design trade-off of our approach.

2 Related Work

Recent works regarding NoC-CNNs employ novel NoC structure designs to reduce energy consumption in computational-heavy layers [8,11]. Other researches on NoC-CNN improve hardware utilization for convolution layers [4,7]. However, these state-of-the-art optimization techniques often bypass pooling layers, though they are essential in CNN models to reduce spatial dimensions.

Two common approaches exist for processing pooling layers. The first is to treat pooling as a standalone layer, as adopted by the aforementioned NoC-CNN architectures [4,7,8,11]. They use local or global buffers to store intermediate layer outputs and conduct inference in a layer-completing order. This approach reduces design complexity and offers adaptability to various workloads. However, it introduces overhead in communication and memory access for distributing and aggregating data. The second way is to merge it with its prior convolution layer from the model side. Alwani et al. first explore the layer fusion technique by creating a computation pyramid across adjacent layers to reduce data transfer [2]. They pipeline the computation in PE to save bandwidth, which may increase the overall latency. Additionally, extra on-chip storage is required for overlapping pyramids. These challenges are intensified when implementing such techniques in NoC-CNN. Simba [14] presents a large-scale CNN inference system using a two-level mesh NoC. They assume the weights remain stationary in PEs and only the neuron outputs are transferred across PE. Then a post-processing unit (PPU) for pooling and non-linear activation is deployed in each PE for cross-layer fusion. This can improve data locality but requires large on-chip buffers. Zhu et al. propose a sparse skipping technique in NoC-CNN to reduce the memory overhead for CNN inference [17]. They make the PPU an independent core in NoC and link it with off-chip memory. It can mitigate the drawback in storage scale. However, the standout PPU creates a bottleneck where every convolution output will be sent to it for pooling.

These layer fusion techniques are beneficial for reducing data movement, but they are also possible to increase end-to-end latency in NoC-CNNs. Inspired by the concept of in-network processing [12], we can offload the pooling function in

PPU from PE to the network for NoC-CNN. Thereby, the pooling operation is combined with the communication in its prior layer to reduce the layer latency.

3 Pooling On-the-Go Design for NoC-CNN

A common NoC-CNN architecture [4] is depicted in Fig. 1. In the mesh network, two types of cores are connected to the network interface (NI) and router. The PE core contains the arithmetic unit and local buffers for neuron computations. The memory controller (MC) core is the portal to the on-chip buffer that transmits data to and from other PE cores through NoC. The on-chip buffer hosts the input feature map (IFMap), weight table, and output feature map (OFMap) for a layer. It updates the buffered weights after completing the current layer from off-chip memory, and OFMap is reused as the next IFMap.

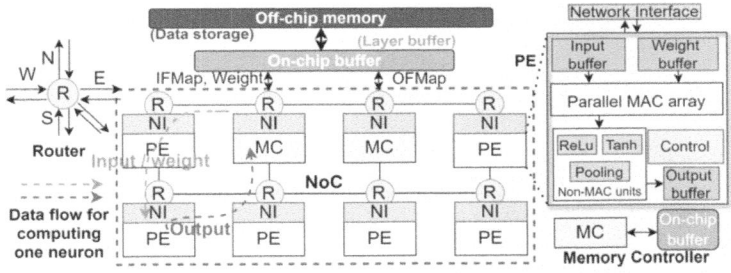

Fig. 1. NoC-based CNN accelerator schematic.

To accommodate various layer types, we utilize the unfolding technique in an output-oriented manner similar to the assumption in [4]. Each layer is represented by a batch of output neurons that equals the size of OFMap. NoC-CNN maps these neurons to PEs during CNN model loading. Assuming a layer's OFMap size is M, and NoC has k PEs, with one PE computing one neuron per round, it necessitates $R = \lceil M/k \rceil$ rounds to complete this layer.

3.1 Pooling On-the-Go Approach

In the pooling standalone NoC-CNN design, the pooling operations are processed in PE. For example, in a DNNoC-like [4] workflow, PE will save the convolution layer (Conv.) outputs to off-chip memory and load it again for pooling operations. This costs extra data moving overhead and lowers the utilization of PE. Therefore, we propose a pooling on-the-go approach to combine the pooling layer computation during transmission, minimizing redundant data movements. Figure 2 illustrated the standalone and on-the-go pooling processes, both starting at T_0. For standalone pooling, the Conv. OFMap is completed at T_1. Then it serves as the pooling layer IFMap and finishes at T_2. Alternatively, in our approach, the pooling operation is done during the transmission of Conv. OFMap from PE to MC. Then MC receives the pooling OFMap at T_2'. The latency improvement of the combined layer is $T_2 - T_2'$.

To realize pooling on-the-go in NoC-CNN, there are three possible positions other than PE, including router, NI, and MC. In flit-based virtual channel (VC) routers, data as payload are unknown to existing routing logic. Therefore, extra decoding units are required for each port in case the pooling happens in the router, introducing a large area and latency overhead. NI and MC are equivalent to pooling block implementation as they are near the end of the data path. Since MC is directly connected to the global buffer, it runs in a slower clock domain than NI. Hence NI is a more suitable position, and only NI connected to MC needs modification. Figure 2 also compares the data path of two pooling designs, where the pooling IFMap transfer is removed in our pooling on-the-go approach.

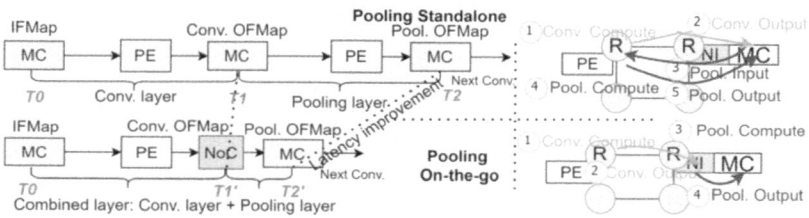

Fig. 2. Timeline (left) and data path (right) of standalone and on-the-go pooling.

3.2 Pooling On-the-Go Implementation

A canonical NI consists of two symmetric ports as the interface between core and router [6]. The original *outport* design is shown at the top of Fig. 3, where core messages are turned into flits and injected into the router. We develop a pooling on-the-go block to offload the pooling layer operations from PE and integrate it in our new *inport* design. The pooling block structure is depicted in the lower half of Fig. 3. We have a temporary buffer to store intermediate pooling values, a pooling function block for calculation, and a controller to manage the whole process. Two multiplexers are used to enable or bypass the new pooling block.

Message Header. A 1-bit **tag** is added to the message header to judge whether a message requires the new pooling service and control the multiplexer. Note that only a combination of a pooling layer after a convolution layer can be optimized from our approach. To correctly perform pooling operations, the message header also includes a 1-bit signal that tells the pooling function, e.g. max pooling and average pooling. Then the channel and ID are given to identify the location in the pooling layer OFMap instead of the initial Conv. OFMap. The remaining bits are reserved for different pooling kernel sizes.

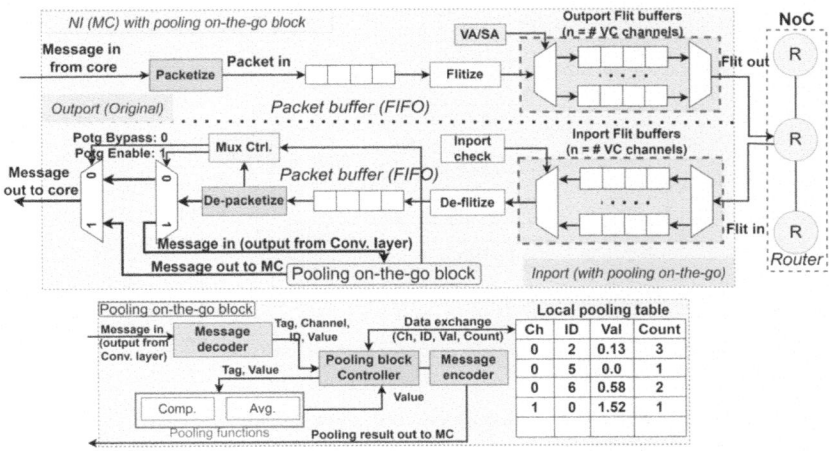

Fig. 3. Network interface with proposed pooling block and the block design.

Local Pooling Table. This is a key component to store the temporary results for pooling, which is organized as a buffer table that can access an entire row at a time. In each row, there are four elements, representing channel, ID, value, and count. "Count" indicates the number of messages received for the same channel and ID. We don't have to allocate the full size of pooling OFMap in the pooling table at once. Since there are multiple MCs in NoC, each will communicate with a fixed number of PEs. Then in each computation round, the number of messages that NI receives is also fixed. So the pooling table only needs the space to hold these messages in one round simultaneously. For example, if in the NoC-CNN, five PEs are communicating with this NI to reach MC, then we only need five rows in the pooling table.

Pooling Block Controller. Figure 4 shows the workflow of the pooling on-the-go controller. The input message from the packet buffer in *inport* is sent to the pooling block when the valid **tag** is given. Then it performs the following steps:

1. The decoder extracts function, channel, ID, and value from the message.
2. Controller checks the pooling table for index comparison on channel and ID.
3. If no matching entry, data is written to an empty row with Count set to 1.
4. If a matching entry exists, we calculate the pooling result of the input value and the stored value. The Count of this row increases by one.
5. If the Count is smaller than the pooling kernel size, the result is written back. Otherwise, a new message is created to deliver the final pooling result.

The controller iteratively processes the valid messages until the whole pooling layer OFMap is completed and stored in the on-chip buffer. Our design ensures that the pooling operation is finished in NI during the transmission of its prior convolution outputs.

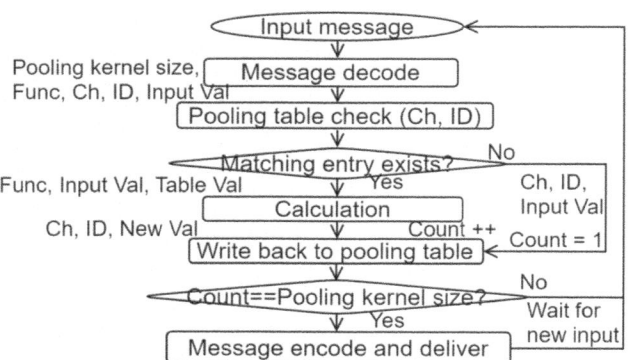

Fig. 4. Pooling block controller workflow.

4 Evaluation and Results

4.1 Experimental Setup

We build a cycle-accurate NoC-CNN simulator based on the NoC simulator in [16] to evaluate our approach. The VC NoC architecture is adopted from Gem5-Garnet [1]. We implement the pooling standalone baseline. Then we deploy our pooling on-the-go functions in the simulator for tests. The inference result and layer latency when running the same CNN model on baseline NoC-CNN and our approach are recorded to validate the correctness and evaluate the latency improvement. Based on Fig. 2, we define the latency reduction P of the pooling layer and the speedup ρ of the combined layer using our approach as

$$P = \frac{T_2 - T_2'}{T_2 - T_1} \times 100\%, \quad \rho = \frac{T_2}{T_2'}. \tag{1}$$

Simulation System Configuration. The default NoC-CNN configurations are summarized in Table 1. We arrange cores in a row-major order, for example, cores with ID 0 to 7 are in the first row. Then we separate the whole network into four identical 4×4 subareas. MCs are positioned at each subarea's center with ID 17, 18, 21, 22, 41, 42, 45, and 46. We simulate an ASIC NoC-CNN in which the NoC components (router, NI) can run at 2 GHz [14,16]. PE and MC are usually slower than routers since they have more complex combinational circuits for calculation. The default PE frequency is 200 MHz as the UNPU in [10]. We also change the PE frequency to 500 MHz and 1 GHz to simulate different hardware designs [14]. The latency results are in the unit of NoC cycles.

We select two representative CNN models, the small LeNet model [9] and the large VGG16 model [15], for evaluation. They both contain the combination of a pooling layer after a convolution layer that our approach applies. The input size is 32 × 32 × 1 for LeNet and 224 × 224 × 3 for VGG16.

LeNet comprises two combined layers that our approach applies. Table 2a gives the parameters for these layers: L1 (Conv1+MaxP1), L2 (Conv2+MaxP2).

Table 1. NoC-CNN default configuration

Item	Amount	Configuration
NoC	64 nodes	8 × 8 mesh network. 2 GHz. X-Y routing. 256-bit link bandwidth. Bidirectional link.
Router	64 routers	4 VCs per port, 4-flit buffers per VC.
Core	64 cores	56 PEs and 8 MCs. 25 MACs per PE cycle. 200 MHz.

ϕ shows the proportion for computation (#OP) of pooling over the total combined layer. VGG16 has 13 convolution layers, five of which are followed by a max pooling layer that can use the pooling on-the-go method. Table 2b summarizes the parameters and the proportion of pooling computation of these five layers. For ease of simulation, we sample VGG16 with the same kernels but smaller feature maps, then scale them up to get the latency for the full model.

Table 2. Layer parameters for pooling on-the-go

(a) LeNet

Layer		Neurons	Kernel size	#OP	ϕ (%)
L1	Conv1	4704	5 × 5	(1 × 5 × 5)×4704	3.846
	MaxP1	1176	2 × 2	(2 × 2)×1176	
L2	Conv2	1600	5 × 5	(6 × 5 × 5)×1600	0.662
	MaxP2	400	2 × 2	(2 × 2)×400	

(b) VGG16

Layer		Neurons	Kernel size	#OP	ϕ (%)
L1	Conv2	3211264	3 × 3	(64 × 3 × 3)×3211264	0.173
	MaxP1	802816	2 × 2	(2 × 2)×802816	
L2	Conv4	1605632	3 × 3	(128 × 3 × 3)×1605632	0.087
	MaxP2	401408	2 × 2	(2 × 2)×401408	
L3	Conv7	802816	3 × 3	(256 × 3 × 3)×802816	0.043
	MaxP3	200704	2 × 2	(2 × 2)×200704	
L4	Conv10	401408	3 × 3	(512 × 3 × 3)×401408	0.022
	MaxP4	100352	2 × 2	(2 × 2)×100352	
L5	Conv13	100352	3 × 3	(512 × 3 × 3)×100352	0.022
	MaxP5	25088	2 × 2	(2 × 2)×25088	

4.2 Experimental Results

The LeNet latency on baseline NoC-CNN and pooling on-the-go approach (with label P) are plotted in Fig. 5. In three evaluated situations, the average latency reductions for MaxP1 and MaxP2 are 98.98% and 97.39%. Speedup ρ for the combined layers L1 and L2 are 1.148x and 1.054x. The more significant improvement in L1 is primarily due to the higher pooling proportion ϕ compared to L2. The core frequency determines the computation latency. Thus a shorter T_1 and T_2 in Eq. (1) are expected for faster PE, while $(T_2' - T_1)$ remains the same. Consequently, the best speedup appears for the 1 GHz setup, which is 1.09x for the full model, 1.16x for L1, and 1.06x for L2. Our observation validates that the proposed approach can achieve a better speedup when PE frequency is higher.

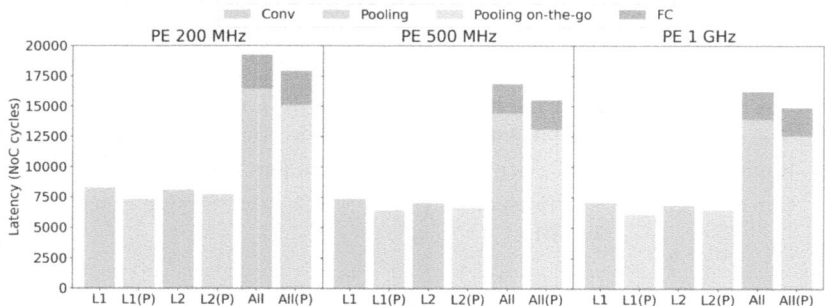

Fig. 5. Inference latency of LeNet.

Figure 6 presents the inference latency of L1 to L5 in VGG16. The full VGG16 model needs 392 million NoC cycles on the baseline NoC-CNN, so we don't plot it here. For five pooling layers MaxP1 to MaxP5, the latency reductions are all over 99.9%. The average speedup of the combined layers from L1 to L5 ranges from 1.016x to 1.0015x. The overall speedup on VGG16 are 1.0036x, 1.0035x, and 1.003x when the PE frequency is 1 GHz, 500 MHz, and 200 MHz, respectively. We can see that the pooling layer latency is almost eliminated using our approach as we expected. However, the pooling operation only occupies a very small proportion of VGG16. For example in the 1 GHz PE setup, it takes around 1.2 million cycles, which is 0.359% of the full model. Therefore, the speedup of our approach on VGG16 is not obvious.

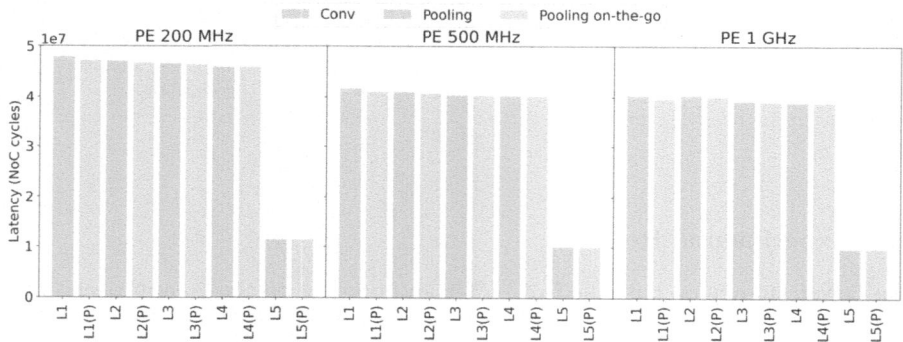

Fig. 6. Inference latency of VGG16.

4.3 Discussion

From the evaluation results, the pooling layer latency is almost eliminated when our approach is applied. The overall speedup depends on the workload proportion of the pooling layer in the CNN model. In LeNet, this proportion is way higher than in VGG16. Thus our method can achieve much better speedup results in LeNet compared with VGG16. Moreover, our approach replaces the standalone pooling units in PE with pooling on-the-go blocks in NI connected to MC. MC constitutes a small fraction of total cores in NoC-CNN, and the area for the extra pooling table and simple controller in the block is not significant. So the proposed approach can maintain or even save area for NoC-CNN. Also, the reduced memory accesses for the standalone pooling layer can improve energy efficiency. Regarding the communication overhead, since the Conv. output packet only contains one output neuron value, the added message header will not affect the packet size as it remains a single-flit packet.

Therefore, the proposed pooling on-the-go approach can improve the performance and efficiency of NoC-CNNs, especially when the target CNNs have lightweight convolution layers followed by normal pooling layers.

5 Conclusion

In this paper, we present a pooling on-the-go approach with a unique pooling block design in the network interface of NoC-CNN. Our method aims to do pooling operations during the transmission of its prior layer outputs, thereby minimizing the pooling layer processing latency. Compared with common standalone pooling, our approach reduces superfluous data transfers to optimize efficiency. We evaluate our method on two CNN models, LeNet and VGG16. The simulation results show that our approach can almost eliminate the pooling layer latency. We achieve 1.09x speedup for the full LeNet model. For the speedup of one combined layer, we reach up to 1.16x for LeNet and 1.016x for VGG16.

This work opens the opportunity for cross-layer optimization using in-network processing in NoC-CNN designs. The RTL implementation of our approach and tradeoffs between timing and power/area will be investigated in future work.

References

1. Agarwal, N., Krishna, T., Peh, L.S., Jha, N.K.: GARNET: a detailed on-chip network model inside a full-system simulator. In: IEEE International Symposium on Performance Analysis of Systems and Software, pp. 33–42. IEEE (2009)
2. Alwani, M., Chen, H., Ferdman, M., Milder, P.: Fused-layer CNN accelerators. In: 49th Annual IEEE/ACM International Symposium on Microarchitecture (MICRO), pp. 1–12. IEEE (2016)
3. Chen, K.C., Ebrahimi, M., Wang, T.Y., Yang, Y.C.: NoC-based DNN accelerator: A future design paradigm. In: 13th IEEE/ACM International Symposium on Networks-on-Chip (NOCS), pp. 1–8 (2019)
4. Chen, K.C., Ebrahimi, M., Wang, T.Y., Yang, Y.C., Liao, Y.H.: A NoC-based simulator for design and evaluation of deep neural networks. Microprocess. Microsyst. **77**, 103145 (2020)

5. Chen, Y.H., Yang, T.J., Emer, J., Sze, V.: Eyeriss v2: a flexible accelerator for emerging deep neural networks on mobile devices. IEEE J. Emerg. Sel. Top. Circ. Syst. **9**(2), 292–308 (2019)
6. Dally, W.J., Towles, B.P.: Principles and Practices of Interconnection Networks. Elsevier, Amsterdam (2004)
7. Hu, X., et al.: High-performance reconfigurable DNN accelerator on a bandwidth-limited embedded system. ACM Trans. Embed. Comput. Syst. **22**, 1–20 (2022)
8. Kwon, H., Samajdar, A., Krishna, T.: MAERI: enabling flexible dataflow mapping over DNN accelerators via reconfigurable interconnects. ACM SIGPLAN Not. **53**(2), 461–475 (2018)
9. LeCun, Y., Bottou, L., Bengio, Y., Haffner, P.: Gradient-based learning applied to document recognition. Proc. IEEE **86**(11), 2278–2324 (1998)
10. Lee, J., Kim, C., Kang, S., Shin, D., Kim, S., Yoo, H.J.: UNPU: an energy-efficient deep neural network accelerator with fully variable weight bit precision. IEEE J. Solid-State Circuits **54**(1), 173–185 (2018)
11. Liu, X., Wen, W., Qian, X., Li, H., Chen, Y.: Neu-NoC: a high-efficient interconnection network for accelerated neuromorphic systems. In: 23rd Asia and South Pacific Design Automation Conference (ASP-DAC), pp. 141–146. IEEE (2018)
12. Lu, Z.: PiN: Processing in Network-on-Chip. IEEE Design & Test (2023)
13. Nabavinejad, S.M., Baharloo, M., Chen, K.C., Palesi, M., Kogel, T., Ebrahimi, M.: An overview of efficient interconnection networks for deep neural network accelerators. IEEE J. Emerg. Sel. Top. Circuits Syst. **10**(3), 268–282 (2020)
14. Shao, Y.S., et al.: Simba: scaling deep-learning inference with multi-chip-module-based architecture. In: 52nd Annual IEEE/ACM International Symposium on Microarchitecture (MICRO), pp. 14–27 (2019)
15. Simonyan, K., Zisserman, A.: Very deep convolutional networks for large-scale image recognition. In: 3rd International Conference on Learning Representations, ICLR (2015)
16. Wang, B., Lu, Z.: Flexible and efficient QoS provisioning in AXI4-based network-on-chip architecture. IEEE Trans. Comput. Aided Des. Integr. Circuits Syst. **41**(5), 1523–1536 (2021)
17. Zhu, L., et al.: A NoC-based spatial DNN inference accelerator with memory-friendly dataflow. IEEE Design & Test (2023)

Vitamin-V: Serverless Cloud Computing Porting on RISC-V

Thrasyvoulos Iliadis[✉], Nikolaos C. Papadopoulos, Kostantinos Nikas, and Dionisios Pnevmatikatos

Institute of Communication and Computer Systems (ICCS), National Technical University of Athens, 15780 Athens, Greece
`filiadis@cslab.ece.ntua.gr`

Abstract. Cloud computing is gaining an ever more important role in global computing nowadays. With the growing demand for cloud computing, existing instruction set architectures (ISA) can burden organizations with heavy fees for licencing and using. Emerging as an alternative, RISC-V is an open source ISA with many customization options. The Vitamin-V project aims to help foster this growth, by developing a comprehensive software-hardware stack for cloud services based on RISC-V. ICCS-NTUA's role in Vitamin-V is to support the RISC-V ecosystem in serverless cloud computing scenarios. To this end, we first show the work done to provide a Function-as-a-Service platform for RISC-V by leveraging lightweight virtualization, and specifically Kata Containers. Second, we show how we modified and used benchmarks for evaluating the RISC-V platforms of the project, using the FunctionBench suite. Future work includes the seamless integration of Kata Containers and Firecracker, as well as extensive testing and evaluation on various RISC-V setups using the ported benchmarks.

1 Introduction

The Vitamin-V project focuses on providing RISC-V based solutions for cloud services. It is looking to develop a complete software-hardware stack based on open source technologies, all built on top of the open source RISC-V ISA. It is considering all relevant RISC-V extensions for virtualization and cloud deployment, including the virtualization, cryptography, and vectorization extensions among others. Vitamin-V will support these extensions and interfaces in three virtual execution environments, i.e. QEMU, gem5, and cloud-FPGA prototype platforms.

The cloud software stack for Vitamin-V includes three aspects:

Classical Cloud Stack. This stack focuses on cloud composed by classical VMs. In this stack OpenStack [11], Rust-VMM [3] and VoSySMonitoRV [7] will be ported.

Modern Cloud Stack. The modern stack revolves around the usage of containers instead of VMs, which mainly uses Kubernetes [1] as a cornerstone.

Serverless Cloud Stack. The serverless cloud stack is a new paradigm for cloud systems with Function-as-a-Service (FaaS) being a typical form example. In this stack the focus is on Lightweight Virtualization, mainly through porting Kata Containers [10] and FunctionBench [8] FaaS workloads.

Section 2 discusses how lightweight virtualization fosters serverless computing, and describes a modern serverless cloud stack. The current status of our work is outlined in Sect. 2.3. Section 3 describes the workloads used in our serverless cloud computing scenarios. In Sect. 3.2 the current status of our work is shown, as well as the complete development environment. Section 4 discusses future work.

2 Function as a Service Platform

Serverless computing, particularly Function-as-a-Service (FaaS), allows developers to create applications using standalone functions without managing the underlying infrastructure. This abstraction allows developers focus on business logic instead of dealing with resource management directly, as a FaaS model can also be beneficial for pricing, with pay-as-you-go models. Cloud providers handle the deployment, resource management, and security isolation of the provided functions, leaving developers are free to use them.

2.1 Lightweight Virtualization

In a FaaS scenario, the provider must make sure that isolation is supported. Isolation is required both from function to function, and from function to other services running on the same system. The two main ways for achieving this are VMs and Containers.

VMs provide isolation by running each workload in a separate environment, with a complete operation system in its disposal. IT is easily understood that this approach offers very strong isolation and security guarantees, but also comes with very big resource overheads for running separate OSes. Containers on the other hand occupy the other end of the spectrum. Containers share the same underlying OS and create lightweight isolated environments for their workloads. They have lower overheads but share vulnerabilities and security levels with their kernel. Also, isolation is not as strong, due to the shared OS.

For getting the best out of both scenarios, AWS developed Firecracker [5], an open source VM Monitor which is already used in production Serverless deployments. It is based on KVM [9] and resembles a stripped-down QEMU [6]. Firecracker offers lightweight virtualization environments called microVMs.

2.2 Modern FaaS Stack

Figure 1 shows the Function-as-a-Service software stack implemented in Vitamin-V. In Vitamin-V's architecture for serverless applications, knative serves as a FaaS framework, seamlessly integrating Kubernetes, which acts as an orchestrator to manage the lifecycle of execution modules in distributed clusters. Containers are managed by containerd, which interfaces with Kubernetes kubelet via the

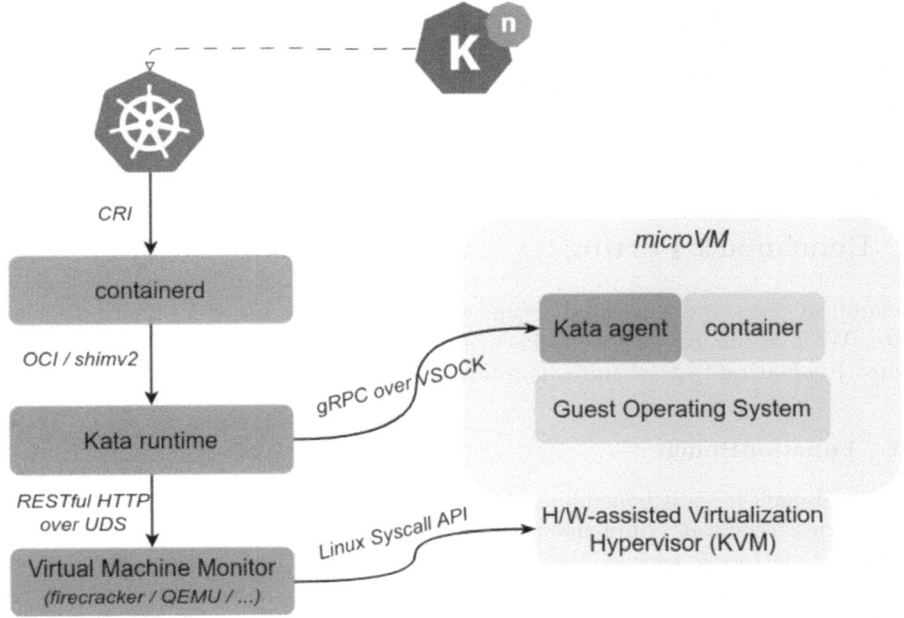

Fig. 1. Function-as-a-Service software stack implemented in VITAMIN-V.

Container Runtime Interface (CRI), ensuring efficient container lifecycle management at node level. For secure container execution, Vitamin-V adopts Kata Containers. This option leverages lightweight microVMs for enhanced security without sacrificing performance. The underlying hypervisor for managing these microVMs is KVM.

2.3 Current Status

Following are our efforts to port a FaaS stack to the RISC-V architecture. Initially, we set up a development environment using Debian for riscv64 but faced limitations with Debian packages that were not yet ported and supported from the community. This led us to manually compile essential components.

One of our first priorities was containerd, written in Golang, which was needed high in the stack. We resolved some issues with the Golang toolchain by using a custom latest installation.

Upon the release of Ubuntu 23.10 with official RISC-V support, we transitioned to Ubuntu. We addressed the unmet dependency of yq v3 for Kata containers by manually building and installing it. Our main focus was on porting the key components of Kata Containers (containerd-shim-kata-v2, kata-runtime, and kata-monitor), adapting the arm64 architecture support for riscv64, adding configuration files, and resolving compilation issues.

Currently, we are testing the kata-runtime with containerd-shim-kata-v2. For the virtual machine manager, we chose KVM with QEMU, and we have already augmented the virtcontainers library with the necessary code to address riscv64-specific parameters, such as various QEMU options, the number of virtual CPUs, suitable kernel parameters, etc. Firecracker is not yet an option due to its reliance on rust-vmm, which has not been ported to RISC-V at the moment of writing.

3 Benchmark Porting

To support the serverless cloud setup, we first target to use the FunctionBench suite. We plan on porting and executing it in VITAMIN-V's evaluation platforms. Evaluating further suites is a target further down the line.

3.1 FunctionBench

FunctionBench [8] is a benchmark suite consisting of workloads highly specific to serverless scenarios. Implementations come written for different major cloud providers' platforms, such as AWS, Azure and Google. The workloads themselves offer a wide range of functionality, with benchmarks covering image and video processing up to more complicated ones in the machine learning domain. The suite offers measurements on computation time and end-to-end latency.

FunctionBench consists of several microbenchmarks and some application-level benchmarks. Microbenchmarks are small functions that only apply lightweight and highly focused computations, and aim to measure specific aspects of the serverless platform. Examples here include cryptography related benchmarks like AES, or float operation benchmarks. Application-level benchmarks simulate more complex functionalities, and chain multiple functions together. With this approach, they can access and stress more platform capabilities and offer more thorough and end-to-end evaluation. The suite is also meant to be extensible, so other benchmarks can be added and written accordingly.

All benchmarks in FunctionBench are written in Python, and include two files - the main code file and a requirements file with the names and versions of python packages required to run the workload. The code is written to be directly integrated with cloud providers, so a function handling the incoming request exists in all benchmarks, alongside the rest of the regular python functions.

The FunctionBench suite was chosen as it encompasses a number of workloads varying in size and resource stressing capabilities. Firstly, FunctionBench includes micro-benchmarks. These micro-benchmarks use system calls to target specific behaviors and only measure the performance of resources. Secondly, the application-benchmarks combine the usage of data and resources and utilize the system in a more complete way. The two approaches together with the easy integration they show to other architectures make FunctionBench a fitting choice for porting to and evaluating RISC-V platforms.

Inside the suite there exist benchmark implementations for three major cloud providers - AWS, Azure and Google. For each provider, the same base set of benchmark is ported. The workloads are written so they integrate with each provider's cloud infrastructure, as some benchmarks require cloud communication to run. We chose the full Google benchmarks set to port, as they were not only straightforward to run online via Google Cloud, but also easy to modify to run locally via *functions-framework* and *Flask*. The function and measurements of the benchmarks remain the same regardless to the cloud provider picked.

3.2 Current Status

The workloads discussed have **not** been designed and written to explicitly work with a RISC-V architecture out-of-the-box. Our effort has focused on porting and building the whole suite from the ground up.

We have successfully built and run all FunctionBench Google benchmarks on a QEMU RISC-V machine running Ubuntu 23.10, with kernel version 6.5.0-40-generic. To achieve this, we had to deal with building the correct dependencies on the system, as well as installing the correct versions of python packages. We used a python virtual environment to install all the required python packages for FunctionBench. In Table 2 we show the packages and their versions after successfully running all benchmarks in the virtual environment (Table 1).

Table 1. Current status of porting benchmarks from FunctionBench in RISC-V for QEMU.

Benchmark	QEMU
float_operation	Completed
linpack	Completed
chameleon	Completed
matmul	Completed
pyaes	Completed
mapreduce	Completed
image_processing	Completed
video_processing	Completed
bucket_down_up	Completed
json_dumps_load	Completed
dd	Completed
gzip_compression	Completed
model_training	Completed
model_serving	Completed

Apart from the package dependencies, there were also system package dependencies. Most dependencies were already installed by default through the Linux Distribution. However, to get the Ubuntu RISC-V system to run the benchmarks

Table 2. Python package names and versions

Name	Version	Name	Version
aiohttp	3.9.3	joblib	1.4.0
aiosignal	1.3.1	joblist	2.0.3
attrs	23.2.0	MarkupSafe	2.1.4
blinker	1.7.0	multidict	6.0.5
cachetools	5.3.2	numpy	1.26.3
certifi	2023.11.17	oauthlib	3.2.2
Chameleon	4.5.2	opencv-python	4.9.0.80
charset-normalizer	3.3.2	packaging	23.2
click	8.1.7	pandas	2.2.1
cloudevents	1.10.1	pillow	10.2.0
decorator	5.1.1	protobuf	4.25.2
deprecation	2.1.0	pyaes	1.6.1
Flask	3.0.1	pyasn1	0.5.1
frozenlist	1.4.1	pyasn1-modules	0.3.0
fsspec	2024.3.1	python-dateutil	2.9.0.post0
functions-framework	3.5.0	pytz	2024.1
gcsfs	2024.3.1	requests	2.31.0
google-api-core	2.16.0	requests-oauthlib	2.0.0
google-auth	2.27.0	rsa	4.9
google-auth-oauthlib	1.2.0	scikit-learn	1.4.2
google-cloud-core	2.4.1	scipy	1.13.0
google-cloud-storage	2.14.0	six	1.16.0
google-crc32c	1.5.0	threadpoolctl	3.4.0
google-resumable-media	2.7.0	tzdata	2024.1
googleapis-common-protos	1.62.0	urllib3	2.2.0
gunicorn	21.2.0	w3lib	2.1.2
idna	3.6	watchdog	3.0.0
itsdangerous	2.1.2	Werkzeug	3.0.1
Jinja2	3.1.3	yarl	1.9.4

properly, the additional packages in Table 3 must be installed. In our case, we used the apt packet manager to install them.

During the work put into porting the workloads, several issues were discovered in the FunctionBench suite itself.

In the "chameleon" benchmark, the file with the list of required packages was not updated. The package "six" was used in the benchmark but was not present in the list, and was not automatically installed. We added the "six" package to the requirements list.

In the "chameleon" benchmark, there was an erroneous line. A line that was probably pasted by accident was added to the benchmark, referencing functions

Table 3. System package dependencies

APT Dependencies
jpeg
libssl-dev
gfortran
libopenblas-dev

and variables that do not exist in the benchmark's scope. We deleted the line and the benchmark ran normally after it.

In the "linpack" benchmark, a component named "asscalar" was included from the "numpy" library. This component is outdated and deprecated, leading to the benchmark not running. Additionally, the component was not used actively in the benchmark. We removed the "asscalar" component from the python include statement.

In the "gzip_compression" benchmark, a file is opened to read with wrong permissions and in the wrong mode. This led to codec errors on runtime when opening the file. We fixed the file permissions by opening the file in binary mode, after which the benchmark ran successfully.

Regarding the above mistakes, we opened a pull request in the FunctionBench project [2].

4 Future Work

Our efforts are currently focused into two parts: Continue porting and integrating the Kata Containers and Firecracker into Function-as-a-Service workflows, and testing and evaluating ported benchmarks on different platforms with different tools.

4.1 Lightweight Virtualization

For lightweight virtualization, next steps include efforts to ensure the correctness of our code, with extensive testing and debugging. We plan to test conainerd-shim-kata-v2 with containerd and verify it is functional. With Kata Containers, we plan to make a pull request to the official repo once we are ready, to work with it together with the community for an industry-quality end result. Finally, once the Kubernetes port is completed, we aim to fully deploy and evaluate our full stack, and test with FaaS workloads.

4.2 Testing and Evaluation

With FunctionBench ported, our next targets include: **RISC-V platform testing, StarFive VisionFive 2** - Running the benchmark suite on actual RISC-V hardware with the Starfive VisionFive 2 board, and take initial measurements as a reference. **RISC-V platform testing, FPGA bitstream from Semidynamics** [4] - Accordingly, we aim to run our tests on the FPGA bitstream we will receive from Semidynamics, and take some reference measurements there as well.

Acknowledgement. This work was supported by project Vitamin-V (Project number: 101093062) funded by the European Union. Views and opinions expressed are, however, those of the author(s) only and do not necessarily reflect those of the European Union or the HaDEA. Neither the European Union nor the granting authority can be held responsible for them.

References

1. Kubernetes. https://kubernetes.io/
2. Pull request on functionbench. https://github.com/ddps-lab/serverless-faas-workbench/pull/47
3. rust-vmm. https://github.com/rust-vmm
4. Semidynamics. https://semidynamics.com/en
5. Agache, A., et al.: Firecracker: lightweight virtualization for serverless applications. In: 17th USENIX Symposium on Networked Systems Design and Implementation (NSDI 2020), pp. 419–434 (2020)
6. Bartholomew, D.: QEMU: a multihost, multitarget emulator. Linux J. **2006**(145), 3 (2006)
7. Caforio, F., Iannicelli, P., Paolino, M., Raho, D.: VoSySmonitoRV: a mixed-criticality solution on linux-capable RISC-V platforms. In: 2021 10th Mediterranean Conference on Embedded Computing (MECO), pp. 1–4. IEEE (2021)
8. Kim, J., Lee, K.: Functionbench: a suite of workloads for serverless cloud function service. In: 2019 IEEE 12th International Conference on Cloud Computing (CLOUD), pp. 502–504. IEEE (2019)
9. Kivity, A., Kamay, Y., Laor, D., Lublin, U., Liguori, A.: KVM: the Linux virtual machine monitor. In: Proceedings of the Linux Symposium, Dttawa, Dntorio, Canada, vol. 1, pp. 225–230 (2007)
10. Randazzo, A., Tinnirello, I.: Kata containers: an emerging architecture for enabling MEC services in fast and secure way. In: 2019 Sixth International Conference on Internet of Things: Systems, Management and Security (IOTSMS), pp. 209–214. IEEE (2019)
11. Sefraoui, O., Aissaoui, M., Eleuldj, M., et al.: OpenStack: toward an open-source solution for cloud computing. Int. J. Comput. Appl. **55**(3), 38–42 (2012)

Design and Implementation of an Open Source OpenGL SC 2.0.1 Installable Client Driver and Offline Compiler

Matina Maria Trompouki[1,2], Marc Solé Bonet[1,2], Josué Pedrajas Pérez[1,2], and Leonidas Kosmidis[1,2(✉)]

[1] Barcelona Supercomputing Center (BSC), Barcelona, Spain
leonidas.kosmidis@bsc.es
[2] Universitat Politècnica de Catalunya (UPC), Barcelona, Spain

Abstract. OpenGL SC 2 is Khronos' Graphics API for safety critical systems. However, unlike other Khronos' APIs, available OpenGL SC 2 drivers are only provided by vendors to their customers. This hinders the wide adoption of OpenGL SC 2, which is limited to a niche market, since there are very limited available resources for it.

In this work, we describe the design and implementation of an Open Source Installable Client Driver (ICD) and offline compiler on top of OpenGL ES 2.0. Thus, our solution enables the development of OpenGL SC 2.0.1 applications on any embedded system, as well as their deployment on selected safety critical platforms, which do not have an available OpenGL SC 2.0.1 driver yet.

Keywords: Safety Critical Systems · Embedded GPUs · OpenGL SC 2 · OpenGL ES 2 · Installable Client Driver · Offline Compiler

1 Introduction

Modern safety critical systems like the ones found in automotive and aerospace systems as well as in medical devices, require the use of embedded graphics processing units (GPUs), either for display purposes [6] or for the acceleration of high performance general purpose computations (GPGPU) [24].

Any malfunction in safety critical systems can have severe consequences in the integrity of the system, which can result in the risk of human lives. For this reason, safety critical systems need to comply with functional safety standards such as ISO 26262 in automotive [9], DO-178C [20] in avionics, ECSS [7] in space and IEC 62304 [8] in medical devices.

While each domain has its own compliance requirements, all functional safety standards provide a description of a rigorous development process, in order to provide high quality assurance.

In order to enable the use of GPUs in such regulated market sectors, as well as their certification with their respective safety standards, Khronos has developed a series of safety critical (SC) standards, such as OpenGL SC 1 [10], OpenGL SC 2 [13], Vulkan SC [14], OpenVX SC [11] and the currently under development SYCL SC [19,21].

However, with the exception of Vulkan SC [15], there are no openly available development tools or drivers for the rest of the Safety Critical Khronos APIs. In particular, OpenGL SC 2 drivers are only available by vendors to their safety critical customers. In combination with the absence of any training resources for OpenGL SC 2, this limits significantly the adoption of this open standard.

In order to overcome this limitation, in this work we implement an open source installable client driver (ICD) for the OpenGL SC 2.0.1 specification [13], as well as an accompanied offline compiler, on top of OpenGL ES 2.

Given the ubiquitous support of OpenGL ES 2, in this way, we enable the development of OpenGL SC 2 software on any embedded platform. In addition, given that certain devices have been deemed appropriate for use in safety critical systems such as AMD's Xilinx Ultrascale+ [2] but currently lack an OpenGL SC 2 driver, we offer a certifiable alternative for their software stack.

Our implementation is portable on any OpenGL ES 2 platform and it has been tested on multiple platforms, using safety critical graphics and GPGPU software.

The rest of the paper is organised as follows. Section 2 provides the Background and Related Work. Section 3 describes the implementation of our ICD and offline compiler. Section 4 describes the experimental validation of our implementation. Finally, Sect. 5 concludes the paper and presents our outlook for future work.

2 Background and Related Work

2.1 OpenGL SC 2

OpenGL SC 2 is (mostly) a subset of OpenGL ES 2, in particular based on the OpenGL ES 2.0.25 specification, which facilitates compliance with safety critical standards and software development requirements.

Similar to all Khronos Safety Critical APIs, dynamic features which increase the implementation size and software complexity, as well as the certification effort and cost, are removed. This includes any dynamic memory management features which are related to deleting/freeing memory allocated for various API objects (e.g. textures, framebuffers etc.), because they can cause memory fragmentation or require the implementation of non deterministic memory management features such as garbage collection.

On the other hand, some OpenGL ES 2 API calls are modified in order to support defensive programming, i.e. additional checks that check for unintentional program defects.

In addition, some calls from later OpenGL ES versions are included in order to make sure that all API calls can be clearly classified as performing memory allocations or not, regardless of the value of their parameters. This allows memory allocation API calls to be used only at application initialisation time, while the rest of the calls to be used within the main application processing phase.

Finally, OpenGL SC 2 removes the ability to compile and link programmable shaders at runtime, which is the default behaviour of OpenGL ES 2. While this sacrifices portability, in this way, the GPU program becomes deterministic and there is no possibility of malfunction due to the failure of online compilation. Moreover, it reduces significantly the certification cost, since otherwise the compiler would be part of the driver, and it would need to be certified, too. For a complex software system such as a compiler, that cost could be prohibitive. Instead, compilers are qualified according to *tool qualification* requirements of the respective functional safety standards, which is a much more cost effective solution [23]. In fact, a compiler might not need to be qualified if the generated code can be manually (or semi-automated) verified, which is a solution frequently employed. In Sect. 4 we provide a detailed analysis of the differences between OpenGL SC 2 and OpenGL ES 2.

Currently, certified OpenGL SC 2 safety critical drivers are available and deployed in systems with the highest criticality defined in their respective standards such as DAL A in avionics according to DO-178C [20] and ASIL D in automotive according to ISO 26262 [9].

Note that the latest OpenGL SC 2 version is 2.0.1 [13] which is a minor update over version 2.0, which fixed several typos in the specification and only changed the default value of the BLEND_COLOR pixel operation.

2.2 OpenGL SC 2 Drivers and Offline Compilers

As already mentioned, OpenGL SC 2 implementations are only available by safety critical driver vendors. In addition to these commercial products, an academic prototype implementation was also provided by Baek and Kim [4,5]. As this prototype implementation was intended to be commercialised later, it is not available as open source.

Both the implementation details and the scope of these works are significantly different from ours. In terms of scope, all previous works aim to provide a standalone, commercial OpenGL SC 2 driver implementation. On the other hand, the primary motivation behind our implementation is to enable OpenGL SC 2 development and training [16,17] without access to a proprietary implementation, thus enabling its widespread use. In addition, our secondary goal is to enable the use of OpenGL SC 2 software on safety critical platforms without an OpenGL SC 2 driver yet.

In terms of implementation, prior works have been implemented from scratch. Conversely, we leverage the similarity between OpenGL ES 2 and OpenGL SC 2, in order to minimise implementation effort and provide an implementation on top of the embedded API version.

2.3 Installable Client Driver

Several Khronos APIs, such as OpenCL [12] and Vulkan SC [15] include an Installable Client Driver (ICD) which provides portability between different vendor implementations. For example, in a system with two GPUs from different vendors, e.g. one NVIDIA and one AMD, the ICD intercepts the OpenCL calls and calls the vendor specific versions, depending on the target GPU. Therefore, these ICDs are implemented as a thin software library, with the same symbols as a vendor driver, which is preloaded before the vendor one (Table 1).

Similar to our case, the Khronos Vulkan SC ICD [15] is targeting development environments, but it is not expected to be used in production environments. However, in the absence of an OpenGL SC 2 safety critical driver for a safety critical device, we explain how our ICD could be used in production environment, too.

Table 1. Modified functions between OpenGL SC 2 and OpenGL ES 2.

OpenGL ES 2	OpenGL SC 2
glDrawElements()	glDrawRangeElements()
glGetUniformfv()	glGetnUniformfv()
glGetUniformiv()	glGetnUniformiv()
glReadPixels()	glReadnPixels()
glTexImage2D()	glTexStorage2D()

3 Design and Implementation

In this section, we provide details about our open source implementation of the ICD and the offline compiler. Our implementation is available at [18]. First, we have performed an analysis of the differences between the OpenGL SC 2 and OpenGL ES 2, which is taken into account in the implementation of the ICD. Then we describe the implementation of the offline compiler.

3.1 ICD Implementation

Unlike OpenCL [12] and Vulkan SC [15] Khronos ICDs, each of which provides a software layer that intercepts and invokes the same type of calls, between different vendor drivers, our ICD implementation expects to interface only with a single vendor OpenGL ES 2 driver.

This has lead us to take the following implementation decisions:
Expose Only the OpenGL SC 2.0.1 Calls to the Applications: Applications only include the OpenGL SC 2.0.1 headers, and link with both our ICD driver as well with the OpenGL ES 2 driver of the system. In this way, all the

Design & Implementation of an OpenGL SC 2.0.1 ICD and Offline Compiler 131

Table 2. Added and removed functions between OpenGL SC 2 and OpenGL ES 2.

Added functions		
glGetGraphicsResetStatus()	glProgramBinary()	
Removed functions		
glAttachShader()	glDeleteShader()	glIsBuffer()
glBindAttribLocation()	glDeleteTextures()	glIsFramebuffer()
glCompileShader()	glDetachShader()	glIsProgram()
glCompressedTexImage2D()	glGetActiveAttrib()	glIsRenderbuffer()
glCopyTexImage2D()	glGetActiveUniform()	glIsShader()
glCopyTexSubImage2D()	glGetAttachedShaders()	glIsTexture()
glCreateShader()	glGetProgramInfoLog()	glLinkProgram()
glDeleteBuffers()	glGetShaderiv()	glReleaseShaderCompiler()
glDeleteFramebuffers()	glGetShaderInfoLog()	glShaderBinary()
glDeleteProgram()	glGetShaderPrecisionFormat()	glShaderSource()
glDeleteRenderbuffers()	glGetShaderSource()	glValidateProgram()

OpenGL ES 2 API calls which have been removed in the OpenGL SC 2.0.1, are hidden from the application and cannot be used. Table 2 shows the list of the removed API function calls.

If there is a need to use our ICD driver in a production environment, e.g. in AMD's Zynq Ultrascale+ which has been certified for use in functional safety applications [2] but does not have an OpenGL SC 2 driver available yet, an additional step needs to performed, in order to ensure that the OpenGL ES 2 functions cannot be called. The reason for this is that in certain functional safety standards e.g. DO-178C additional provisions need to be taken to ensure that deactivated code cannot be inadvertently used. In this case, we include the option to enable a preloaded library that redefines the removed OpenGL ES 2 API calls and raises an error when this happens.

Implement Only the Added and Modified API Calls. Since the majority of calls remain identical between the two standards, not every API call is implemented in our ICD. Instead we only provide an implementation for the calls which are unique. Table 2 shows the list of the added API function calls. This includes only 2 API calls, glGetGraphicsResetStatus() and glProgramBinary(). The former provides information about the graphics reset context in case of an error, while the latter allows to load a program binary. Our implementation uses the optional OpenGL ES 2 functionality glProgramBinaryOES internally, therefore an explicit requirement for our ICD to work is that the underlying OpenGL ES 2 implementation supports loading binary shaders, which we test through the `OES_get_program_binary` extension.

Modified API Calls Implementation. OpenGL SC 2.0.1 modifies several OpenGL ES 2 API calls in the direction of defensive programming. In this case, these API calls in our ICD are wrappers to the original OpenGL ES 2, which perform the necessary tests before invoking them. The only significantly modified API call is glTexImage2D(), which depending on whether its last argument is a NULL pointer, a new texture allocation takes place. Instead, it is replaced with glTexStorage2D() which has been borrowed from the OpenGL ES 3 specification, in order to perform the allocation.

In order to guarantee that our implementation works also on systems which support only OpenGL ES 2 but not OpenGL ES 3, like the ARM Mali-400 GPU found in the AMD Zynq Ultrascale+, we implement glTexStorage2D() using glTexImage2D().

Information Tracking and Restricted Limit Emulation. Our ICD implementation tracks information flow before calling the corresponding OpenGL ES 2 calls. This allows to enable additional checks and emulate behaviour in constrained environments. For example, even though the underlying device and driver may have plenty of GPU resources available, we can emulate constraint environments and evaluate the application's robustness in such cases. For example, we can set a virtual limit to the size of the maximum texture memory (or other dynamically allocated objects), and cause an application failure when this limit is exceeded.

3.2 Offline Compiler

By default OpenGL ES 2 supports online shader compilation, while some vendors implement the optional extension glShaderBinaryOES which allows loading precompiled vertex or fragment shaders.

Some vendors like ARM and AMD, provide an offline compiler [1,3] which can be used to precompile shaders for use with the aforementioned extension. Other vendors although they support the extension, they only ship their online compiler with their driver. In order to enable the use of OpenGL SC 2.0.1 even on these targets, we have created an offline compiler that uses the underlying online compiler of the OpenGL ES 2 driver, in order to obtain the compiled binary.

Obviously, the requirement for our offline compiler to work on a given platform is the support of the `OES_get_program_binary` extension, as in the case of our ICD implementation. In this case, we are using the glGetProgramBinaryOES call in order to obtain the binary shader.

4 Implementation Validation

We have tested our implementation on several embedded platforms with varying hardware and software capabilities, which are used in safety critical systems. In particular we have verified that it works on NVIDIA's Xavier AGX, Zynq Ultrascale+ and on an avionics-grade AMD E8860. The 2 first platforms are widely used in automotive while the last one in aerospace systems. Xavier and E8860 support up to the latest version of OpenGL ES, while the Zynq supports only OpenGL ES 2.

On the software side we have used existing OpenGL SC 2 software we have developed in the past. In particular, we have used two versions of a proprietary prototype avionics application provided by Airbus Defence and Space [6], one using directly hand-written OpenGL SC 2 code, and another one written in the Brook Auto CUDA-like language [22], which internally uses the BRASIL [23] source-to-source compiler which converts Brook Auto to OpenGL SC 2. The functionality of the application is identical to the one obtained on top of Core-AVI's Argus Core 2 OpenGL SC 2 avionics certified driver on AMD E8860 [6].

In addition to this application, we have also used GPGPU software written in OpenGL SC 2 [24], which we released as open source [17] and we use for teaching OpenGL SC 2 tutorials [16].

In addition to the nominal use of our software, we have emulated a scenario in which we have configured our ICD driver to appear to have fewer resources than the application needs, in order to observe the application's behaviour in faulty modes.

For the ARM and AMD GPUs we perform all our tests using both our offline compiler and the vendor provided offline compiler, without change in the functionality. In all cases, the behaviour of the applications on top of our ICD driver is functionally equivalent to their behaviour when executed on top of the CoreAVI's Argus Core 2 OpenGL SC 2 driver on the avionics-grade AMD E8860 [6].

Based on these results, we have a good indication that our OpenGL SC 2 implementation can be used for the development of OpenGL SC 2 software as well as for OpenGL SC 2 training, without need for access to commercial tools.

Finally, for the AMD Zynq Ultrascale+ we have emulated an additional scenario, in which our ICD could be used in a production safety critical environment. For this purpose, we ensure that the deleted OpenGL ES 2 API calls shown in Table 2 are hidden behind our preloaded library. We confirm that a modified version of the tested software which erroneously includes the OpenGL ES 2 header and tried to execute an API call which is not allowed in the OpenGL SC 2 specification is failing, as it is supposed to.

5 Conclusions and Future Work

In this paper we have described the design and implementation of an OpenGL SC 2 ICD and offline compiler. Our implementation is open source [18] and can contribute to the wider adoption of OpenGL SC 2, since it allows development and training [16,17] for this Khronos API, without the need of proprietary tools.

Although our evaluation shows promising results, it cannot be considered complete yet. As future steps we plan to evaluate our implementation with the OpenGL SC 2 conformance suite, as well as to contribute our code to Khronos, in order to become available as an official Khronos OpenGL SC 2 ICD, similar to the cases of OpenCL and Vulkan SC ICDs. Finally, we will reuse our lessons learnt in order to develop a similar approach for SYCL SC, when its specification is released.

Acknowledgments. The authors thank CoreAVI for providing access to their Argus Core 2 OpenGL SC 2 driver and to an avionics-grade AMD E8860 GPU.

This work was supported by the European Union's Horizon Europe programme under the METASAT project (grant agreement 101082622). It was also partially supported by the Spanish Ministry of Economy and Competitiveness under grants PID2019-107255GB-C21 and IJC-2020-045931-I (Spanish State Research Agency/Agencia Española de Investigación (AEI)/http://dx.doi.org/10.13039/501100011033) and by the Department of Research and Universities of the Government of Catalonia with a grant to the CAOS Research Group (Code: 2021 SGR 00637).

References

1. AMD: RGA (Radeon GPU Analyzer) (2018). https://github.com/GPUOpen-Tools/radeon_gpu_analyzer
2. AMD: Zynq UltraScale+ Milestone: First SoC Certified for Automotive Functional Safety Applications (2022). https://community.amd.com/t5/adaptive-computing/zynq-ultrascale-milestone-first-soc-certified-for-automotive/ba-p/562152
3. ARM: Mali Offline Compiler (2012). https://developer.arm.com/Tools%20and%20Software/Mali%20Offline%20Compiler
4. Baek, N., Kim, K.J.: Design and implementation of OpenGL SC 2.0 rendering pipeline. Cluster Comput. **22**(1), 931–936 (2019)
5. Baek, N., Kim, K.J.: Prototype implementation of the OpenGL ES 2.0 shading language offline compiler. Cluster Comput. **22**(1), 943–948 (2019)
6. Benito, M., Trompouki, M.M., Kosmidis, L., Garcia, J.D., Carretero, S., Wenger, K.: Comparison of GPU computing methodologies for safety-critical systems: an avionics case study. In: Design, Automation & Test in Europe Conference (DATE) (2021)
7. European Cooperation for Space Standardization: ECSS-E-ST-40C Software (2009)
8. International Organization for Standardization: IEC 62304 Medical Device Software - Software Life Cycle Processes (2006)
9. International Organization for Standardization: ISO 26262. Road Vehicles – Functional Safety (2018)
10. Khronos Group: OpenGL SC Safety-Critical Profile Specification 1.0.1 (2009)
11. Khronos Group: The OpenVX SC Specification **1**, 1 (2017)
12. Khronos Group: Opencl icd loader (2018). https://github.com/KhronosGroup/OpenCL-ICD-Loader
13. Khronos Group: OpenGL SC 2.0.1 (Full Specification) (2019)
14. Khronos Group: Vulkan SC 1.0.10 - A Specification (2022)
15. Khronos Group: Vulkan SC Loader (2023). https://github.com/KhronosGroup/VulkanSC-Loader
16. Kosmidis, L., Trompouki, M.M.: Introduction to Certifiable General Purpose GPU Programming for Avionics Systems. Tutorial at the 42nd Digital Avionics Systems Conference (DASC) (2023)
17. Kosmidis, L., Trompouki, M.M.: OpenGL SC 2 GPGPU Tutorial Repository (2023). https://gitlab.bsc.es/lkosmidi/opengl_sc_2_tutorial
18. Kosmidis, L., Trompouki, M.M.: OpenGL SC 2.0.1 ICD and Offline Compiler Repository (2023). https://gitlab.bsc.es/lkosmidi/opengl_sc_2_icd

19. Peralta, C.Q., Trompouki, M.M., Kosmidis, L.: Evaluation of SYCL's suitability for high-performance critical systems. In: Proceedings of the 2023 International Workshop on OpenCL, IWOCL 2023. Association for Computing Machinery, New York (2023). https://doi.org/10.1145/3585341.3585378
20. RTCA and EUROCAE: DO-178C / ED-12C, Software Considerations in Airborne Systems and Equipment Certification (2012)
21. Tomusk, E., Beckham, V.: What's new in SYCL for safety critical systems. In: Proceedings of the 2023 International Workshop on OpenCL, IWOCL 2023, Association for Computing Machinery, New York (2023). https://doi.org/10.1145/3585341.3585367
22. Trompouki, M.M., Kosmidis, L.: Brook auto: high-level certification-friendly programming for GPU-powered automotive systems. In: Proceedings of the 55th Annual Design Automation Conference, DAC 2018, San Francisco, CA, USA, 24–29 June 2018, pp. 100:1–100:6. ACM (2018). https://doi.org/10.1145/3195970.3196002
23. Trompouki, M.M., Kosmidis, L.: BRASIL: A high-integrity GPGPU toolchain for automotive systems. In: 37th IEEE International Conference on Computer Design, ICCD 2019, Abu Dhabi, United Arab Emirates, 17–20 November 2019, pp. 660–663. IEEE (2019). https://doi.org/10.1109/ICCD46524.2019.00094
24. Trompouki, M.M., Kosmidis, L.: DO-178C certification of general-purpose GPU software: review of existing methods and future directions. In: 40th Digital Avionics Systems Conference (DASC) (2021). https://doi.org/10.1109/DASC52595.2021.9594412

Special Session on Security

Plan Your Defense: A Comparative Analysis of Leakage Detection Methods on RISC-V Cores

Konstantina Miteloudi[✉], Asmita Adhikary, Niels van Drueten, Lejla Batina, and Ileana Buhan

Digital Security Group, Radboud University, Nijmgegen, The Netherlands
{konstantina.miteloudi,asmita.adhikary,lejla.batina,ileana.buhan}@ru.nl,
niels@vandrueten.nl

Abstract. Hardening microprocessors against side-channel attacks is a critical aspect of ensuring their security. A key step in this process is identifying and mitigating "leaky" hardware modules, which leak information during the execution of cryptographic algorithms. In this paper, we explore how different leakage detection methods, the Side-channel Vulnerability Factor (SVF) and the Test Vector Leakage Assessment (TVLA), contribute to hardening of microprocessors. We conduct experiments on two RISC-V cores, SHAKTI and Ibex, using two cryptographic algorithms, SHA-3 and AES. Our findings suggest that SVF and TVLA can provide valuable insights into identifying leaky modules. However, the effectiveness of these methods can vary depending on the specific core and cryptographic algorithm in use. We conclude that the choice of leakage detection method should be based not only on computational cost but also on the specific requirements of the system, the implementation of the algorithm examined and the nature of the potential threats.

Keywords: Pre-Silicon Design · Side-Channel Analysis · Leakage Detection Methods · Hardening Microprocessors

1 Introduction

Microprocessors are at the heart of modern digital systems, from everyday consumer electronics to critical infrastructure. Ensuring their security against various forms of attacks is crucial. One such form of attack, side-channel attacks, exploits information leaked during the execution of cryptographic algorithms, potentially compromising the system's security. As such, a key step in hardening microprocessors against side-channel attacks is identifying and mitigating these "leaky" hardware modules.

Several methods exist for detecting such leakages, each with strengths and weaknesses. Two methods, the Side-channel Vulnerability Factor (SVF) [5] and the Test Vector Leakage Assessment (TVLA) [9], have been commonly used in the field. SVF provides a measure of the potential exploitability of a leak, while

TVLA offers a statistical framework for identifying whether a device under test is vulnerable to information leakage. However, the effectiveness of these methods can vary depending on the specific hardware and algorithm in use [2,20]. In this work, we applied these leakage assessment methods on two RISC-V cores: SHAKTI and Ibex. These cores, popular in various applications for their open-source nature, present a range of opportunities and challenges for security.

Our research question is: "How effectively can we harden microprocessors of varying sizes that run full cryptographic algorithms against side-channel attacks?". We aim to provide insights into how SVF and TVLA can be used to identify vulnerabilities in RISC-V cores of different sizes and how these findings can enforce the best strategies for hardening these cores. Through our experiments with different cryptographic algorithms, i.e. SHA-3 and AES, we seek to offer a comprehensive understanding of the ways these leakage detection methods can contribute to the hardening of RISC-V cores. Our findings will be of interest to security designers and architects, contributing to the development of more secure microprocessors/tools [18].

2 Related Work

Several approaches have been developed to identify and eliminate leaks during the pre-silicon phase [12]. These approaches can be roughly divided based on which device layer or development phase they aim to harden [4]. The level of leakage can be detected at top architectural choices [1] or/and can emerge from the micro-architectural behaviour [14].

De Mulder et al. [15] proposed a solution to protect an AES implementation against side channel leakage related to memory accesses on a RISC-V core. Gigerl et al. [8] introduced COCO, a tool that can detect gate-level leakage by simulating execution with Verilator. They annotate the registers and memory that hold secret data and trace their flow through the circuit to find possible sources of leakage. He et al. [10] estimate the power profile of a hardware design using functional simulation at the RTL level. Gao et al. [7] designed and implemented an ISE (Instruction Set Extension) called FENL that localizes and reduces microarchitectural leakage. The ISE acts as a leakage fence that prevents interaction between instructions. A similar approach is taken by Pham et al. [16], which combines a diversified ISE with hardware diversification through a co-processor to achieve leakage mitigation. Bloem et al. [3] extended the concept of hardware-software contracts to power-side channels and formally verified a wide range of instructions for implementing cryptographic algorithms for the RISC-V Ibex core. ACA [19] uses a gate-level model for a target design, typically available after logic synthesis and a side-channel leakage model. Kiaei and Schaumont proposed Root Canal [11], a framework to help a designer with white-box access to the embedded CPU system uncover the origin of a side-channel leak. Root Canal can eliminate side-channel leaks before tape-out. After tape-out, changes to the hardware are no longer possible.

To our knowledge, none of the previous work investigates the impact of the leakage detection methods on identifying leaky modules. Arsath et al. [6] developed a framework, PLAN, that analyzes the RTL description of a processor and reports the information leakage in each of the processor modules. In PLAN, they use a modified version of SVF as a leakage detection method, and they apply this method to a simulated RISC-V core running different cryptographic algorithms. The results of their analysis provide a ranking of the hardware modules based on their contribution to the overall leakage. In our work, we replicate the experimental setup of [6], applying both the SVF and the TVLA methods to compare their effectiveness in identifying leaky modules. This replication is the foundation for further exploration and comparison of these two leakage detection methods.

3 Preliminaries

3.1 Leakage Detection Methods

Let $\mathcal{X}(N, d)$ be a set of N traces. A *trace* is a time series with d samples recorded during the processing of an algorithm on a given device (e.g., an encryption operation) for a given input x.

Test Vector Leakage Assessment. (TVLA) [9] is the most popular leakage detection method due to its simplicity and relative effectiveness. It comes in two flavours: *specific* and *non-specific*. The 'fixed-vs-random' is the most common non-specific test and compares a set of traces acquired with a fixed plaintext with another set of traces acquired with random plaintext. In the case of a specific test, the traces are divided according to a known intermediate value tested for leakage. Welch's two-sample t-value for equality of means applies to all trace samples in both cases. A difference between two sets larger than a given threshold is evidence of a leak's presence.

Side-Channel Vulnerability Factor. (SVF) [5] measures side-channel information leakage by recognizing leaked execution patterns. SVF quantifies the similarity between patterns in the observations of the attackers or *side-channel traces* ($\mathcal{S}$, defined in (1), with the actual execution patterns of the victim or *oracle traces* ($\mathcal{O}$, defined in (2)).

$$\mathcal{S} = \{(x_i; s_1^i, s_2^i, ... s_d^i), \text{where } 1 \leq x_i \leq N\} \quad (1)$$

$$\mathcal{O} = \{(x_i; o_1^i, o_2^i, ... o_d^i), \text{where } 1 \leq x_i \leq N\} \quad (2)$$

where s_j^i (and o_j^i) is sample j in side channel trace (and oracle trace, respectively) corresponding to input x_i.

The original version of the SVF algorithm proposed in [5], which we denote with SVF_{time}, quantifies *patterns in the time-domain* between an oracle and a side-channel trace. Arsath et al. [6] implemented a modified version of $\text{SVF}_{\text{input}}$ that is adapted to capture *patterns related to changes in the input data*, the typical cause of side-channel vulnerabilities. After data collection, both algorithms extract patterns in parallel for the oracle and side-channel trace. The difference between the implementation of SVF_{time} and $\text{SVF}_{\text{input}}$ is apparent in the construction of the similarity matrices as shown in Eq. (3), (4) and (5), (6) respectively.

$$M^{\mathcal{S}}_{\text{time}}(s^i_j, s^i_k) = \begin{cases} D(s^i_j, s^i_k), & \text{if } j < k \\ 0, & \text{if not.} \end{cases} \quad (3)$$

and

$$M^{\mathcal{O}}_{\text{time}}(o^i_j, o^i_k) = \begin{cases} D'(o^i_j, o^i_k), & \text{if } j < k \\ 0, & \text{if not.} \end{cases} \quad (4)$$

When computing SVF_{time}, the first step is to construct $M^{\mathcal{S}}_{\text{time}}$, the similarity matrix for a side-channel trace, using Eq. (3), where D is a distance (of choice) between samples s^i_j, s^i_k. The next step is to compute the similarity matrix, $M^{\mathcal{O}}_{\text{time}}$, for the oracle trace by computing the distance D' between the samples in the same power trace o_i, o_j, using Eq. (4). The correlation between $M^{\mathcal{S}}_{\text{time}}$ and $M^{\mathcal{O}}_{\text{time}}$ will give the SVF_{time} value.

$$M^{\mathcal{S}}_{\text{input}}(s^i_t, s^j_t) = \begin{cases} \tilde{D}(s^i_t, s^j_t), & \text{if } i < j \\ 0, & \text{if not.} \end{cases} \quad (5)$$

and

$$M^{\mathcal{O}}_{\text{input}}(o^i_t, o^j_t) = \begin{cases} \tilde{D}(o^i_t; o^j_t), & \text{if } i < j \\ 0, & \text{if not.} \end{cases} \quad (6)$$

For computing SVF_{time}, one side-channel trace is sufficient however for computing $\text{SVF}_{\text{input}}$, multiple side-channel traces are required (to capture changes in the input). The procedure for computing $\text{SVF}_{\text{input}}$ is very similar to SVF_{time}. The difference is in the choice of samples for computing the similarity matrix is illustrated in Eq. (5) and (6). We first construct $M^{\mathcal{S}}_{\text{input}}$, the similarity matrix for the side-channel traces by computing the distance $\tilde{D}$ between the sample s_t corresponding to different input values x_i, x_j. In the same way, we calculate $M^{\mathcal{O}}_{\text{input}}$, the similarity matrix for the oracle traces, by computing the distance $\tilde{D}$ between the sample o_t and the input x_i, x_j. All similarity matrices are triangular, as the main diagonal, which contains only zero values, is removed, and distance measures are commutative. In this work we implement $\text{SVF}_{\text{input}}$.

4 Experimental Setup

Simulation Setup. In our setup, we use two different 32-bit RISC-V cores, SHAKTI-C and Ibex, and two different algorithms, AES and SHA-3. SHAKTI-C [17] is a 5-stage pipeline in-order processor, while Ibex [13] is a 2-stage in-order processor. From each core, we selected specific modules to examine. We targeted the ones responsible for processing data and instructions and we excluded those that do other work, such as error checking. Specifically, for SHAKTI-C, we examine:

1. RF (Register File): integer and floating point registers.
2. CSR (Control and Status Register): raises interrupts on the processor.
3. ALU (Arithmetic Logic Unit): performs the arithmetic and logic operations.
4. FPU (Floating Point Unit): handles operations with floating point numbers.
5. Dcache: cache memory connected with the ALU.
6. MBOX: implements the multiplication and division operations.
7. BPU (Branch Prediction Unit): decides the next program counter.
8. ITLB (Instruction Translation-Look aside Buffer): keeps track of instructions recently used to avoid second access to memory.
9. DTLB (Data Translation Look aside Buffer): keeps track of data recently used to avoid second access to memory.

For Ibex, we examine modules with the same functionality:

1. RF (Register File): integer registers.
2. CSR (Control and Status Register): raises interrupts on the processor.
3. ALU (Arithmetic Logic Unit): performs the arithmetic and logic operations.
4. MULT/DIV (Multiplier/Divider Block): performs multiplication and division.
5. PF-BUF (Prefetch Buffer): fetches instructions from the memory.
6. LSU (Load-Store Unit): interfaces with the RF and the main memory to deal with load/store operations.

We ran simulations of every algorithm with Verilator simulator (Ver. 4.210) for 256 different inputs, randomly generated. For each simulation run, we took one Value Change Dump (VCD) file. VCD files show the value of every signal, of every module of the RISC-V core for every timestamp of an implementation. We processed the vcd files, as well as analyzed them, using Python. We parsed every file, and for each module, signals were concatenated for each timestamp, creating a composite signal. This signal represents the collective behaviour of all signals and the module's state at that specific point in time. Then, all the concatenated signals for all the selected timestamps, were processed differently, depending on the methodology selected.

SVF Computation. For SVF computation, the concatenated signals are retained in their original form. These signals serve as a complex representation of the module's state. Each module contains N rows of signal values per timestamp s_t. Computing SVF requires the generation of oracle traces, which contain the intermediate values of the cryptographic algorithm during its execution. They are the expected values that the algorithm will produce at each time step given a particular input. We run simulations with the gcc compiler on a Linux system, using the same 256 inputs that we used in the simulations on RISC-V. We record different intermediate values in order to examine how the choice of the oracle trace affects the SVF. For the oracle set, we use the Hamming distance metric to compute $M^{\mathcal{O}}_{\text{input}}$, as described in 5 and 6. The oracle set will contain one sample for each input, so the size of $\mathcal{O}$ is N.

The next step is to calculate a similarity matrix for the oracle trace and a similarity matrix for the side channel trace as described in Sect. 3.1. This step is necessary for correlation because the two traces contain different information and cannot be compared directly. We get two lists of Hamming distance values, and for each timestamp, we compute the Pearson correlation value between the oracle list and the side-channel list. This value shows whether there is a linear correlation between the two lists in our implementation. The SVF value of a module and an oracle is the maximum of all Pearson correlation values. A module's final SVF value is the oracles' maximum SVF value. Arsath et al. [6] use 4 categories to show how much a module leaks: (1) 0.0–0.1: No leakage, (2) 0.1–0.3: Mild leakage, (3) 0.3–0.6: Medium leakage, (4) 0.6–1.0: Severe leakage.

TVLA Computation. Our TVLA computation is based on the nonspecific fixed versus random test as specified in [9]. Since we worked on simulated executions, we needed a hypothetical power consumption model. This model is implemented with the Hamming weight (HW), and every timestamp of the concatenated signals takes an HW value. To calculate the t-value per timestamp, we used the ttest_ind function from the SciPy Python library, that calculates the t-value for the means of two independent samples of values. The non-specific fixed versus random test executes the fixed set multiple times to eliminate noise during a run. In our case, the runs do not contain noise because the run is simulated, and we know exactly all the signal values at any given time. Once all data for TVLA had been collected, we computed a t-value per cycle. This t-value is calculated from the fixed set of size one and the random set of size $N = 128$ for SHAKTI and $N = 256$ for Ibex.

4.1 Target Cryptographic Implementations

We chose unprotected implementations without any countermeasures, as our goal was to examine how leaks impact the different hardware modules. We ran the full algorithms, then chose to zoom in on different parts of them. We wanted to find any vulnerabilities that could arise, regardless of their nature or the specific type of data that might be exposed.

AES: We used the Tiny-AES[1] implementation, written in C. There are options for 128-bit, 192-bit, or 256-bit key sizes and options for ECB, CTR, and CBC modes. We used a key size of 128 bits in the ECB mode, and we encrypted one block of data.

SHA-3: We used the tiny_sha3[2] implementation, written in C. SHA-3 is a sponge function with the KECCAK-f[1600] as permutation function. We provided 832 bits of data as input, so we did not need padding. The output of SHA-3 is 384 bits.

---

[1] https://github.com/kokke/tiny-AES-c.
[2] https://github.com/mjosaarinen/tiny_sha3.

5 Experimental Results

To determine whether the choice of the leakage detection function influences the decision about the leakiness of a module, we used the experimental setup described in Sect. 4. We selected nine and six modules for the SHAKTI core and the Ibex core, respectively, that target processing instructions and data. We determined how "leaky" a module is by recording the maximum SVF value. In addition, we ran TVLA in fixed versus random mode. As this is a nonspecific test, we did not explicitly target intermediate variables. When comparing the results of TVLA with the results of SVF, we expected that TVLA will reveal more leaky points since our SVF procedure did not target all the intermediates.

AES. For experiments, we chose the typical candidate intermediate variables as the target: the first byte of the S-box output, sbox_out$_1$, fifth byte of the S-box output, sbox_out$_5$, and the first byte of the S-box input, $p \oplus k$ (sbox_in$_1$). For the round output, we have oracles for the full round output (mc_out) and for the first byte of the round output (mc_out$_1$).

SHA3. SHA-3 is the other implementation we analyzed. From the first round of the Keccak permutation function, we targeted χ as the only nonlinear operation. We defined three oracles based on the χ step: bc, a SHA-3 implementation-specific operation $bc[i] = st[j + i]$ where $i = 0$ and $j = 0$, not operation in $x \leftarrow x \oplus (\neg y \& z)$ where $i = 0$ and $j = 0$ and xor operation in $x \leftarrow x \oplus (\neg y \& z)$ where $i = 0$ and $j = 0$.

5.1 Case Study: The SHAKTI Core

Figure 1 shows the leakage in ALU from the SHAKTI core, for both AES and SHA-3. The first plot shows the evolution in time of the SVF value, during the first round of AES. We represented the different target intermediates with different unique symbols. Horizontal dotted lines are drawn to indicate leakage thresholds. The yellow dotted line at 0.3 shows the minimum threshold for what we consider to be medium leakage and the red dotted line at 0.6 is for the severe leakage. Also, the oracles are highlighted with yellow where the SVF value is ≥ 0.3 and red when SVF ≥ 0.6. The second plot shows the combined SVF with the t-value for the same module, i.e., ALU. In TVLA, we see leaks in almost all cycles and for most of the cycles, it shows leaks unrelated to the SVF oracles. For example, during the execution of the SubBytes operation (cycle 23.000 - 25.000), the SVF only finds leaks when the first or fifth S-box is computed. TVLA looks at all S-box operations and shows more leaks in cycles 23.000–25.000. This observation also holds for the cycles after SubBytes. TVLA indicates leaks in cycles where SVF does not show leakage. There are two possible explanations for this behaviour. The first is that TVLA shows false positives. The second is that the Hamming distance between the power traces and the oracles, that were used to calculate the SVF values, does not capture all the relations between the samples. The third plot shows the evolution in time of the SVF value, during the first round of the first execution of KECCAK-f, the SHA-3 permutation, for ALU.

The fourth plot shows the combined SVF with the t-value for the same module and implementation, i.e., ALU and SHA3. We observe that SHA-3 is extremely leaky, according to TVLA. While SHA-3 executes the KECCAK-f function multiple times, and one execution of KECCAK-f takes multiple rounds, SVF will only find leaks in the intermediate values we target. TVLA finds multiple leaks during the whole execution of SHA3.

5.2 Case Study: The Ibex Core

Figure 2 shows the leakage in ALU from the Ibex core for both AES and SHA-3. Similar to SHAKTI, the first plot shows the evolution in time of the SVF value, during the first round of AES and the second plot shows combined the SVF with the t-value. Also, the third plot shows the evolution in time of the SVF value during the first execution of SHA3 and the fourth plot shows the combined SVF with the t-value for the same module, ALU. As we observed in SHAKTI, for ALU, TVLA shows leakage in almost all cycles, while SVF shows only at some. We also observe that both methods find the same pattern of leaky cycles. This might indicate that the leakage is not caused only by one instruction but by a sequence of instructions as they are processed over time.

Figure 3 shows the leakage in the Register File from Ibex core for both AES and SHA-3. The second plot shows the SVF combined with the t-value for the same module. The Register File and ALU identify the same sequence of leaky operations. Again, TVLA shows more leaky points than SVF. The third plot shows the leakage value for SHA3, and the fourth plot, the combined SVF-TVLA. We observe that SVF shows severe leakage in the second half of this execution timing window. Specifically, the oracle *not* shows the same leaky points as TVLA, while in the first half of the execution, it identifies only a couple of leaky instructions. We also observe that oracle *xor* identifies leaky instructions, while oracle *bc* does not.

Figure 4 shows the combined SVF-TVLA on module MBOX from SHAKTI and Mult/Div from Ibex. Both modules are responsible for multiplication division. The first two plots show AES and SHA-3, respectively, for MBOX, while the last two show AES and SHA3, respectively, for Mult/Div. If we compare these plots with the plots from ALU, we observe a similar pattern of leakage, unexpected given the absence of multiplications or divisions in our code. Our examination of Ibex's RTL code revealed that the Register File outputs are

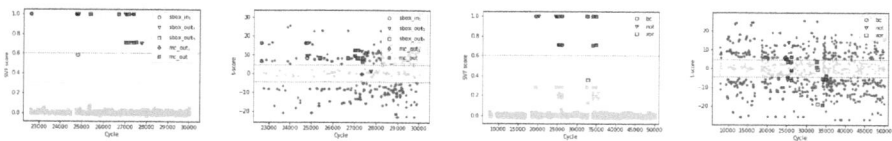

Fig. 1. SVF AES, combined SVF-TVLA AES, SVF SHA-3, combined SVF-TVLA SHA-3. For ALU module on SHAKTI core (left to right).

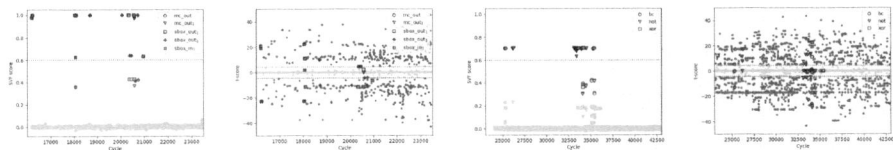

Fig. 2. SVF AES, combined SVF-TVLA AES, SVF SHA-3, combined SVF-TVLA SHA-3. For ALU module on Ibex core (left to right).

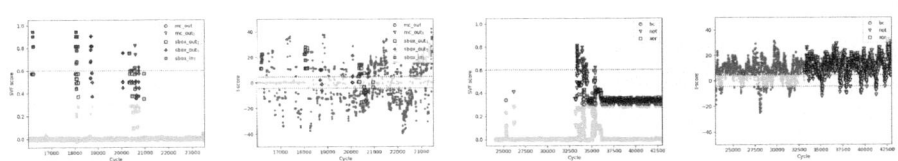

Fig. 3. SVF AES, combined SVF-TVLA AES, SVF SHA-3, combined SVF-TVLA SHA-3. For Register File on Ibex core (left to right).

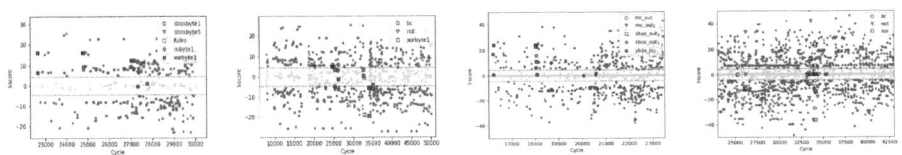

Fig. 4. SVF-TVLA for: AES MBOX(SHAKTI), SHA-3 MBOX(SHAKTI), AES Mult/Div(Ibex) and SHA-3 Mult/Div(Ibex) (left to right).

Table 1. Results for AES and SHA-3 on SHAKTI core

	AES						SHA-3			
Type	max(SVF)					TVLA	max(SVF)			TVLA
	$sbox\_in_1$	$sbox\_out_1$	$sbox\_out_5$	mc_out_1	mc_out		bc	not	xor	
Dcache	1	1	1	1	0.05	✓	0.99	1	1	✓
RF	1	1	1	1	0.05	✓	1	1	1	✓
CSR	0.98	0.98	0.98	0.98	0.05	✓	0.97	0.97	.97	✓
ALU	1	1	1	1	0.05	✓	1	1	1	✓
FPU	1	1	1	1	0.05	✓	1	1	1	✓
MBox	1	1	1	1	0.05	✓	1	1	1	✓
BPU	0	0	0	0	0	–	0	0	0	–
ITLB	0	0	0	0	0	–	0	0	0	–
DTLB	0.87	0.87	0.87	0.87	0.06	✓	0.3	0.3	0.31	✓

directly connected to both the ALU and Mult/Div unit, keeping both components active within the processor, regardless of their usage. Similar behavior was observed between the Register File and LSU, with leakage patterns on LSU mirroring those of the Register File, even while not only load/store instructions were executed. These observations confirmed that even non-utilized components within the processor can become sources of information leakage.

5.3 Performance Results

All experiments, for both the SHAKTI and the Ibex core, were done on an AMD Ryzen THREADRIPPER 3990X 4.3 GHz CPU with 128 cores and 256 GB RAM. On this PC, the run-time of the two methods is significantly different. For the SHAKTI core, the SVF computation of all the modules for the AES case study took around 30k cycles, which lasted approximately eight hours. The same experiment for the SHA-3 case study took around one day of computation. On the other hand, TVLA computation lasted about an hour for all modules for all case studies. For the Ibex core, the SVF computation of the algorithms took about twice the time compared to the SHAKTI core. The TVLA computation lasted less than an hour for all the modules of AES and SHA3. We can easily observe the contrast in run-time efficiency between the SVF and TVLA, which is crucial when choosing the appropriate method.

Table 2. Results for AES and SHA-3 on Ibex core

Type	AES max(SVF)					TVLA	SHA-3 max(SVF)			TVLA
	$sbox\_in_1$	$sbox\_out_1$	$sbox\_out_5$	mc_out_1	mc_out		bc	not	xor	
RF	0.94	0.9	0.9	0.82	0.05	✓	0.59	0.81	0.58	✓
CSR	0.97	0.97	0.97	0.95	0.05	✓	0.69	0.70	0.70	✓
ALU	1	0.99	1	0.99	0.06	✓	0.70	0.70	0.70	✓
MULT/DIV	0.99	0.99	1	0.84	0.04	✓	0.63	0.63	0.64	✓
PF-BUF	0	0	0	0	0	–	0	0	0	–
LSU	1	0.99	1	0.98	0.06	✓	0.96	0.96	0.96	✓

6 Conclusions and Future Work

In this study, we compared the performance of two different leakage detection methods, SVF and TVLA, in detecting leaky modules on microprocessors. We have conducted experiments on two RISC-V cores, SHAKTI and Ibex, using the cryptographic algorithms AES and SHA3. Our investigation has revealed interesting differences in how these methods identify potential leaks. Specifically, we observe peaks in cycles where SVF does not find any correlation between the oracle trace and the side-channel trace. In contrast, TVLA identifies a difference in the probability density functions of our fixed set and random set. This distinction can be explained by the fact that SVF targets an intermediate computation when determining leaks. Consequently, leakage points of any other intermediate data value are not included in a single SVF test. TVLA, on the other hand, adopts a much broader approach, evaluating the overall difference in probability density functions between the fixed and random sets, which allows it to detect potential leaks that SVF might miss.

Our results, presented in Table 1 and Table 2 for SHAKTI and Ibex cores respectively, for all examined modules, reveal no leaks in the BPU and ITLB modules on SHAKTI or the Prefetch buffer on Ibex, with both algorithms. This finding shows the importance of selecting the appropriate method based on the desired level of analysis granularity. For more coarse-grained analysis where a broad overview is beneficial, TVLA is recommended due to its lower computational effort and quicker results. On the other hand, SVF is better suited for fine-grained analysis that requires examining micro-architectural behavior in detail.

Moreover, our analysis highlights that TVLA and SVF show leaks in different cycles, opening questions about which metric more indicates the "correct" leak. This aspect, alongside the critical role of selecting the appropriate oracles, emphasizes the complexity of accurately detecting leakage. Not all oracles show leakage, potentially leading to incorrect conclusions about a module's security. Also, SVF uses the Pearson correlation coefficient to detect linear correlations. This means it might not find any non-linear relationships between the oracle trace and the side-channel trace. The generality of TVLA allows for broader applications, while the specificity of SVF, although powerful, necessitates careful oracle selection to ensure comprehensive leakage detection.

Moving forward, we plan to investigate further the differences between the SVF and TVLA methods, aiming to refine the process of hardening microprocessors against side-channel attacks. We also aim to explore other leakage detection methods and the impact of different implementations of cryptographic algorithms on the leakage profile of microprocessors. Ultimately, our goal is to contribute to developing more secure microprocessors that are robust against side-channel attacks.

Acknowledgments. This work was partially funded by the Dutch Research Council (NWO) through the PROACT project (NWA.1215.18.014).

References

1. Althoff, A., et al.: Hiding intermittent information leakage with architectural support for blinking. In: 45th ACM/IEEE Annual International Symposium on Computer Architecture, ISCA, Los Angeles, CA, USA, pp. 638–649 (2018). https://doi.org/10.1109/ISCA.2018.00059
2. Arora, V., Buhan, I., Perin, G., Picek, S.: A tale of two boards: on the influence of microarchitecture on side-channel leakage. In: Grosso, V., Pöppelmann, T. (eds.)

CARDIS 2021. LNCS, vol. 13173, pp. 80–96. Springer, Cham (2021). https://doi.org/10.1007/978-3-030-97348-3_5
3. Bloem, R., Gigerl, B., Gourjon, M., Hadzic, V., Mangard, S., Primas, R.: Power contracts: provably complete power leakage models for processors. In: Conference on Computer and Communications Security, CCS , Los Angeles, CA, USA, pp. 381–395. ACM (2022). https://doi.org/10.1145/3548606.3560600
4. Buhan, I., Batina, L., Yarom, Y., Schaumont, P.: SoK: design tools for side-channel-aware implementations. In: ASIA CCS 2022: ACM Asia Conference on Computer and Communications Security, Nagasaki, Japan, pp. 756–770. ACM (2022). https://doi.org/10.1145/3488932.3517415
5. Demme, J., Martin, R., Waksman, A., Sethumadhavan, S.: Side-channel vulnerability factor: a metric for measuring information leakage. In: 39th International Symposium on Computer Architecture (ISCA), pp. 106–117 (2012). https://doi.org/10.1109/ISCA.2012.6237010
6. F, M.A.K., Ganesan, V., Bodduna, R., Rebeiro, C.: PARAM: a microprocessor hardened for power side-channel attack resistance. In: International Symposium on Hardware Oriented Security and Trust, HOST, San Jose, CA, USA, pp. 23–34. IEEE (2020). https://doi.org/10.1109/HOST45689.2020.9300263
7. Gao, S., Großschädl, J., Marshall, B., Page, D., Pham, T.H., Regazzoni, F.: An instruction set extension to support software-based masking. IACR Trans. Cryptogr. Hardw. Embed. Syst., 283–325 (2021). https://doi.org/10.46586/tches.v2021.i4.283-325
8. Gigerl, B., Hadzic, V., Primas, R., Mangard, S., Bloem, R.: COCO: co-design and co-verification of masked software implementations on CPUs. In: 30th USENIX Security Symposium, USENIX, pp. 1469–1468 (2021)
9. Gilbert Goodwill, B.J., Jaffe, J., Rohatgi, P., et al.: A testing methodology for side-channel resistance validation. In: NIST Non-invasive Attack Testing Workshop, vol. 7, pp. 115–136 (2011)
10. He, M.T., Park, J., Nahiyan, A., Vassilev, A., Jin, Y., Tehranipoor, M.M.: RTL-PSC: automated power side-channel leakage assessment at register-transfer level. In: 37th IEEE VLSI Test Symposium, VTS Monterey, CA, USA, pp. 1–6 (2019). https://doi.org/10.1109/VTS.2019.8758600
11. Kiaei, P., Schaumont, P.: SoC root canal! Root cause analysis of power side-channel leakage in system-on-chip designs. IACR Trans. Cryptogr. Hardw. Embed. Syst., 751–773 (2022). https://doi.org/10.46586/tches.v2022.i4.751-773
12. Lakshmy, A.V., Rebeiro, C., Bhunia, S.: FORTIFY: analytical pre-silicon side-channel characterization of digital designs. In: 27th Asia and South Pacific Design Automation Conference, ASP-DAC, pp. 660–665. IEEE (2022). https://doi.org/10.1109/ASP-DAC52403.2022.9712551
13. lowRISC: Lowrisc/ibex-demo-system: A demo system for ibex. https://github.com/lowRISC/ibex-demo-system
14. Marshall, B., Page, D., Webb, J.: MIRACLE: micro-architectural leakage evaluation a study of micro-architectural power leakage across many devices. IACR Trans. Cryptogr. Hardw. Embed. Syst., 175–220 (2022). https://doi.org/10.46586/TCHES.V2022.I1.175-220
15. Mulder, E.D., Gummalla, S., Hutter, M.: Protecting RISC-V against side-channel attacks. In: Proceedings of the 56th Annual Design Automation Conference 2019, DAC, Las Vegas, NV, USA, p. 45 (2019). https://doi.org/10.1145/3316781.3323485
16. Pham, T.H., Marshall, B., Fell, A., Lam, S., Page, D.: XDIVINSA: extended diversifying instruction agent to mitigate power side-channel leakage. In: 32nd

IEEE International Conference on Application-specific Systems, Architectures and Processors, ASAP, pp. 179–186 (2021). https://doi.org/10.1109/ASAP52443.2021.00034
17. SHAKTI: Family of processors (2021). https://shakti.org.in/processors.html
18. SLPSK, P., Vairam, P.K., Rebeiro, C., Kamakoti, V.: Karna: a gate-sizing based security aware EDA flow for improved power side-channel attack protection. In: Proceedings of the International Conference on Computer-Aided Design, pp. 1–8 (2019). https://doi.org/10.1109/ICCAD45719.2019.8942173
19. Yao, Y., Kathuria, T., Ege, B., Schaumont, P.: Architecture correlation analysis (ACA): identifying the source of side-channel leakage at gate-level. In: International Symposium on Hardware Oriented Security and Trust, HOST, San Jose, CA, USA, pp. 188–196. IEEE (2020). https://doi.org/10.1109/HOST45689.2020.9300271
20. Zhang, T., Liu, F., Chen, S., Lee, R.B.: Side channel vulnerability metrics: the promise and the pitfalls. In: HASP 2013, The Second Workshop on Hardware and Architectural Support for Security and Privacy, Tel-Aviv, Israel, p. 2. ACM (2013). https://doi.org/10.1145/2487726.2487728

iVault: Architectural Code Concealing Techniques to Protect Cryptographic Keys

George Christou[1](✉), Giorgos Vasiliadis[2,3], Apostolis Zarras[3,4], and Sotiris Ioannidis[1,3]

[1] Technical University of Crete, Chania, Greece
gchristou@tuc.gr
[2] Department of Management Science and Technology, Hellenic Mediterranean University, Agios Nikolaos, Greece
[3] Foundation for Research and Technology – Hellas, Heraklion, Greece
[4] University of Piraeus, Piraeus, Greece

Abstract. Memory corruption bugs remain a significant concern in applications developed using memory-unsafe languages, such as C/C++. Adversaries can exploit these bugs and perform arbitrary read and write operations. These arbitrary reads can target cryptographic keys, severely compromising their secure operation. In this paper, we introduce iVault a lightweight approach to securely store private and secret cryptographic keys. iVault encodes cryptographic keys within the machine instruction immediates and leverage architectural mechanisms to protect the .text segment from being disclosed. We assess iVault in terms of performance and code size expansion, and we show that it represents a viable solution for safeguarding cryptographic keys.

Keywords: Hardware Assisted Security · Key Management

1 Introduction

Modern cryptography is typically used to protect sensitive or private data from being intercepted and/or leaked when transferred over the network or stored in memory. The adoption of cryptographic hardware extensions within commodity CPUs has reduced the overheads imposed from cryptographic operations on data, making cryptography mainstream and widely used in diverse set of applications [16,22]. Besides performance, cryptography is only effective in terms of security, as long as the cryptographic keys are adequately protected [15]. In fact, the process of securely storing and managing cryptographic keys used for encryption and decryption, known as key management, forms the basis for the end-to-end security of a system.

Key management is often considered quite challenging though, especially in cases where the keys must be accessed frequently, such as real-time processing or streaming applications. This is further exacerbated by the fact that the majority of crypto libraries are written in low-level languages, such as C/C++, mainly to access the architectural extensions available in modern CPUs for accelerating cryptography. Unfortunately, these low-level languages are not memory safe, and thus, memory corruption bugs can allow attackers to manipulate the memory contents and access sensitive information, such as secret or private cryptographic keys. One such example is the Heartbleed bug that allowed buffer over-reads due to improper input validation [14]. This bug can be exploited to disclose the cryptographic keys from the main memory and has affected an enormous amount of computing systems and users, due to the popularity of the affected library [8].

To tackle this problem, several academic works have been proposed to define safe regions for storing sensitive data [23,24]. These works mostly focus on intra-process isolation, since traditional operating systems offer strong isolation guarantees between processes. Among these, the deployment of memory safety mechanisms to the C and C++ programming languages can restrict memory accesses and eliminate memory corruption vulnerabilities. However, these mechanisms lack practicality due to high performance overhead. Other approaches utilize hardware-based Trusted Execution Environments (TEEs), such as Intel SGX [17], AMD SEV [1], or ARM TrustZone [2]. These TEEs provide secure and isolated environments where the code and the keys can reside, preventing unauthorized access or tampering from any outside entity. Still, current hardware-based TEEs do not guarantee the memory safety of code that has been developed with memory unsafe languages such as C and C++. As a consequence, programs running inside TEEs face the same memory corruption vulnerabilities as traditional software, allowing attackers to violate their confidentiality.

In this work, we propose `iVault`, a lightweight approach to securely store private and secret cryptographic keys as immediates in machine code. The machine code is then protected using hardware-assisted techniques that are able to *hide* the `.text` segment of binaries. By doing so, the encoded keys are sufficiently protected in case of memory corruption vulnerabilities that allow an attacker to disclose arbitrary memory regions. `iVault` implements a representative set of popular cryptographic algorithms, in which the cryptographic keys are encoded as immediates in the corresponding machine code. `iVault` also provides a set of API functions that allow to easily encode the cryptographic keys on demand.

We implement `iVault` in two different architectures: SPARC and x86. For SPARC, we employ a modified Leon3 processor that is equipped with Instruction Set Randomization. In the case of the x86, we take advantage of Intel Memory Protection Keys (MPKs), a feature available on recent Intel processor models. Our evaluation shows that `iVault` can effectively prevent the exploitation of memory disclosure bugs that target cryptographic keys, with an average overhead of 0.36% in x86 and 8.93% in SPARC.

2 Background

In this section we briefly describe the two architectural features that we utilize for the implementation of `iVault` in regards to the protection of the .text segment: Instruction Set Randomization and Memory Protection Keys.

2.1 Instruction Set Randomization

Instruction Set Randomization (ISR) aims to fortify applications against code injection attacks [20]. Its fundamental concept involves the randomization of the instruction set of each process through encryption. Thus, any injected code will likely fail to execute, as decryption takes place before entering into the processor's instruction cache, potentially resulting in invalid code. Originally, ISR was not conceived to defend against Code Reuse Attacks (CRAs) such as Return Oriented Programming (ROP) [25] and Jump Oriented Programming (JOP) [6]. However, ISR schemes with strong encryption can thwart CRAs by obstructing the disclosure of useful gadgets. In ISR, the .text segment is encrypted, causing data accesses on this section to return encrypted bytes. In `iVault`, we leverage ASIST [10], a modified Leon3 processor [13], which provides three distinct encryption modes for ISR: XOR, Transposition, and AES. In `iVault` we opt for the AES variant due to its ability to also defend against CRAs and its resilience against cryptographic attacks such as known-plaintext-ciphertext.

Overall, `iVault` relies on the capability of ISR to prevent the disclosure of the .text segment, thereby enabling us to *conceal* cryptographic keys. Consequently, any arbitrary memory read attempt will fail to unveil this information to potential attackers.

2.2 Memory Protection Keys

Memory Protection Keys (MPK) is a mechanism introduced recently in Intel processors [18]. It allows user-space applications to directly modify the access rights on groups of memory pages. Each group of pages is associated with a unique key, with applications capable of managing up to 16 page groups. The access rights for each page group are delineated in a thread-local and user-accessible register known as the Protection Keys Rights Register (for users), denoted as %pkru. Given that the %pkru register is specific to each thread, MPK facilitates a per-thread perspective of the process's memory. For instance, distinct application threads possess different access rights configured for each key within their respective %pkru register.

If a memory page is marked as executable in the page table but configured with no access in the %pkru register, the memory page is treated as execute-only. This occurs since any attempt at data access will lead to a mismatch between the rights specified in the page table and those in the %pkru register. Linux leverages MPK to support execute-only memory pages. Invoking `mprotect` with only PROT_EXEC specified as permissions will result in the allocation of a

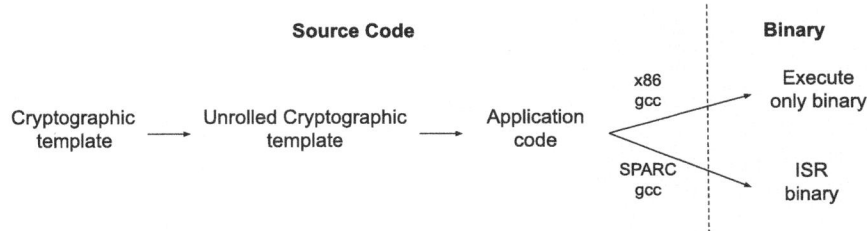

Fig. 1. iVault template inclusion in applications.

protection key associated with the memory pages passed to mprotect. Subsequently, the %pkru register will be set to DISABLE_ACCESS for the newly allocated protection key, while the page table rights will be configured as executable and readable. Any attempt to access execute-only pages, except for instruction fetching, will trigger a memory violation exception.

In iVault, we leverage execute-only memory to achieve similar properties as with ISR. By preventing read access on the .text segment, the embedded keys will not be disclosed due to memory corruption bugs.

3 Threat Model

Our threat model assumes adversaries can exploit memory and type unsafety in applications that utilize cryptography. Consequently, an attacker can exploit memory corruption vulnerabilities to enable arbitrary memory read capabilities. These vulnerabilities can lead to unauthorized access to sensitive data. Finally, we consider side-channel attacks and hardware faults as out of scope.

To secure keys stored in the .text segment, specific OS and hardware features are necessary. We presume the $W^\wedge X$ policy is enforced, and the application excludes self-modifying code. Our cryptographic implementations are designed to coexist with other security mechanisms, such as AppArmor and RELRO, which can further enhance application protection. The hardware must include Memory Protection Keys or a functionally equivalent mechanism. For our Leon3 implementation, we employ ISR. Although our required hardware feature is not as standard as our OS prerequisites, it is included in the latest Intel server CPU series. Additionally, the MPK functionality can be emulated through memory tagging, which is available in ARM's latest processor series [4].

4 Design

We outline the design of iVault and the cryptographic suite that implements. For each cryptographic algorithm, iVault uses templates that can be employed to encode the keys as immediate operands at various stages of the application's life-cycle, such as post-compilation, program initialization, or program execution.

4.1 Source Code Transformations

To correctly embed the keys for each cryptographic algorithm, it is essential to ensure that every cryptographic operation is implemented as a block of instructions with only one entry and exit point, namely *basic block*. This is required because, otherwise, it would be impractical to modify the instruction immediates at runtime, on every iteration of an encryption algorithm (e.g., AES requires 10 loops). To unroll the loops, we serialize and transform each round of the block ciphers implemented in iVault as shown in Fig. 1, ensuring that all data operations are executed without any branch present.

4.2 Cryptographic Key Set

The cryptographic keys are set at various stages of an application's life cycle. Initially, the immediates of the key instructions are set to dummy values. Each cryptographic function is analyzed to produce a map of the key byte locations. The real key is embedded by iterating through the map that locates key part positions within the binary. At this stage, instructions that carry key parts are patched to incorporate the key used during the application's execution. Next, the key can be modified during the application's runtime, a functionality that varies with the architecture in which iVault is implemented. For the x86 architecture, the function included in the cryptographic library modifies the key parts at runtime, utilizing the key map. In contrast, in our ISR-based implementation, where the .text area is encrypted, and the ISR key is stored in the kernel process table; we depend on the ISR-aware operating system to correctly encrypt the rewritten cryptographic functions—those patched with the new encryption key. As we show in Sect. 6, encoding the cryptographic keys in the instructions immediates reduces the memory accesses required during each cryptographic operation.

5 Implementation

We now describe the implementation details of iVault for symmetric and asymmetric key cryptography, respectively.

5.1 Symmetric Cryptography

We implement two block ciphers to evaluate the design of iVault: XTEA and AES. XTEA is a block cipher encryption algorithm that operates on 64-bit data blocks using a 128-bit key and employs a Feistel network structure [28]. This involves splitting the input data into two halves, performing a series of operations on each, and then merging the outcomes. The key generates multiple round keys that alter the data during each Feistel cycle, with a typical configuration of 64 rounds, enhancing its security. Due to its simplicity, speed, and compact code size, XTEA is frequently chosen for embedded systems. We unroll the algorithm loops for the cryptographic key embedding and replace key array accesses with dummy constant values. We then compile this modified code into a binary that embeds these dummy parts as immediates in the machine instructions. Now, a script associates each key part with the corresponding instruction and patches the binary with the real key.

We also implement AES algorithm in ECB mode, in which the input data is partitioned into fixed-size blocks (128 bits for AES), that are encrypted separately using the same key. This direct encryption process requires no extra data or computations beyond the key and the input data. Identical plaintext blocks will consistently yield the same ciphertext blocks. Our approach to implement ECB is similar to XTEA: we unroll all rounds, use constant values as a dummy key, and later patch the actual key to be used in the targeted binary.

5.2 Asymmetric Cryptography

In `iVault`, we incorporate the 256-bit Elliptic Curve Digital Signature Algorithm (ECDSA) [19], which is a digital signature algorithm that leverages elliptic curve cryptography (ECC). ECDSA is widely used to verify the authenticity, integrity, and non-repudiation of digital messages and transactions. The ECDSA process involves a pair of public and private keys; the private key generates digital signatures, whereas the public key is used for their verification.

The algorithm initiates by creating a random number, known as a nonce, to determine a point on an elliptic curve. This point is then used to calculate the signature, comprising a pair of integers: the x-coordinate and a value derived from the nonce and the elliptic curve point. For signature verification, the receiver employs the sender's public key to compute the corresponding elliptic curve point and verifies its congruence with the point involved in the signature creation. The receiver then validates the signature using the same mathematical procedures originally used to generate it. In `iVault`, we have implemented the sign function, the sole function that employs the private key. A notable distinction from the block ciphers we have developed is that ECDSA utilizes a large integer for the key rather than a byte array.

5.3 Architectural Specific Implementations

We implement `iVault` on two different architectures: x86 and SPARC. A notable distinction in our approach is that our x86 processor operates on a 64-bit architecture, whereas our SPARC processor is a 32-bit. This architectural difference does not affect our block ciphers; however, for ECDSA, the key division involves four instructions on the x86 architecture and eight on the SPARC architecture.

We also employ different architectural extensions specific to each architecture to enhance security. For the x86 implementation, we use MPK to designate the page containing the cryptographic functions as execute-only. Conversely, we use ISR for the SPARC implementation to encrypt the entire `.text` segment of the application that employs the `iVault` cryptographic suite. A notable difference is that in our ISR implementation, the whole `.text` segment is protected, whereas, in x86, only the pages containing the cryptographic operations are configured as execute only. Thus, in our x86 implementation, we have to page-align the first sensitive function and the first non-sensitive function to avoid the co-existence of cryptographic functions with normal ones on the same page.

5.4 Changing Encryption Keys

In each of our implementations, we have developed functions that enable the cryptographic key to be changed at runtime. For the x86 architecture, this function employs *mprotect* to mark the page containing the cryptographic function as writable. Then, the new key is patched into the immediates of the instructions using the map we produced during the initial stages of the implementation. This map includes the address offset of key parts in the cryptographic functions, calculating the true address by adding the function's base load address to the offset in the map. After patching the new key, the key change function uses *mprotect* again to set the access rights to execute only.

In our ISR implementation, direct modification of the cryptographic functions' code is not feasible, as it is encrypted, and the key resides solely in kernel space. Therefore, we first use *mprotect* to make the pages containing the cryptographic functions writable and then completely overwrite them with a new function embedded with the new cryptographic key. We then use the *asist_encrypt* system call to encrypt the new function with the process's ISR key. Finally, we call *mprotect* once more to set the access rights to executable.

6 Evaluation

We evaluate iVault in terms of security and in terms of performance. To achieve this, we use a set of popular cryptographic algorithms both in standalone setups and real-world scenarios. Our aim is to answer the following evaluation questions:

EQ1: Can iVault protect cryptographic keys against memory disclosure?
EQ2: What is the impact of iVault on the binary code size?
EQ3: What is the impact of iVault on the runtime performance?

6.1 Security Analysis (EQ1)

We assess the resilience of iVault by delineating attacks conforming to our threat model, described in Sect. 3. We also implement synthetic attack scenarios to showcase how iVault prevents the extraction of cryptographic keys from an application.

Arbitrary Memory Reads. In iVault, the cryptographic keys reside only within the .text area of an application, which is sufficiently isolated in both implementations (i.e., x86 and SPARC). On x86 architectures, accesses to the .text segment are prohibited because it is configured with execute-only permissions. Similarly, in our customized SPARC V8 processor, the .text segment

Table 1. The code size growth (in bytes) of iVault in the execute-only memory version (x86).

Bench	Vanilla	iVault	Overhead
XTEA	1205	16981	1309.21%
AES	6789	13189	94.27 %
ECC	30581	34677	13.39 %
SQLite	868564	881412	1.48 %

Table 2. The code size growth (in bytes) of iVault in the Instruction Set Randomization version (SPARC).

Bench	Vanilla	iVault	Overhead
XTEA	29496	44428	50.62%
AES	49852	56624	13.58 %
ECC	87780	94312	7.44 %
SQLite	1207720	1221992	1.18 %

is encrypted. Consequently, any attempts at arbitrary read primitives, such as buffer over-reads and use-after-free, will fail to disclose the cryptographic keys.

Extracting Intermediate States. In iVault, each cryptographic algorithm is realized as a basic block, implemented as a code block without any branches. During every cryptographic operation, the function executes independently of any other variables in the application. At the epilogue of each function, we ensure that any intermediate states generated during the cryptographic operation are nullified and, therefore, cannot be retrieved (e.g., through arbitrary reads accessible from other code blocks).

Code Reuse Attacks. A major class of exploitation techniques that target memory vulnerabilities is code reuse attacks. In this scenario, the attacker exploits arbitrary memory writes to overwrite control-flow variables. Still, an attacker might use the iVault's API to alter the cryptographic keys. Nonetheless, this action would not disclose any data encrypted with previous keys. For code reuse attacks to succeed, the attacker must know in advance the location of the code snippets necessary to implement the payload. However, the .text segments of iVault are unreadable, rendering the attacker unaware of the location of useful code. The idea of removing read access from the code segment has been studied [3]. Advanced code reuse attack techniques have demonstrated that applications can still be exploited even without knowledge of the layout of the .text segment [5]. However, concealing the code segment significantly raises the bar for a successful code reuse attack.

Take Away: iVault can effectively protect cryptographic keys in applications against arbitrary reads.

6.2 Overhead on the Code Size (EQ2)

As we mention in Sect. 4.1, iVault unrolls each and every loop contained in the targeted cryptographic algorithm in order to have only a *large* basic block that contains all the instructions that will encrypt or decrypt a block of data. This inevitably expands the .text segment size of the final binary, which we measure by comparing the original versions of the algorithms utilized for prototyping iVault with the modified binaries. As depicted in Table 1, the growth of the .text segment in our execute-only memory implementation surpasses that of our ISR implementation. This disparity stems from MPKs operating on a per-page granularity. Thus, we page-aligned the first *sensitive* function and the first subsequent non-sensitive function of the binary. In the case of XTEA algorithm, this increases .text by half a page (approximately). One could argue that the execute-only memory could be applied to the whole .text segment in order to reduce growth. However, this is not always possible since compilers may emit data (e.g., jump tables) in the .text segment.

We note that the ISR implementation does not require page-aligning sensitive functions, since the whole application is protected. To protect binaries, we compile them statically and without jump tables and strict aliasing (emit data to the .text segment). We also use the same compilation flags for both vanilla and iVault binaries in order to gather consistent measurements for code size growth and runtime performance. As we observe in Table 2, the percentage of the code added is lower since the binaries are statically linked and are amortized in both cases when the implementations are included in larger code bases (i.e. in ECC and SQLite).

Take Away: iVault code size overhead is not prohibitive in applications with large code base.

6.3 Runtime Performance Evaluation (EQ3)

To assess the runtime performance of iVault, we run benchmarks on popular cryptographic algorithms and real application scenarios. The standalone execution of cryptographic operations can pinpoint the performance impact of our modifications, while large applications provide us more insights with regards to the real-world expected impact.

Setup. We evaluate iVault on x86 and SPARC V8 architectures. Our x86 system features an Intel Core i9-10900 CPU with 32GB RAM and runs Linux version 5.4.0–84. To ensure consistent measurements, we disable frequency scaling and turbo boost. For evaluating iVault on the ISR-enabled SPARC V8 processor, we utilize a Leon3 processor configured with a 64-KB (4-way associative) instruction cache. The cache operates with a single level and follows a pure Harvard architecture. We synthesize and map the ISR-enabled Leon3 processor onto a Xilinx XUPV5 ML509 FPGA board with 256 MB DDR2 SDRAM memory, operated at 80-MHz core clock frequency. Our measurements include the overhead imposed by the ISR, as we run the vanilla results on a non-ISR Leon3 with identical configuration (frequency, RAM).

Algorithms and Applications. We first evaluate iVault by executing standalone cryptographic functions of individual algorithms. We measure the execution time of iVault by executing 1M cryptographic operations (encryption and decryption) for XTEA and AES and 1K ECDSA operations. We then modify SQLite and Mbed TLS to validate our approach in real-world scenarios further. Our modified SQLite utilizes AES to provide fully encrypted databases, while in Mbed TLS, we alter the ECDSA signing and verification functions. For SQLite, we run the default benchmark values in x86 (100K entries), while in Leon3, we configured the benchmark to operate on 100 entries due to the system's limited capabilities.

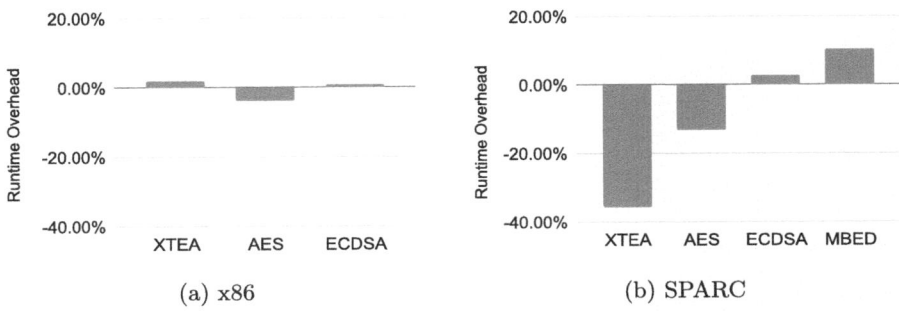

Fig. 2. The runtime overheads of iVault for different cryptographic algorithms.

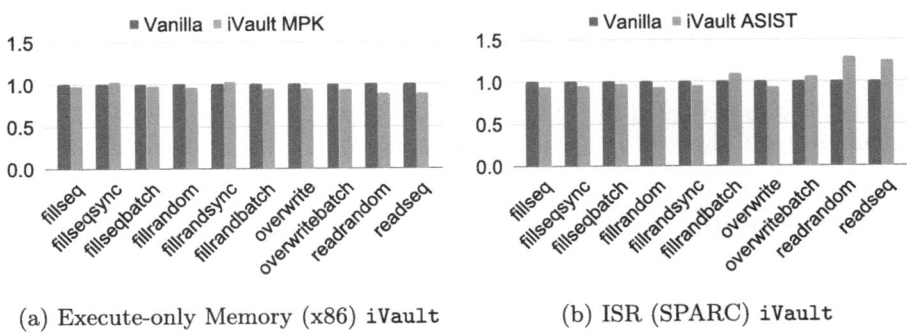

Fig. 3. The performance overheads of iVault when running SQLite benchmarks

Our findings suggest that iVault is a practical security strategy. In x86 (Fig. 2a), the runtime performance ranges between -3.8% to 2% and is affected negatively by the code size growth and reduced cache locality (due to page-alignment) and positively by the reduced number of memory operations required for each cryptographic operations. This is especially prevalent in our SPARC implementation (Fig. 2b), where the reduced amount of memory operations amortize the overhead imposed due to ISR, while ECC and Mbed TLS are negatively affected since they do not stress the memory subsystem (128-bit*10 round keys for AES vs. 256-bit private key for ECDSA).

In SQLite, both implementations enhance the performance of most benchmarks (Fig. 3). Slowdowns can be observed in our ISR implementation (Fig. 3b) when random and read sequences are introduced. This might be because SQLite's code size is two times larger than Leon3's instruction cache, and the cache evictions will require the invocation of the ISR unit when the instructions are cached again.

Take Away: `iVault` is practical in terms of runtime performance and benefits from the reduced stress on the memory subsystem.

7 Related Work

A number of works aim to protect cryptographic keys from memory bugs. PixelVault [27] and GRIM [21] use similar code concealing techniques, but for GPU programs. Other frameworks have been designed to safeguard data. For instance, AEGIS framework [26] supports secure operational environments and essential trusted computing functionalities for handling security-sensitive applications. Similarly, Bastion [9] integrates a memory authentication mechanism into the microprocessor, delivering safeguards against software and physical threats. These academic proposals paved the way to include TEEs in commodity processors. Intel Software Guard eXtensions (SGX) [11] aim to provide integrity and privacy guarantees to security-sensitive applications while narrowing the trusted computing base to just the processor's chip. Proposals like Sanctum [12] and MI6 [7] aim to exceed Intel SGX's security capabilities for the RISC-V CPU architecture but also add safeguards against micro-architectural side-channels.

8 Conclusions

We propose `iVault`, a novel mechanism to safeguard cryptographic keys by utilizing architectural extensions for code concealment. Our strategy was implemented on both x86 and SRARC architectures, demonstrating the advantages of execute-only memory and Instruction Set Randomization in protecting cryptographic keys. Our findings indicate that even though `iVault` leads to an increase in the size of the `.text` segment, it also decreases memory operations and enhances the performance of cryptographic functions.

Acknowledgements. This work has been supported by the European Union's Horizon Europe research and innovation programme under grant agreements No. 101070599 (SecOPERA), 101120962 (RESCALE), and 101120726 (dAIEDGE). Views and opinions expressed are however those of the authors only and do not necessarily reflect those of the European Union or REA. Neither the European Union nor the granting authority can be held responsible for them.

References

1. AMD: Secure Encrypted Virtualization (SEV). https://www.amd.com/en/developer/sev.html
2. ARM: Trustzone. https://www.arm.com/products/security-on-arm/trustzone
3. Backes, M., Holz, T., Kollenda, B., Koppe, P., Nürnberger, S., Pewny, J.: You can run but you can't read: preventing disclosure exploits in executable code. In: ACM SIGSAC Conference on Computer and Communications Security (2014)
4. Bannister, S.: Memory tagging extension: Enhancing memory safety through architecture. ARM Community (2018)
5. Bittau, A., Belay, A., Mashtizadeh, A., Mazières, D., Boneh, D.: Hacking blind. In: IEEE Symposium on Security and Privacy (2014)
6. Bletsch, T., Jiang, X., Freeh, V.W., Liang, Z.: Jump-oriented programming: a new class of code-reuse attack. In: ACM ASIACCS (2011)
7. Bourgeat, T., Lebedev, I., Wright, A., Zhang, S., Arvind, Devadas, S.: Mi6: Secure enclaves in a speculative out-of-order processor. In: IEEE/ACM Micro (2019)
8. Carvalho, M., DeMott, J., Ford, R., Wheeler, D.A.: Heartbleed 101. IEEE Sec. Priv. **12**(4), 63–67 (2014)
9. Champagne, D., Lee, R.B.: Scalable architectural support for trusted software. In: International Symposium on High-Performance Computer Architecture (2010)
10. Christou, G., Vasiliadis, G., Papaefstathiou, V., Papadogiannakis, A., Ioannidis, S.: On architectural support for instruction set randomization. ACM Trans. Architect. Code Optimiz. (TACO) **17**(4), 1–26 (2020)
11. Costan, V., Devadas, S.: Intel SGX explained. Cryptology ePrint Archive (2016)
12. Costan, V., Lebedev, I., Devadas, S.: Sanctum: minimal hardware extensions for strong software isolation. In: USENIX Security Symposium (2016)
13. Daněk, M., et al.: The leon3 processor. UTLEON3: Exploring Fine-Grain Multi-Threading in FPGAs, pp. 9–14 (2013)
14. Durumeric, Z et al.: The matter of heartbleed. In: Internet Measurement Conference (IMC) (2014)
15. Harrison, K., Xu, S.: Protecting cryptographic keys from memory disclosure attacks. In: 37th IEEE/IFIP DSN, pp. 137–143. IEEE (2007)
16. Hofemeier, G., Chesebrough, R.: Introduction to Intel AES-NI and Intel Secure Key Instructions. Intel, White Paper **62** (2012)
17. Intel: Software Guard Extensions. https://www.intel.com/content/dam/develop/external/us/en/documents/329298-002-629101.pdf
18. Intel: Intel Memory Protection Keys (2022). https://www.kernel.org/doc/html/latest/core-api/protection-keys.html
19. Johnson, D., Menezes, A., Vanstone, S.: The elliptic curve digital signature algorithm (ecdsa). Int. J. Inf. Secur. **1**, 36–63 (2001)
20. Kc, G.S., Keromytis, A.D., Prevelakis, V.: Countering code-injection attacks with instruction-set randomization. In: ACM CCS (2003)
21. Koromilas, L., Vasiliadis, G., Athanasopoulos, E., Ioannidis, S.: GRIM: Leveraging GPUs for Kernel Integrity Monitoring. In: Monrose, F., Dacier, M., Blanc, G., Garcia-Alfaro, J. (eds.) RAID 2016. LNCS, vol. 9854, pp. 3–23. Springer, Cham (2016). https://doi.org/10.1007/978-3-319-45719-2_1
22. Kounavis, M.E., Kang, X., Grewal, K., Eszenyi, M., Gueron, S., Durham, D.: Encrypting the Internet. ACM SIGCOMM CCR **40**(4), 135–146 (2010)
23. Mao, Y., Chen, H., Zhou, D., Wang, X., Zeldovich, N., Kaashoek, M.F.: Software fault isolation with API integrity and multi-principal modules. In: ACM SOSP (2011)

24. McCamant, S., Morrisett, G.: Evaluating sfi for a cisc architecture. In: USENIX Security Symposium (2006)
25. Shacham, H.: The Geometry of Innocent Flesh on the Bone: Return-into-libc Without Function Calls (on the x86). In: ACM CCS (2007)
26. Suh, G.E., Clarke, D., Gassend, B., Van Dijk, M., Devadas, S.: AEGIS: Architecture for tamper-evident and tamper-resistant processing. In: ACM ICS (2003)
27. Vasiliadis, G., Athanasopoulos, E., Polychronakis, M., Ioannidis, S.: PixelVault: Using GPUs for securing cryptographic operations. In: ACM SIGSAC CCS (2014)
28. Wheeler, D.J., Needham, R.M.: Correction to xtea. Unpublished manuscript, Computer Laboratory, Cambridge University, England **1**(2), 17 (1998)

I2DS: FPGA-Based Deep Learning Industrial Intrusion Detection System

Ioannis Morianos[1,2(✉)], Konstantinos Georgopoulos[1], Andreas Brokalakis[1], Thomas Kyriakakis[1,2], and Sotiris Ioannidis[1,2]

[1] Technical University of Crete, Chania, Crete, Greece
{imorianos,kgeorgopoulos,abrokalakis,tkyriakakis,sioannidis}@tuc.gr
[2] Dienekes, Heraklion, Crete, Greece

Abstract. The use of IoT systems in industrial environments provides tremendous benefits and economic value leading to an exponential rise in their adoption. Their extended use, however, does not come without concerns related to potential security threats, thereby creating an obstacle in their further use in the field. To address these security concerns, we introduce a specialized Industrial Intrusion Detection System (I2DS). Our proposed system merges the capabilities of deep learning (DL) with FPGA-based hardware acceleration techniques, enabling it to detect subtle anomalies and potential cyber threats that may evade conventional rule-based intrusion detection systems (IDS) in an effective way. More specifically, by implementing the system on FPGA hardware, we achieve low-latency, high-throughput processing of network traffic, essential for real-time intrusion detection in industrial settings. Our architecture is scalable and can be adapted according to network bandwidth requirements, while remaining lightweight, making it an ideal solution for the stringent resource constraints often encountered in IoT environments. The proposed solution has been validated with the modbus TON-IoT dataset, achieving up to two orders of magnitude higher performance compared to a software equivalent implementation.

Keywords: Intrusion detection systems · Deep learning · Industrial environments · Hardware Acceleration · FPGA

1 Introduction

With the proliferation of Internet of Things (IoT) devices and the expanding inter-connectivity of industrial networks, the exposure to cyber threats has escalated considerably [5,23]. As a result, Industrial Intrusion Detection Systems (I2DS) schemes play a crucial role in mitigating these risks by actively monitoring network traffic for suspicious activities.

Traditionally, Intrusion Detection Systems (IDS) like SNORT[1] have relied on rules and signatures [16,17] to identify known patterns of malicious behavior. While effective for known threats, these rule-based approaches struggle to adapt to the evolving landscape of cyber threats, leaving industrial systems vulnerable to novel attacks and sophisticated adversaries.

Consequently, during the past decade we have witnessed a notable surge in the adoption and development of Deep Learning (DL) and Machine Learning (ML) techniques [11,19,26] applied to intrusion detection systems. Driven by the availability of large-scale datasets (containing both normal and malicious network traffic), advances in computing power and breakthroughs in algorithmic innovation, it has been able to train those IDSes to distinguish between benign and suspicious behavior and report new and previously unseen threats. As such, ML- and DL-based IDSes (e.g. [7,8,20,22,27]) have emerged as a powerful alternative to traditional rule-based IDSes.

However, the use of ML-based IDSes is not without challenges and compared to rule-based IDSes, they can generate more false positives although in the case of industrial environments, where security is paramount, this may be an acceptable tradeoff. ML-based IDSes, however, require significantly more computational resources than typical IDS systems and this can be challenging for an Industrial IoT installation. Cost, latency issues (especially when real-time monitoring is required) and scalability concerns when multiple nodes and high-bandwidth network traffic have to be handled can be a show-stopper for such computationally-heavy solutions.

To mitigate this challenge, custom hardware solutions may prove to be an efficient alternative. In particular, Field-Programmable Gate Arrays (FPGAs) can offer a promising solution by providing hardware acceleration for ML tasks. Unlike CPUs and GPUs, which are general-purpose processors, FPGAs can be tailored to specific applications at the hardware-level, offering higher efficiency, lower latency and lower power consumption for computational tasks. At the same time, compared to ASICs, they retain their flexibility and are able to adapt to changes and updates post-deployment, which is crucial for security solutions.

As such, in this paper, we propose a novel approach that combines the power of ML-based approaches with the efficiency of FPGA-based hardware acceleration to develop an Industrial Intrusion Detection System (I2DS) tailored to industrial data requirements. Our contributions are the following:

- By leveraging ML/DL techniques, our I2DS can detect subtle anomalies and potential cyber threats that may evade traditional rule-based IDS. Furthermore, by accelerating the computational tasks on FPGA hardware, we achieve low-latency, high-throughput processing of network traffic, essential for real-time intrusion detection in industrial environments.
- Our implementation targets devices that integrate ARM CPU cores and FPGA hardware providing high degrees of flexibility and performance.

---

[1] https://www.snort.org/.

- Our architecture is scalable by employing parallelization techniques to enhance throughput, thus it can be adapted to different scenarios of varying performance requirements.
- Compared to equivalent software solutions, the proposed solution offers orders of magnitude higher performance at power envelopes that are suitable for deployment at almost all levels of IoT environments.

The paper is structured as follows. Section 2 summarises previous work on FPGA-based IDSes and ML-based IDSes and the background of this paper. Section 3 describes the process required for the preparation and training of the I2DS ML model. Section 4 describes the proposed hardware architecture. Section 5 presents the experimental setup and the results of our work. Finally, Sect. 6 concludes the paper and comments on future work directions.

2 Background and Related Work

The concept of using hardware accelerators in the form of FPGA devices for intrusion detection systems is by no means a new one. Implementations such as those reported in [2,10,21,28] have gained significant traction, due to their ability to efficiently process and analyze network traffic in real-time. By offloading processing tasks onto specialized hardware [4,15], these systems can perform deep packet inspection, pattern matching, and anomaly detection with minimal impact on network performance.

Ioannou et al. [9] trained a three-layer fully connected neural network with one hidden layer containing 21 hidden neurons on the NSL-KDD dataset. They accelerated this network using a Xilinx Zynq Z-7020 FPGA and their architecture reportedly supports a throughput of more than 10 Gbps, while achieving an accuracy of 80.52%.

While the aforementioned solutions follow a fully-custom hardware design approach, several frameworks have emerged that assist the mapping of a software-based model to an FPGA. AMD (Xilinx) has developed Vitis AI[2], a tool that produces Deep-Learning Processor Units (DPUs) that can be instantiated in the fabric of the FPGA and support a rich set of AI models that can be accelerated.

Similarly, frameworks exist for a more model-specific/custom hardware design implementations such as HLS4ML[3], which is a Python package for machine learning inference in FPGAs. Fahim et al. [6] propose a framework that translates traditional open-source machine learning package models into C++ code that can be employed by modern High Level Synthesis (HLS) tools.

Recently, AMD (Xilinx) introduced FINN [3,18,25], an open-source framework designed to implement specialized accelerators on FPGAs by harnessing reduced-precision datatypes and streaming dataflow architectures. This framework tailors hardware architectures to suit the specific requirements of Deep

---

[2] https://www.xilinx.com/products/design-tools/vitis/vitis-ai.html.
[3] https://opensource.web.cern.ch/HLS4ML.

Neural Network (DNN) topologies and precise datatypes. Each layer is instantiated with dedicated compute units in hardware and on-chip data streams connect these units to establish the desired network topology. By leveraging the compact size of reduced-precision DNNs, FINN enables the storage of all parameters on the chip, thereby, circumventing potential memory bottlenecks associated with off-chip memory access. To describe the generated Quantized Neural Network (QNN) accelerators, FINN generates synthesizable C++-based HLS code.

Using the FINN toolchain for FPGA implementation, Le Jeune et al. [12] present a near real-time NIDS trained using UNSW-NB15 and CICIDS2017 datasets. They propose the utilization of flow buckets for extraction of raw traffic-based features and the acceleration of neural network architectures for intrusion detection. They additionally demonstrate that their deep learning architectures retain performance even when quantized towards 2-bit weights and activations.

Umuroglu et al. [24] introduced LogicNets as an approach to co-design neural networks and hardware circuits specifically targeted to extreme-throughput applications. By representing neurons as truth tables with defined input and output bit sizes, LogicNets enable scalable designs capable of high clock frequencies of up to 471 MHz while maintaining strong performance with 91.30% accuracy on a network architecture trained with the UNSW-NB15 dataset.

Lastly, Ngo et al. [14] deployed an FPGA anomaly-based AI-assisted IDS for IoT devices by using the IoT-23 dataset. Their results show 40.5x speedup over the Quadro M2000 GPU. They use DMA for the communication between the Programmable Logic (PL) and Processing System (PS) and the performance of the hardware accelerated IDS is bounded only by the memory access overheads.

The aforementioned works demonstrate the performance benefits that FPGA acceleration offers to ML-based IDSes. However, because of the complexity of the designs at the hardware level, almost all modern solutions rely on high-level frameworks to generate the hardware accelerators that are mapped to the reconfigurable resources. While for productivity and functional verification purposes, this is definitely the design approach that is most beneficial, we recognize that such high-level approaches introduce overheads that cannot be ignored, both at the performance level and at the resources that are required. As such, we propose a design approach that on one hand leverages this high-level workflow from model design to hardware generation, but employs a more custom architecture and replaces python-related structures with lower level C code aiming to provide higher performance and minimize associated overheads (Fig. 1).

3 QNN Model Design

3.1 Industrial Enviroment Dataset

Our work targets the industrial IoT environments. As such, the model we designed was trained with the TON IoT[4] Modbus dataset of the UNSW [1,13]. Modbusservice simulates the functionality of the Modbus devices found in many

---

[4] https://research.unsw.edu.au/projects/toniot-datasets.

industrial applications. These devices interact with each other using a master-slave communication to transmit register types such as input, discrete, holding and Coil over serial lines.

Feature	Description
ts	Timestamp of sensor reading data
date	Date of logging Modbus register's data
time	Time of logging Modbus register's data
FC1_Read_Input_Register	Modbus function code that is responsible for reading an input register
FC2_Read_Discrete_Value	Modbus function code that is in charge of reading a discrete value
FC3_Read_Holding_Register	Modbus function code that is responsible for reading a holding register
FC4_Read_Coil	Modbus function code that is responsible for reading a coil
label	Identify normal and attack records, where '0' indicates normal and '1' indicates attacks
type	A tag with normal or attack sub-classes, such as DoS, DDoS and backdoor attacks

Fig. 1. TON IoT Modbus description. [1]

3.2 Quantization and Training

For the quantiazation-training and evaluation of the model we used the Pytorch framework with the Brevitas library. The model is a Multi Layer Perceptron (MLP) that initially undergoes quantization, through the utilization of Quantization Aware Training (QAT) within Brevitas. By integrating quantization directly into the training pipeline, Brevitas enables deep learning models to learn parameters that are aware of the reduced precision requirements imposed by FPGA hardware. This approach addresses the challenge of accuracy degradation often associated with low-bit precision quantization, as the model adapts and optimizes its parameters during training to account for quantization effects. Our neural network was trained using 2-bit quantization for both weights and activations. The MLP consists of four Fully-Connected (FC) layers: three hidden layers, each with 64 neurons, and a final output layer with a single output. The model underwent training using a Stochastic Gradient Descent (SGD) optimizer with an initial learning rate of 0.001. During the learning process, the learning rate was reduced by a factor of 10, whenever no improvement was observed over the last 10 epochs. As a result, training proceeded for a total of 100 epochs while the training dataset was a quantized version of the TON IoT modbus dataset. Eventually, the trained model achieved an accuracy of 96.37%, with 99% precision and 89% recall leading to 94% f1-score.

4 Hardware Implementation

4.1 Mapping the Software Model to a Hardware Implementation

Following the training process, we employ the FINN compiler for the construction of hardware layers to deployed in the FPGA resources. The process involves several key steps. Initially, optimization techniques are employed to eliminate floating-point operations from the model. This involves redistributing and consolidating these operations within multi-thresholding layers, facilitating their transformation into HLS layers. Once all non-supported operations have been addressed, the model is synthesized into hardware using Xilinx Vivado through FINN. The initial hardware designed produced by FINN can be further customized, optimized and re-synthesized using the Vivado manually (as is the case for our work). Subsequently, this synthesized hardware can been deployed to the actual FPGA hardware device. For our work, we have used the ZYNQ UltraScale+ XCZU7EV MPSoC device hosted on a ZCU104 prototyping board[5].

4.2 Hardware Model

Figure 2 demonstrates the basic hardware component architecture, i.e. the hardware-based model component. This component consists of the four hardware layers, each one having as many Processing Elements (PEs) as the neurons of the layer, for both inter- as well as intra-layer parallelization. The weights are integrated at the layers, minimizing the cost of weight loading.

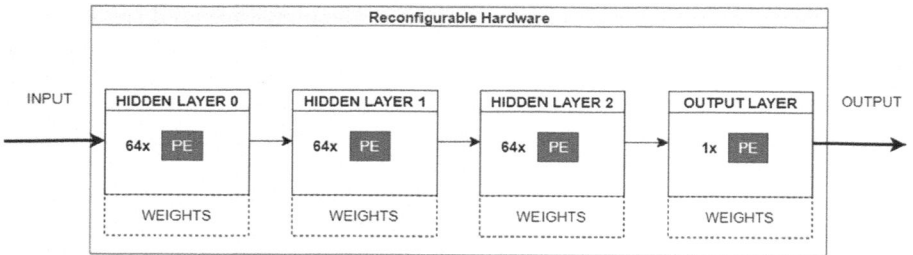

Fig. 2. Hardware layers of accelerated model.

4.3 I2DS Architecture

The aforementioned hardware model is the main computational kernel that performs the intrusion detection tasks. To produce a working IDS system, an engine that can properly feed this computational kernel with the network data streams is required, as well as a controller for its operation. For the former, the hardware model is integrated with a Direct Memory Access (DMA) engine that moves data from the data packet memory to the accelerator. Network data is written in a DDR4 memory connected directly to the FPGA resources (PL side of the MPSoC chip) and through the DMA engine they are loaded to a FIFO structure. The hardware accelerator accesses the network data sequencially from the FIFO memory that acts as a buffer. Both DMA engine and FIFO memory are connected through high performance AXI4 interfaces.

The control of the process is handled by software running on the general purpose CPU cores of the MPSoC device (ARM Cortex-A53). The CPU employs

---

[5] https://www.xilinx.com/products/boards-and-kits/zcu104.html.

AXI4-lite interfaces to communicate with the memory resources and pass configuration data to the accelerator. Detection alerts are laso conveyed from the accelerator to the software components through this interface.

According to the application performance requirements, the aforementioned architecture can be scaled. As there are no practical dependencies between data, several I2DS modules (a module consists of a hardware detection engine, a DMA core and a FIFO memory) can be used in parallel to simultaneously process different network packets or streams. The practical limiting factors for scaling is the performance of the memory interface and the available reconfigurable resources of the FPGA device. In the device of our development board, we have been able to scale our architecture up to four instances and this system is depicted in Fig. 3.

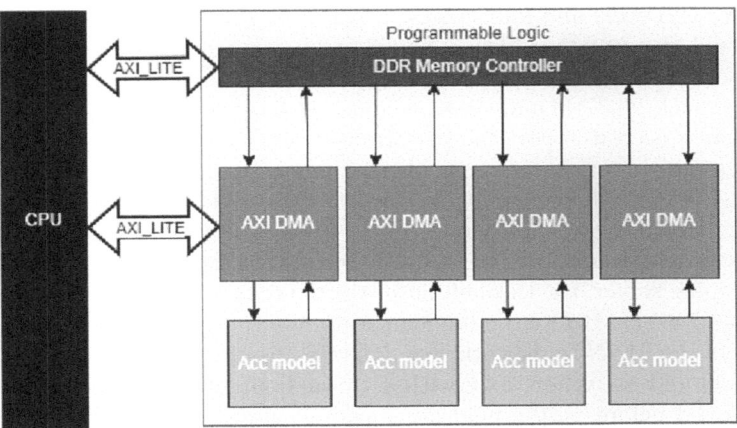

Fig. 3. I2DS architecture.

4.4 Implementation

For the implementation of the hardware system, we have used Vivado 2020.2, targeting the XCZU7EV-2FFVC1156 FPGA device. The hardware accelerator has been implemented through FINN, according to the process described in Sect. 4.2. Although FINN can generate both the bitstream that is used to program the reconfigurable hardware resources as well as the python code that targets the Processing System (PS), we opted for a semi-custom solution. On the hardware side, we used the synthesizable hardware kernel for the model that FINN produced and manually connected it to the AXI DMA and FIFO components as well as the different interfaces and other components required to produced the system decsribed in Fig. 3. The software components handling control and communications, produced in python code by the FINN framework, were also replaced by our C code to remove the performance overheads introduced by the high-level interpreted software.

5 Evaluation

5.1 System Performance and Resources Utilization

To evaluate the performance of our proposed solution, we have produced three implementations. A software-equivalent (marked as SW-EQ in the figures below) inference of the model is executed on an AMD Ryzen 9 3900X 3.80GHz, while the hardware accelerated implementation is loaded on the ZYNQ UltraScale+ MPSoC ZCU104 development board hosting an UltraScale+ FPGA integrated with ARM Cortex-A53 (1.3GHz). Two hardware accelerated implementations are provided. The first one (FINN) is the hardware accelerated version of the IDS using the FINN framework (marked as FINN), while the other is based on the modifications and optimizations discussed in the previous section. For the latter, three different configurations have been produced, with one (marked as I2DS), two (I2DSx2) and four (I2DSx4) accelerator engines.

It should be noted that both software and hardware-accelerated implementations are equivalent: the hardware model provides the exact same accuracy as the software model (96.37%) and the same data set has been used in both cases. The metric that is used to report the performance is records per second (rps). Every record is a new input of data from the dataset with all the modbus headers. In every experiment a dataset of 10,000 records was used for equal comparison. By measuring the inference runtime for every implementation we can estimate the performance in rps (records per second). During the verification of the model at the developing server, the throughput of the SW-EQ of the model has been measured at 84,746 rps. Before the implementation of the proposed architecture, the full steps of the FINN framework were followed, resulting in an accelerated hardware model and a Python code with a throughput of 4,878,048 rps combined. As mentioned before, in the final implementation of our architecture, a custom design was used, incorporating the model-IP generated by FINN, DMA, and FIFOs targeting the PL part of the MPSoC, along with optimized C code in the PS part. The experimental results of the I2DS using C code showed a throughput of 14,285,714 rps, almost four times higher than the performance provided by initial FINN generated system. Finally, the parallel optimized architecture with two parallel models and four parallel models achieved throughputs of 28,011,204 and 52,631,579 rps respectively. Figure 4 demonstrates the performance achieved in all cases.

Our system targets IoT-Industrial environments that usually are resource constrained. Vivado reports (provided in Table 2) show that our implementations consume less than 30% of the total resources of the FPGA fabric even with four levels of parallelization. As such, smaller FPGA devices than our prototype platform can be adopted to reduce costs and/or energy consumption or additional logic may be integrated in the FPGA (for example the model can be extended or refined, while other components providing additional functionality can also be implemented alongside our accelerator). It should be noted that all hardware implementations are using a 100 MHz clock.

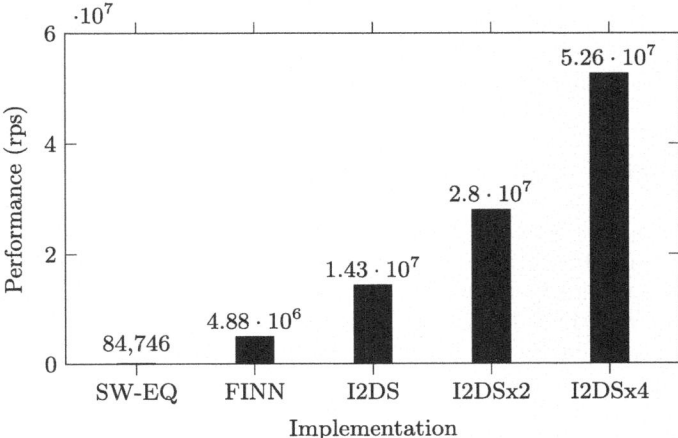

Fig. 4. Performance (in terms of records per second) of software and hardware implementations.

Table 1. Relative performance comparison of software and hardware implementations.

	SW-EQ	FINN	I2DS	I2DSx2
FINN	57.6x			
I2DS	168.6x	2.9x		
I2DSx2	330.6x	5.7x	1.9x	
I2DSx4	620.9x	11x	3.7x	1.9x

Table 2. Resource utilization of hardware implementations on a ZCU104 board.

Resources	Available	FINN	I2DS	I2DSx2	I2DSx4
LUT	230400	20733 (9.00%)	16423 (7.13%)	32072 (13.92%)	62746 (27.23%)
LUTRAM	101760	996 (0.98%)	881 (0.87%)	1672 (1.64%)	3178 (3.12%)
FF	460800	11079 (1.64%)	12010 (2.61%)	23414 (5.08%)	45345 (9.84%)
BRAM	312	2 (0.64%)	7 (2.24%)	14 (4.49%)	28 (8.97%)

5.2 Discussion

Hardware implementations achieve up to two orders of magnitude higher performance compared to the software equivalent implementation, thus demonstrating clearly the benefit of employing hardware acceleration in the specific application. Furthermore, while FINN generated solutions are clearly beneficial, we demonstrate that our optimizations have tangible impact without sacrificing ease of use or resolving to a full custom solution that can be pretty hard to complete. Our directly comparable solution (one core I2DS system) with the FINN generated one, provides 2.9x higher throughput while consuming less logic resources (at the cost of more memory resources). Beyond that, our solution can also scale to multiple cores, practically doubling performance at each step (resource cost is also doubled as expected) as can be seen at Fig. 4 and Table 1.

6 Conclusion and Future Work

This paper proposes a hardware-accelerated ML-based IDS that targets industrial IoT systems. Our ML-model is trained on industry datasets and manages to achieve high detection performance, despite using low bit precision. By adopting the high-level FINN framework, a rather straightforward path to produce an FPGA-accelerated I2DS system is provided. Indeed, this system is able to outperform the purely software solution by a significant margin (57.6x higher throughput can be achieved), proving that hardware acceleration of ML computational tasks is extremely beneficial.

When using the high-level FINN framework, it becomes apparent that a number of significant overheads hinder the unlocking of further performance potential of the hardware platform. We identify that most of these overheads are attributed to the adoption of python structures and support in both the software part of the application and on the actual hardware to provide support for these high-level abstractions. Instead of adopting a full custom design approach, which may have detrimental impact to the effort, cost, development time and expertise required to produce a working solution, we retain the main computational kernels produced by FINN and modify the software parts as well as the high level organization of the overall system architecture. The end result is an I2DS system that provides 2.9x times higher performance than the comparable FINN generated design, while consuming less overall resources. Furthermore, this design can easily scale by adopting a parallel network stream processing, in which case performance scales almost perfectly linear with the number of processing units added.

Acknowledgements. This work has been supported by EU Horizon 2020 research projects PANDORA (101135775) and EMERALDS (101093051).

References

1. Alsaedi, A., Moustafa, N., Tari, Z., Mahmood, A., Anwar, A.: TON_IoT telemetry dataset: a new generation dataset of IoT and IIoT for data-driven intrusion detection systems. IEEE Access **8**, 165130–165150 (2020). https://doi.org/10.1109/ACCESS.2020.3022862
2. Baker, Z.K., Prasanna, V.K.: Automatic synthesis of efficient intrusion detection systems on FPGAs. IEEE Trans. Dependable Secure Comput. **3**(4), 289–300 (2006). https://doi.org/10.1109/TDSC.2006.44
3. Blott, M., et al.: FINN-R: an end-to-end deep-learning framework for fast exploration of quantized neural networks. ACM Trans. Reconfigurable Technol. Syst. **11**(3) (2018). https://doi.org/10.1145/3242897

4. Deyannis, D., Papadogiannaki, E., Chrysos, G., Georgopoulos, K., Ioannidis, S.: The diversification and enhancement of an ids scheme for the cybersecurity needs of modern supply chains. Electronics **11**(13) (2022). https://doi.org/10.3390/electronics11131944
5. Dhirani, L.L., Armstrong, E., Newe, T.: Industrial IoT, cyber threats, and standards landscape: evaluation and roadmap. Sensors **21**(11) (2021). https://doi.org/10.3390/s21113901
6. Fahim, F., et al.: hls4ml: An open-source codesign workflow to empower scientific low-power machine learning devices (2021)
7. García-Teodoro, P., Díaz-Verdejo, J., Maciá-Fernández, G., Vázquez, E.: Anomaly-based network intrusion detection: techniques, systems and challenges. Comput. Secur. **28**(1), 18–28 (2009). https://doi.org/10.1016/j.cose.2008.08.003
8. Hidayat, I., Ali, M., Arshad, A.: Machine learning-based intrusion detection system: an experimental comparison. J. Comput. Cogn. Eng. **2** (2022). https://doi.org/10.47852/bonviewJCCE2202270
9. Ioannou, L., Fahmy, S.A.: Network intrusion detection using neural networks on FPGA SoCs. In: 2019 29th International Conference on Field Programmable Logic and Applications (FPL), pp. 232–238 (2019). https://doi.org/10.1109/FPL.2019.00043
10. Kim, J., Park, J.: FPGA-based network intrusion detection for IEC 61850-based industrial network. ICT Express **4**(1), 1–5 (2018). https://doi.org/10.1016/j.icte.2018.01.002 , sI: CI Smart Grid Cyber Security
11. Krizhevsky, A., Sutskever, I., Hinton, G.E.: Imagenet classification with deep convolutional neural networks. In: Pereira, F., Burges, C., Bottou, L., Weinberger, K. (eds.) Adv. Neural Inf. Process. Syst. **25**. Curran Associates, Inc. (2012)
12. Le Jeune, L., Goedemé, T., Mentens, N.: Towards real-time deep learning-based network intrusion detection on FPGA. In: Applied Cryptography and Network Security Workshops, pp. 133–150. Springer International Publishing, Cham (2021)
13. Moustafa, N.: A new distributed architecture for evaluating AI-based security systems at the edge: Network TON_IoT datasets. Sustain. Urban Areas **72**, 102994 (2021). https://doi.org/10.1016/j.scs.2021.102994
14. Ngo, D.M., Temko, A., Murphy, C.C., Popovici, E.: FPGA hardware acceleration framework for anomaly-based intrusion detection system in IoT. In: 2021 31st International Conference on Field-Programmable Logic and Applications (FPL), pp. 69–75. IEEE (2021)
15. Papadogiannaki, E., Chrysos, G., Georgopoulos, K., Ioannidis, S.: A reconfigurable IDS framework for encrypted and non-encrypted network data in supply chains. In: 9th International Conference on Engineering and Emerging Technologies (ICEET), pp. 1–6 (2023)
16. Bro, P.V.: A system for detecting network intruders in Real-Time. In: 7th USENIX Security Symposium (USENIX Security 98). USENIX Association, San Antonio, TX (1998)
17. Roesch, M.: Snort - lightweight intrusion detection for networks. In: Proceedings of the 13th USENIX Conference on System Administration, p. 229–238. LISA 1999, USENIX Association, USA (1999)
18. Rybalkin, V., Pappalardo, A., Ghaffar, M., Gambardella, G., Wehn, N., Blott, M.: FINN-L: library extensions and design trade-off analysis for variable precision LSTM networks on FPGAs. In: 2018 28th International Conference on Field Programmable Logic and Applications (FPL), pp. 89–897. IEEE Computer Society, Los Alamitos, CA, USA (2018). https://doi.org/10.1109/FPL.2018.00024

19. Schmidhuber, J.: Deep learning in neural networks: an overview. Neural Netw. **61**, 85–117 (2015). https://doi.org/10.1016/j.neunet.2014.09.003
20. Shone, N., Ngoc, T.N., Phai, V.D., Shi, Q.: A deep learning approach to network intrusion detection. IEEE Trans. Emerg. Top. Comput. Intell. **2**(1), 41–50 (2018). https://doi.org/10.1109/TETCI.2017.2772792
21. Sourdis, I., Pnevmatikatos, D.: Fast, large-scale string match for a 10Gbps FPGA-based network intrusion detection system. In: Y.K. Cheung, P., Constantinides, G.A. (eds.) Field Programmable Logic and Application, pp. 880–889. Springer Berlin Heidelberg, Berlin, Heidelberg (2003)
22. Tsai, C.F., Hsu, Y.F., Lin, C.Y., Lin, W.Y.: Intrusion detection by machine learning: a review. Expert Syst. Appl. **36**(10), 11994–12000 (2009). https://doi.org/10.1016/j.eswa.2009.05.029
23. Tsiknas, K., Taketzis, D., Demertzis, K., Skianis, C.: Cyber threats to industrial IoT: a survey on attacks and countermeasures. IoT **2**(1), 163–186 (2021). https://doi.org/10.3390/iot2010009
24. Umuroglu, Y., Akhauri, Y., Fraser, N.J., Blott, M.: LogicNets: co-designed neural networks and circuits for extreme-throughput applications. In: Proceedings of the International Conference on Field-Programmable Logic and Applications, pp. 291–297. IEEE Computer Society, Los Alamitos, CA, USA (2020)
25. Umuroglu, Y., et al.: FINN: a framework for fast, scalable binarized neural network inference. In: Proceedings of the 2017 ACM/SIGDA International Symposium on Field-Programmable Gate Arrays, p. 65–74. FPGA 2017, Association for Computing Machinery, New York, NY, USA (2017). https://doi.org/10.1145/3020078.3021744
26. Weyand, T., Kostrikov, I., Philbin, J.: PlaNet - photo geolocation with convolutional neural networks. In: Computer Vision–ECCV 2016: 14th European Conference, Amsterdam, The Netherlands, October 11-14, 2016, Proceedings, Part VIII 14, pp. 37–55. Springer International Publishing (2016). https://doi.org/10.1007/978-3-319-46484-8_3
27. Zhang, Y., Chen, X., Guo, D., Song, M., Teng, Y., Wang, X.: PCCN: parallel cross convolutional neural network for abnormal network traffic flows detection in multi-class imbalanced network traffic flows. IEEE Access **7**, 119904–119916 (2019). https://doi.org/10.1109/ACCESS.2019.2933165
28. Zhao, Z., Sadok, H., Atre, N., Hoe, J.C., Sekar, V., Sherry, J.: Achieving 100gbps intrusion prevention on a single server. In: 14th USENIX Symposium on Operating Systems Design and Implementation (OSDI 20), pp. 1083–1100. USENIX Association (2020)

Special Session on European Projects: Actions towards Security, Digital Rights, and Crime Investigation in the Cyberspace

ACRA: A Cutting-Edge Analytics Platform for Advanced Real-Time Corruption Risk Assessment and Investigation Prioritization

Nikolaos Peppes, Emmanouil Daskalakis(✉), Theodoros Alexakis, and Evgenia Adamopoulou

Institute of Communication and Computer Systems, School of Electrical and Computer Engineering, National Technical University of Athens, Zografou 15773, Athens, Greece
edaskalakis@cn.ntua.gr

Abstract. In the realm of anti-corruption initiatives, critical challenges need to be addressed for reinforcing the global fight against corruption. FALCON, a Horizon Europe research program, employs a multi-actor, evidence-based approach to develop actionable indicators and data-driven tools aiming to offer comprehensive corruption intelligence. In this context, the proposed prototype tool, ACRA (Advanced Corruption Risk Assessment), addresses FALCON's objectives. Designed for Law Enforcement Agencies and Anti-corruption Authorities, ACRA enables real-time analysis for identifying high risks related to corruption cases. The platform allows for anomaly detection in ownership structures, generating corruption probability scores based on diverse risk indicators, providing an overall risk assessment report based on likelihood and impact, integrating inputs from various sources, and tracing cross-border links. ACRA stands as a customizable, real-time analytical platform prototype, facilitating the identification and prioritization of investigations. The current study contributes to the scope of the SAMOSXXIV conference by presenting the capabilities of the ACRA tool and the challenges addressed by it, focusing on transparency and on the sharing of insights that may benefit the broader research community.

Keywords: corruption crime investigation · risk assessment · decision making · predictive analytics · risk classification

1 Introduction

According to a prevalent definition, corruption is "the abuse of entrusted power for private gain" [20]. It is a widespread global phenomenon which hampers economic development, exacerbates poverty and inequality, and may also threaten democracy as a whole [24]. Therefore, tackling corruption effectively is an increasing focus of many national governments, companies, and global institutions. Anticorruption measures can play an important role in the mitigation of corruption phenomena and may cover a wide spectrum from the prevention of corruption and the endorsement of a culture of integrity, to ensuring effective investigation of corruption cases and prosecution of corruption. This paper has been developed in the context of FALCON [9], a three-year Horizon Europe research project in the field of anti-corruption. This project aims to address the significant challenges of the global fight against corruption by developing new, data-driven indicators and tools. It started in September 2023 and follows an evidence-based, multi-actor, and interdisciplinary approach.

The ACRA tool presented in this paper conducts corruption risk assessment. Corruption risk assessment constitutes a diagnostic tool aiming at detecting the weaknesses of a system which may serve as a breeding ground for corruption cases [16]. One important difference from other risk assessment tools is that corruption risk assessment mainly revolves around the probability of corruption rather than the existence of corruption and its extent. ACRA tool offers a variety of services which enable end-users to collect, analyze, and visualize data from heterogeneous data sources, thus helping them gain valuable insights into different corruption risks, and make informed decisions, utilizing diverse predefined corruption indicators.

The remainder of this paper is structured as follows:

– Section 2 contains related research works from the scientific literature.
– Section 3 describes the architecture of the ACRA tool.
– Section 4 revolves around the services offered by the ACRA tool.
– Section 5 concludes the deliverable.

2 Related Works

The use of Information and Communication Technologies (ICT) can play a key role in tackling corruption. Benítez-Martínez et al. [4] presented a governance approach utilizing Blockchain [22] and Smart Contract [14] technologies. More specifically, the authors made use of a neural blockchain whose nodes can host both public and private information. Smart contracts were contained in the block which encompasses all relevant data and records from procurement processes. The authors' approach was validated by means of an e-Delphi Panel [7], involving 20 experts on the Blockchain/Public Administration transformation domains. The authors' approach offered important benefits in terms of increasing transparency and immutability while helping avoid corruption in diverse public procurement cases. Another approach which used smart contracts for mitigating corruption in public procurement was presented by Weingaertner et al.[26]. The authors' work mainly revolved around three aspects of public procurement, i.e., the bidding process, the compliance of suppliers with diverse legal prerequisites, and the delivery verification. In the above aspects, corruption may be present by means of hidden agreements, illegal information disclosure, biased bidding processes, etc. The feasibility of this approach was tested by creating a prototype based on the design science method [11], leading to more automated procurement processes with increased transparency and disintermediation. Caruso et al. [6] described a model for advanced and simplified monitoring of procurement processes of public organizations which aimed at preventing and detecting cases of corruption. There is a vast amount of data and a large number of Key Performance Indicators (KPIs) which need to be monitored and processed for tackling corruption in public procurement processes, leading to the so-called "KPI overload" problem. By conducting classification based on supervised neural networks [21], the model could identify transactions, buyers or suppliers which were suspected to be parts of corruption cases. A database was then built for collecting data related to public procurement, and KPIs were calculated (e.g., number and value of items purchased from a single supplier, which helped to identify if there was a pattern for procurement from this supplier) and visualization techniques were implemented that simplified the monitoring of large amounts of data. The model was found capable of providing a first-screening evaluation, reducing the number of KPIs which need to be monitored and simplifying the overall anticorruption monitoring process. Despite the reduced number of parameters which need to be monitored by the user, there was only a 0.3% probability of missing important alarms.

Another possible indicator of corruption in public procurement processes, is the existence of fake suppliers who have limited or no capacity of delivering goods. Wacker et al.[25] presented a model for fast and efficient image analysis of images of different suppliers. The main goal of the authors was to automatically distinguish between random images of buildings and landscapes from legitimate supplier locations. For this, deep features were extracted from Google Street View images, utilizing Convolutional Neural Networks [1]. The classification results were very encouraging, yielding a 78% precision, while having a recall rate of about 100%. Making use of this model, a user needed to discard only 22% of the cases which were automatically proposed as suspected of fraud. In another research work published by Noerlina et al. [17], a web application was developed which helped at monitoring corruption cases per area. More specifically, the application made use of web crawling and web scraping techniques for collecting news from different news portals as well as of a Backpropagation Artificial Neural Network [5] for classifying the news. After detecting news related to corruption cases in a specific region, further analysis was conducted to extract more information about the corruption cases which could be used by Law Enforcement Authorities or decision makers. Experimental testing of the proposed application indicated a high classification accuracy of 96.91% between news related to corruption and news not related to corruption.

Risk assessment is an active research topic in various domains where different solutions for automated risk assessment tools are present. Thus, the existing solutions of automated risk assessment vary in terms of the methodologies and algorithms used. More specifically, there are qualitative and quantitative risk assessment solutions. In the next paragraphs there is an overview of such solutions with different approaches.

One of the most common and widely studied methodologies concerning risk assessment is the establishment of predefined indicators which can lead to several risks. This methodology is often a combination of quantitative and qualitative attributes. Thus, quantitative attributes are mainly measurements that can lead to indicators and having numerical values whilst the result of the risk assessment of such measures has a more qualitative nature by providing a label for the risk as severe or non-severe. Such an approach was followed by Aznar-Siguan and Bresch in their study about the so-called CLIMADA framework [3]. Their study was based on several different factors and their combinations in order to provide a probabilistic event-based risk assessment. More specifically, the CLIMADA framework contained a detailed mapping of hazards and exposures, by integrating probabilistic models. In addition, it evaluated the socio-economic impact of climate phenomena and assessed a wide range of adaptation measures that could alleviate the outcomes of natural disasters. In a similar approach but for a different domain, Kandasamy et al. [12] presented a unique risk ranking method which quantified Internet of Things (IoT) risk vectors in order to calculate the cyber risk for IoT systems. IoT risks were divided into 4 categories, i.e., ethical, privacy, security and technical. Similar to the previous study which quantified specific metrics into a qualitative result, Kandasamy et al. also proposed a risk computational model which provided risk impact and likelihood and finally produced a risk score.

Another widely used approach for automated or adaptive risk assessment systems is the fuzzy logic [8]. A fuzzy logic system is a system that tries to imitate how humans are thinking. Thus, a fuzzy logic system tries to combine the precise numerical problem-solving approach that a computer system performs with imprecise linguistic inputs [15]. Towards this direction, Atlam et al. [2] proposed an adaptive and dynamic risk based IoT access control model utilizing a fuzzy logic system with expert judgment. The proposed solution used IoT real-time and contextual information associated with the access request to automatically determine the access decision. The proposed model used user attributes collected while making the access request, sensitivity of data to be accessed, severity of actions to be performed and user risk history as inputs to estimate the risk value regarding each access request. Also, Gallab et al. [10] proposed a fuzzy logic solution for risk assessment. Their approach quantified the qualitative values of risk. For this reason, the proposed system calculated the Risk Priority Number (RPN) based on the severity, the frequency, the detectability, and a predefined set of rules or events. In general, the utilization of fuzzy logic approaches can lift the barrier of imprecise and insufficient data.

The evolution of computer science and specifically the emergence and the establishment of Artificial Intelligence in various domains consists a new field for exploration concerning risk assessment solutions. In this light, Paltrinieri et al. [19] presented a Deep Neural Network (DNN) [27] approach which estimated the risk in an industrial application. More specifically, their approach involved a DNN model which took several indicators observed during the past 30 years as inputs. These indicators were used to calculate the risk of a drill drive-off in an oil and gas drilling site. Their approach was directly compared to a Multiple Linear Regression (MLR) [13] model which was used as a risk assessment solution and indicated that the DNN performance surpassed the MLR model. Also, their study indicated that AI solutions were feasible for risk assessment and could perform well where conventional models lacked performance in cases such as the "black swan" effect. A "black swan" effect describes an unforeseen event that in case it happens can have major effect. The theory of the "black swan" effect developed by Nassim Nicholas Taleb in 2001 [23]. This means that AI can predict and estimate the risk even of unknown events as they can retrain and adapt to new sets of data. On the contrary, statistical methods and models could only provide reliable predictions in predefined known events. However, the DNN approach of Paltrinieri et al.[19] had some restrictions as the authors faced over/under-fitting phenomena.

As obvious from the above, there are many different approaches concerning risk assessment and for various different domains. In the next sections of the current study there is a detailed description of the proposed automated risk assessment solution for fighting corruption. This solution hosts different approaches into a unified framework and aims to automate the risk assessment in the domain of fighting corruption.

3   ACRA Platform Architecture

3.1   Crafting ACRA: Unravelling the Advanced Corruption Risk Assessment Design

ACRA, the Advanced Corruption Risk Assessment tool, emerges as a user-friendly, consistent, and adaptable risk assessment system within the FALCON project framework. Operating as a decision support system, ACRA navigates users through the intricacies of corruption risk assessment by combining outputs from various sources, including mitigation measures, corruption indices, and impact assessment methods.

The tool features a risk modeling user interface supported by simulation services and a model graph, crucial for effective corruption risk assessment. ACRA enables users to seamlessly select assessment scenarios, estimating likelihood and impact based on diverse data inputs, eliminating the need for repetitive data handling and model employment.

ACRA determines risk levels by evaluating the impact and frequency of identified risks, resulting in a prioritized list crucial for subsequent evaluation and risk treatment. Employing a comprehensive risk analysis approach, ACRA leverages various methods, including DL-based classification, fuzzy logic-based risk assessment, and rule-based risk estimation. This flexibility allows for a qualitative, quantitative, and hybrid examination of potential corruption risks.

Furthermore, ACRA integrates linguistic representation to preserve user feedback, collecting and incorporating information and requirements into the overall system logic.

The architecture of the tool is comprised of three levels: a backend service layer managing analysis procedures, an intermediate RESTful service responsible for serving analysis results in a machine-readable format and facilitating real-time interaction based on end-user specifications through the ACRA Graphical User Interface (GUI), and the frontend/graphical user interface for visual representation and further user interaction. The diagram presented in Fig. 1 illustrates the comprehensive architecture of the ACRA platform.

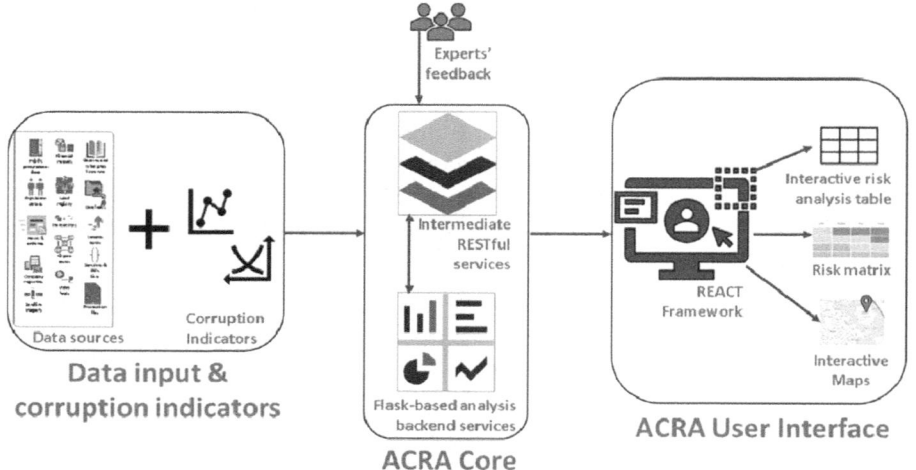

Fig. 1. ACRA concept architecture

3.2 Overview of the Flask-Based Backend Framework

Flask, a micro web framework crafted and implemented in Python [18], drives the backend architecture of the ACRA tool. Functioning as a microframework, Flask stands out for its minimalistic design, free from specific tools or libraries. In contrast to frameworks featuring built-in database abstraction layers or form validation, Flask encourages flexibility through its support for extensions, seamlessly incorporating extra features into the application. These extensions span diverse functionalities like object-relational mappers, form validation, upload handling, and compatibility with various authentication technologies. In essence, Flask embraces simplicity and speed, offering a lightweight foundation for our system.

3.3 Intermediate RESTful Architecture

RESTful is a design style within software architecture, yet it doesn't constitute a standard itself. Its primary responsibility lies in structuring the interaction between the system's front-end (client side) and back-end (server side). Representational State Transfer (REST) played a key role in formulating the rules of the hypertext transfer protocol (HTTP). REST encompasses a set of architectural constraints and principles, and if an architecture adheres to these criteria, it qualifies as RESTful. Beyond architectural conditions, it offers a straightforward application programming interface (API) that clearly presents the system's services. A RESTful system comprises a client requesting resources and a server holding those resources. Adhering to industry standards in creating REST APIs is crucial for development ease and increased client adoption. RESTful APIs have six architectural constraints:

- Uniform Interface
- Stateless
- Cacheable
- Client-Server
- Layered System
- Code on Demand (optional)

Uniform Interface is a fundamental constraint, differentiating between REST and non-REST APIs. It emphasizes a consistent way of interacting with a server, regardless of the device or type of application (website, mobile app). Consequently, RESTful systems are developed in alignment with the REST philosophy and principles.

3.4 ACRA Graphical User Interface

The GUI of ACRA has been meticulously crafted with the React framework at its core. As a widely embraced JavaScript library for UI development, React framework lays the foundation for our project. Recognizing that React alone may not offer a complete solution for web application development, we acknowledge the importance of incorporating additional tools and frameworks. These complementary elements are essential to augment React's capabilities, addressing key areas such as routing, state management, data fetching, testing, and styling. By leveraging a React framework, we create an out-of-the-box environment tailored specifically for ACRA's development, streamlining the intricate setup process. This approach allows us to focus on the application's logic, freeing the overall process from dealing with boilerplate code and technical intricacies.

Moreover, the outlined functional and non-functional requirements play a key role in shaping the development of the ACRA tool. The functional requirements emphasize crucial functionalities including data segmentation based on time, user-adjustable training and testing data ratios, sampling method selection, threshold selection and customization, and more. On the non-functional front, the ACRA tool is expected to be user-friendly, easily maintainable, and accessible across various operating environments, ensuring a seamless and efficient user experience.

4 ACRA Services

The ACRA platform is being developed within the FALCON project framework to deliver a comprehensive assessment of total risk. This objective is achieved by analyzing the likelihood and associated impact of various scenarios sourced from diverse data streams. Through its advanced analytics services and capabilities, ACRA enables users to gain valuable insights into corruption risk, empowering them to make informed decisions and take appropriate actions.

ACRA, an Advanced Corruption Risk Assessment data analytics platform, is currently in development, integrating robust visualization and analysis components and capabilities. Its primary objective is to uncover hidden patterns, extract valuable insights, and offer guidance for decision-making processes, particularly to aid in managing corruption incidents with high-risk probability. Notably, ACRA excels in handling high-velocity data streams and real-time data processing. The platform comprises a suite of services enabling end-users to collect, analyze, and visualize diverse data and data sources, leveraging valuable information alongside predefined corruption indicators. ACRA manages a wide range of data types, encompassing text, images, satellite imagery, and cryptocurrency data, while assisting end-users across the analytics lifecycle. It offers an intuitive, customizable dashboard for user interaction. ACRA integrates data catalogues in the form of tables, which export the analytic results and enable searches on specific data aspects. Additionally, it includes analytic charts tailored to the end-users' needs and interactive maps that visualize the events detected in correlation with their calculated risk and further information. Furthermore, users can generate reports containing the extracted analytic information for collaborative sharing purposes. Figure 2 showcases the Home page interface of the ACRA platform.

Fig. 2. Home Page of the ACRA platform

These tables visualize information such as the corruption incident, corruption domain, and use case within the FALCON project, along with the likelihood and impact calculated based on predefined thresholds provided in collaboration with project experts. Additionally, the estimated risk is depicted, and advanced features such as global search filtering, column filtering, pagination, and further customization of the tables and extracted information are provided. In addition to the analytic metrics, diagrams are developed and integrated to provide an intuition of the risks calculated both qualitatively and quantitatively. Figure 3 illustrates one of these analytics dashboards integrated into the ACRA platform.

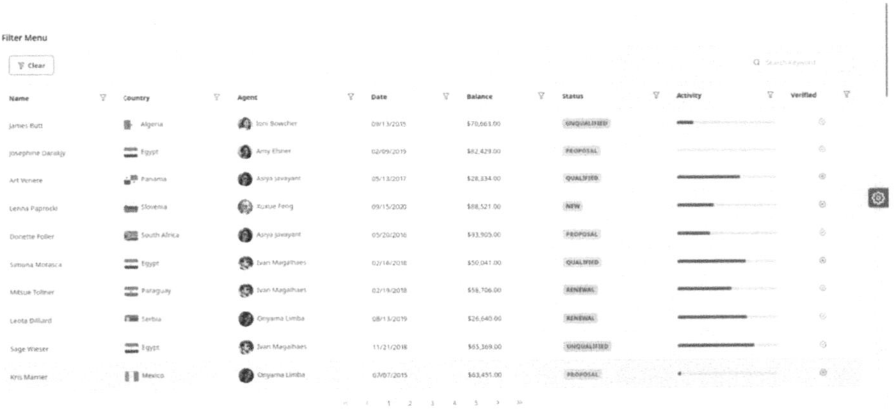

Fig. 3. Corruption analytic results in ACRA platform

Another crucial service integrated for risk analysis assessment by the project's experts is the real-time creation of a risk matrix. This matrix, also known as a probability and severity (or likelihood and impact risk) matrix, is derived from preprocessed events analyzed for risk likelihood, impact, and estimated risk in real-time. It aids in visualizing the probability versus the severity of potential risks. Depending on the likelihood and severity of each event, risks can be categorized in terms of qualitative risk analysis as high, moderate, or low (the exact number of categories can be specified based on expert preferences). The risk matrix further empowers Falcon's end-users to cultivate a solid understanding of the risk environment, facilitating the management and mitigation of risks before they occur. Figure 4 illustrates a risk matrix based on the risks calculated within ACRA's analytic mechanisms.

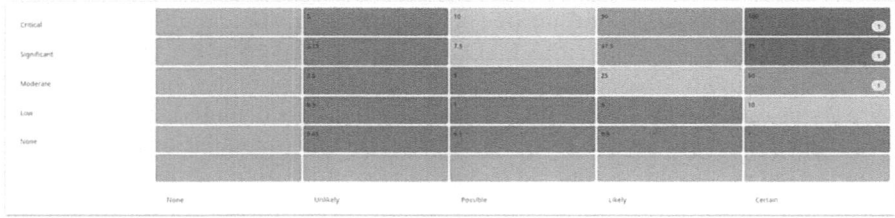

Fig. 4. Risk Matrix in ACRA platform

5 Conclusions

Despite the increasing digitalization in modern times, corruption continues to cast a pall over societies at a global scale, negatively affecting the economic development and exacerbating inequality. The use of state-of-the-art technologies can aid in tackling corruption, and automated corruption risk assessment models and methodologies are no exception. The present research work presents the ACRA prototype corruption risk assessment tool, which is being developed in the context of FALCON Horizon Europe project. ACRA can serve as a user-friendly, adaptable, and efficient corruption risk assessment system. Built upon a 3-layer architecture, ACRA comprises a DL-based decision support tool, which enables users to seamlessly collect, analyze, and visualize heterogeneous data sources, and extract valuable corruption risk related information, based on predefined corruption indicators. Through a meticulously crafted user GUI tailored to the specific needs of Law Enforcement Agencies and Anticorruption Authorities, users have access to different services, including analytics charts and a corruption risk matrix, which can facilitate the management and mitigation of corruption risks, even before they occur.

Acknowledgments. Co-funded by the European Union within the Horizon Europe programme, under FALCON project - grant agreement No. 101121281. Views and opinions expressed are however those of the author(s) only and do not necessarily reflect those of the European Union or the European Research Executive Agency. Neither the European Union nor the the granting authority can be held responsible for them.

Disclosure of Interests. The authors have no competing interests to declare that are relevant to the content of this article.

References

1. Albawi, S., Mohammed, T.A., Al-Zawi, S.: Understanding of a convolutional neural network. In: 2017 International Conference on Engineering and Technology (ICET), pp. 1–6 (2017). https://doi.org/10.1109/ICEngTechnol.2017.8308186
2. Atlam, H.F., Walters, R.J., Wills, G.B., Daniel, J.: Fuzzy logic with expert judgment to implement an adaptive risk-based access control model for IoT. Mob. Networks Appl. 1–13 (2019). https://doi.org/10.1007/s11036-019-01214-w
3. Aznar-Siguan, G., Bresch, D.N.: CLIMADA v1: a global weather and climate risk assessment platform. Geoscientific Model Dev. **12**(7), 3085–3097 (2019). https://doi.org/10.5194/gmd-12-3085-2019
4. Benítez-Martínez, F.L., Romero-Frías, E., Hurtado-Torres, M.V.: Neural blockchain technology for a new anticorruption token: towards a novel governance model. J. Inf. Technol. Politics **20**(1), 1–18 (2023). https://doi.org/10.1080/19331681.2022.2027317
5. Buscema, M.: Back propagation neural networks. Subst. Use Misuse **33**(2), 233–270 (1998). https://doi.org/10.3109/10826089809115863
6. Caruso, S., Bruccoleri, M., Pietrosi, A., Scaccianoce, A.: Artificial intelligence to counteract KPI overload in business process monitoring: the case of anti-corruption in public organizations. Bus. Process Manage. J. **29** (2023). https://doi.org/10.1108/BPMJ-11-2022-0578
7. Donohoe, H., Stellefson, M., Tennant, B.: Advantages and limitations of the e-Delphi technique. Am. J. Health Educ. **43**(1), 38–46 (2012). https://doi.org/10.1080/19325037.2012.10599216
8. Dote, Y.: Introduction to fuzzy logic. In: Proceedings of IECON 1995 - 21st Annual Conference on IEEE Industrial Electronics, vol. 1, pp. 50–56 (1995). https://doi.org/10.1109/IECON.1995.483332
9. FALCON: FALCON research project. https://www.falcon-horizon.eu
10. Gallab, M., Bouloiz, H., Alaoui, Y.L., Tkiouat, M.: Risk assessment of maintenance activities using fuzzy logic. Procedia Comput. Sci. **148**, 226–235 (2019). https://doi.org/10.1016/j.procs.2019.01.065
11. Hevner, A.R., March, S.T., Park, J., Ram, S.: Design science in information systems research. MIS Q. **28**(1), 75–105 (2004). https://doi.org/10.2307/25148625
12. Kandasamy, K., Srinivas, S., Achuthan, K., Rangan, V.P.: IoT cyber risk: a holistic analysis of cyber risk assessment frameworks, risk vectors, and risk ranking process. EURASIP J. Inf. Secur. **2020**(1), 1–18 (2020). https://doi.org/10.1186/s13635-020-00111-0
13. Kaya Uyanık, G., Güler, N.: A study on multiple linear regression analysis. Procedia. Soc. Behav. Sci. **106**, 234–240 (2013). https://doi.org/10.1016/j.sbspro.2013.12.027
14. Kõlvart, M., Poola, M., Rull, A.: Smart contracts. In: Kerikmäe, T., Rull, A. (eds.) The Future of Law and eTechnologies, pp. 133–147. Springer, Cham (2016). https://doi.org/10.1007/978-3-319-26896-5_7
15. Kose, U.: Fundamentals of fuzzy logic with an easy-to-use, interactive fuzzy control application. Int. J. Mod. Eng. Res. **2**(3), 1198–1203 (2012)
16. McDevitt, A.: Corruption Risk Assessment Topic Guide. Tech. rep, Transparency International (2011)
17. Noerlina et al.: Development of a web based corruption case mapping using machine learning with artificial neural network. In: 2018 International Conference on Information Management and Technology (ICIMTech), pp. 400–405 (2018). https://doi.org/10.1109/ICIMTech.2018.8528150

18. Pallets Projects: Flask. https://flask.palletsprojects.com/en/3.0.x/
19. Paltrinieri, N., Comfort, L., Reniers, G.: Learning about risk: machine learning for risk assessment. Saf. Sci. **118**, 475–486 (2019). https://doi.org/10.1016/j.ssci.2019.06.001
20. Pozsgai-Alvarez, J.: The abuse of entrusted power for private gain: meaning, nature and theoretical evolution. Crime Law Soc. Chang. **74**(4), 433–455 (2020). https://doi.org/10.1007/s10611-020-09903-4
21. Sperduti, A., Starita, A.: Supervised neural networks for the classification of structures. IEEE Trans. Neural Networks **8**(3), 714–735 (1997). https://doi.org/10.1109/72.572108
22. Swan, M.: Blockchain: Blueprint for a New Economy. O'Reilly Media (2015)
23. Taleb, N.: The Black Swan. Random House, A Random House International Edition (2009)
24. Transparency International: What is corruption? https://www.transparency.org/en/what-is-corruption
25. Wacker, J., Ferreira, R.P., Ladeira, M.: Detecting fake suppliers using deep image features. In: 2018 7th Brazilian Conference on Intelligent Systems (BRACIS), pp. 224–229 (2018). https://doi.org/10.1109/BRACIS.2018.00046
26. Weingärtner, T., Batista, D., Köchli, S., Voutat, G.: Prototyping a smart contract based public procurement to fight corruption. Computers **10**(7) (2021). https://doi.org/10.3390/computers10070085
27. Yi, H., Shiyu, S., Xiusheng, D., Zhigang, C.: A study on deep neural networks framework. In: 2016 IEEE Advanced Information Management, Communicates, Electronic and Automation Control Conference (IMCEC), pp. 1519–1522 (2016). https://doi.org/10.1109/IMCEC.2016.7867471

Post Quantum Cryptography Research Lines in the Italian Center for Security and Rights in Cyberspace

Alessandro Barenghi and Gerardo Pelosi

Politecnico di Milano, Milan 20133, Italy
{alessandro.barenghi,gerardo.pelosi}@polimi.it

Abstract. The Italian foundation for Security and Rights in Cyberspace (SERICS) is in charge of managing the current, broad range, research in a variety of computer security domains, ranging from strictly computer related aspects, such as OS and Virtualization security, to the development of new cryptographic techniques, up to tackling human, social and legal problems related to computer security and privacy. The SERICS project is founded by the Italian National Recovery and Resilience Plan (NRRP), which in turn receives funding from the EU - NextGenerationEU programme. The SERICS foundation is managing the STRIDE project, to tackle the aforementioned research challenges. In the context of the STRIDE projects, a cascade call was made to tackle specific aspects of the overall reseach challenges. The two-years AQuSDIT project, winner of the aforementioned cascade call, aims to tackle the current open problems in the digital identity realm, with a particular focus on resistance to quantum computer-based attacks, and ledger-based technologies for identification and supply chain tracking. In this context, the research activities at Politecnico di Milano focus on the design of post quantum cryptosystems, and their secure and efficient realization as hardware components, either in the form of full accelerators, or support to existing computing infrastructures. In the following, we will present an overview of the research activities of the 2-year AQuSDIT project, together with an outlook on the first research results which have been obtained by the group of participants from Politecnico di Milano.

Keywords: Computer security · Cryptography · Post quantum cryptography

1 Introduction

The Italian SERICS Foundation [30] - Security and Rights in CyberSpace was established to be the entity implementing the extended partnerships among national research institutions and companies, to submit funding applications for the development of fundamental scientific research projects - under the Italian National Recovery and Resilience Plan (NRRP), Mission 4 "Education and

Research" - Component 2 "From Research to Enterprise" - Investment 1.3, funded by the European Union - NextGenerationEU [19]. The creation of the whole structure received an important organizational push from the Cybersecurity Italian National Lab, which in turn represents the coordination point of a network of 59 interconnected entities, which include the main Italian Universities, Research Institutes and Military Academies. The Cybersecurity Italian National Lab has played a key role in gathering the Italian cybersecurity community around the unique SERICS foundation structure that will be the recipient of funds for research in one of the most relevant fields of this century, that is cybersecurity. From an operative perspective, the SERICS foundation aggregates activities across ten different scientific fields, and it is organised according to a Hub and Spoke model. The Hub is meant to validate and manage the research programmes, whose activities will be led by the Spokes, which in turn include universities, research organizations and companies to build a synergy between the scientific communities and the industrial world. The 10 spokes are focused on 10 thematic areas of interest, which are: *Human, social and legal aspects, Misinformation and Fake News, Attacks and Defences, Operating Systems and Virtualization Security, Cryptography and Distributed Systems Security, Software and Platform Security, Infrastructure Security, Risk Management and Governance, Securing Digital Transformation, Data Governance and Protection*. The objectives of the projects developed by the partnerships in each spoke are focused on identifying key problems in computer and network security and privacy that cause societal harm, economic losses and hinder the adoption of smart city technologies. Each project consortium is the result of a planning action made by the SERICS foundation that led to the definition of a broad research agenda that as previously mentioned, encompasses technical, legal, and societal issues related to security and privacy and includes the best academic and industrial researchers with the expertise needed to make progress on these issues.

In particular, Spoke 5 is primarily concerned with research activities in the domains of cryptography and distributed system security. Given the vastness of these domains and the necessity of identifying concrete objectives aimed at obtaining long-term results of high technological value and possible impact on the country, the activities of this spoke recognize the necessity of coexistence of two distinct yet interrelated souls. Among the subtopics *(i)* cryptographic primitives and protocols, *(ii)* foundational cryptography and cryptanalysis, *(iii)* post-quantum cryptography, *(iv)* digital identity, authentication, and accountability, and *(v)* distributed ledgers and blockchain, the two main directions are the continuous search for advancing the knowledge in all the fields mentioned above and the plan to apply this investigative approach to applied research goals with low- and medium-term societal impacts. Such an objective is pursued by implementing a single unifying project, named STRIDE - *Secure and TRaceable Identities in Distributed Environments*, focused on the notion of digital identification and tracing, with an emphasis on unconventional perspectives. STRIDE project as well as the EU funded projects pursued by other spokes received the needed financial support from the European Commission with the funding mechanism named "Financial Support for Third Parties (FSTP)", which has been envisioned to distribute 80% of the public funding, received by the subject in charge of pursuing the research activities in the first place, through issuing further open calls to the end of creating a domino effect, where funding flows from one EC funded project to another, enlarging effectively the set of relevant competencies contributing to the digital innovation. However, the performance of the activities pursued in the projects selected with a cascade call is critically evaluated, with a keen focus on deliverables and the successful achievement of Key Performance Indicators (KPIs). In response to the cascade call issued by SERICS-Spoke 5, a Consortium composed by 10 Italian Universities (Politecnico di Milano, Università di Camerino, Università dell'Insubria, Università di Perugia, Università di Pisa, Università Politecnica delle Marche, Università di Trento, Università di Reggio Calabria, Università di Palermo, Università di Roma 3), gathering competencies in mathematics, physics, computer science, computer engineering, telecommunications and law, proposed to pursue the research activities related to post quantum cryptographic techniques and technologies that realize one of the pillars of the 2-year project (2024–2025) named AQuSDIT - *Advanced and Quantum-safe Solutions for Digital Identity and digital Tracing.*

2 AQuSDIT Project

Cryptography is a fundamental discipline for safeguarding the integrity and confidentiality of data in a multitude of contexts, including critical infrastructure, business applications, and personal data management. The availability of modern and robust cryptographic tools is also crucial for the competitiveness and attractiveness of Italian companies and institutions. Moreover, cryptography is now a pivotal component in the functioning of public administration, defense, and social security. Despite their continued use, traditional cryptographic tools are becoming inadequate to address modern challenges such as the need to protect data at rest (secure storage), the need to protect data in transit (secure communication), and the need to protect data in use (secure computation). These challenges are to be considered in combination with the technological advancements in quantum computing and decentralized systems, calling for substantial investment in research, development, and education to enable the medium- and long-term design and implementation of robust cryptographic tools that can be used as building blocks for protecting data in cyberspace. Cryptography is also at the basis of modern decentralized infrastructures, which are commonly referred to as blockchains. These technologies, which originated with the introduction of cryptocurrencies, are now widespread and can be applied in a wide variety of contexts: supply chain tracking, electronic voting, and certification of artworks. Cryptographic primitives and protocols provide the foundation for the security and immutability of such digital infrastructures. Consequently, they must be adapted and modernized to withstand new threats, including those posed by quantum computing. This project aims to strengthen the national community

through the development, validation, and implementation of cryptographic tools and innovative blockchain technologies to address the above challenges, with particular reference to digital identity and digital traceability applications.
The research will be structured along two main lines:

(1) The design, analysis, and experimental validation of new cryptographic primitives and protocols capable of withstanding quantum computer-based attacks for application in digital identity systems.
(2) The design, analysis, and experimental validation of new methods based on distributed ledger technologies for digital identification of things or people and for traceability of products and processes.

2.1 Originality, Methodology, and Organization

The research activity will address some open challenges that are recognized to be of significant interest by the national and international scientific community. Such challenges include:

- The definition and validation of new asymmetric cryptographic primitives, with a particular focus on digital signatures. The aim is to develop primitives that are capable of withstanding quantum computer-based attacks and achieve higher levels of security and efficiency than those currently available in the state of the art. This will be achieved aiming at reducing the size of digital signatures and the size of the corresponding public verification keys.
- The definition and validation of new zero-knowledge identification protocols (ZK-IDs) that offer resistance to quantum computer-based attacks and achieve better performance than those currently available in the state of the art, in terms of key size and amount of information transmitted, is also a key objective.
- The definition and validation of functional encryption methods that enable the disclosure of secret data functions in a concise and publicly verifiable manner, with numerous applications in the areas of distributed systems, blockchain, and distributed ledger technologies.
- The definition of new decentralized protocols and systems, based on blockchain and distributed ledger technologies, to overcome the fragmentation of existing state of the art solutions and define common and scientifically validated approaches for use in applications for digital identity and traceability of products and processes.
- The study and definition of techniques for attacking cryptographic primitives and protocols that provide the foundations for decentralized systems, with a particular interest being taken into systems for self-sovereign identity, electronic voting, digital currency and traceability.
- The study of new models and solutions for advanced blockchain-based applications that support traceability, transparency, verifiability and accountability, possibly based on paradigms of self-sovereign identity.

- The analysis of protocols to reconcile privacy and identification needs in distributed applications (including those based on location and proximity), possibly based on models of self-sovereign identity and zero-knowledge proof.
- The definition of methods and protocols for action identification (supply chain, notarization, process tracking) possibly based on smart contracts with automatic synthesis and security verifiable.
- The definition of smart contract specification techniques and new model-driven approaches for design, execution and auditing of business processes on blockchain platforms.

The methodology that will be adopted in addressing the research challenges described above will be strictly bound to the scientific method, and aimed at producing reliable and verifiable knowledge advancement. It will start from the analysis of existing models and the development of new models for the solutions, algorithms and protocols under study, while defining which key performance indicators (KPIs) are suitable to characterize them. Typical information engineering methodologies will be used to design new solutions and improve existing ones, as well as to implement the new solutions for experimental validation. The scientific activity and its findings will be documented in scientific papers proposed for publication in proceedings of national and international conferences and workshops and in scientific journals of international relevance. Scientific publications resulting from the project activities will be made available in open access, and following the principles of the San Francisco Declaration on Research Assessment (DORA).

Organization. Two main research lines on "Quantum-safe cryptographic primitives and protocols for digital identity" (RL1) and "Advanced digital identification and tracing and distributed ledger technologies" (RL2) will be pursued by the consortium members, maintaining four milestones, at months 4, 8, 19 and 24, to provide detailed deliverables and artifacts. The research activities of RL1 will aim to achieve the following objectives.

- RL1.O1. Design and implement post-quantum digital signature and cryptographic systems and public key cryptography based on lattices and codes, as per the STRIDE call on lattices and code-based, with or without homomorphic properties. This will be done taking into account their computational and engineering security as well as hardware and software tradeoffs in their practical implementation.
- RL1.O2. Design code-based techniques for blockchain security.
- RL1.O3. Design of functional and post-quantum cryptography, and realization of related hardware support.
- RL1.O4. Design and implementation of secure (quantum-safe) cryptographic mechanisms for distributed systems. This includes advanced cryptographic primitives (e.g., homomorphic/functional cryptography.) cryptography), multiparty computation security, and the design of new cryptographic primitives.

The research activities of RL2 will aim to achieve the following objectives.

- RL2.O1. New models and solutions for advanced blockchain-based applications supporting traceability, transparency, auditability, and accountability, possibly based on self-sovereign-identity paradigms. Protocols to reconcile privacy and identification needs in distributed applications (including location-based and proximity-based), possibly based on self-sovereign-identity models and zero-knowledge proofs. Legal aspects should also be addressed concerning both digital identity and privacy.
- RL2.O2. Methods and protocols for action identification (supply chain, notarization, process tracing) possibly based on smart contracts with automatic synthesis and verifiable security.
- RL2.O3. Study of methodologies for secure smart contracts: secure design, runtime enforcement techniques, innovative off-chain models and protocols that enable the secure and efficient execution of smart contracts.
- RL2.O4. Study of multiple blockchain platforms and generation of related smart contracts. Model-driven techniques for the design, development, and execution of business process-based applications should be adopted.

3 Activities at Politecnico di Milano and Preliminary Results

The research activities of the group of participants from Politecnico di Milano will be focused entirely on the topics included in RL1 - "Quantum-safe cryptographic primitives and protocols for digital identity".

Motivation and State of the Art. The advent of large-scale quantum computing has the potential to compromise the security of digital identities due to its ability to circumvent the cryptographic algorithms that currently underpin secure communication and digital identity systems. The main risks are:

(i) Compromising Digital Certificates: digital certificates play a pivotal role in binding digital identities to the means of verifying validating the signatures made by them, and allowing them to entertain confidential communications. For a quantum computer-enabled attacker it would be trivial to obtain the private signing key corresponding to a RSA or ECDSA public verification key contained in a certificate, in turn allowing her to impersonate the subject of the certificate itself. Similarly, if the certificate is binding an identity to a public encryption key, the attacker would be able to retrieve the corresponding private decryption key, jeopardizing secure communications.

(ii) The *store now, decrypt later threat*: The potential exists for quantum computers to decrypt encrypted data that was intercepted in the past. If an attacker stores encrypted communication until a quantum computer is available, they could use quantum algorithms to decrypt the information. This puts previously intercepted data at risk of being exposed.

(iii) Identity Theft and Fraud: Quantum computing can enable attackers to break the encryption protecting personal information like passwords and credit card numbers. This could lead to identity theft, fraud, and unauthorized access to personal accounts or systems.

Several industry standards are currently being developed and evaluated for post-quantum cryptography. Although the field is still evolving, there are some of the major standardization organizations and initiatives that are actively contributing to the development of industry standards for post-quantum cryptography. Their efforts aim to provide new guidelines, new algorithms, and updated protocols that will ensure the security of digital systems and communications in the presence of powerful quantum computers. The research and development of post-quantum cryptography are currently witnessing the creation of several national and industry standards. The US National Institute of Standards and Technology (NIST) has been leading a standardization process for post-quantum cryptography, started in late 2016, to evaluate and select quantum-resistant cryptographic algorithms [25]. The initiative evolved over four rounds of public scrutiny and selection among the candidates, discarding either the ones affected by cryptanalytic breaks, or the ones which exhibit worse performance figures (execution times, or size of the signatures/ciphertexts). Upon closure of the third round, NIST has selected four algorithms which it will standardize as a result of the Post-Quantum Cryptography (PQC) Standardization Process: CRYSTALS–Kyber, along with three digital signature schemes: CRYSTALS–Dilithium, FALCON, and SPHINCS$^+$. The standardization process is continuing with a fourth round, involving alternate candidates for encryption schemes, as the only selected one after the third round relies on problems related to finding the closest vector in a finite dimensional lattice. The decision to have a fourth round was taken with the intent of standardizing alternatives to CRYSTALS-Kyber relying on alternative computationally hard problems, such as the ones coming from coding theory. Finally, we note that the International Organization for Standardization (ISO) has established a working group, ISO/IEC JTC 1/SC 27/WG 2, dedicated to the standardization of quantum-resistant cryptographic algorithms.

Code-based Cryptosystem Design. The research on the design of cryptosystems based on computationally hard problems coming from coding theory is currently tackled from different directions at Politecnico di Milano.

The first one involves quantifying the amount of cryptanalytic efforts required to solve computationally hard problems on which post-quantum cryptosystems are built. Indeed, while the computational complexity of the best current solvers for the *syndrome decoding problem* on random codes, currently one of the most popular candidates to build code-based cryptosystems, is exponential in the number of errors, finite regime estimates provide the means to match the security margin provided by symmetric ciphers without the need of sacrificing performance in the designed cryptosystem. In this direction, the estimation of the finite-regime, concrete quantum cryptanalytic effort required to break code based cryptosystems, started from the design of a quantum algorithm to speed up a combinatorial search taking place in Lee and Brickell's Information Set Decoding [23] (ISD) cryptanalytic technique [27]. This work lead to the acceleration of a full ISD algorithm (namely, the one devised by Prange) in [26,28,29]. Further investigations have lead to a complete description of a quantum walk approach to solve the subset sum problem [6], a key component to design a quantum circuit for the currently most advanced ISD techniques, such as the ones proposed by Both and May in [17]. These investigations allow to provide reliable parameters (e.g., key sizes) for post-quantum cryptosystems, as closed-formulas to determine the quantum gate count of a cryptanalytic approach can be employed in an automated parameter space exploration, following the approach employed during the design of LEDACrypt [10,11]. A further improvement point for post-quantum encryption algorithms, such as LEDACrypt and the current fourth round candidate BIKE is represented by accurate estimates of the decryption failure rate, due to a decoding failure in the underlying bit flipping decoder. Decoding failures have a direct impact on the security, revealing information on the private key being employed in the decryption procedure. At Politecnico di Milano, recent advancements on providing accurate and reliable estimates for the decoding failure rate of bit flipping decoders [1] allow for improvements up to 30% in keysize with respect to the best previous bounds [12]. A different direction being pursued in Politecnico di Milano is the design of post quantum signature schemes, relying on the Fiat-Shamir transformation [20] to turn instances of a zero-knowledge interactive identification protocol into digital signatures. Indeed, such an approach allows to use instances of a problem which is computationally hard also for a quantum computer, where the problem instance itself becomes the public verification key of the signature scheme, while its solution represents the private signature key. The framework provides a way to prove, non interactively, the knowledge of the private signature key to anyone willing to verify the signature, without revealing provably anything but the fact that the signer knows the private key. The key generation process, given the intractability of the computational problem, starts by randomly sampling the private key (i.e., the problem solution) and then constructing a problem around it. In this direction, Politecnico di Milano is currently active in two signature schemes, LESS [8] and CROSS [9], both relying on the Fiat-Shamir transformation, and two separate, coding theory related hard problems, namely linear code equivalence for LESS, and restricted syndrome decoding for CROSS. The linear code equivalence problem employed in LESS allows greater flexibility in building signature schemes with richer features [14], while the NP-complete nature of the restricted syndrome decoding problem provides sound guarantees on the impracticality of a polynomial time solver [13].

Code-based Cryptosystem Engineering. Post quantum cryptosystem engineering requires both to design implementations which provide good resource-performance tradeoffs, and to provide protection against implementation attacks, among which, a prime threat is represented by *side channel attacks*. Post quantum cryptosystems, both code-based ones and lattice-based ones require efficient arithmetic operations among matrices (e.g., matrix- vector multiplications). However, it is a very common choice, in order to improve the computation speed of the cryptosystems, to select matrices with a particular property, i.e., block circulant matrices. Block circulant matrices are built splitting a rectangular matrix in square equally sized blocks. Each square block is in turn a square matrix that is fully defined by its first row, as all other rows are obtained from cyclic shifts of the first row itself. It can be proven that such matrices are isomorphic to the one of the remainders of polynomials with coefficients taken over the same field as the matrix elements, divided by $x^n - 1$, where n is the length of the side of the square matrix. Properties similar to the ones of block circulant matrices can also be obtained considering directly polynomial rings modulo $x^n + 1$, which behave, arithmetically speaking, in a similar fashion.

At Politecnico di Milano, these facts were exploited to the design unified polynomial multipliers [3,5] supporting multiple lattice-based cryptosystems, in particular, different NTRU variants [18,22] and CRYSTALS-Kyber. The research efforts in designing hardware implementations of post quantum cryptosystems lead to the development of a complete hardware accelerator [2] for the NTRU cryptosystem proposal to the NIST standardization effort [18]. While not being selected for standardization, NTRU is explicitly considered by NIST a sound alternative to CRYSTALS-Kyber, in case the patent issues surrounding Kyber are a hindrance to its deployment. A further research direction pursued at Politecnico di Milano is the one of implementing code-based post quantum cryptosystems. The efforts in this direction have lead to the design of a full cryptographic accelerator for the HQC cryptosystem [4,7]. HQC [24], currently one of the three remaining candidates for the fourth round of NIST's standardization effort, is one of the few existing cryptosystems that has a direct security reduction to a computationally hard problem, in the regime where the parameters of the cryptosystem are selected. Furthermore, its efficient arithmetic choice (binary polynomials) allow for compact and high performing implementations.

The sound engineering of post quantum cryptosystems also requires to tackle the issue of side channel attacks. This class of techniques exploits the measurement of physical parameters from a cryptosystem implementation, such as power consumption, electromagnetic radiations and computation time, to extract information from the computation itself. Typically the attacker attempts to deduce either the value of an encrypted message, or a private key, regardless of whether it is a signature or decryption key, from side channel information. A further step forward with respect to the aforementioned approach is to induce errors in the computation of a cryptographic primitive. While these errors will likely result in an unusable result (e.g., a mangled ciphertext, or an incorrect signature), the attacker may be able to derive useful information by either comparing the result with the corresponding correct one, or inferring information on the private key from the erroneous values. Such side channel attack techniques, known as fault attacks, have steadily proven to be extremely effective in disrupting the security guarantees of pre- and post-quantum cryptosystems alike [15,21,31]. In this direction, the research activity at Politecnico di Milano is tackling the study of the effectiveness of fault attacks against post-quantum cryptosystems, with a special focus on signature schemes [16]. Indeed, signature schemes built with the Fiat-Shamir transform start from a zero knowledge interactive identification scheme, which in principle, provides no information whatsoever to the attacker, when run interactively. However, the introduction of faults in the computation of the corresponding signature scheme may lead to the disclosure of the private key, or allow the splicing of a valid signature from its legitimate message, making the attacker able to reuse the said signature on a different document [16].

4 Concluding Remarks

Advancing the state of the art in computer security requires to tackle a variety of challenges, among which, the ones related to providing quantum computing resistant alternatives to current asymmetric cryptographic primitives. In this work, we described the current research directions of the Politecnico di Milano group, highlighting the research efforts in designing and engineering secure and efficient post quantum cryptosystems.

Acknowledgements. This work was supported in part by project SERICS (PE00000014) under the NRRP MUR program funded by the EU - NGEU.

References

1. Annechini, A., Barenghi, A., Pelosi, G.: Bit-flipping decoder failure rate estimation for (v,w)-regular Codes. In: IEEE International Symposium on Information Theory, ISIT 2024, July 7–12, Athens, Greece, 2024, pp. 1–6. IEEE (2024)
2. Antognazza, F., Barenghi, A., Pelosi, G., Susella, R.: A flexible ASIC-oriented design for a full NTRU accelerator. In: Takahashi, A. (ed.) Proceedings of the 28th Asia and South Pacific Design Automation Conference, ASPDAC 2023, Tokyo, Japan, January 16–19, 2023, pp. 591–597. ACM (2023). https://doi.org/10.1145/3566097.3567916
3. Antognazza, F., Barenghi, A., Pelosi, G., Susella, R.: An efficient unified architecture for polynomial multiplications in lattice-based cryptoschemes. In: Mori, P., Lenzini, G., Furnell, S. (eds.) Proceedings of the 9th International Conference on Information Systems Security and Privacy, ICISSP 2023, Lisbon, Portugal, February 22–24, 2023, pp. 81–88. SciTePress (2023). https://doi.org/10.5220/0011654200003405
4. Antognazza, F., Barenghi, A., Pelosi, G., Susella, R.: A high efficiency hardware design for the post-quantum KEM HQC. In: IEEE International Symposium on Hardware Oriented Security and Trust, HOST 2024, Washington, DC, USA, May 6–9, 2024, pp. 431–441. IEEE (2024). https://doi.org/10.1109/host55342.2024.10545409
5. Antognazza, F., Barenghi, A., Pelosi, G., Susella, R.: Performance and efficiency exploration of hardware polynomial multipliers for post-quantum lattice-based cryptosystems. SN Comput. Sci. **5**(2), 212 (2024). https://doi.org/10.1007/s42979-023-02547-w
6. Antognazza, F., Barenghi, A., Pelosi, G., Susella, R.: Poster: A versatile and unified HQC hardware accelerator. In: 61st ACM/IEEE Design Automation Conference (DAC 2024), June 23–27, 2024, San Francisco, CA, USA. ACM (2024). https://doi.org/10.1145/3649329.3657337

7. Antognazza, F., Barenghi, A., Pelosi, G., Susella, R.: Poster: A versatile and unified HQC hardware accelerator. In: 5th ACNS Workshop on Secure Cryptographic Implementation (SCI 2024) - n Martin Andreoni (Editor) Applied Cryptography and Network Security Workshops. ACNS 2024 Satellite Workshops, AIBlock, AIHWS, AIoTS, SCI, AAC, SiMLA, LLE, and CIMSS. Lecture Notes in Computer Science, vol. 14586–14587. Springer (2024). https://doi.org/10.1007/BFb0054868
8. Baldi, M., et al.: Linear Equivalence Signature Scheme. https://www.less-project.com/
9. Baldi, M., et al.: Codes and Restricted Objects Signature Scheme. https://www.cross-crypto.com/
10. Baldi, M., Barenghi, A., Chiaraluce, F., Pelosi, G., Santini, P.: LEDAkem: a post-quantum key encapsulation mechanism based on QC-LDPC codes. In: Lange, T., Steinwandt, R. (eds.) PQCrypto 2018. LNCS, vol. 10786, pp. 3–24. Springer, Cham (2018). https://doi.org/10.1007/978-3-319-79063-3_1
11. Baldi, M., Barenghi, A., Chiaraluce, F., Pelosi, G., Santini, P.: LEDAcrypt: QC-LDPC code-based cryptosystems with bounded decryption failure rate. In: Baldi, M., Persichetti, E., Santini, P. (eds.) CBC 2019. LNCS, vol. 11666, pp. 11–43. Springer, Cham (2019). https://doi.org/10.1007/978-3-030-25922-8_2
12. Baldi, M., Barenghi, A., Chiaraluce, F., Pelosi, G., Santini, P.: Performance bounds for QC-MDPC codes decoders. In: Wachter-Zeh, A., Bartz, H., Liva, G. (eds.) Code-Based Cryptography - 9th International Workshop, CBCrypto 2021, Munich, Germany, June 21–22, 2021 Revised Selected Papers. Lecture Notes in Computer Science, vol. 13150, pp. 95–122. Springer (2021). https://doi.org/10.1007/978-3-030-98365-9_6
13. Baldi, M., Bitzer, S., Pavoni, A., Santini, P., Wachter-Zeh, A., Weger, V.: Zero knowledge protocols and signatures from the restricted syndrome decoding problem. In: Tang, Q., Teague, V. (eds.) Public-Key Cryptography - PKC 2024 - 27th IACR International Conference on Practice and Theory of Public-Key Cryptography, Sydney, NSW, Australia, April 15–17, 2024, Proceedings, Part II. Lecture Notes in Computer Science, vol. 14602, pp. 243–274. Springer (2024). https://doi.org/10.1007/978-3-031-57722-2_8
14. Barenghi, A., Biasse, J., Persichetti, E., Santini, P.: On the computational hardness of the code equivalence problem in cryptography. Adv. Math. Commun. **17**(1), 23–55 (2023). https://doi.org/10.3934/amc.2022064
15. Barenghi, A., Breveglieri, L., Koren, I., Naccache, D.: Fault injection attacks on cryptographic devices: theory, practice, and countermeasures. In: Proc. IEEE **100**(11), 3056–3076 (2012). https://doi.org/10.1109/JPROC.2012.2188769
16. Barenghi, A., Pelosi, G.: Fault attacks friendliness of post-quantum cryptosystems. In: Workshop on Fault Detection and Tolerance in Cryptography, FDTC 2023, Prague, Czech Republic, September 10, 2023, p. 1. IEEE (2023). https://doi.org/10.1109/FDTC60478.2023.00006
17. Both, L., May, A.: Decoding linear codes with high error rate and its impact for LPN security. In: Lange, T., Steinwandt, R. (eds.) PQCrypto 2018. LNCS, vol. 10786, pp. 25–46. Springer, Cham (2018). https://doi.org/10.1007/978-3-319-79063-3_2
18. Chen, C., et al.: NTRU - A submission to the NIST post-quantum standardization effort. https://www.cross-crypto.com/
19. European Commission: NextGenerationEU - more than a recovery plan. https://next-generation-eu.europa.eu/index_en (2021)
20. Feige, U., Fiat, A., Shamir, A.: Zero-knowledge proofs of identity. J. Cryptol. **1**(2), 77–94 (1988). https://doi.org/10.1007/BF02351717

21. Genêt, A.: On protecting SPHINCS+ against fault attacks. IACR Trans. Cryptogr. Hardw. Embed. Syst. **2023**(2), 80–114 (2023). https://doi.org/10.46586/tches.v2023.i2.80-114
22. Hoffstein, J., Pipher, J., Silverman, J.H.: NTRU: a ring-based public key cryptosystem. In: Buhler, J.P. (ed.) ANTS 1998. LNCS, vol. 1423, pp. 267–288. Springer, Heidelberg (1998). https://doi.org/10.1007/BFb0054868
23. Lee, P.J., Brickell, E.F.: An observation on the security of McEliece's public-key cryptosystem. In: Günther, C.G. (ed.) Advances in Cryptology - EUROCRYPT 1988, Workshop on the Theory and Application of of Cryptographic Techniques, Davos, Switzerland, May 25-27, 1988, Proceedings. Lecture Notes in Computer Science, vol. 330, pp. 275–280. Springer (1988). https://doi.org/10.1007/3-540-45961-8_25
24. Melchor, C.A., Blazy, O., Deneuville, J., Gaborit, P., Zémor, G.: Efficient encryption from random quasi-cyclic codes. IEEE Trans. Inf. Theory **64**(5), 3927–3943 (2018). https://doi.org/10.1109/TIT.2018.2804444
25. National Institute of Standards and Technology: Post-Quantum Cryptography Standardization Initiative. https://csrc.nist.gov/projects/post-quantum-cryptography
26. Perriello, S., Barenghi, A., Pelosi, G.: A complete quantum circuit to solve the information set decoding problem. In: Müller, H.A., Byrd, G., Culhane, C., Humble, T.S. (eds.) IEEE International Conference on Quantum Computing and Engineering, QCE 2021, Broomfield, CO, USA, October 17-22, 2021. pp. 366–377. IEEE (2021). https://doi.org/10.1109/QCE52317.2021.00056
27. Perriello, S., Barenghi, A., Pelosi, G.: A quantum circuit to speed-up the cryptanalysis of code-based cryptosystems. In: Garcia-Alfaro, J., Li, S., Poovendran, R., Debar, H., Yung, M. (eds.) SecureComm 2021. LNICSSITE, vol. 399, pp. 458–474. Springer, Cham (2021). https://doi.org/10.1007/978-3-030-90022-9_25
28. Perriello, S., Barenghi, A., Pelosi, G.: Improving the efficiency of quantum circuits for information set decoding. ACM Trans. Quantum Comput. (2023). https://doi.org/10.1145/3607256
29. Perriello, S., Barenghi, A., Pelosi, G.: Quantum circuit design for the lee-brickell based information set decoding. In: 5th ACNS Workshop on Secure Cryptographic Implementation (SCI 2024) - n Martin Andreoni (Editor) Applied Cryptography and Network Security Workshops. ACNS 2024 Satellite Workshops, AIBlock, AIHWS, AIoTS, SCI, AAC, SiMLA, LLE, and CIMSS. Lecture Notes in Computer Science, vol. 14586–14587. Springer (2024). https://doi.org/10.1007/BFb0054868
30. SERICS Foundation: SERICS - Security and Rights in CyberSpace. https://serics.eu (2022)
31. Ulitzsch, V.Q., Marzougui, S., Bagia, A., Tibouchi, M., Seifert, J.: Loop aborts strike back: defeating fault countermeasures in lattice signatures with ILP. IACR Trans. Cryptogr. Hardw. Embed. Syst. **2023**(4), 367–392 (2023). https://doi.org/10.46586/tches.v2023.i4.367-392

Advancing Future 5G/B5G Systems: The Int5Gent Approach

Evrydiki Kyriazi[1], Panagiotis Toumasis[1], Alexandros Valadasis[2], Georgios P. Katsikas[2], Ilias Papalamprou[1], Ioannis Stratakos[1(✉)], George Lentaris[1,3], Giannis Giannoulis[1], Dimitris Apostolopoulos[1], Dimitrios Soudris[1], and Hercules Avramopoulos[1]

[1] National Technical University of Athens, Athens, Greece
{evkyriazi,ptoumasis,jgiannou,apostold,hav}@mail.ntua.gr,
{ipapalambrou,istratak,glentaris,dsoudris}@microlab.ntua.gr
[2] UBITECH, Athens, Greece
{avalantasis,gkatsikas}@ubitech.eu
[3] University of West Attica, Athens, Greece

Abstract. The evolution of mobile networks (5G/B5G) relies on different hybrid transport architectures that enable flexible and scalable interconnection between devices and services with different interfaces and requirements. Despite significant improvements in data rates, device capabilities and data volumes compared to previous generations, technology choices are still under consideration and new proposals are constantly emerging. To address these challenges, Int5Gent proposes and develops a 5G/B5G system that integrates innovative data plane technology building blocks within a flexible orchestration framework. The proposed platform provides a complete 5G system for validating advanced services and Internet of Things solutions, facilitating the transition beyond current 5G network capabilities, and evaluating state-of-the-art data transport and edge processing solutions.

Keywords: 5G · Beyond 5G · SDN/NFV · Edge processing · Network Orchestration · mmWave

1 Introduction

The deployment of a robust 5G infrastructure, incorporating data plane technology blocks, control plane, and application deployment layer, is of paramount importance for maintaining the momentum of 5G market penetration. This infrastructure must meet key performance indicators (KPIs) and support the development of innovative vertical markets [1]. The growing demand for use cases with strict latency requirements, rapid service deployment, dynamicity, and trustworthiness is driving a shift towards distributed network models implemented through edge computing [2]. This approach necessitates the deployment of advanced infrastructure in the access and metro segments to provide reliable data transport and to manage both physical and virtualised network functions for numerous distributed nodes. This is because execution resources (compute and storage) must be positioned close to end users and data generation sources.

The advent of the edge computing model in 5G represents a significant shift in the conventional cloud-based connectivity paradigm (access-core-cloud). In this novel model, certain functions are now executed at the network edge, providing near-real-time feedback to end-user devices. Meanwhile, other data portions are processed in the cloud. This complexity is further compounded by the varying types of edge nodes, which range from simple gateway servers to mini-data centres (DCs), each with different connectivity requirements.

From the perspective of the data plane, new technology building blocks must enable 5G infrastructure to provide flexible, high-capacity, and scalable connectivity between 5G terminals, edge computing nodes, and core infrastructure, including legacy cloud computing. This necessitates transitioning to higher operating bands (V, W, and D-band) and deploying photonic interconnection solutions, which require efficient data distribution elements and advanced RF electronic system designs. Furthermore, the necessity for low latency at the service level and the deployment of new intelligent processing algorithms at the edge node necessitates the development of edge processing units capable of real-time, flexible resource handling. In particular, GPU-assisted edge processing is of significant importance for applications requiring extensive parallelism, such as AI, video processing, and data analytics services [3].

1.1 Future 5G Systems: Envisioning Key Technological Aspects and Challenges

Dedicated edge computing node deployments are increasingly utilized in vertical sectors such as manufacturing, transportation logistics, and smart city gateways. Conversely, fog computing leverages larger processing nodes deployed between the edge and cloud segments of the network, facilitating infrastructure and computing resource sharing among multiple attached subnetworks This approach is practical for services requiring moderate latency and offers better deployment economics due to resource-sharing principles.The typical 5G concept relies on a pool of collocated baseband units (BBUs) at the central office (CO) site, connected to remote radio head (RRH) units via the operator's fronthaul infrastructure. Recent partnerships between major cloud service operators and telecom operators aim to advance this concept, bringing edge computing service deployment closer to reality [4].

Despite cloud service providers moving closer to the edge, distributed edge computing at the end-user site remains essential for meeting advanced 5G requirements, including reliability, security, ultra-low latency, and user-centric services. Sharing edge computing nodes over telecom operator infrastructure introduces a powerful business model, benefiting infrastructure owners, end-users, application developers, and service providers. This model allows operators to expand their portfolio with new tailored user-centric services.

The Int5Gent vision entails the coexistence of edge and fog computing nodes within a 5G fronthaul-backhaul infrastructure, which supports vertical services and IoT devices at access networks. A network orchestrator oversees the entire 5G system, with distributed edge/fog node management and centralized application deployment and monitoring, linked to the cloud for service delivery. Realizing this 5G platform necessitates significant advancements in both hardware and network/service orchestration.

2 The Int5Gent Proposed Architecture

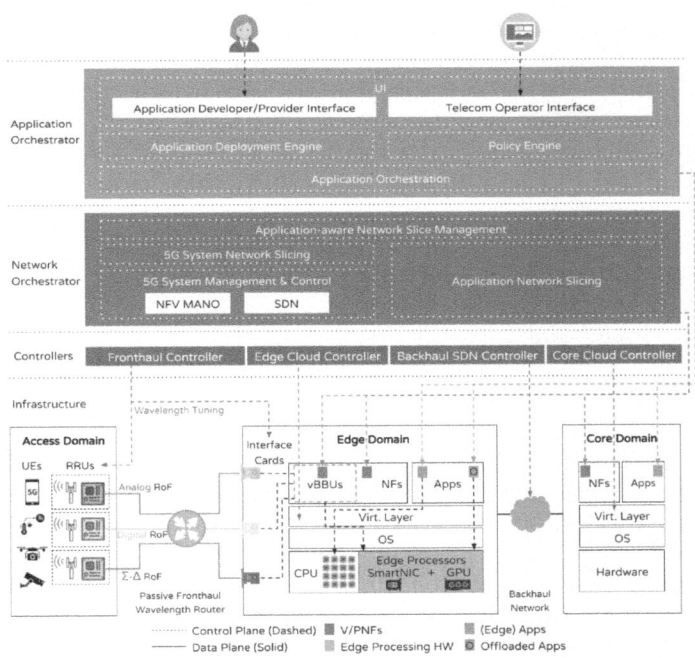

Fig. 1. Overview of the Int5Gent architecture.

Figure 1 presents a global overview of the Int5Gent architecture, organized into several layers: 1) Infrastructure, 2) Controllers, 3) Network Orchestrator, and 4) Application Orchestrator. The Infrastructure layer is further divided into Access, Edge, and Core domains. The architecture also supports three types of Radio over Fiber (RoF): i) Analog, ii) Digital, and iii) Sigma-Delta. In the Access domain, Remote Radio Units (RRUs) connect to Baseband Units (BBUs) in the Edge domain via a wavelength-routed Wavelength Division Multiplex.

2.1 Infrastructure Layer Architecture

Digital Radio-over-Fiber (DRoF): 5G New Radio has driven the creation of disaggregated RAN and efficient connectivity between Remote Radio Units (RRUs) and Baseband Units (BBUs), resulting in packet-based fronthaul networks such as eCPRI. These networks achieve radio data transmission by fragmenting and encapsulating it using standards like IP or Ethernet [5,6]. The data stream is then multiplexed with other network traffic, switched through Ethernet switches, and routed via IP routers.

This approach offers several distinct benefits. Firstly, it enhances the flexibility of the fronthaul network. A single baseband unit can manage multiple radio units using a single network port, with traffic to each radio unit distributed by an Ethernet switch. Secondly, this method allows for the dynamic allocation of fronthaul network and baseband processing capacity to radio cells with varying loads. For instance, cells experiencing a temporary increase in load can receive a greater proportion of the available fronthaul bandwidth and baseband processing resources. Furthermore, this approach facilitates interoperability among equipment from different vendors, as the fronthaul network medium (Ethernet) is standardised by a well-established consortium, with hardware components widely available from various manufacturers. The O-RAN Alliance [7] is the leading standardisation body and community, established to foster interoperability among 5G Radio Access Network (RAN) equipment providers and users.

In order to integrate digital radio-over-fiber capabilities into the Int5Gent environment, commercial CPRI/eCPRI-based RRUs (split 8) and NR digital signal processing cards will be provided. These will be integrated via PCIe interface with COTS x86 hardware, such as a portable edge server. The portable edge server will be prepared as an Int5Gent-compliant Network Functions Virtualization Infrastructure (NFVI) and used for the deployment of commercial BBU software binaries. These binaries, packaged as Docker images with Helm charts, will interface with the provided driver of the PCIe-based 5G NR digital signal processing card.

For fronthaul connectivity, point-to-point (P2P) multi-mode fiber will be employed to link the RRU SFP port with the SFP port on the CPRI/eCPRI-based signal processing card. The integrated radio and signal processing elements on the portable edge server will ensure that the 5G RAN capabilities, specifically 5G NR SA mode operating on band n78 (3500 MHz) with a 50 MHz channel bandwidth and TDD mode [8], are fully operational. These capabilities will be fully interconnected with the Int5Gent network and services orchestration environment.

Analog Intermediate Frequency-over-Fiber. In the context of the evolving 5G RAN ecosystem [9], it is of paramount importance to address the limitations of current deployments in terms of bandwidth efficiency, synchronicity, network availability, and cost. In order to achieve this, the investigation of the SDoF modulation scheme is aimed at achieving tight synchronisation among numerous antenna units. Simultaneously, the emergence of A-RoF-based transport schemes is seeking to deliver extreme bandwidth connectivity. Specifically, the deployment of Analog Intermediate Frequency over Fiber (A-IFoF) transport technology within the Int5Gent multi-RAT access network provides a high-capacity pathway, offering multi-Gbps connectivity over both fiber and converged fiber-wireless network segments. This takes advantage of the extensive bandwidth availability at mmWaves.

Centralised baseband processing techniques are essential for supporting A-IFoF-based fiber and fiber-wireless transmission links. The design and development of corresponding DSP algorithms on real-time platforms are critical for integrating this scheme with legacy deployments. Relocating baseband processing from remote sites to a central office (CO) can significantly reduce network ownership, operation, and maintenance costs by centralising resources in RANs. Given the inherent vulnerability of A-IFoF to distortions, transmission impairments, and nonlinearities in both fiber and wireless components, the design of centralised DSP platforms for the BBUs is of crucial importance for the deployment of flexible, cost-efficient RAN topologies.

In recent years, a number of different A-IFoF fronthaul implementation concepts have been proposed. These implementations demonstrate the scheme's efficiency in dense deployments by eliminating the need for Digital-to-Analog (DAC) conversion and Analog-to-Digital (ADC) conversion units at the remote units (RUs), leveraging advanced bandwidth availability, and enabling the convergence of multiple optical and radio technologies. This has been demonstrated through proof-of-concept experiments. The coexistence of both analog and legacy optical transceivers within the same core infrastructure represents a significant challenge in the implementation of hybrid transport systems. To address this, state-of-the-art Field-Programmable Gate Arrays (FPGAs) have been investigated as Ethernet-compatible baseband processor platforms for creating and processing IF-upconverted signals and integrating them into legacy infrastructures to deliver real-world services.

In the Int5Gent environment, the digital baseband processing platform that is intended to modulate the analog IFoF signals is the AMD RFSoC XCZU28DR-2 device. This device is capable of supporting circuits up to 425K LUTs and integrates 8 SD-FEC hard IPs, as well as 8+8 DAC/ADCs for the purpose of handling analog waveforms sampled at 4 Gsps. The RFSoC device will feature one digital interface and four analog interfaces. The digital interface will be a 10/25G Ethernet port connected via an SFP28 cable to input and output Ethernet data towards the backhaul network. The analog interfaces for recirculating traffic towards the fronthaul will comprise two DAC converters and two ADC converters, which will be connected via SMA cables to the analog components of Int5Gent's A-IFoF link, specifically to the EML and the photodiode.

Sigma-Delta-over-Fiber. The Sigma-Delta Modulation over Fiber (SDMoF) RAN technology provides a PCIe interface at the central unit side (edge box), enabling the exchange of I/Q samples with various RRUs and seamless integration into the Int5Gent baseband platform. At the RRU, a baseband analog interface connects with the RF front-end modules.

SDMoF RAN technology employs sigma-delta modulation to convert a multi-bit digital baseband signal into a single-bit stream. This process enables the transmission of multiple SDM signals over fiber. At the RRU, the analog signal is extracted by filtering out out-of-band quantisation noise, eliminating the need for DAC converters, local oscillators, and mixers. This approach is anticipated to result in a notable reduction in costs when compared to A-RoF technology. This is due to the fact that mass-market optical transceivers can be reused, as they are compatible with the digital nature of SDMoF. Furthermore, the interleaving of multiple sigma-delta streams allows for the efficient utilisation of optical layer bandwidth and the support of multiple antennas. The extraction of a reference clock from the sigma-delta stream at the remote radio units (RRUs) ensures tight phase synchronisation among numerous RRUs, which is beneficial for cooperation in distributed beamforming for cell-free massive MIMO communications [14]. A high-end FPGA will be integrated with commercial-off-the-shelf (COTS) hardware via a PCIe interface. The FPGA will utilise high-speed sigma-delta modulators to convert multi-bit digital baseband I/Q signals from the PCIe interface into a single-bit stream for the downlink. This will be followed by reverse DSP processing for the uplink.

The interoperability of the SDMoF fronthaul and 5G NR will be demonstrated by interfacing with a commercially available baseband unit (BBU) software package, such as Amarisoft, which will be prepared and deployed on the server. Drivers will be developed to connect the BBU and the DU-FPGA over the PCIe interface. Furthermore, a set of RRUs with antenna systems (3.5GHz/n78) will be employed to provide a fully operational gNB. The integration of baseline BBU software packages will ensure that the proposed SDoF-assured gNB is fully compatible with existing 5G gNB implementations, facilitating straightforward interconnection with commercial 5G core networks. To test and verify the gNB's operation, integration and verification with a 5G core network will be conducted in a controlled laboratory environment. In order to demonstrate an operational 5G mobile system, the gNB will be interconnected with a 5G core network using standardised 3GPP-based interfaces (N2 and N3).

The SDoF-RU is compatible with the 5G New Radio frequency band n78 (3300–3800 MHz), which features four RF transceivers (4 × 4 MIMO) and Time-Division Duplexing (TDD). A QSFP28 module enables the RRU to be connected to the DU-FPGA via either multi-mode or single-mode fiber. The recovered clock from the bit-interleaved sigma-delta stream will synchronise the RRU with the DU. Two different versions will be provided. The first COTS version can be integrated into the complete Int5Gent network and demonstrates tight phase synchronisation among two different RRUs, with a phase difference of less than 10 ps within five minutes. A second version, featuring a dedicated integrated circuit with clock-and-data recovery and similar downlink blocks as the COTS counterpart, will also be designed to further improve phase synchronization and reduce RRU costs.

2.2 Transport Network Layer Architecture

This section outlines the design of the Int5Gent transport network, which employs a software-defined approach divided into two distinct domains.

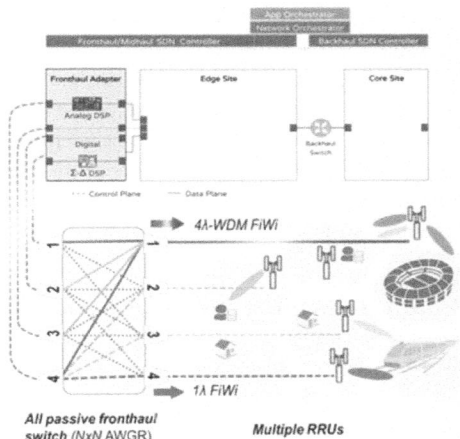

Fig. 2. Conceptual diagram of the proposed P2Mp FiWi C-RAN fronthaul architecture.

AWGR-Based Fronthaul Transport Network. The Int5Gent project aims to develop a Fiber-Wireless (FiWi) millimetre-wave (mmWave) architecture that connects various optical fronthaul interfaces with multiple mmWave antennas in a Point-to-Multipoint (PtMP) system. This architecture dynamically allocates fronthaul bandwidth and steers beams based on service requirements and traffic demands, as outlined in reference [10]. It is capable of directing up to 16 Wavelength Division Multiplexing (WDM) channels to mmWave antennas through high-capacity FiWi links.

The system functions as an any-to-any optical interconnect, routing interfaces from the edge box unit to mmWave antennas with capacities up to 10 Gb/s, using an all-passive Arrayed Waveguide Grating Router (AWGR). This enables the system to meet peak-traffic KPIs. The following key features are noteworthy:

1. Coexistence of analog and digital RoF FiWi links, including Sigma Delta.
2. AWGR deployment as an all-passive fronthaul switch for different modulation formats.
3. Parallel transport of multiple radio waveforms.

Figure 2 illustrates the reconfigurable architecture with four access interfaces (N=4). The edge-box interface utilises a four-wavelength optical transmitter array, which is fiber-connected to the AWGR's input ports and then to multi-beam mmWave antennas. The proposed system is designed to support the reconfigurable allocation of four-wavelength FiWi mmWave downlink traffic to four AWGR output ports and mmWave antennas. Furthermore, it is capable of aggregating four downlink wavelengths into a single WDM stream, which is beneficial for high-traffic sites.

The wavelength routing through the AWGR is developed using software tools, interfacing commercial wavelength tunable SFP+ transceivers with a Mellanox Network Interface Card (NIC) at the edge box fronthaul interface. Int5Gent aims to develop a fronthaul architecture that can interconnect various optical fronthaul interfaces to several mmWave antennas. This architecture will eventually form a point-to-multipoint (PtMP) system that is capable of dynamically steering the fronthaul bandwidth and transported beams according to the service requirements and traffic demands.

SDN-Enabled Backhaul Transport Network. An optical backhaul transport network is defined as a system of interconnected network elements (NE) that utilise optical fibres and control and management software to deliver transport services for digital clients on dense wavelength division multiplexing (DWDM) media channels [11]. Essential components include:

- **Optical Terminals (OT):** Facilitate digital to WDM adaptation, comprising Transponders (1:1 client-to-line interface mapping), Muxponders (N:1 mapping and multiplexing), and Switchponders (N:M mapping, digital switching, and multiplexing).
- **Reconfigurable Optical Add Drop Multiplexers (ROADMs):** Provide optical switching, amplification, equalization, and add/drop functions for specific optical signals.
- **In-Line Optical Amplifiers (ILAs):** Installed in transmission spans between Mux/Demux NEs or ROADMs for signal amplification.
- **Standard Single-mode Fibers (SSMF):** Connect the network elements.

The backhaul transport network of Int5Gent follows the trend of open optical network disaggregation. This model involves the assembly of network components from multiple vendors, allowing for the selection of the best components, incremental upgrades, and the avoidance of vendor lock-in. In partially disaggregated networks, Optical Transponders (OTs) are separated from the Optical Line System (OLS) and can be sourced from different vendors. This decoupling is driven by the differing life cycles of transponders and OLS, and the rapid innovation in coherent Dense Wavelength Division Multiplexing (DWDM) transponders. This approach supports multiple generations of transponders, promotes competition, and protects against industrial risks. The long-term goal is to ensure data plane and control/management interoperability, enabling terminal devices from any vendor to transmit over an OLS deployed by another vendor.

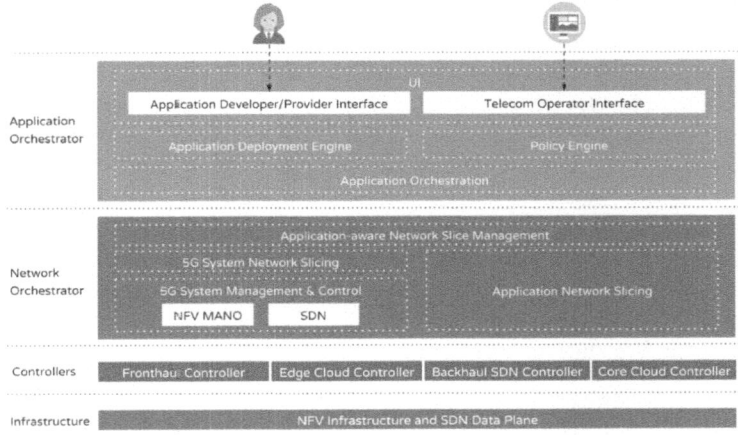

Fig. 3. Application and Network orchestration layers in the Int5Gent architecture.

2.3 Orchestration Layer

Int5Gent has developed a complete 5G system that integrates a range of cutting-edge components, including: (i) fronthaul radio access technologies, (ii) SDN-based transport networking across the entire 5G network, and (iii) decentralised cloud resources at both the edge and core levels. The effective management of the extensive heterogeneity of this geographically distributed pool of devices, while dynamically provisioning the appropriate amount of resources across multiple tenants, necessitates the implementation of fine-grained application and network orchestration mechanisms.

In order to achieve this objective, the Int5Gent orchestration framework architecture is presented in Fig. 3. As illustrated, the Int5Gent Orchestration Framework is comprised of two primary layers, each of which is discussed next:

- **The Vertical Application Orchestrator (VAO):** The VAO is a tool that leverages containers and Infrastructure as a Service (IaaS) cloud platforms to automate service deployment, localization, lifecycle management (LCM), and scaling. It implements an innovative policy framework that links application components with high-level policies. The VAO provides a user-friendly interface for service onboarding and allows stakeholders and applications (APs) to define high-level policies for each service component. Furthermore, the VAO frontend incorporates a dashboard component for intelligent application-level analytics and visualization tools. The VAO supports componentized applications in the form of microservices, organized as Directed Acyclic Graphs (DAGs). Application developers can register components using the VAO UI, which then associates each component with the necessary high-level policies, such as cloud-level, network-level, or scaling policies. The deployment of applications involves three distinct steps. Firstly, the application graph is

converted into a VAS intent. Secondly, the corresponding end-to-end Network Service (NS) is realised by the Network Orchestrator (NOr). Thirdly, the target application is deployed over the created VAS by the VAO.
- **The Network Orchestrator (NOr):** The Network Orchestrator (NOr) represents a pivotal element within the Int5Gent Orchestration Framework Architecture, tasked with overseeing the lifecycle of End-to-End Network Slices (E2E NSs) associated with Vertical Applications (VAs). It is responsible for the allocation, orchestration, and coordination of slice subnets across various network segments, interacting with technology-specific platforms to facilitate these processes. Furthermore, the NOr is responsible for the provisioning of 5G and transport network slices and the allocation of computing resources for VA slice subnets.

In order to facilitate the dynamic management of both application and network resources, these two layers interact with the underlying SDN and cloud infrastructure controllers.

3 Int5Gent Use Cases and Scenarios

The objective of 5G technology is to deliver high capacity, low latency, and also massive connectivity for machine-type communications (mMTC) in a multi-tenant manner over the same network infrastructure through network slicing. This allows for network sharing beyond traditional infrastructure sharing models by running multiple logical networks as independent business operations on a common physical infrastructure. In order to achieve this objective, Int5Gent will present two use cases: the Barcelona Use Case (BCN UC) and the Athens Use Case (ATH UC). This section outlines the Int5Gent use cases, specifying the objectives, planned activities, targeted deployment options, testbed and demonstration activities, and outcomes, with a particular focus on specific components of the architecture.

3.1 Barcelona Use Case

The principal objective of BCN US is to assess and advance the integrated network and vertical application orchestrator framework within a fully operational environment. This environment encompasses a 5G-enabled physical railway infrastructure, an optical/packet transport network, and cloud/edge computing infrastructure for the deployment of various end-user-oriented services. This use case involves two primary users/stakeholders and utilises real-world data from critical infrastructure. The railway operator will request network slices to deploy safety, monitoring, and maintenance-related applications for the rail network, utilising data provided by sensors deployed in an actual railway network. The railway maintenance platform will manage the information collected by the rail sensors in real-time, as well as its historical data, enabling the setup of certain rail line stabilisation actions before dangerous situations occur.

The BCN UC serves to illustrate the validation of two independent network slices that share the same physical infrastructure but provide distinct Quality-of-Service (QoS) parameters:

1. **Mission-critical mMTC with guaranteed QoS:** This scenario features a sensor network deployed on rail tracks that can swiftly respond to safety hazards by triggering alarms to alert the control center and potentially halt service in affected areas for immediate security responses. A mission-critical safety application runs in a 5G User Plane Function (UPF) deployed at the mobile edge to ensure guaranteed QoS [12], while monitoring and maintenance applications operate in the cloud.
2. **Regular mMTC:** This scenario concerns the typical operation of a range of applications without the imposition of strict quality of service (QoS) policies. The 5G core and railway applications for monitoring, maintenance, and safety are deployed on cloud infrastructure.

3.2 Athens Use Case

The ATH UC is designed to demonstrate the deployment of critical services over advanced technology infrastructures and dynamically provisioned heterogeneous 5G access segments, which are tailored for Public Protection and Disaster Relief (PPDR) operations [12]. PPDR day-to-day operations require on-demand, scheduled network coverage and mission-critical services in areas lacking public network coverage. In the event of a disaster where the public core network is partially or completely unavailable, PPDR requires a resilient solution for all network segments. Int5Gent proposes the ad-hoc automatic deployment of a complete 5G-assured PPDR network, including gNB, MEC, and 5GC segments, dedicated to the PPDR sector on a compact server (edge box) in the form of a Non-Public Network (NPN) as defined in 5G terminology. This solution facilitates the rapid and automated deployment of dependable PPDR services through the use of drone-based and camera-based real-time video streaming, which employs cloud-native principles and edge-offloaded AI-based processing.

To illustrate this, the ATH UC will utilise key technological blocks with enhanced physical layer KPIs to support the infrastructure needs. In particular, high-throughput Analog FiWi IFoF/D-band connections will be established to provide up to 3 Gbps connectivity in both indoor and outdoor environments. The tight synchronization requirements of RU/DU connections will be met by deploying SD-RoF cards and SD-RoF-compatible RRU nodes throughout the fronthaul physical infrastructure of the access domain. Furthermore, wavelength reconfiguration and passive optical switching functionalities will be available in the fronthaul transport domain to multiplex fronthaul streams assigned to each transport scenario.

4 Conclusions

This paper presents the future 5G/B5G system that is being developed and finalised within the Int5Gent project. The main objective of Int5Gent is to create an end-to-end next-generation platform that covers all aspects of an advanced communication network, from the data plane to the service layer. The system employs advanced physical layer communication infrastructures (D-RoF, A-RoF, SDoF) and high-performance compute edge nodes to provide a comprehensive solution for application execution and advanced service delivery. The NFV/SDN-based network orchestration layer spans the edge and access domains, managing platform resources. Additionally, the intelligent overlay application orchestration module facilitates communication between application developers and vertical end-users, enabling service management and deployment across the network.

Acknowledgments. This project has been funded by the European Union's Horizon 2020 Research and Innovation Programme under Grant Agreement No. 957403.

References

1. Ericsson – Ericsson Mobility Report (2019)
2. Ericsson white paper – Edge computing and 5G: Harnessing the distributed cloud for 5G success (2019)
3. NVIDIA blog – What Is Edge Computing? by SCOTT MARTIN (2019)
4. Business Insider, Hirsh Chitkara – AWS's new partnership with network operators will help enable latency-sensitive 5G applications (2019)
5. 3GPP TS 23.501 Technical Specification Group Services and System Aspects; System architecture for the 5G System (5GS); Stage 2, (Rel-17) (2021)
6. Ericsson AB, Huawei Technologies Co. Ltd, NEC Corporation and Nokia, eCPRI Specification V2.0. Interface Specification. http://www.cpri.info/downloads/eCPRI_v_2.0_2019_05_10c.pdf
7. O-RAN Alliance. https://www.o-ran.org/about
8. Time and Phase Synchronization Aspects of Packet Networks, ITU-T Recommendation G.8271/Y.1366, 2012; Network limits for time synchronization in packet networks with full timing support from the network, ITU-T Recommendation G.8271.1/Y.1366.1, 2020
9. Global 5G: Implications of a Transformational Technology (2019). https://www.5gamericas.org/global-5g-implications-of-a-transformational-technology/
10. Petrov, V., et al.: Achieving end-to-end reliability of mission-critical traffic in softwarized 5G networks. IEEE J. Sel. Areas Commun. **36**(3), 485–501 (2018)
11. ITU-T Recommendation G.694 ", Spectral grids for WDM applications: DWDM frequency grid", 10/20 https://www.itu.int/rec/T-REC-G.694.1/en
12. Mezzavilla, M., et al.: Public safety communications above 6 GHz: challenges and opportunities. IEEE Access **6**, 316–329 (2018)
13. Kumbhar, A., Koohifar, F., Guvenc, I., Mueller, B.: A survey on legacy and emerging technologies for public safety communications", IEEE Commun. Surveys Tuts. **19**(1), 97–124, 1st Quart (2017)
14. IEEE standard for a precision clock synchronization protocol for networked measurement and control systems. In: IEEE Std 1588-2019 (Revision of IEEE Std 1588-2008), pp. 1–499 (2020)

RISC-V Accelerators, Enablement and Applications for Automotive and Smart Home in the ISOLDE Project

Cătălin Bogdan Ciobanu[1,2(✉)], Honorius Gâlmeanu[2,5],
Alexandru Puşcaşu[1,2], Mihai Gologanu[1], Octavian Buiu[1],
Mihai Antonescu[3], Vlad-Gabriel Serbu[3], Vasile-Mădălin Moise[3],
Cristian-Tiberius Axinte[4], Alexandru-Tudor Popovici[4],
George-Iulian Uleru[4], Andrei Stan[4], Mihai Munteanu[5],
Alexandru Drîmbărean[9], Csaba Nemeti[5], Dănuţ Rotar[6],
Daniel Grosu[6], Cosmin Moişă[6], Bogdan Ditu[7], Petre Cristian Trusca[7],
Marius Antache[7], Simona Costinescu[7], Mari-Anais Sachian[8],
George Suciu[8], Cristian Gheorghe[8], Cristina Tudor[8], and Kejsi Koci[8]

[1] National Institute for Research and Development in Microtechnologies - IMT Bucharest,
Voluntari, Romania
{catalin.ciobanu,alexandru.puscasu,mihai.gologanu,octavian.buiu}@imt.ro
[2] Transilvania University of Braşov, Braşov, Romania
{catalin.ciobanu,alexandru.puscasu,galmeanu}@unitbv.ro
[3] National University of Science and Technology Politehnica Bucharest, Bucharest, Romania
{vlad_gabriel.serbu,madalin.moise,mihai.antonescu}@upb.ro
[4] Gheorghe Asachi Technical University of Iaşi, Iaşi, Romania
{cristian-tiberius.axinte,alexandru-tudor.popovici,george-iulian.uleru,
andrei.stan}@academic.tuiasi.ro
[5] FotoNation SRL, Braşov, Romania
{honorius.galmeanu,mihai.munteanu,csaba.nemeti}@fotonation.com
[6] Continental Automotive Romania, Timişoara, Romania
{danut.2.rotar,daniel.grosu,cosmin.moisa}@continental-corporation.com
[7] NXP Semiconductors Romania, Bucharest, Romania
{bogdan.ditu,petrecristian.trusca,marius.antache,
simona.costinescu}@nxp.com
[8] BEIA Consult International, Bucharest, Romania
{anais.sachian,george,cristian.gheorghe,cristina.tudor,
kejsi.koci}@beia.ro
[9] FotoNation Ltd, Galway, Ireland
alexandru.drimbarean@fotonation.com

Abstract. With Artificial Intelligence applications becoming ubiquitous, both industrial and consumer applications require more computing availability. The increasing need for power-constrained Artificial Intelligence computing asks for new and innovative solutions, on both hardware design as well as on software toolchains that leverage them. At the same time, the challenge of EU technological sovereignty encourages an industry trend oriented to developing its own solutions for power efficient

High Performance Computing (HPC). In this context, as partners in the ISOLDE project started in 2023, we propose the development of new power efficient embedded HPC accelerators, HPC design platforms, as well as High Level Synthesis (HLS) approaches and toolchain technology designs for RISC-V based applications. Specifically, we envisage applications such as Fast Fourier Transform, Number Theoretic Transforms, Post Quantum Computing and artificial intelligence, as well as designing ONNX targeted toolchains based on the LLVM compiler, open solutions for Neural Networks (NN) accelerators and new OpenMP extensions. Within the ISOLDE framework, the envisaged applications to prove the readiness of these technologies are the Automotive and the Smart Home demonstrators.

Keywords: RISC-V · HPC · Polymorphic Register File · PolyMem · AI Accelerator · HLS · AI Compiler · ONNX · LLVM · OpenMP

1 Introduction

Chips are strategic assets for key industrial value chains. As the digital transformation gathers more momentum, new markets are emerging in the industry. Computing capabilities leverage all industrial activities: from automated cars, cloud and Internet of Things (IoT), to connectivity infrastructure, space technologies and defence industries.

The European Union (EU) initiative to bolster Europe's competitiveness and resilience in semiconductor technologies and applications formalized by the European Chips Act entered into force as a regulation in September 2023 [1]. It will reinforce the semiconductor ecosystem in the EU, ensure resilience of supply chains and reduce external dependencies, all seen as key steps in EU technological sovereignty. It is also expected to double Europe's share in the semiconductor global market to 20%.

Industry demands for chips are expected to double by 2030. There will be challenges in meeting this demand, and the EU will address this through the European Chips Act initiative. This will strengthen the EU technological leadership and will mobilise more than €43 billion of public and private investments.

The European Chips Act has identified RISC-V [2–4] as one of the next-generation technologies where Europe should invest, to preserve and strengthen its leadership in research, innovation and computer-based equipment manufacturing [5]. Although ubiquitous and energy efficient, RISC-V computational capabilities are situated on the lower-end of the performance scale [6]. For high-performing computation capabilities, academia and industry players employ proprietary technology developed mainly by United States (US)-based companies. As general industry interest in high-performance computing increases, mainly driven by the development and adoption of Artificial Intelligence (AI) [7], the RISC-V initiative is seen as an opportunity for EU to leverage this technology to address the high performance computing's surging market.

Within this context, the ISOLDE (High Performance, Safe, Secure, Open-Source Leveraged RISC-V Domain-Specific Ecosystems) Chips-JU (previously

KDT-JU) project aims at developing high performance RISC-V processing systems and platforms, and targets at least Technology Readiness Level (TRL) 7 for the majority of its building blocks. It will demonstrate the created technologies for application domains such as Automotive, Space and IoT [8]. More specifically, it aims to build on top of the European developed RISC-V CPUs by developing advanced accelerator architectures and embedded High-Performance Computing (HPC) IPs that address the entire value chain [9].

The scope of this work is to present a cross-cutting facet of the activities of the Romanian cluster in the ISOLDE project, starting from hardware accelerators design and development together with the software tools required to program them, up to the implementation and integration into the Automotive and Smart Home demonstrators. We approach this from two perspectives: the hardware design, be it custom or automated, and the software perspective, that describes the approaches used to design the compilers that target the embedded HPC accelerators and subsystems.

The remainder of this paper is organized as follows: Sect. 2 presents the concepts of FFT split-radix and Number Theoretic Transforms algorithms to be accelerated into dedicated hardware as well as the tightly-coupled SIMD/Vector accelerator. Section 3 shows a High Level Synthesis (HLS) approach to building efficient HPC solutions using Processing Elements, followed by a Smart Home RISC-V use case in Sect. 4. Section 5 transitions from hardware, describing the architecture of the proposed AI/ML (Machine Learning) accelerator, to software, by addressing the associated compiler. Next, we describe the design process for Application Specific RISC-V Hardware Accelerators in Sect. 6. The software toolchain tailored for neural network accelerators is presented in Sect. 7. Section 8 presents the development ideas for an extension of OpenMP and its applicability on a generic-designed Hardware Abstraction Layer, whereas Sect. 9 concludes the paper.

2 Split-Radix Algorithms, Number Theoretic Transforms for PQC and SIMD/Vector Accelerator

In the ISOLDE Project, the National Institute for Research and Development in Microtechnologies (IMT) contributes to both algorithm and digital designs. We adapt split-radix algorithms for hardware acceleration of Fast Fourier Transform (FFT) and of Number Theoretic Transforms (NTT) used for post-quantum cryptography. We also design an accelerator for SIMD/Vector operation.

2.1 Algorithms

FFT is a fast algorithm to calculate the discrete Fourier transform for a periodic array. We use FFT for signal processing (designing coded sequences for time-of-flight acoustic sensors) and HPC (estimating macroscopic properties of a composite from a 2D or 3D image of its micro-structure). Both applications require hardware acceleration for real-time systems.

Based on [10], Bernstein has provided a public domain implementation of a split-radix, in-place, recursive, decimation-in-frequency FFT algorithm [11]. We adapted it to SIMD-like parallelism with short vectors of length V. When reaching FFT levels of order V^2, elements are permuted by interpreting the V^2 array as a $V \times V$ matrix and transposing it in place. Then we may continue with V-type parallelism to the last level of the FFT transform. The proposed algorithm can be implemented in hardware as a tightly-coupled accelerator, where the split-radix conjugate type butterfly is implemented with SIMD-type parallelism. For real arrays, power can be saved by gating the unneeded "conjugate root" part of the circuit. We explore the use of the vector accelerator with two-dimensional registers (see Sect. 2.2) to skip the in-place transpose. We also consider a loosely-coupled accelerator for FFTs with arbitrary lengths (power of 2). For RISC-V vector accelerators with long vectors, the previous approach is not applicable; thus we explore split-radix algorithms adapted to this use case.

In a separate development, we explore algorithms for Number Theoretic Transforms (NTT), the equivalent of FFT for integer arithmetic in finite fields, with application to the fast multiplication of polynomials in finite polynomial rings $Z_q(X)/(X^n - 1)$. This is one of the most time and energy consuming operations for Post-Quantum Cryptography (PQC) based on learning with errors. The problem here is that only few choices of (n, q) admit NTT. Some PQC algorithms are specially devised around NTT friendly pairs, while others on purpose shun such choices in order to decrease the attack surface. This work is focused on *universal* NTT algorithms using either complex transforms for generalized Mersenne primes, or real transforms for generalized Fermat primes. The hardware implementations for such algorithms are also being examined.

2.2 Digital Design

IMT's contribution to SIMD/Vector accelerators is a tightly coupled accelerator for RISC-V cores. It features software-defined two-dimensional registers, acceleration of matrix operations (commonly used for Artificial Intelligence, AI - specifically Machine Learning, ML), and the coupling of the accelerator with the main core by means of the new CoreV-eXtension-Interface (CV-X-IF).

The IMT accelerator was designed to be flexible, with generic AI applications in mind. It has software defined 2D registers based on the Polymorphic Register File Organization [12], with a table storing the width, height and data type for each register specified by the user. The supported operations of this 2D accelerator are common matrix operations used in AI, like addition, subtraction, cross product, dot product and convolution.

The proposed accelerator has two interfaces: one to the main core and another one to the main memory; the latter is used to unload memory operations from the core. The new CV-X-IF interface for RISC-V cores allows the extension of the Instruction Set Architecture (ISA) with new opcodes and provides access to core registers, thus largely simplifying the design of tightly-coupled accelerators [13]. Figure 1a shows the accelerator's place in the system and its interactions with other components. Figure 1b shows the internal architecture of the accelerator

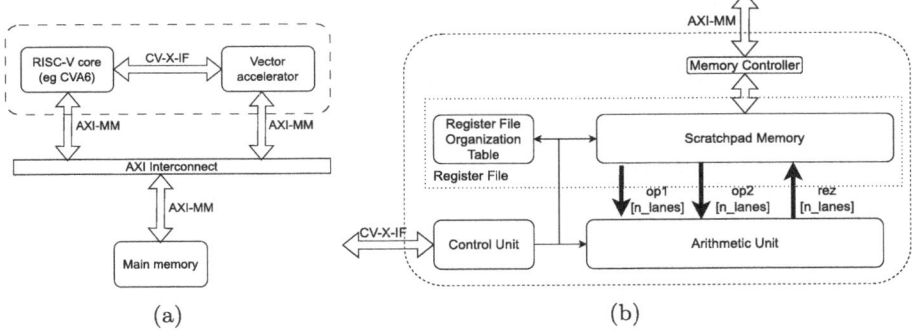

Fig. 1. SIMD/Vector accelerator. **(a)**: Interfaces **(b)**: Internal architecture

that includes a scratchpad memory based on PolyMem [14]. This allows for multi-lane conflict-free access to the stored data and for reading of 2D data in multiple patterns. For example, one could read multiple elements from the same line, from the same column or from the transposed matrix, without in-memory transposing [12,14]. This two dimensional memory organization largely simplifies and speeds up data accesses.

3 Flexible Extensions Platform Architecture for HPC Design

3.1 An HLS Approach to DSP Accelerators

High-Level Synthesis (HLS) is a design flow for digital systems. The input to this process is an abstract (high-level) behavioral specification together with the design parameters and constraints. The output is a register-transfer level (RTL) description that implements the input behavior. Two examples of proprietary HLS tools are AMD Vitis^{TM} – which accepts algorithms and dataflows described in C/C++ [15] – and MATLAB Simulink®. Examples of free open-source synthesis frameworks include SGen [16] based on Scala and SPIRAL [17].

3.2 Architecture Description

Technical University of Iași proposes an architecture (see Fig. 2) that offers a flexible approach towards building efficient high performance computational solutions for specialized uses cases. It aims at flexibly chaining a set of Processing Elements (PEs) with predictable throughput and latency. This in turn helps reduce the complexity of design space exploration phase of processing intensive projects.

This architecture encompasses the fundamental components typically found in a computing engine, including data processing units, memory blocks, an interconnection network and the required control logic. The set of PEs consists of digital designs employed to accelerate the computation of trigonometric functions

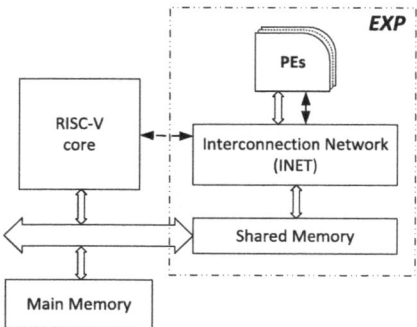

Fig. 2. RISC-V system Extensions Platform (EXP) architecture for vector processing.

(e.g., CORDIC [18]) and digital signal processing specific operators (e.g. Discrete Fourier Transform). With the help of PEs, these operators can be sequenced, thus achieving composite computations.

Furthermore, the PEs can synchronize their execution to create a low latency dataflow type of architecture. This is partially achieved by using vector queues feeding the pipeline of each PE with streamed data. This type of organization is characteristic to Kahn process networks, which have proved their usefulness in modeling the embedded systems, HPC systems, signal processing systems, stream processing systems, and dataflow programming languages.

The Shared Memory serves as a local repository for data blocks on which the PEs operate on. External modules such as DMAs can access its contents. To facilitate parallel access by PEs, it employs multiple memory banks (modules). They could take the form of standard memory blocks or FIFOs and are linked to PEs via the interconnection network.

3.3 Interconnection Network

The Interconnection Network (INET) serves as the communication backbone that facilitates data transfer between the PEs and the other system components (RISC-V core and shared memory). The INET is responsible for scheduling the data flows, dynamically interconnecting PEs and storage elements according to specific computation requirements.

4 Custom RISC-V Open-Source Designs for Smart Home

The ISOLDE Project, a pioneering initiative in the realm of computing architecture, is making significant steps in the integration of RISC-V accelerators into the automotive and smart home sectors [19]. The RISC-V open-source ISA is revolutionizing the way we think about processing power and efficiency, offering a customizable and scalable solution that is rapidly gaining traction. BEIA is providing customization of open-source RISC-V designs targeting efficient, safe, secure and interoperable Smart Home applications.

Smart Home. The smart home market is another area where RISC-V is making an impact. The ISOLDE Project's work with RISC-V accelerators allows for more intelligent and energy-efficient home automation systems. From managing lighting and temperature to ensuring security, RISC-V's flexibility facilitates the development of customized smart home applications that enhance user convenience and comfort. Innovations in technology are constantly reshaping our lives, and the realm of Smart Homes is no exception. While the ISOLDE Project has traditionally focused on automotive and space applications, its principles find new relevance in the context of Smart Homes.

Energy Efficiency. Due to its adaptable design, RISC-V provides a special opportunity to minimize power consumption in the field of smart home technologies. Manufacturers can design solutions that improve user experience and support larger sustainability initiatives by customizing products to meet specific energy-saving criteria [20]. RISC-V facilitates the creation of energy-efficient smart home ecosystems by allowing the implementation of creative power-saving features and the adaptation of processing power based on real-time consumption patterns. By lowering the energy waste, it helps customers to save money on electricity bills and also supports the international efforts on mitigation of climate change causes. In the end, RISC-V adoption in smart home technology is a big step toward building a more ecologically friendly and sustainable future [21].

Customization. The open-source nature of RISC-V empowers manufacturers to craft bespoke processors tailored for specific Smart Home applications. From smart thermostats to security systems, RISC-V enables the creation of devices finely tuned to the unique needs of each home [22].

Security. Because user privacy is so important and the data involved is sensitive, it is imperative that Smart Homes maintain strong security measures. The modular architecture of RISC-V makes it easier to incorporate cutting-edge security measures designed to meet the unique requirements of smart home environments [23]. RISC-V facilitates the deployment of encryption protocols, secure boot methods, and authentication protocols with seamless integration, thereby mitigating illegal access and any breaches to user data. Therefore, smart home systems can guarantee that security stays a primary concern and give customers trust about the confidentiality and integrity of their personal data by utilizing RISC-V's adaptable design [24].

Interoperability. RISC-V's standardized ISA facilitates interoperability among Smart Home devices, enabling seamless communication and integration. This enhances user's experience by ensuring that devices coming from different manufacturers can interact effortlessly within the home ecosystem, promoting convenience and versatility [25].

Customization of Open-Source RISC-V Designs. BEIA actively participates in the design and development of customizable and domain-specific open-source RISC-V processors within the ISOLDE framework. Their contribution extends beyond generic architectures, tailoring processors specifically for Smart Home applications. By leveraging RISC-V's open-source nature, BEIA ensures that Smart Home devices benefit from energy-efficient designs, security enhancements, and seamless interoperability.

Through fine-tuning processor designs, optimizing power management, and integrating specialized accelerators, BEIA contributes to sustainable Smart Home ecosystems. Their focus on energy efficiency directly impacts the longevity of devices and reduces the overall carbon footprint.

By ensuring that ISOLDE's high-performance components reside within Europe, BEIA contributes to the unification and focus of a robust RISC-V ecosystem. This ecosystem, supported by industry stakeholders, strengthens the EU's microelectronics industry and fosters breakthrough designs.

RISC-V stands as a powerful enabler of innovation in Smart Homes, offering unparalleled flexibility, efficiency, security, and interoperability. As the world moves towards increasingly interconnected living spaces, RISC-V emerges as a cornerstone technology driving the evolution of Smart Home ecosystems.

5 AI/ML Accelerator and Toolchain

For the ISOLDE project, FotoNation is leveraging its designs of a convolutional neural network accelerator [26,27]. A targeted architecture compiler is developed in order to better make use of the hardware capabilities of the accelerator.

5.1 AI/ML Accelerator Architecture

The accelerator system integration is depicted in Fig. 3. All interfaces are standard AXI4 128-bit wide, making the accelerator easily to be integrated in the majority of systems. It is a loosely coupled architecture.

Current implementation of the host processor features a RISC-V CPU. This is connected to the same AXI bus and controls the accelerator by taking care of configuring its registers, starting it and monitoring its running program. When required, it can access the accelerator's Cache (internal Memory Banks) to perform custom operations, and can also assist in debugging accelerator's program.

One interrupt line is mandatory and it will be used by the accelerator to signal its program completion status. System memory is required for storing the CPU routines, the accelerator program, the neural network parameters, the intermediary computed feature maps as well as the input and output data.

Figure 3 also presents the block diagram of the AI/ML accelerator. It supports the most common operations of a standard convolutional neural network, such as convolution, pooling, non-linear activation functions, element-wise addition and multiplication, as well as matrix multiplication (supporting the fully-connected layer inference). An operation is defined by an instruction; instructions are then aggregated, making up the neural network inference process.

A typical processing sequence on the AI/ML accelerator is detailed by the following timeline:

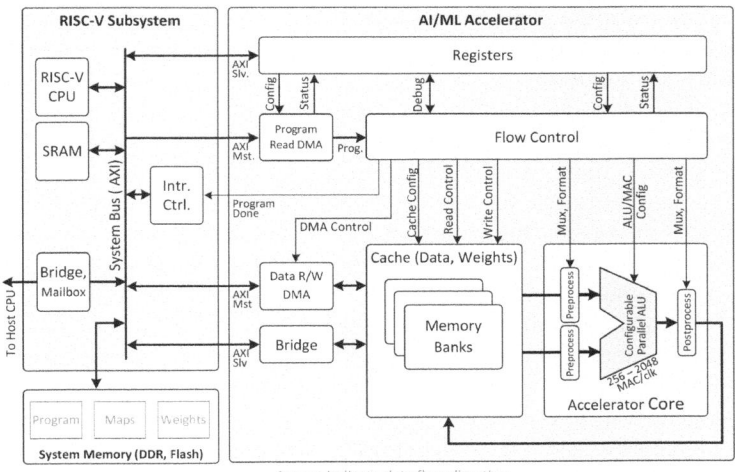

Fig. 3. AI/ML accelerator: AXI bus integration and internal architecture

1. Load of the compiled neural network program, its parameters (weights) and associated input data into the System Memory;
2. Start the accelerator's clock, followed by configuration of its Registers. These contain the accelerator's status bits and give the CPU full control over the Accelerator Core when complex interactions (or debugging) is needed;
3. Configure the Program DMA and start the accelerator's program transfer using the DMA. Data is prepared by the DMA block, before instruction execution;
4. Instruction execution starts in the Accelerator Core. This contains a configurable Parallel ALU that processes the data from the Cache and writes the results back into the same Cache. Operations can work on 8 or 16 bit data, as they use high precision accumulators. The number of MAC operations is parameterised, from 256 to 2048 MACs;
5. Read/Write DMA transfers are controlled within accelerator's program;
6. The Host CPU monitors program's progress by interrupts or status registers;
7. The accelerator raises the "program completed" interrupt, and the CPU can post-process the results.

The AI/ML accelerator has two clock domains: the AI/ML accelerator clock and the AXI interface clock. Both clocks can be gated externally when the module is not in use.

5.2 Toolchain for AI/ML Accelerator

FotoNation has gained substantial expertise in optimizing convolutional neural network architectures to accelerate their execution on low-power hardware, with minimal computational requirements [28]. The current implementation of the toolchain comprises three modules: the accelerator driver, the compiler itself and the software simulator.

The optimization and compilation of the given neural network is achieved by FotoNation's custom compiler, that leverages ONNX-MLIR [29]. It pre-processes the input network given as an ONNX model, for example fusing together Convolution followed by BatchNorm nodes, absorbing activation functions into Convolution nodes or considering Constant nodes containing parameters as integral part of Convolution nodes. The ONNX nodes, seen as operations, are later converted into corresponding successions of AI/ML instructions. This is performed such that the memory traffic for intermediary activation maps (from Cache to System Memory and back) is minimized. Typical AI/ML instructions are Load, Save (used for transfers in-between the Cache and the System Memory) and the operators referred in Subsect. 5.1.

On implementing the SW toolchain, the developer needs to ensure that the results of the implemented operation decomposition are still consistent with the original results of the operation as produced by a standard implementation. Moreover, the results of composing several operations, as these build on top of each other, are also required to be verified as being accurate. Systematic testing is thus implemented by creating a SW model of accelerator's operations; their computational result is then verified against the standard implementation.

6 Application-Specific RISC-V Hardware Accelerator Platform

Automotive applications can be classified as: i) compute-intensive modules: modulate data flow, lots of number crunching and few decisions, e.g. machine learning inference, digital signal processing, or cryptography and ii) regular modules: modulate instruction flow, little number crunching and making a lot of decisions.

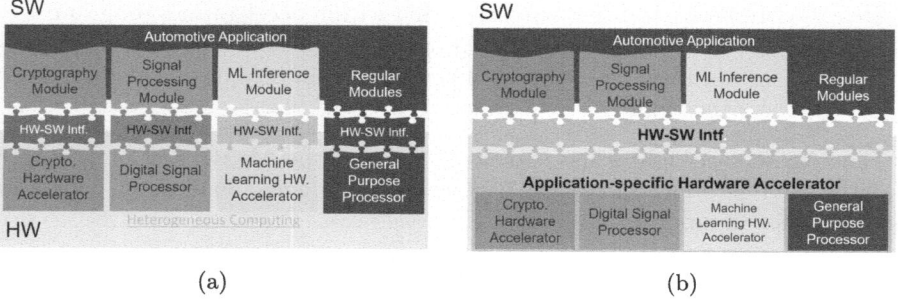

Fig. 4. Heterogeneous computing: **(a)** Fragmented HW-SW interface **(b)** Unified HW-SW interface.

In order to improve performance, compute-intensive module should be executed on a dedicated hardware accelerator. In general, each selected hardware accelerator comes with its own hardware software (HW-SW) interface (Fig. 4a). This approach leads to a heterogeneous hardware setup - General Purpose Processors (GPPs), hardware accelerators and associated interconnection network - which can become a programming challenge due to the fragmented HW-SW Interface (Fig. 4a). A hardware façade built on top of this heterogeneous accelerators set can make the programmer's life less challenging (Fig. 4b).

The benefits of this approach are the following: i) **SW First!** - hardware is tailored to the application needs, i.e. the selected hardware accelerator(s) shall match the required performance/Watt; ii) A **single hardware-software interface** will ease the programming of the system; iii) **Synergies at hardware level** can be acquired, enforcing better performance/Watt.

The above approach is known as Application-Specific Instruction-set Processor (ASIP). This delivers high performance and energy efficiency by tailoring the processor architecture and instruction set to the specific requirements of a particular application domain.

The HW-SW interface of a computing system is known as Instruction Set Architecture (ISA). It defines the following, among others: i) instruction set and instruction encoding; ii) architectural state (register set, control & status register, etc.); iii) memory specification - addressing and alignment; iv) virtual memory architecture.

The microarchitecture consists of an implementation of the ISA in a particular GPP. A compiler will translate the high-level language into a flow of instructions defined by the ISA. Thus, the ISA is essentially a compiler target (Fig. 5a).

Continental Romania (CAR) introduces the Application-specific RISC-V Hardware Accelerator (AIDA) platform (Fig. 5b), designed from the perspective of the following goals: i) **performance**, measured using throughput (operations per second) and latency (time to complete a task); and ii) **flexibility**, the degree to which the accelerator can cope with variations of the application.

The hardware façade in this case is the RISC-V RV32I processor with custom extensions. These are tailored to make the hardware accelerator programmable from the RISC-V software ecosystem perspective. To accommodate the ML model complexity, a ML compiler shall translate the model's execution graph into a flow of RISC-V like instructions. The software toolchain is able to translate ONNX machine learning models and/or C++ applications into binary code to be executed by AIDA. The toolchain development effort is equally balanced between the ONNX frontend and the RISC-V backend, while leveraging all optimizations already available in the LLVM framework [30].

7 Toolchain for Neural Network Accelerators

In the ISOLDE Project, the National University of Science and Technology Politehnica Bucharest (UPB) spearheads the creation of a sophisticated soft-

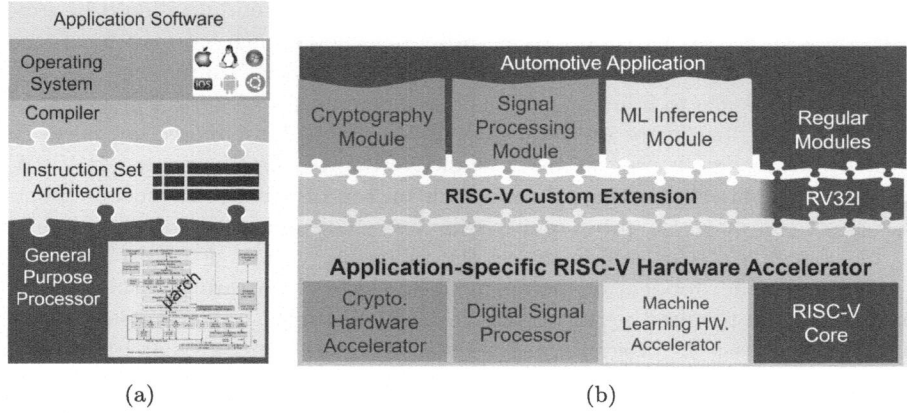

Fig. 5. Instruction Set Architecture: **(a)** SW stack **(b)** AIDA.

ware toolchain tailored for neural network accelerators such as [31] with hardware improvements described in [32], and optimized data transfers described in [33]. By providing developers with specialized development tools for the platform, UPB aims to improve user experience, enabling them to craft high-quality software more efficiently. The toolchain is designed to streamline the testing and implementation of established neural network architectures, thereby minimizing developer workload.

The toolchain is structured as seen in Fig. 6. It is split into two components: the functionality operating on the accelerator host, such as a RISC-V processor like CVA6, and the Software Development Kit (SDK) executed on a remote computer, a follow-up framework for [34,35].

At the application level, end-users have access to a sophisticated Graphical User Interface (GUI) to seamlessly upload both the neural network architecture and input data onto the runtime. Using its previous experience with complementary tools described in [36,37], UPB's team develops better software aimed at enhancing user experience and boosting productivity.

On the host system, a dedicated runtime environment manages all communications between the remote computer and the physical accelerator. User connectivity is facilitated through Ethernet, while interactions with the hardware accelerator are conducted via AXI interfaces: AXI Lite for control and AXI Stream for data transfers. The runtime will also oversee accelerator memory management and, when necessary, dynamically adapt the accelerator's computing behavior.

Although the majority of the work will focus on software development, UPB's team also plays a pivotal role in defining packaging requirements and adapting hardware interfaces for the automotive demonstrator.

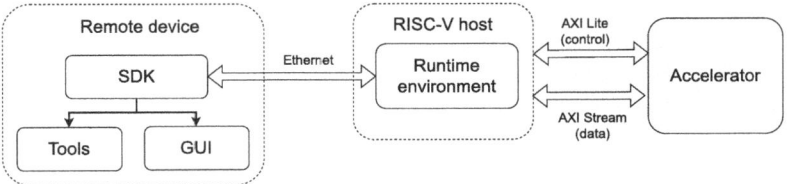

Fig. 6. Toolchain general structure

8 OpenMP Support for RISC-V Subsystems

As part of ISOLDE European Project, NXP Romania is contributing to OpenMP support for a bare-metal multicore RISC-V based subsystem, called OpenMP Lite. In the domain of OpenMP, NXP has initiated a shift towards the development of a Hardware Abstraction Layer (HAL) for the multicore target subsystem.

NXP's initial efforts have been concentrated on the analysis and testing of various frameworks, such as Software-Hardware Interface for Multi-Many-Core (SHIM) [38], that could serve as the foundation for this abstraction. NXP currently analyzes and evaluates the requirements to transition its existing runtime to operating on a HAL instead of running on a particular architecture. This approach ensures that NXP's HAL is not only robust and efficient, but also versatile with respect to the evolving hardware trends. This would enable multiple architectures to reuse the runtime being developed; this requires only defining the 3rd party architecture within the HAL framework. Development of a HAL specification under the OpenMP runtime represents a strategic move towards enhancing system's adaptability and versatility.

When it comes to OpenMP using multiple devices (i.e., host and target(s)), the offloading paradigm comes into place. This becomes handy when Asymmetric Multi-Processors (AMPs) programming is considered.

Offloading is a mechanism that helps applications to distribute their workload (in part or completely) to specialized accelerators while the host core can continue with other independent tasks. Even though the OpenMP standard has defined the offloading workflow, most of the current implementations are heavily relying on the host operating system. Although justified, embedded systems could face certain situations where the host benefits only from a minimal OS support, or no OS at all (bare metal). When it comes to the lowest parts of the offloading stack on the host, the OpenMP runtime requires specific interactions with target low-level drivers.

From this perspective, the OpenMP runtime library is quite hard to be retargeted to systems where the host OS and target drivers are not following the mainstream of current implementations. Even though one is targeting OpenMP for offloading on a multi-core RISC-V accelerator, he/she could face different configurations of host processors and integration scenarios. NXP plans to approach this problem focusing on high retargetability.

To meet this high retargetability, NXP started to identify all pieces of OS dependencies in the OpenMP runtime implementation and to re-design them using an abstraction layer. The same dependencies are being identified regarding the interaction between the host and its target. The purpose is to keep the abstraction layer as simple as possible, designing with retargetability as the objective. NXP is also evaluating the possibility of remapping the abstraction layer (either entirely, or by pieces) with other specific standards, like SHIM.

To prove the retargetability of this solution, NXP intends to validate the concept on different Asymmetric Multiprocessing (AMP) configurations, as little related with NXP's current targets as possible. The measure of the success will be the monitoring of the retargetability time and the performance of the resulting implementation, compared with dedicated solutions.

To verify and validate the ongoing development process, NXP is porting a set of OpenMP benchmarks from the community, namely the integration tests from Rodinia 3.1 [39] and unit tests from the Mercurium project [40]. Comprehensive unit tests for all of OpenMP Lite supported directives and clauses based on OpenMP 5.0 specifications [41] are planned to be developed.

9 Conclusions

As part of the Chips JU initiative, the ISOLDE project targets to enrich the development of Open Source hardware, a critical need for EU technological sovereignty. ISOLDE raises the Technology Readiness Level for RISC-V based applications, providing reusable technology components as building blocks, including both the hardware components such as HPC accelerators as well as the system software like compilers and associated extensions. The Romanian cluster, composed of four companies, two Universities and one Research Institute, are involved in the Automotive and Smart Home use-cases. This covers the development of HPC accelerators targeting domains such as physical phenomenons observation, post-quantum computing processing and artificial intelligence applications, as well as development of automated High Level Synthesis of embedded HPC architectures and creation of flexible design methodologies for toolchains targeting RISC-V accelerator-based subsystems.

Acknowledgements. This work was supported by grants of the Ministry of Research, Innovation and Digitization, CNCS/CCCDI - UEFISCDI, project numbers PN-IV-P8-8.1-PME-2024-0006, PN-IV-P8-8.1-PME-2024-0009, PN-IV-P8-8.1-PME-2024-0012, PN-IV-P8-8.1-PME-2024-0020, PN-IV-P8-8.1-PME-2024-0022, PN-IV-P8-8.1-PME-2024-0024 and PN-IV-P8-8.1-PME-2024-0025 within PNCDI IV.

The ISOLDE project, nr. 101112274 is supported by the Chips Joint Undertaking and its members Austria, Czechia, France, Germany, Italy, Romania, Spain, Sweden, Switzerland.

References

1. European Commission. A Europe fit for the digital age - European Chips Act (2023). https://commission.europa.eu/strategy-and-policy/priorities-2019-2024/europe-fit-digital-age/european-chips-act_en
2. RISC-V International. About RISC-V, 2024. https://riscv.org/about/
3. Urquhart, R.: What Does RISC-V Stand For? A brief history of the open ISA. (2021). https://semiengineering.com/what-does-risc-v-stand-for/
4. Dahad, N.: DAC 2023: RISC-V is not in the future, it's now (2023). https://www.embedded.com/dac-2023-risc-v-is-not-in-the-future-its-now/
5. EuroHPC-JU. New call for developing an HPC ecosystem based on RISC-V (2023). https://eurohpc-ju.europa.eu/new-call-developing-hpc-ecosystem-based-risc-v-2023-02-01_en
6. Shah, A.: RISC-V Is Far from Being an Alternative to x86 and Arm in HPC (2022). https://www.hpcwire.com/2022/11/18/risc-v-is-far-from-being-an-alternative-to-x86-and-arm-in-hpc/
7. HPCWire. Artificial Intelligence Supercomputer Market Predicted Worth of $6.43 Billion by 2030, 2024. https://www.hpcwire.com/off-the-wire/artificial-intelligence-supercomputer-market-predicted-worth-of-6-43-billion-by-2030/
8. ISOLDE. High Performance, Safe, Secure, Open-Source Leveraged RISC-V Domain-Specific Ecosystems (ISOLDE) (2023). https://www.isolde-project.eu/
9. Fornaciari, W., et al.: RISC-V processor technologies for aerospace applications in the ISOLDE project. In: SAMOS, pp. 363–378 (2023)
10. Bernstein, D.: Multidigit multiplication for mathematicians (2001). https://cr.yp.to/papers/m3.pdf
11. Bernstein, D.: DJBFFT - an extremely fast library for floating-point convolution (1999). https://cr.yp.to/djbfft.html
12. Ciobanu, C.B.: Customizable Register Files for Multidimensional SIMD Architectures. Delft University of Technology (TUDelft), 2013. ISBN 978-94-6186-121-4. https://doi.org/10.4233/uuid:6da2ee07-99df-450d-93bd-2367725f4f70
13. OpenHW Group. Core-V eXtension interface (CV-X-IF) (2024). https://docs.openhwgroup.org/projects/openhw-group-core-v-xif/en/latest/
14. Ciobanu, C.B., et al.: MAX-PolyMem: high-bandwidth Polymorphic parallel memories for DFEs. In: IPDPSW 2018, pp. 107–114 (2018)
15. AMD. Vitis HLS (2020). https://www.amd.com/en/products/software/adaptive-socs-and-fpgas/vitis.html
16. Serre, F., et al.: A DSL-based FFT hardware generator in scala. In: Proceedings of FPL 2018, pp. 315–3157 (2018)
17. Franchetti, F., et al.: SPIRAL: extreme performance portability. Proc. IEEE **106**, 1935–1968 (2018)
18. Walther, J.S.: The Story of Unified Cordic. J. VLSI Signal Process. Syst. **25**(2), 107-112 (2000). ISSN 0922-5773
19. Suciu, G., et al.: IoT platform for personal data protection. Ann. Disaster Risk Sci. ADRS **3**(1), 0–0 (2020)
20. Cui, E., et al.: RISC-V Instruction Set Architecture extensions: A Survey (2023)
21. Yitmen, I., et al.: BIM-Enabled Cognitive Computing for Smart Built Environment. Taylor & Francis. (2023)
22. Calice, F.: SystemC Simulation of Extra-functional properties for RISC-V-based systems. Diss. Politecnico di Torino (2023)

23. Desbiens, F.: The Hardware Building Enterprise IoT Solutions with Eclipse IoT Technologies: An Open Source Approach to Edge Computing. Berkeley. Berkeley, CA: Apress, pp. 189–216 (2022)
24. Oyinloye, T.A.: Software exploitation and software protection measures enhancing software protection via inter-process control flow integrity (2023)
25. Baccelli, E.: Internet of Things (IoT): Societal Challenges & Scientific Research Fields for IoT (2021)
26. Munteanu, M.C.: Neural network engine (2020). https://patents.google.com/patent/US20190317730A1/en
27. Munteanu, M.C., et al.: Convolutional neural network (2021). https://patents.google.com/patent/US20200126178A1/en
28. Lemley, J., et al.: Convolutional neural network implementation for eye-gaze estimation on low-quality consumer imaging systems. IEEE Trans. Consum. Electron. **65**(2), 179–187 (2019)
29. Jin, T., et al.: Compiling ONNX Neural Network Models Using MLIR. ArXiv preprint arxiv: abs/2008.08272 (2020). https://arxiv.org/abs/2008.08272v2
30. Lattner, C., et al.: LLVM: a compilation framework for lifelong program analysis and transformation. In: CGO, pp. 75–88, San Jose, USA (2004)
31. Ștefan, G.M., et al.: FPGA-based programmable accelerator for hybrid processing. ROMJIST, **19**(1-2), 148–165 (2016). ISSN 1453-8245
32. Antonescu, M., Ștefan, G.M.: Multi-function scan circuit. In: 2020 International Semiconductor Conference (CAS), pp. 123–126 (2020)
33. Popescu, G.V.: Improvements in data transfer for a mapreduce accelerator. ROMJIST, **25**(3-4), 368–380 (2022). ISSN 1453-8245
34. Bîră, C.: OPINCAA OPcode INjection for Connex-Arm Architecture (A Programming Environment For Parallel Accelerators). MATRIX ROM (2021)
35. Popescu, G.V., et al.: Python-based programming framework for a heterogeneous MapReduce architecture. In: COMM 2022, pp. 1–6 (2022)
36. Bîră, C., et al.: Functional virtual prototyping environment for a family of MapReduce embedded accelerators. In: MCSI 2016, pp. 155–160 (2016)
37. Bîră, C., et al.: Parallel machine simulator using racket/scheme functional programming language. In: Proceedings of SPIE Volume 11718. SPIE (2020)
38. IEEE Standard for Software-Hardware Interface for Multi-Many-Core (2020)
39. Che, S.: A benchmark suite for heterogeneous computing. Proceedings of IISWC 2009, (2009). https://github.com/SOLLVE/benchmarks/tree/master/rodinia_3.1/openmp
40. Ferrer, R.: Mercurium: Design Decisions for a S2S Compiler. Cetus Users and Compiler Infastructure Workshop in conjunction with PACT, 2011 (2011). https://github.com/bsc-pm/mcxx
41. OpenMP Architecture Review Board. OpenMP API Specification 5.0., 2020. https://www.openmp.org/wp-content/uploads/OpenMP-API-Specification-5.0.pdf

PMDI: An AI-Enabled Ecosystem for Cooperative Urban Mobility

William Fornaciari[1]( ), Giovanni Agosta[1], Massimo Fioravanti[1],
Paolo Giuseppetti[4], Alessandro Solinas[4], Luigi Gallo[4], Manuel Pernigotto[4],
Mario Pedol[4], Francesco Pro[2], Irene Amerini[2], Lorenzo Papa[2], Luca Maiano[2],
Giovanni Trovini[3], Mauro Di Giamberardino[3], and Paolo Satta[3]

[1] Politecnico di Milano, Milano, Italy
{william.fornaciari,giovanni.agosta,massimo.fioravanti}@polimi.it
[2] Università di Roma "La Sapienza", Roma, Italy
{Francesco.pro,irene.amerini,lorenzo.papa,luca.maiano}@uniroma1.it
[3] Smart Interaction, Roma, Italy
giovanni@smart-interaction.com
[4] Vodafone Automotive, Italia, Italy
{paolo.giuseppetti1,alessandro.solinas,luigi.gallo,manuel.pernigotto,
mario.pedol}@vodafone.com
https://heaplab.deib.polimi.it , https://automotive.vodafone.com ,
https://www.uniroma1.it , https://www.smart-interaction.com

Abstract. The PMDI project aims at radically improving the safety of urban mobility by extending STEP, an automotive data management and analytics platform, to support real-time and near-real-time use cases, particularly focusing on dangerous crossings at urban intersections. Such capabilities will be achieved by deploying STEP on Multi-access Edge Computing (MEC) hardware modules, and integrating within the platform fast AI video and image analytics as well as danger detection algorithms taking as inputs V2X messages from a variety of sources, including (virtual) on-board units and infrastructural sensors. To ensure that dangerous conditions are correctly learnt by AI algorithms, digital twins of the road sections under examination will be built leveraging domain specific language technologies designed to ease the integration.

Keywords: Urban Mobility · V2X · Cooperative Cyber-physical Systems · AI video analytics

1 Introduction

Road accidents are a major cause of death in urban areas. As many as 22800 people were killed in road accidents in the EU in 2019, of which 47.5% involved vulnerable road users, such as riders, bikers, and pedestrians. The latter fraction increases to 75% when considering urban roads. According to the U.S. Department of Transportation, up to 80% of automobile accidents can be prevented with improved vehicle connectivity, using Vehicle-to-Anything (V2X) communications [22]. It is projected that over 10% of the driving time is wasted in traffic jams, 12% of urban traffic is created by vehicles trying to park, and up to 17% of urban fuel is wasted at traffic lights when there is no cross-traffic. Cooperative-Intelligent Transportation Systems (C-ITS) [20] can be very useful in situations such as construction site warnings and traffic congestion in highways caused by an accident or road damage. With vehicles connected together and connected with roadside infrastructure, all of these problems can be mitigated. Data fragmentation currently limits the benefits that connectivity services can bring to road safety. Fragmented data from unconnected sources mean the ecosystem cannot coordinate to improve safety.

The PMDI project is centred around a "Dangerous Cross Junction" scenario, where a connected ecosystem, dynamically composed by vehicles transiting at the cross, vulnerable users, pedestrians, bikes, motorbikes, infrastructure elements, traffic lights, video cameras, attempts to predict and manage the behaviour of the actors, to send real-time warning messages to prevent accidents. The collision risk is detected between connected and not connected mobility consumers, whose trajectories cross in the conflict zone of an intersection.

The adoption of Vodafone's Safer Transport for Europe Platform (STEP) Service Oriented Architecture, will allow to overcome the challenge of data fragmentation, by building models and scenarios, using both real data and synthetic data from digital twins, to simulate the events at the cross. A variety of messages will be supported to allow the platform to ingest information from both vehicles and infrastructural sensors, and AI-based algorithms will allow a real-time prediction of dangerous events, which will then be notified through appropriate messages to the connected vehicles, allowing drivers to react promptly and appropriately to avoid the danger.

Consortium. To successfully complete this ambitious program, the ITS-ETSI project brings together expertise from widely different sectors: *Vodafone Automotive* provides the key expertise in automotive telematics and data analytics, as well as the STEP data management platform; *Politecnico di Milano*, through the HEAP Laboratory, contributes scientific advances in domain specific languages for simulation and digital twins; *Università di Roma "La Sapienza"* provides expertise in AI algorithms for image and video analytics; and *Smart Interaction* provides hardware modules for video analytics.

Organization of the Paper. The rest of the paper is organized as follows. In Sect. 2 we present the overall architecture of the proposed system. In Sect. 3 we introduce the STEP platform, as well as the extensions for ETSI message generation, while in Sect. 4 we propose efficient AI-based algorithms for danger detection and collision forecasting. In Sect. 5 we introduce the proposed extensions towards edge computing for real-time danger detection, while in Sect. 6 we introduce the simulation system for micro-scale urban mobility employed for scenario analysis. Finally, in Sect. 7 we draw some conclusions and outline the roadmap for the project.

2   Cooperative Urban Mobility Architecture

The PMDI platform will host an ecosystem of mobility players, to make roads safer and mobility more efficient. Through Multi-access Edge Computing (MEC) deployment [5], it will be able to achieve the required real-time performance to support the timely generation of warnings for supported intersections, thus addressing local needs, as well as collecting data at the Cloud level to address larger scale requirements. The platform will accommodate C-ITS Day 1, Day 1.5 and subsequent use cases and all vertical mobility applications for event detection, monitoring, notifications and mobility simulation, and benefits from integrated AI models, dedicated HW and algorithms developed to mobility management and control applications [19]. MEC/Cloud deployment will also address the critical issues of data fragmentation, standardization, the low latency required in many applications, the scale and sustainability factor, and the need for ecosystem.

The platform relies on a cooperative system of systems architecture, obtained through the integration of multiple devices, including infrastructural sensors such as road-side cameras and actuators such as intelligent traffic lights, as well as mobile devices such as automotive on-board units and virtual on-board units provided as Android/iOS applications. The ecosystem generated by this integration will provide the following capabilities:

- signaling the presence of pedestrians or cyclists even they are not visible to a vehicle's driver;
- reporting construction sites or roadblocks, as well as related speed limit changes, to improve driving decisions;
- signaling incoming emergency vehicles and optimization of the traffic light system to ensure their rapid passage;
- possibility for a pedestrian or cyclist to notify their presence to approaching vehicles via V2X messages;
- real-time video analytics to identify VRUs and obstacles that do not notify their presence via V2X messages.

To achieve these capabilities, the platform needs, from a technological perspective, to provide three main components: 1. Real and near-real-time tools for dynamic and predictive mobility monitoring; 2. Real and near-real-time detection and notification tools; 3. Forecasting and planning tools.

The rest of this section provides an overview of each of the three components.

2.1   Dynamic and Predictive Mobility Monitoring

Based on standards widely present in the transport domain (ETSI, 5GAA and 3GPP) STEP collects and processes data from various sources, including cars, pedestrians, trucks, cyclists, traffic lights, and other infrastructural sensors, pooling these data to draw significant information for mobility purposes and transmitting it intelligently to the sectors and actors involved. All significant elements of road traffic, be they people, vehicles, infrastructures, directly or indirectly, are equipped with the ability to produce data and dialogue by inserting them into the ecosystem:

To support this scenario, edge computing enables a near-real-time processing of the locally collected data [19], while 5G networks enable efficient data transmission without large and costly fixed infrastructure [3]. The combination of these technologies allows a platform such as STEP to be extended to cover near-real-time applications, such as detecting and notifying a pedestrian that is crossing at an intersection to incoming drivers that are turning at the same intersection, but whose field of vision is obstructed by obstacles such as a parked truck.

2.2 Detection and Notification Tools

The above-mentioned data, collected from the mobility ecosystem, can be combined and processed in an intelligent way. The value of the results, though, lies in making them quickly available to the users, as well as forming a knowledge base that can be used for different, although related, purposes.

Timely detection and notification of events can serve a wide range of scenarios, improving road safety by promptly notifying the appropriate first respondents (local police, health services) when accidents are detected; helping drivers, as well as other road users, in avoiding accidents by notifying dangerous conditions in advance; and supporting crisis management by interoperating with elements of the ecosystems, e.g., prompting intelligent traffic lights to change their behaviour to minimize the risk of further damage after an accident.

2.3 Forecasting and Planning

At a coarser time scale, the STEP platform will collect wide amounts of real time data and historical data, which not only allow the above-described danger detection and management functions, but provide the essential qualitative and quantitative basis to allow system actors (e.g., local authorities in charge of traffic management) to create forecasting tools.

Such tools can address a wide range of scenarios, including predictive and reactive maintenance of traffic lights, planning of intelligent traffic light policies, and efficient management and planning of both routine activities (e.g., waste collection routes) and occasional planned events (e.g., fairs or renovation works).

3 The STEP Platform

The Safer Transport for Europe (STEP) Platform was created with the goal of enhancing road safety across the European Union through the use of Cooperative Intelligent Transport Systems (C-ITS). A key focus of STEP is facilitating reliable communication between all elements of the transportation network, including vehicles, pedestrians, infrastructure such as traffic signals or traffic management systems, and road operators. This communication is enabled through standardized protocols defined by the European Telecommunications Standards Institute (ETSI) to ensure seamless interoperability between diverse C-ITS applications and technologies.

By supporting the secure and efficient transmission of critical safety data between all transportation stakeholders, STEP addresses many of the ongoing challenges associated with C-ITS deployment. One such challenge is managing the massive volumes of high-priority event data generated every moment by thousands of connected devices across countries and cities. Another challenge is the inherent complexity that stems from the need to process this data in near real-time despite variable latency conditions. To overpass these obstacles, STEP employs a sophisticated architecture that leverages the latest technologies for data management, connectivity, and analysis. At its core is integration with a specialized V2X SDK optimized for low-latency communication. Standards-based protocols defined by ETSI provide the rules and framework for accurate, reliable cross-border communication.

The overarching objective of the STEP platform is to proactively enhance road safety across Europe through timely situational awareness and risk mitigation initiatives. This is achieved primarily by disseminating real-time alerts regarding hazards, traffic disruptions, or other safety-critical events detected using technologies like 5G cellular connectivity, multi-access edge computing infrastructure, computer vision, and artificial intelligence models. The architecture incorporates a diverse set of components to support these functions, including a V2X SDK, relevant standards defined by ETSI, and standardized message formats for sharing presence data, hazard warnings, traffic management signals, intersection maps, and more.

Widespread adoption of the STEP platform by all levels of transportation stakeholders is important to maximizing its benefits. To facilitate this, considerable effort has been made toward collaborative deployment and integration with existing transportation systems across the EU. Pilot testing of various technical solutions is also ongoing to address challenges involving latency, data throughput, scalability, and reliability under real-world operating conditions. For example, private cloud architectures and multi-access edge computing deployments are being evaluated for their suitability in minimizing critical response times between event detection and alerts.

Diverse communications protocols manage interactions with STEP to suit the needs of different user and device types. Standardized back-end technologies provide a high-performance framework for routing messages between subscribed users and applications at nationwide scale. Together, these elements form a unified C-ITS environment empowering safer, more efficient transportation across Europe through cooperative data sharing.

3.1 Extensions of the STEP Cooperative Platform and SDK

The Vodafone STEP platform provides a Software Development Kit (SDK) supporting multiple devices, including Android, iOS, and embedded platforms such as automotive black boxes, which enables devices to exchange ETSI messages with the STEP platform itself. Figure 1 reports STEP SDK architecture.

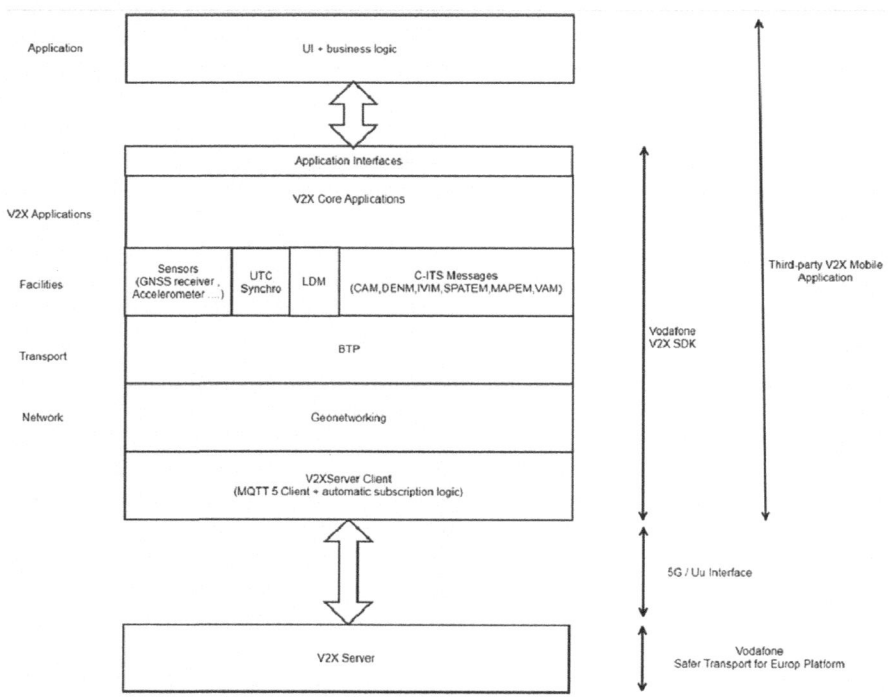

Fig. 1. STEP SDK Architecture to enable interactions between third party applications and the STEP platform

The SDK makes available a wide range of messages, including CAM, DENM, SPATEM, MAPEM, VAM, IVIM, and CMP, and provides the appropriate entry points, events and listeners for easy integration. The V2XSDK class acts as the unique entry point for interacting with the SDK functionalities, and provides methods to subscribe and unsubscribe to a range of events, which third party applications can receive by implementing the EventListener interface. STEP, through the extensions brought on in PMDI, will support a wide range of events notifying changes in the message queues, as well as enabling the application to monitor the status of the connection with STEP, thus allowing a graceful degradation of performance under irregular network conditions.

3.2 ETSI Message Generation and Notification

PMDI aims to enhance STEP by utilizing risk assessment information capable of identifying risk conditions. It evaluates signaling strategies and consequent implementations to fulfill the primary project objective of reducing mobility incidents and accidents. The identified key actors can be categorized into different main groups: vulnerable users (VRU); drivers, encompassing individuals utilizing motorized vehicles with more than a certain power threshold; special vehicles, such as ambulances, law enforcement, firefighters, and other special categories (e.g., electric wheelchairs). All involved actors and infrastructures contribute to providing elements to the infrastructure manager for real-time modulation, such as traffic light logic adjustments or contributing to the braking logic of a vehicle equipped with cooperative implementing applications, to alert non-implementing cooperative vehicle drivers or VRUs of imminent danger.

One of the main risks of such an infrastructure lies in redundancy and/or inadequate synchronization and latency of alert notifications to different actors. An excessive frequency of messages could confuse the users or even push them to switch the notifications off. To mitigate this risk, careful analysis is required to keep track of end user notification frequency and of the time for which each notification is shown.

Taking into account the risk analysis, as well as context data such as the intersection topology, traffic light status, and position and speed of road users, detected via V2X messages, it is possible to formulate optimal signaling strategies for each user category to maximize the usefulness of messages and avoid information overload.

Assuming a collision has been predicted for a pair of actors, both road users are alerted: while V2X messages from vehicles are cyclically emitted, events such as warning messages are sent only for a specific period and are encoded within decentralized environmental notification messages. An advantage of V2X is the standardized message format: any application only needs to insert its parameters according to the standard. A vehicle capable of receiving V2X can decode and interpret it without being programmed for this specific application. Thus, the protection system can send a coded message to warn of the presence of people on the road at a certain distance. How this is presented is entirely at the discretion of the device/vehicle manufacturer and therefore allows complete implementation freedom. The target system decides on its own whether a received message is relevant thanks to two elements: firstly, the position reference, and secondly, the destination area. The target platform will include at least platforms for different mobile operating systems such as Android and iOS.

To improve the effectiveness of alerts and their impact on users, it is useful to incorporate the principles of user experience design (UX). Understanding how users respond to alerts can significantly improve the overall safety and usability of the platform. UX design principles can guide the development of intuitive and visually appealing alert interfaces, ensuring that users can quickly understand and act upon the information provided. By leveraging UX design techniques such as user research, prototyping, and usability testing, developers can iteratively refine alert interfaces to better align with user needs and preferences. For example, using visually distinctive elements can enhance the perceived urgency of alerts, increasing the likelihood that users will take appropriate action.

Furthermore, considering individual differences in cognitive processing and emotional response can lead to personalized alert experiences tailored to the specific needs and characteristics of different user groups. The ultimate goal is to minimize the possibility of collisions among road users. To achieve this goal, it is imperative to share information across networks, utilizing a cooperative system that enables communication between various devices such as V2X, and ensuring that such information generates consumable notification messages for end users in reasonable times and manners.

The most significant challenge lies in intercepting VRUs, as their adoption rate of the solution is crucial. Since VRUs have personal devices that are not remotely controllable, they may experience temporary disconnections from the system (due to network unavailability) and exhibit behaviors that are not always predictable through statistical simulations. Consequently, it follows that the behavior of the simulator must closely mimic human behavior, implementing corrective actions as a VRU, a driver, or any other actor present on or near the roadway would. The greatest risk associated with simulator usage is the failure to emulate human-compliant behavior, which is influenced by factors such as mood, adoption rate, trust in the presented solution, and technical hindrances.

4 Efficient AI Algorithms for Urban Mobility Scenarios

4.1 Collision Forecasting for Urban Mobility

Collision forecasting in urban mobility is a crucial aspect of modern transportation management, which aims to prevent accidents, improving road safety and traffic flow by anticipating potential collision events before they occur. Collision avoidance systems are designed to prevent or mitigate a vehicle collision with other vehicles or with Vulnerable Road Users (VRUs). The task of a collision avoidance system is to track objects of potential collision risk and determine any action to avoid or mitigate a collision [11]. The importance of collision avoidance lies in its ability to significantly reduce the incidence of traffic accidents, which are a major cause of death and injury worldwide. Literature in this field often explores various technologies and methodologies for effective collision prediction and avoidance, including sensor technology, artificial intelligence, and network communication systems [23].

The vehicle trajectory prediction problem has garnered significant attention in research, particularly focusing on highway scenarios or limited road infrastructure data. However, extending these solutions to urban intersections proves challenging due to the dynamic nature of driver behavior. Previous approaches either statically categorize driving styles or employ Gaussian Processes, which struggle to scale and accurately predict maneuvers at intersections due to the multitude of possible actions [17]. Fewer studies address urban intersections directly. Some predict drivers' maneuver intentions rather than full trajectories, while others introduce group trajectory prediction frameworks considering vehicle interactions [27]. Recent advancements incorporate Graph Neural Networks (GNNs) for interaction-aware single-vehicle trajectory predictions [15].

A multi-modal trajectory prediction framework generating multiple potential trajectories for each vehicle has been proposed, but increases computational complexity significantly [6]. Alternative approaches include monitoring specific areas via Multi-access Edge Computing (MEC) servers, but suffer from quantization effects. Some leverage various sensor inputs to select the best trajectory prediction based on uncertainty estimation but lack precision compared to multi-source predictions [18]. Only a few of the existing approaches integrate trajectory prediction with preemptive collision forecasting, leaving uncertainty about their suitability for collision avoidance applications with critical time-sensitive requirements. Finally, while numerous approaches exist for vehicle trajectory prediction, few adequately address the challenges of urban intersections and collision avoidance with critical time sensitivity [23]. Traditionally, collision avoidance has relied on rule-based systems that use sensors and pre-defined algorithms to detect potential hazards and act accordingly. These systems, while effective in many scenarios, face challenges such as limited sensor range, and the inability to adapt to complex dynamic environments. State-of-the-art research in traditional collision avoidance has focused on enhancing sensor technology and integrating more sophisticated algorithms to improve detection accuracy and decision-making capabilities.

Our methodology to address the collision forecasting challenge will exploit machine learning, deep learning, and reinforcement learning techniques. Within our framework, we intend to analyze various types of data to comprehend vehicle behavior and environmental conditions. This includes data from sensors measuring motion, location-based data, and information about road infrastructure. Furthermore, we aim to incorporate external data sources, to enrich our predictive models. By amalgamating diverse data sources and leveraging advanced algorithms we expect to significantly enhance the accuracy and reliability of our forecasts. Through this approach, we aim to develop a sophisticated collision forecasting system that not only improves safety but also contributes to smarter and more efficient urban traffic management.

The architecture of our solution involves real-time trajectory predictions for each road agent. This involves dynamically collecting and processing data from diverse sources. Trajectory forecasts are derived through the seamless integration of these various data streams. The predictions will be computed on a Multi-access Edge Computing (MEC) platform, which enables swift processing and response times critical for effective collision avoidance. The utilization of MEC not only ensures rapid computation but also facilitates the handling of large volumes of heterogeneous data from disparate sources, ensuring that predictions are both timely and relevant.

By leveraging these advanced technologies and integrating different data sources, our approach aims to contribute to safer and more efficient urban mobility solutions.

4.2 Danger Detection in Urban Mobility Scenarios

In urban mobility scenarios, danger detection is crucial in guaranteeing safety. Timely notifications of potentially dangerous situations can allow the avoidance of accidents, not only for vehicles but also for Vulnerable Road Users (VRUs). In the context of Computer Vision, this is a widely studied task that lies in the huge research field of Object Detection [12]. It is the task of locating and classifying one or multiple objects inside an image.

Traditional object detector [30] techniques are based on three phases: 1. Identification, which is the selection of possible regions where the objects are located; 2. Feature extraction, to highlight the main features of the objects through for example HOG [7] or SIFT [16]; 3. Classification, where each object is assigned a belonging class. A sliding window technique was used for highlighting objects through bounding boxes.

In recent years, through the advent of Deep Learning, Object Detectors had a big increase in performance. They can be mainly divided into two-stage detectors [9,10] and one-stage detectors [21,26]. Two-stage detectors are characterized by two phases: 1. Localization, where the objects are located inside the image through for example Selective Search [28]; 2. Classification, where the objects are classified. These methods are also called region-based frameworks. One-stage detectors instead are based on classification or regression and perform the step of localization and classification simultaneously.

Among state-of-the-art techniques, the crucial point for an object detector is the dataset on which it is trained. Our goal is to create a dataset ad hoc for our problem. A good dataset needs to contain a good quantity of significant samples. In addition to this, in a road environment, a detector can suffer from atmospheric and light conditions changes, so we need to make the model able to detect in every possible condition providing the dataset with good samples.

Another critical point in our problem is the latency of the framework. To prevent accidents in real-time, the detection and notification of a dangerous situation should have the lowest possible latency. Our solution will exploit the use of Deep Learning techniques, to provide a fast and efficient model. With this solution, we want to make an additional step to safer urban mobility.

5 MEC Platform

Multi-Access Edge Computing (MEC) is an infrastructure that provides an IT service environment and cloud computing capabilities at the edge of the cellular network. Rather than placing computing resources in centralized cloud data centers, MEC moves them to the edge - to cellular base stations and other network access points. This reduces latency and allows for real-time, context-aware services and applications [14,29].

5.1 A MEC Platform for AI Video Analytics

One of the central figures in this project is the IVA (Intelligent Video Analytics) hardware module. Comprised of a processing board integrated with an AI edge acceleration module and a 5G modem, encased in plastic, its pivotal function is to capture, pre-process, and transmit video streams sourced from pre-installed IP cameras. The final iteration of this module accommodates up to four AI accelerators from the Google Coral TPU family, capable of efficiently processing data streams originating from as many as 20 high-resolution CCTV cameras. Employing sophisticated Computer Vision and Machine Learning techniques, it preprocesses the incoming streams before real-time transmission via 5G to the AI engine situated in the MEC infrastructure, where our groundbreaking AI deductive models are hosted. This IVA module is meticulously designed for effortless scalability, adapting seamlessly to varying quantities and qualities of video streams utilized. The IVA module captures video streams from the surveillance cameras deployed in the designated area, conducts preprocessing operations, and forwards them to the MEC platform. Within this platform, artificial intelligence algorithms are deployed to conduct diverse detections within the frames. In scenarios involving hazardous events, integration with Vodafone's STEP platform is anticipated through APIs utilizing the cooperative SDK developed by Vodafone. The aim is to ensure that alerts triggered by the AI algorithms process, signaling hazardous situations, are transmitted to the STEP platform in compliance with ETSI standards. These alerts will then serve as inputs for the platform to generate actionable messages for end users. Upon receiving a hazard alert from the MEC 5G, the software identifies the critical zone, analyzes vehicle dynamics within it using processed video images, and determines the appropriate alert messages for each detected event. This process aligns with the technical and textual specifications outlined by ETSI standards. ETSI has outlined telecommunications specifications tailored to each unique use case. These specifications encompass technical parameters such as frequency and latency, as well as the nature of information to be conveyed, such as position and speed data, along with the precise text messages to be communicated to drivers. These requirements are meticulously crafted through dedicated simulations and testing procedures, continually updated by ETSI to ensure the highest standard of reliability, thereby mitigating potential issues.

5.2 MEC Deployment of STEP

The deployment of STEP on MEC infrastructure involves a integration process aimed at leveraging MEC's low-latency processing capabilities at the network edge to enhance the platform's performance and efficiency. Firstly, STEP's architecture is optimized to accommodate deployment on MEC, considering the unique characteristics and requirements of MEC environments. This entails adapting STEP's components, such as edge nodes and edge applications, to seamlessly integrate with MEC infrastructure. Next, the deployment process involves the installation of STEP's components, including edge nodes, within MEC environments. These edge nodes serve as physical servers hosting STEP applications and services, thereby bringing STEP's functionality closer to end users and data sources. In summary, deploying STEP on MEC involves optimizing STEP's architecture for MEC environments, installing STEP components within MEC infrastructure, leveraging edge orchestration mechanisms for efficient resource management, and tailoring edge applications to capitalize on MEC's low-latency processing capabilities. This integration enhances STEP's ability to deliver real-time safety services and applications, ultimately improving road safety across Europe.

6 Micro-scale Urban Mobility Simulation

Urban traffic scenarios, which are usually studied at the macro level as network flow problems, acquire additional depth when ADAS systems, V2X communications, and dynamic traffic light policies are added to the scenario. Such scenarios have been previously studied employing macroscopic simulation tools [2] within the SafeCOP ECSEL project [1].

Simulation systems operating at the macroscopic level, such as SUMO [13], are unsuitable to address small scale scenarios where the impact of anomalous behaviours and the potential reactions of the various actors, under different warning availability and timing, need to be assessed. Some European tools, such as Aimsun[1] and SymuVia[2], provide microscopic simulation [4], which is more suitable for the scope of the project. Another alternative is provided by tools employed for the microscopic simulation of autonomous driving, such as CARLA[3] [8], which have since been extended to support real driver behaviors [24,25]. Tools like CARLA provide essential features for the evaluation of anomalous events such as accidents. For instance, collision resolution via physical simulation, while obviously creating a significant performance overhead that is not desirable in simulators aimed primarily at assessing the efficiency of traffic systems, is quite useful when attempting to detect accidents and estimate their effects and impacts. Another key point for this purpose is that most microscopic simulation tools ignore collisions with static objects such as guard rails or buildings, and force vehicles to stick to lanes, which is not useful when trying to integrate driver behaviour patterns. On the contrary, tools for autonomous driving already require the autonomous driving algorithm to operate independently of the simulated lanes.

In perspective, highly efficient microscopic simulation systems could be used as *digital twins* of the real scenario, employing data fed by sensors through the V2X connectivity, to train AI-based tools for detecting dangerous conditions that cannot be easily replicated in the real world. To this end, there is a need for such tools to enable the exploration of multiple scenarios, taking into account different reactions of the human actors, considering the timing of the warning messages emitted by different detection algorithms.

In the project, we plan to extend CARLA and bridging it to realistic models of driver behaviour. To this end, we develop a domain specific language (DSL), *Rulebook*, that is suitable for wrapping the simulator and exposing it to external

---

[1] https://www.aimsun.com/aimsun-next-overview/.
[2] https://github.com/licit-lab/symuvia.
[3] https://carla.org/.

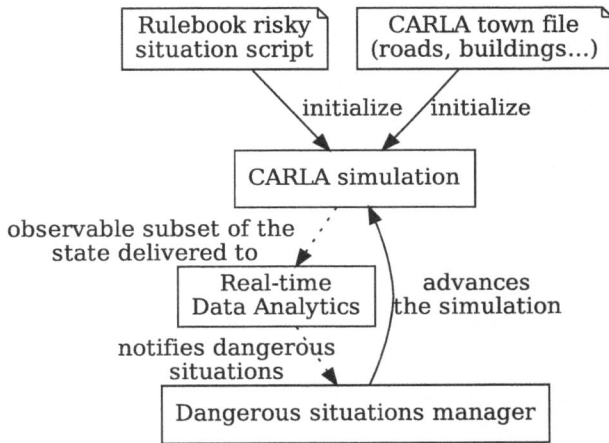

Fig. 2. Block diagram of the simulation. Dashed edges represent simulated network connections, while solid edges represent internal operations of the simulator.

decision-making algorithms. Furthermore, we plan to employ our DSL to connect CARLA to the network simulation, to ensure a realistic assessment of the V2X communication delays. The overall architecture of the simulation system is depicted in Fig. 2.

This will enable to plug in the simulation a variety of subsystems, including ADAS messages, together with their SIL/ASIL safety levels (thus enabling a dynamic composition of such messages, and the application of runtime safety

Fig. 3. A map of the area around Politecnico di Milano in Milan, rendered in CARLA with programmatically generated buildings.

policies to exclude potentially misleading or late warnings), and dynamic traffic light management policies, to evaluate their impact on traffic safety.

Scenarios for such microscopic simulation will be drawn from the real world, employing open source street maps such as those offered by the OpenStreetMap project[4], initially populated with programmatically generated buildings to simulate visibility and wireless connectivity issues. An example of the resulting scenario is shown in Fig. 3, and an example road with vehicles is shown in Fig. 4.

Fig. 4. A close up view on one of the roads in Fig. 3, including vehicles.

7 Concluding Remarks

This paper presents the PMDI project, a collaborative industrial research and development effort aiming at improving safety of urban mobility by enhancing the Vodafone Safer Transport for Europe Platform (STEP) with near-real-time capabilities, achieved through Multi-access Edge Computing (MEC). Such near-real-time capabilities enables a wide range of scenarios, including danger detection and prediction, as well as timely notification of these conditions to the road users and relevant authorities.

The project will develop several components, from the MEC hardware modules to the AI video analytics algorithms and the digital twin tools needed to train them.

Acknowledgements. This work is partially supported by the Italian Ministry of Enterprises and Made in Italy (MIMIT) under the program "Accordi per l'innovazione nella filiera del settore automotive", through the grant "Piattaforma ed ecosistema cooperativo, C- ITS ETSI standard per la mobilità digitale integrata".

---

[4] https://www.openstreetmap.org

References

1. Agosta, G., et al.: V2i cooperation for traffic management with safecop. In: 2016 Euromicro Conference on Digital System Design (DSD), pp. 621–627. IEEE (2016). https://doi.org/10.1109/DSD.2016.18
2. Agosta, G., et al.: Toward a v2i-based solution for traffic lights optimization. In: 2019 11th International Congress on Ultra Modern Telecommunications and Control Systems and Workshops (ICUMT), pp. 1–6 (2019). https://doi.org/10.1109/ICUMT48472.2019.8970697
3. Balador, A., et al.: Wireless communication technologies for safe cooperative cyber physical systems. Sensors **18**(11) (2018). https://doi.org/10.3390/s18114075
4. Boukhellouf, M., Buisson, C., Chiabaut, N.: Merging and diverging operations: benchmark of three European microscopic simulation tools and comparison with analytical formulations. Eur. Transp. Res. Rev. **15**(1), 12 (2023)
5. Casademont, J., et al.: Multi-radio v2x communications interoperability through a multi-access edge computing (mec). In: 2020 22nd International Conference on Transparent Optical Networks (ICTON), pp. 1–4. IEEE (2020)
6. Cui, H., et al.: Multimodal trajectory predictions for autonomous driving using deep convolutional networks. In: 2019 International Conference on Robotics and Automation (ICRA), pp. 2090–2096 (2019). https://doi.org/10.1109/ICRA.2019.8793868
7. Dalal, N., Triggs, B.: Histograms of oriented gradients for human detection. In: 2005 IEEE Computer Society Conference on Computer Vision and Pattern Recognition (CVPR'05). vol. 1, pp. 886–893 (2005). https://doi.org/10.1109/CVPR.2005.177
8. Dosovitskiy, A., Ros, G., Codevilla, F., Lopez, A., Koltun, V.: Carla: An open urban driving simulator. In: Conference on robot learning, pp. 1–16. PMLR (2017)
9. Girshick, R.: Fast r-cnn. In: 2015 IEEE International Conference on Computer Vision (ICCV), pp. 1440–1448 (2015). https://doi.org/10.1109/ICCV.2015.169
10. Girshick, R., Donahue, J., Darrell, T., Malik, J.: Rich feature hierarchies for accurate object detection and semantic segmentation (2014)
11. Jansson, J.: Collision avoidance theory : with application to automotive collision mitigation (2005). https://api.semanticscholar.org/CorpusID:107312197
12. Kaur, R., Singh, S.: A comprehensive review of object detection with deep learning. Digit. Signal Process. **132** (2023). https://doi.org/10.1016/j.dsp.2022.103812
13. Krajzewicz, D.: Traffic simulation with sumo–simulation of urban mobility. Fundam. Traffic Simul. 269–293 (2010)
14. Liang, B., Gregory, M.A., Li, S.: Multi-access edge computing fundamentals, services, enablers and challenges: a complete survey. J. Netw. Comput. Appl. **199**, 103308 (2022)
15. Liang, M., et al.: Learning lane graph representations for motion forecasting. In: Vedaldi, A., Bischof, H., Brox, T., Frahm, J.-M. (eds.) ECCV 2020. LNCS, vol. 12347, pp. 541–556. Springer, Cham (2020). https://doi.org/10.1007/978-3-030-58536-5_32
16. Lindeberg, T.: Scale invariant feature transform. **7** (2012). https://doi.org/10.4249/scholarpedia.10491
17. Liu, J., et al.: An integrated approach to probabilistic vehicle trajectory prediction via driver characteristic and intention estimation. In: 2019 IEEE Intelligent Transportation Systems Conference (ITSC), pp. 3526–3532 (2019). https://doi.org/10.1109/ITSC.2019.8917039

18. Liu, W., Shoji, Y.: Edge-assisted vehicle mobility prediction to support v2x communications. IEEE Trans. Veh. Technol. **68**(10), 10227–10238 (2019). https://doi.org/10.1109/TVT.2019.2937825
19. Lu, M., et al.: C-its (cooperative intelligent transport systems) deployment in Europe: challenges and key findings. In: 25th ITS World Congress, Copenhagen, Denmark, pp. 17–21 (2018)
20. Pagano, P., et al.: Is ICT mature for an Eu-wide intelligent transport system? IET Intell. Transp. Syst. **7**(1), 151–159 (2013). https://doi.org/10.1049/iet-its.2011.0161
21. Redmon, J., Divvala, S., Girshick, R., Farhadi, A.: You only look once: Unified, real-time object detection. In: Proceedings of the IEEE Conference on Computer Vision and Pattern Recognition (CVPR) (2016)
22. Saini, M., Alelaiwi, A., Saddik, A.E.: How close are we to realizing a pragmatic vanet solution? a meta-survey. ACM Comput. Surv. **48**(2) (2015). https://doi.org/10.1145/2817552
23. Selvaraj, D.C., Vitale, C., Panayiotou, T., Kolios, P., Chiasserini, C.F., Ellinas, G.: Edge-assisted ml-aided uncertainty-aware vehicle collision avoidance at urban intersections. IEEE Trans. Intell. Vehicles 1–17 (2023). https://doi.org/10.1109/TIV.2023.3296190
24. Serrano, S.M., et al.: Insertion of real agents behaviors in Carla autonomous driving simulator. In: Proceedings of the 6th International Conference on Computer-Human Interaction Research and Applications - CHIRA, pp. 23–31. INSTICC, SciTePress (2022). https://doi.org/10.5220/0011352400003323
25. Stefansson, E., Jiang, F.J., Nekouei, E., Nilsson, H., Johansson, K.H.: Modeling the decision-making in human driver overtaking. IFAC-PapersOnLine **53**(2), 15338–15345 (2020). https://doi.org/10.1016/j.ifacol.2020.12.2346
26. Szegedy, C., Toshev, A., Erhan, D.: Deep neural networks for object detection. Adv. Neural Inf. Process. Syst. **26**, Curran Associates, Inc. (2013)
27. Tran, Q., Firl, J.: Online maneuver recognition and multimodal trajectory prediction for intersection assistance using non-parametric regression. In: 2014 IEEE Intelligent Vehicles Symposium Proceedings, pp. 918–923 (2014). https://doi.org/10.1109/IVS.2014.6856480
28. Uijlings, J.R.R., van de Sande, K.E.A., Gevers, T., Smeulders, A.W.M.: Selective search for object recognition. Int. J. Comput. Vision **104**(2), 154–171 (2013). https://ivi.fnwi.uva.nl/isis/publications/2013/UijlingsIJCV2013
29. Yousaf, et al.: Understanding multi-access edge computing: Fundamentals, standards, and deployment considerations. IEEE Network (2019)
30. Zhao, Z.Q., Zheng, P., Xu, S.T., Wu, X.: Object detection with deep learning: a review. IEEE Trans. Neural Netw. Learn. Syst. **30**(11), 3212–3232 (2019). https://doi.org/10.1109/TNNLS.2018.2876865

Open Source Software Randomisation Framework for Probabilistic WCET Prediction on Multicore CPUs, GPUs and Accelerators

Leonidas Kosmidis[1,2](✉)[iD], Matina Maria Trompouki[1,2][iD], Pau López Castillón[1,2], Eric Rufart Blasco[1,2], Javier Fernandez Salgado[3], and Andreas Jung[3]

[1] Barcelona Supercomputing Center (BSC), Barcelona, Spain
[2] Universitat Politècnica de Catalunya (UPC), Barcelona, Spain
[3] European Space Agency (ESA), Noordwijk, The Netherlands

Abstract. High criticality space systems frequently have real-time requirements. Therefore, it is important to be able to compute the Worst Case Execution Time (WCET) of its software. However, with the complexity of modern processor architectures, it is very difficult to compute the WCET with traditional methods, such as static timing analysis or measurement based solutions. Recently, a novel timing analysis method was introduced, known as Measurement Based Probabilistic Timing Analysis (MBPTA). A unique characteristic of MBPTA compared to traditional methods is that it produces a Probabilistic WCET (pWCET) which instead of a single overestimated value is a curve that associates execution times with probabilities which can reach arbitrary low values (e.g. 10^{-14}). MBPTA simplifies the estimation of pWCET by simply requiring the collection of execution times which are independent and identically distributed (i.i.d.). However, this property is not satisfied in conventional hardware and software systems. Special hardware designs have been proposed which provide hardware-based time-randomisation, including a probabilistic version of Cobham Gaisler's LEON3 as well as software solutions in the form of software randomisation. However, existing software randomisation methods only support CPUs, are very restrictive (i.e. support only ANSI C) and more importantly are not open source. This limits significantly the applicability of these methods in space, although ESA has supported in the past activities related to MBPTA hardware and software (P4S-PROARTIS for Space and EFL-Eviction Frequency Limitation). In this ESA-funded project, we implement an open source, qualifiable software randomisation tool which will be able to software randomise code for CPUs, including multicores as well as GPUs, which to our knowledge are not amenable to any WCET solution.

Keywords: Real-time Systems · Worst Cased Execution Time (WCET) · Open Source · Source-to-source Compiler · Measurement

Based Probabilistic Timing Analysis (MBPTA) · Software Randomisation

1 Introduction

For certain systems, timing can be a factor as important as functional correctness. This is preeminently true in Hard Real-Time Systems where timing failures can have catastrophic impacts. These timing requirements make the Worst Case Execution Time (WCET) estimations, which denote the highest possible execution time of a given software being run on a specific processor for any possible input, a vital aspect of these kinds of computing systems.

The first and most commonly used approach to compute the WCET is the static one. In Static Deterministic Timing Analysis [3,33], abstract models of the architecture are generated, and then they are used to produce the WCET applying a symbolic execution of the software that takes into account all possible input paths. This method is not always usable, due to the reluctance of hardware vendors to disclose information about their internal designs. Furthermore, even with this information, the complexity of modern processor designs and some of the features they include such as multi-level, unified L2 caches [15] cannot be modelled, leading to disabling some key features from these processors to estimate the WCET. This in turn causes the expected performance to greatly diminish and overly pessimistic estimations to be made.

Another approach commonly used in industry is deterministic Measurement Based Timing Analysis [3,33]. Instead of abstract execution, MBPTA performs its estimations using actual execution time measurements, which are obtained under stressful conditions. However, it is hard to ensure that measurements have been collected under the worst hardware state or input conditions. For this reason, an engineering margin is usually applied on top of the maximum observed execution time (MOET). This margin is specific for a given processor and configuration and it is based on long, prior industrial experience. Similar to the Static Timing Analysis case, some high performance features are disabled in order to reduce uncertainty, and keep the engineering margin low. For example, in the commercial avionics sector, a typical engineering margin used on the MPC755 [31] is 20%, provided that the unified L2 cache is disabled.

Another approach for timing analysis, which has been gaining traction in recent years, is Probabilistic Timing Analysis [6]. The WCET estimations obtained with this method are more favorable compared to the overly pessimistic ones generated using a static approach and can handle much more complex designs such as those found in modern processor architectures, like unified multi-level caches [15].

MBPTA instead of a single value, provides a probabilistic Worst Case Execution Time (pWCET) curve. Figure 1 shows an example of such pWCET curve, which can associate a target probability value e.g. 10^{-14} in this example, with an execution time of 1.2×10^8 processor cycles. This means that the probability of this execution time to be exceeded is 10^{-14}, which is comparable to failure probability of the hardware, and therefore safe to use.

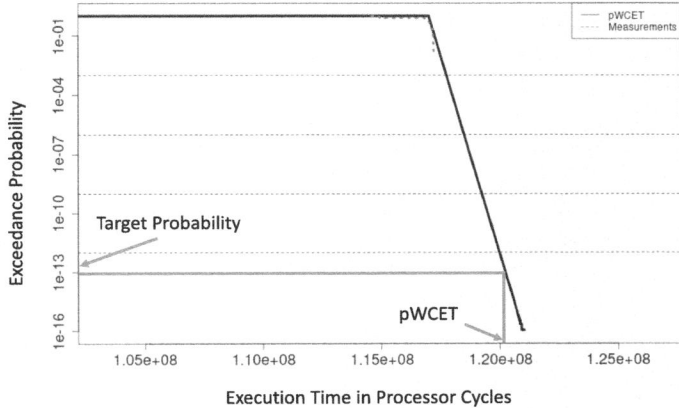

Fig. 1. Example of a pWCET curve.

MBPTA relies on a well established mathematical method known as Extreme Value Theory (EVT) [23], which has been successfully used in several domains such as for the prediction of extreme physical phenomena like floods and tsunamis, or stock market values. EVT is applied on a series of execution time observations, which allow the prediction of the maximum execution time of the program, by modelling the extreme of the probabilistic execution time distribution.

However, probabilistic timing analysis can only be used on MBPTA-compliant microarchitectures [20,21]. Such hardware designs, require small modifications to existing hardware designs, which provide time-randomisation, such as time-randomised caches.

When an architecture is not MBPTA-compliant, it can obtain MBPTA compliance through *software randomisation* means. In this case, program elements are placed in random positions in memory achieving an equivalent effect with hardware randomisation.

In the ESA activity "Open Source Software Randomisation Framework for Probabilistic WCET Prediction and Security on (multicore) CPUs, GPUs and Accelerators" [10] with ESA Contract No. 4000140111/22/NL/GLC/ov, we are developing an open source software randomisation tool known as TASA (Toolchain Agnostic Software rAndomisation) in the Clang source-to-source compiler framework, in order to enable software randomisation in almost any conventional architecture.

In particular, we reimplement TASA [22], a software randomisation tool that relies on source code transformations of the application (i) requiring no changes in existing toolchains, which heavily reduces tool qualification and implementation costs; and (ii) enables the use of MBPTA in conventional, deterministic platforms. Our implementation is based on the Clang compiler framework. The reason for this is that so far the original TASA [22] has only been prototyped as a proof of concept with a hand written C-parser which only supports ANSI C and does not support the C preprocessor, which limits significantly its use with complex code.

Although a later re-implementation of TASA in the CIL (C Intermediate Language) [24] source to source transformation framework was performed, including support for the GPU language CUDA [28], it suffered from the same limitation as CIL, which is the fact that it is only able to parse C code.

Re-implementation in Clang allows TASA to be applied in industrial grade code and to be extended to other languages supported by Clang such as C++, CUDA, OpenCL and other parallel programming models.

2 Project Objectives

The main objective of the project is to lift the barriers of the commercial and academic use of Measurement-Based Probabilistic Timing Analysis (MBPTA). This is achieved by the development of open source tools and their corresponding documentation, so that they are used correctly. These objectives are further decomposed to the following objectives:

- Develop an open source, qualifiable and platform agnostic software randomisation source-to-source compiler framework which will be able to software randomise code for CPUs, including multicores as well as GPUs.
- Document the procedure of applying MBPTA using the compiler framework developed in the project, collecting execution times, ensuring that the collected execution times comply with MBPTA requirements and processing them with the existing open source MBPTA tools [12] in order to produce the pWCET curve.
- Demonstrate the effectiveness of the produced tool on a complex space case study.

Finally, two minor objectives defined by ESA during the project execution and which can be used in order to guide th definition of the next European space processors are:

- Compare the results obtained with the software randomisation implementation with a hardware randomisation implementation.
- Perform a state-of-the-art collection of documents and reports related to hardware and software randomisation.

3 Background and Related Work

Measurement Based Probabilistic Timing Analysis [8] was introduced a decade ago in order to allow the computation of the Worst Case Execution Time (WCET) on complex hardware designs, which cannot be effectively analysed with traditional deterministic timing analysis methods. Traditional methods like static analysis, either do not scale computationally for large programs and/or complex hardware due to the state explosion, or need to make pessimistic assumptions to remain scalable at the expensive of a sound but significantly overestimated WCET which in modern hardware can be impractical.

In a similar way, traditional deterministic measurement based analysis has also limitations with hardware and software complexity. In particular, it is hard to guarantee that the hardware state during the analysis time (which is typically performed under stressful conditions), is representative of the one actually happen when the system is integrated and deployed. This leads to underutilisation of complex hardware and the introduction of arbitrary engineering margins over high execution times, to account for this uncertainty. A representative example comes from the commercial avionics world, where the high performance PowerPC 750 is used. While the processor features a Level 2 (L2) cache, it is disabled and an engineering margin of 20% is added on top of the highest observed execution times, based on the long years of experience of Airbus with this processor [32]. However, this reduces significantly the average performance of the processor, since the memory hierarchy is one of the most significant performance enablers. On the other hand, had the L2 was enabled, an even higher engineering margin would need to be applied, which would degrade further the worst case performance of the processor.

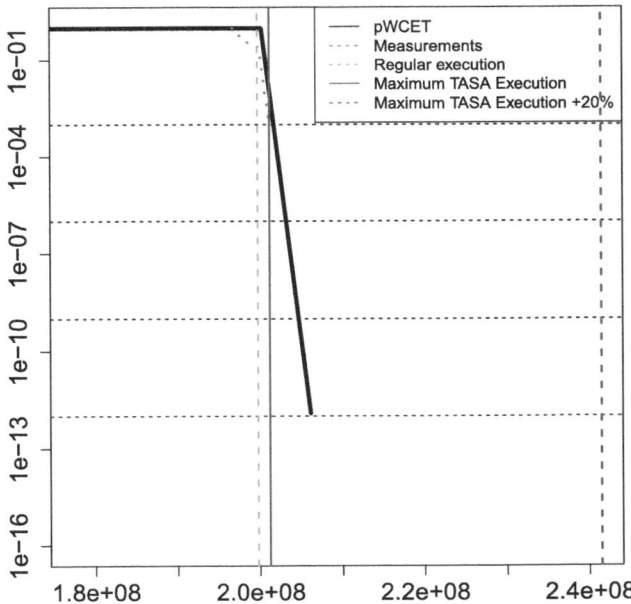

Fig. 2. Comparison between a deterministic WCET estimation and a pWCET curve.

While the traditional methods provide a single value as a worst case execution time (i.e. the purple dashed line in Fig. 2 which represents a 20% engineering margin over the maximum observed execution time), MBPTA provides a probabilistic Worst Case Execution Time (pwCET) curve which associates a probability with a worst case execution time (black line). By selecting a point on this curve we can assess what is the probability (known as exceedance probability) for a given execution time to be exceeded. For example, the probability that the execution time exceeds 210 million cycles is 10^{-16}.

MBPTA relies on a well established mathematical theory called Extreme Value Theory (EVT), which is widely used in the prediction of rare events such as the water level in order to determine the maximum height of damns or flood protection constructions around rivers, or the prediction of minimum and maximum values in the stock market. This sound mathematical theory allows to predict arbitrary low exceedance probabilities much lower than hardware failure rates.

However, in order to work, MBPTA has two fundamental requirements [8]:

1. MBPTA only works when the events that affect the execution time of a program (i.e. cache misses or other events related to hardware state) are random events which are independent and identically distributed (i.i.d.). Independent mean that there must be no execution time correlation between program executions. Identical means that every time that a random event happens, follows the same probability distribution.
2. The hardware events which happen during analysis time (when test measurements are collected), must be the same or worse than the events which will happen at integration/deployment time.

Obviously none of these properties are satisfied on conventional deterministic systems and therefore MBPTA cannot be safely used without proper provisions. In particular, MBPTA requires the platform to become time-randomised, e.g. its hardware events to be randomised which in turn will make the resulting execution time random. In such a system, the big benefit is that the more tests are performed, the more we are sampling a random distribution, and therefore we can better estimate its distribution, including its maximum value, using EVT. In fact, this random distribution remains the same both at analysis and deployment time, thus complying with the second requirement, too. Note however, that this property does not hold in a deterministic system which we may test it for long time, but there is no guarantee that a distribution exists and it is captured. For example a slight change in the memory layout at integration time can change completely the execution time observed at analysis.

In order to enable the use of MBPTA in practice, Dr. Leonidas Kosmidis' PhD thesis [14] proposed hardware and software solutions for time-randomisation, building on the original MBPTA paper [8] which introduced this timing analysis method. The hardware and equivalent software randomisation methods proposed in his thesis have been evaluated in realistic conditions with several industrial case studies, within several European (PROARTIS, PROXIMA) and ESA-funded projects (P4S-PROARTIS for Space and EFL-Eviction Frequency Limitation).

The idea behind software solutions is that while hardware randomisation targets future processors (e.g. LEON3 Probabilistic Platform [11]), software randomisation can enable MBPTA on existing processors, which implement conventional hardware [17]. The principle of software randomisation lies on the fact that the mapping of addresses in a cache is performed based on the address in main memory. Therefore, if the address in main memory is randomised, the cache mapping is also randomised, which creates different cache conflicts between different executions. This results in random execution times, since each execution experiences a different number of cache conflicts.

The main difference between the hardware and software randomisation is the granularity in which randomisation is applied. In a random placement cache, the granularity is a cache line size, while in the case of software randomisation, it depends on the part of the software that is randomised. In the solutions developed in Dr. Kosmidis' thesis, the software elements which are randomised are code (functions), stack, global data and heap. However, despite this small difference, we have shown in several works with industrial case studies that software randomisation has the capability of enabling MBPTA even in the most deterministic platforms, like the automotive microcontroller Aurix TriCore from Infineon [16], which to our experience is the only platform which does not experience any execution time jitter when executing the same program with the same input. In this platform, software randomisation is able to generate random execution times as expected.

In Dr. Kosmidis' thesis, 3 ways of dynamic software randomisation were proposed. Dynamic software randomisation [17] is based on Stabilizer [9], an LLVM compiler pass and a runtime system. As the name indicates, this randomisation takes place dynamically, during the program execution. This method has was ported in several platforms (SPARC/LEON3, PowerPC/PowerPC 750 and P4080) and has been evaluated with avionics case studies [18,32] and a space case study [7]. In particular, in [32] a comparison was performed between hardware and software randomisation using two avionics applications provided by Airbus, Toulouse. The conclusion was that although both were capable of enabling MBPTA, the software randomisation had an additional overhead. However, the even with the additional overhead of software randomisation, there is a benefit in the reduction of pWCET, since the estimated WCET is lower than the typical 20% engineering margin which is used in the avionics industry over high watermark execution times.

In [7] a very interesting result was reported by software randomising a space case study provided by Airbus Defence and Space, Toulouse on a conventional LEON3 platform. Despite its overhead, the software randomised version not only had a better WCET, but also a better average execution time. The reason is that the default memory layout produced by the compiler was pathological and incurred several misses. However, the software randomised versions resulted in better memory layouts, reducing the overall number of cache misses, and therefore improving also the execution times of the application.

Although dynamic memory randomisation has been the most mature software randomisation developed in Dr. Kosmidis' thesis, it has some shortcomings. First, it is based on LLVM which is changing rapidly. Therefore, the compiler pass requires porting it to each new version of LLVM which is released every couple of months. Simply staying with an old version of LLVM is not an option, since the SPARC backed of the LLVM version 3.4 which supports Stabilizer is very old, and has several limitations that prevented us executing software randomisation on another case study from Airbus Defence and Space, Toulouse, the Gaia VPU software within the Proartis4Space ESA-funded activity. Second, this method uses dynamic memory allocation and self modifying code which is forbidden in safety critical systems, since it complicates their qualification. Although we improved our implementation in [7,18] so that the dynamic memory used by this method is bounded e.g. by employing an eager allocation and randomisation scheme, still the method was not seen positively by certification authorities, especially in the automotive sector, where static memory mappings are preferred.

This led to [19] which implemented static randomisation, using only compiler modifications for the stack randomisation, and reordering at linker level. This method removes certification issues of dynamic software randomisation and does not have any runtime overheads. However, it still required access to the compiler source code.

When in the PROXIMA project [5] we needed to apply software randomisation to the AURIX TriCore microcontroller, which didn't have an open source compiler, we needed another solution. That led another variant of static software randomisation, which is applied at source code level [22]. This method has the same benefit of [19], while it is completely independent of any compiler. In our paper we have compared also static software randomisation with dynamic one, confirming that the overhead of the static variant is smaller, while both are able to enable MBPTA. Moreover, the same static variant was used in [16], showing for the first time that it is possible to enable MBPTA through a software method even in the most deterministic platform.

For this reason, this version of static software randomisation, TASA, is the most appropriate one and it is the one we consider for this project. However, since the original implementation was prototyped quickly as a proof of concept, it had several limitations, such as the fact that it can only parse ANSI C code, and only code that it is already preprocessed and belongs to a single file.

4 Project Innovations and Impact

In this project we are reimplementing TASA [22] properly within a source-to-source compiler, Clang. This will allow its usage beyond single core code, in other environments which support extensions of the C and C++ languages. For example it could be applied in multicore environments by software randomising OpenMP or Pthread based programs, or even in OpenCL/CUDA GPU code, allowing the computation of WCET not only on single core programs but also on parallel CPU and GPU programs.

In fact, having a software randomisation tool developed in such a compiler framework, allows randomising large code bases, even for example the operating system itself, such as RTEMS SMP.

In our implementation, we plan to investigate additional randomisation features, which allows additional randomisation elements which have not been considered by prior works. For example, we have ideas about randomising the branch predictor which is available in some processors, as well as the compiler register allocation, with similar source code transformations.

We believe that enabling the computation of WCET using MBPTA is going to be a big benefit for space systems, especially for multicore CPUs and GPUs which due to their complexity, WCET computation is challenging. For example, in the ESA-funded activity "CoreSight based execution monitoring for space applications" presented in ESA's final presentation days December 2020 (https://indico.esa.int/event/347/timetable/), a conventional high watermark measurement based solution was used in order to compute WCET of a multi-core execution based on the performance counters information extracted using CoreSight events. The reason why MBPTA was not used, was that an open source software randomisation solution was not available at the time. Therefore, there is a need for the development of such an open source software randomisation tool, that could enable the benefits of MBPTA WCET computation in several platforms used in space or in other critical domains.

Another reason that has limited the applicability of MBPTA so far, is that despite the existence of the open source MBPTA timing analysis tools from BSC [2,4], the process of using them is not well documented. Although our team at BSC has taught a tutorial on their usage in ESWEEK 2015, this knowledge needs to be codified in a document to facilitate its use and most importantly to make sure its correct use. For example, there are several examples of scientific papers in the literature which tried to apply MBPTA on execution times collected on deterministic systems, without any randomisation. While the execution times might seem random due to the inherent variability (jitter) of high performance systems, such data do not comply with the MBPTA properties we described earlier, and such estimations are not trustworthy. Therefore, an important outcome of our project is also to make sure that these tools are used properly.

5 Methodology

In order to achieve the project goals, we follow a structured approach, which leverages our prior work in this domain.

5.1 Source to Source Compiler Implementation

For the implementation of the TASA source-to-source compiler we are using the Clang infrastructure for each of the identified C-based languages. First we start with the implementation of software randomisation for the C language, which is functionally equivalent to our previous CIL-based implementation [13,28].

The C implementation will be followed by support for OpenMP parallel programs. Next we will extend the software randomisation concept to C++.

This will enable the application of software randomisation to the C++ based GPU programming languages such as CUDA and OpenCL. The CUDA implementation will be functionally equivalent to our CIL-based TASA implementation [13,28], which was only capable to work with the C CUDA subset. Therefore, a comparison between these two implementations will be performed, too.

In total we target 5 different Clang based TASA compilers for each C/C++ based programming languages: C, OpenMP, C++, CUDA and OpenCL.

5.2 Software

In order to evaluate our software randomisation compilers we will have to use appropriate software written in its target language. For the C implementation, our initial approach is to use the EEMBC Autobench [1], which represents automotive tasks and has been used in the original TASA publication [22]. This benchmarking suite is widely used in the real-time research community for WCET estimation. In addition to that, an ESA-provided use case of on-board processing tasks will be used.

For the evaluation of the OpenMP, CUDA and OpenCL implementations, we plan to use the open source ESA benchmarking suite GPU4S Bench [27]/OBPMark Kernels [26,29], which we developed in the GPU4S (GPU for Space) ESA-funded project [12] and to our knowledge is the only space-relevant parallel benchmarking suite which supports all targeting programming models. In this way, we will avoid additional effort for parallelising safety critical software for the evaluation of our compilers. Finally, the open source pedestrian detection application we have developed in multiple programming models [25,30] and we have used in [28] is also a potential candidate for the CUDA and C++ implementations. Moreover, the availability of pWCET results for CUDA will allow the comparison between the CIL-based and our Clang implementation.

5.3 Hardware Randomisation Comparison

In order to compare our software randomisation implementation with hardware randomisation, we will implement an MBPTA-compliant processor, ideally based on RISC-V. Frontgrade Gaisler's NOEL-V space processor is a potential option, however a deterministic processor such as Chips Alliance's VeeR core is also a good candidate.

The MBPTA modifications of the processor's implementation will be performed in its RTL (Register Transfer Level) description. In order to obtain the execution times required for the pWCET estimation will be performed either on a cycle accurate simulation or an FPGA implementation of the processor.

A trade-off will be performed for the method selection since simulation allows several executions in parallel but each execution time can be potentially long. On the other hand, an FPGA implementation provides very short execution times compared to simulation, but the execution of the experiments needs to be serialised.

5.4 Target Hardware Platforms

Since each of the programming languages we will software randomise targets a different platform, we will evaluate their TASA compiler in the appropriate platform.

For the C language, which we will use also for comparison with hardware randomisation, we will use the same RISC-V processor we will make MBPTA-compliant, as described in the previous subsection. This will allow a fair comparison between hardware and software randomisation.

For the OpenMP evaluation, we will need a multicore platform, while for the CUDA and OpenCL implementation we will need a GPU platform. We plan to use the embedded multicore and GPU platforms used in the GPU4S project [12]. This includes the NVIDIA Xavier which was also used for the CUDA software randomisation in [28].

All the selected platforms will provide hardware monitoring facilities such as performance counters, in order to be able to reason about the effectiveness of the software randomisation, as we did in [7].

5.5 pWCET Estimation

In order to generate the pWCET curve, we will generate 1000 source code variants for each target application, which will be executed on the target platforms. For the hardware randomisation comparison, we will collect the same number of executions using the executable generated with the default compiler toolchain.

For each execution, we will collect the end-to-end execution times of the software, as well as performance counters.

We will then compare the performance counters (i.e. cache misses) of the original executable with the performance counters of the software and hardware randomised executions.

The execution time measurements will be processed using the open source MBPTA-CV set of R scripts. The tool will first validate that the measurements are independent and identically distributed using the appropriate statistical tests. If this condition is satisfied, the MBPTA curve fitting process will be performed. If the tool detects that there are not enough measurements belonging to the tail of the distribution, the process stops and asks the user to provide more measurements, otherwise the pWCET curve is generated.

In order to validate the tightness of the computed distribution, the pWCET will be compared also with the default execution time, as well as with the maximum observed execution time (MOET) and MOET+20% engineering margin, as it is used in deterministic measurement based timing analysis, as shown in Fig. 2.

6 Conclusions and Future Work

In this paper we described the work we are performing within the "Open Source Software Randomisation Framework for Probabilistic WCET Prediction on Multicore CPUs, GPUs and Accelerators" ESA-funded project. We have described the project objectives and the necessary background on prior software randomisation activities. As we have explained, while the Measurement Based Probabilistic Timing Analysis (MBPTA) has shown very promising results with the computation of the Probabilistic Worst Case Execution Time (pWCET) of industrial case studies, there is a lack of tools and documentation in order to be widely adopted by industry.

For this reason, in this project we are developing open source source-to-source compilers for all C/C++ based languages supported by Clang, which will be able to be used to software randomise industrial-grade code. Moreover, we are documenting the process of obtaining pWCET in a way that satisfies all MBPTA required properties, using open source timing analysis tools. Finally, as part of the project, we will perform a comparison of software randomisation with hardware randomisation, and we will provide a survey of the published project reports and scientific papers on MBPTA hardware and software support, in order to facilitate the definition of future European Space Processors.

Acknowledgments. This work is supported by the European Space Agency under the "Open Source Software Randomisation Framework for Probabilistic WCET Prediction and Security on (multicore) CPUs, GPUs and Accelerators" with ESA Contract No. 4000140111/22/NL/GLC/ov.

It was also partially supported by the Spanish Ministry of Economy and Competitiveness under grants PID2019-107255GB-C21 and IJC-2020–045931-I (Spanish State Research Agency / Agencia Española de Investigación (AEI) / http://dx.doi.org/10.13039/501100011033) and by the Department of Research and Universities of the Government of Catalonia with a grant to the CAOS Research Group (Code: 2021 SGR 00637).

References

1. EEMBC — eembc.org. https://www.eembc.org/autobench/ Accessed 13 Oct 2023
2. Abella, J.: MBPTA CV, Open Source Download page at BSC website. https://www.bsc.es/research-and-development/software-and-apps/software-list/mbpta-cv
3. Abella, J., et al.: WCET analysis methods: pitfalls and challenges on their trustworthiness. In: 10th IEEE International Symposium on Industrial Embedded Systems (SIES), pp. 39–48 (2015)
4. Abella, J., Padilla, M., del Castillo, J., Cazorla, F.J.: Measurement-based worst-case execution time estimation using the coefficient of variation. ACM Trans. Design Autom. Electr. Syst. **22**(4), 72:1–72:29 (2017)

5. Cazorla, F.J., et al.: PROXIMA: improving measurement-based timing analysis through randomisation and probabilistic analysis. In: 2016 Euromicro Conference on Digital System Design (DSD), pp. 276–285 (2016)
6. Cazorla, F.J., Kosmidis, L., Mezzetti, E., Hernández, C., Abella, J., Vardanega, T.: Probabilistic worst-case timing analysis: taxonomy and comprehensive survey. ACM Comput. Surv. **52**(1), 14:1–14:35 (2019)
7. Cros, F., et al.: Dynamic software randomisation: lessons learned from an aerospace case study. In: Design, Automation and Test in Europe Conference and Exhibition (DATE) (2017)
8. Cucu-Grosjean, L., et al.: Measurement-based probabilistic timing analysis for multi-path programs. In: 24th Euromicro Conference on Real-Time Systems (ECRTS), pp. 91–101 (2012)
9. Curtsinger, C., Berger, E.D.: STABILIZER: statistically sound performance evaluation. In: Architectural Support for Programming Languages and Operating Systems (ASPLOS), pp. 219–228 (2013)
10. ESA: Open Source Software Randomisation Framework for Probabilistic WCET Prediction and Security on (multicore) CPUs, GPUs and Accelerators. https://activities.esa.int/4000140111
11. Gaisler: LEON3 Probabilistic Platform. https://www.gaisler.com/index.php/products/processors/leon3
12. Kosmidis, L., et al.: GPU4S: major project outcomes, lessons learnt and way forward. In: Design, Automation and Test in Europe Conference (DATE) (2021)
13. Kosmidis, L.: TASA-CIL repository. https://gitlab.bsc.es/lkosmidi/tasa_cil
14. Kosmidis, L.: Enabling Caches in Probabilistic Timing Analysis. Ph.D. thesis, Polytechnic University of Catalonia, Spain (2017). http://hdl.handle.net/10803/460819
15. Kosmidis, L., Abella, J., Quiñones, E., Cazorla, F.J.: Multi-level unified caches for probabilistically time analysable real-time systems. In: Proceedings of the IEEE 34th Real-Time Systems Symposium (RTSS), pp. 360–371 (2013)
16. Kosmidis, L., et al.: Measurement-based timing analysis of the AURIX caches. In: 16th International Workshop on Worst-Case Execution Time Analysis (WCET). vol. 55, pp. 9:1–9:11 (2016)
17. Kosmidis, L., Curtsinger, C., Quiñones, E., Abella, J., Berger, E.D., Cazorla, F.J.: Probabilistic timing analysis on conventional cache designs. In: Design, Automation and Test in Europe (DATE), pp. 603–606 (2013)
18. Kosmidis, L., Maxim, C., Jégu, V., Vatrinet, F., Cazorla, F.J.: Industrial experiences with resource management under software randomization in ARINC653 avionics environments. In: Proceedings of the International Conference on Computer-Aided Design (ICCAD), pp. 108 (2018)
19. Kosmidis, L., Quiñones, E., Abella, J., Farrall, G., Wartel, F., Cazorla, F.J.: Containing timing-related certification cost in automotive systems deploying complex hardware. In: The 51st Annual Design Automation Conference (DAC), pp. 22:1–22:6 (2014)
20. Kosmidis, L., Quiñones, E., Abella, J., Vardanega, T., Broster, I., Cazorla, F.J.: Measurement-based probabilistic timing analysis and its impact on processor architecture. In: 17th Euromicro Conference on Digital System Design (DSD), pp. 401–410 (2014)
21. Kosmidis, L., et al.: Fitting processor architectures for measurement-based probabilistic timing analysis. Microprocess. Microsyst. **47**, 287–302 (2016)

22. Kosmidis, L., Vargas, R., Morales, D., Quiñones, E., Abella, J., Cazorla, F.J.: TASA: Toolchain-agnostic Static Software Randomisation for Critical Real-time Systems. In: Proceedings of the 35th International Conference on Computer-Aided Design (ICCAD) (2016)
23. Kotz, S., Nadarajah, S.: Extreme Value Distributions: Theory and Applications. World Scientific (2000)
24. Necula, G.C., McPeak, S., Rahul, S.P., Weimer, W.: CIL: intermediate language and tools for analysis and transformation of C programs. In: Horspool, R.N. (ed.) CC 2002. LNCS, vol. 2304, pp. 213–228. Springer, Heidelberg (2002). https://doi.org/10.1007/3-540-45937-5_16
25. Peralta, C.Q., Trompouki, M.M., Kosmidis, L.: Evaluation of SYCL's suitability for high-performance critical systems. In: Proceedings of the 2023 International Workshop on OpenCL (IWOCL) (2023)
26. Rodriguez, I., A., J., Kosmidis, L., Steenari, D.: GPU4S Bench Code Repository. https://github.com/OBPMark/GPU4S_Bench (2020)
27. Rodriguez, I., Kosmidis, L., Lachaize, J., Notebaert, O., Steenari, D.: GPU4S Bench: design and implementation of an open GPU benchmarking suite for space on-board processing. Tech. Rep. UPC-DAC-RR-CAP-2019-1, Universitat Politècnica de Catalunya (2019). https://www.ac.upc.edu/app/research-reports/public/html/research_center_index-CAP-2019,en.html
28. Rodriguez Ferrandez, I., Jover Alvarez, A., Trompouki, M.M., Kosmidis, L., Cazorla, F.J.: Worst case execution time and power estimation of multicore and GPU software: a pedestrian detection use case. Ada Lett. **43**(1) (2023)
29. Steenari, D., Kosmidis, L., Rodriquez, I., Jover, A., Förster, K.: OBPMark (On-Board Processing Benchmarks) - open source computational performance benchmarks for space applications. In: European Workshop on On-Board Data Processing (OBDP) (2021). https://doi.org/10.5281/zenodo.5638577
30. Trompouki, M.M., Kosmidis, L., Navarro, N.: An open benchmark implementation for multi-CPU multi-GPU pedestrian detection in automotive systems. In: 2017 IEEE/ACM International Conference on Computer-Aided Design (ICCAD) (2017)
31. Wartel, F., et al.: Timing analysis of an avionics case study on complex hardware/software platforms. In: Proceedings of the 2015 Design, Automation and Test in Europe Conference and Exhibition (DATE), pp. 397–402 (2015)
32. Wartel, F., et al.: Measurement-based probabilistic timing analysis: lessons from an integrated-modular avionics case study. In: 8th IEEE International Symposium on Industrial Embedded Systems (SIES), pp. 241–248 (2013)
33. Wilhelm, R., et al.: The Worst-case Execution-time Problem - overview of methods and survey of tools. ACM Trans. Embed. Comput. Syst. **7**(3), 36:1–36:53 (2008)

A Hypervisor Based Platform for the Development and Verification of Reliable Software Applications

N. Petrellis[1]([✉]) [iD], M. Mavropoulos[1] [iD], V. Kelefouras[2] [iD], G. Keramidas[3] [iD], K. Radonjic[4], and N. Voros[1] [iD]

[1] Electrical and Computer Engineering Department, University of Peloponnese, Patra, Greece
npetrellis@uop.gr
[2] School of Engineering, Computing and Mathematics, University of Plymouth, Plymouth, UK
[3] School of Informatics, Aristotle University of Thessaloniki, Thessaloniki, Greece
[4] Power, Electronics, and Communication Engineering Department, University of Novi Sad, Novi Sad, Serbia

Abstract. In the XANDAR project, a holistic model-based toolchain has been formulated that follows the X-by-Construction (XbC) paradigm i.e., a "step-wise refinement from specifications to executable code" that results in systems with guaranteed non-functional properties. XANDAR defined also meta-model extensions, a library of safety, fault-tolerance, and security patterns, and investigated many further techniques for design automation, verification, and validation. In the project, the actual code generation procedure is performed by the XbC backend that efficiently performs the code optimizations, code parallelization, scheduling, mapping, and run-time system generation of the input software modules on the target platform ensuring that the predefined deadlines are met. This paper describes the main features of the XbC backend including the generation of the hypervisor configuration files that are customized for the target multicore platform. The use cases analyzed in XANDAR showcased that the proposed XbC backend was able to output acceptable solutions in an efficient manner.

Keywords: Code Optimizations · HEFT Scheduling · EDF Scheduling · Hypervisor · Software Components · Runnables

1 Introduction to the XANDAR Project Framework

The next generation of networked embedded systems has caused the need for software technologies that combine high performance with a sufficient degree of resilience from both a safety and a security perspective. The toolchain allows designers to make use of the XANDAR design methodology and, at the same time, is an implementation of the XANDAR process [1]. In XANDAR toolchain, the application requirements determine the system architecture modeling, annotating the appropriate building blocks and generating the application framework based on Software Components (SWC) [3]. In the model-based frontend of XANDAR, the user interacts with the toolchain to describe relevant requirements and to specify a high-level representation of the envisaged software system. A SWC represents a certain functionality to be implemented in software. The XbC backend is responsible to generate the actual code to be executed by a SWC where a continuous refinement and analysis takes place. The latter process can identify potential failures, enforcing the frontend developers of the toolchain to adopt alternative solutions in their design.

The overall flow of the XbC backend is divided into three phases: i) software-hardware mapping and scheduling, ii) fine/coarse-grained parallelization, and iii) artefact generation. The fine/coarse-grain parallelization, mapping, and scheduling target to optimize the resulting system implementation wrt. certain properties by translating the model-based specifications into implementation artefacts to be executed on the XtratuM hypervisor XNG [4, 5]. More specifically, the XbC backend generates one or more binary images to be deployed to the target device. Each binary image is assembled from user-specified SWC code, toolchain-provided management and runtime logic (e.g., a hypervisor kernel), and platform configuration files (e.g., an auto-generated hypervisor configuration). Note that a SWC includes one or more processing tasks, called runnables that can be executed in parallel in one or more CPU cores as multiple threads. In addition, the XbC backend generates a hardware description that captures the mapping between images and their target platforms.

The main steps of the XbC backend (shown also in Fig. 1) are: i) applying loop transformations to each runnable individually to reduce their execution time; a tool is developed which is built upon Pluto tool [6], ii) scheduling/mapping the runnables of each SWC to minimize the scheduling length and scheduling time of each SWC individually; a tool is developed extending the popular Heterogeneous Earliest Finish Time (HEFT) algorithm [7], iii) scheduling/mapping the SWCs to minimize the scheduling length; a tool is developed extending the popular Earlier Deadline First (EDF) algorithm [8], iv) gather all scheduling parameters found in (i)–(iii) above (e.g., starting/ending execution times of the SWCs and number of CPU cores used per SWC) and generate the hypervisor script, so as the Hypervisor can schedule the SWCs on the right hardware resources and on the right time slots. It is important to note that two different scheduling algorithms are used as the two scheduling problems are very different. Finally, we need to mention that the output of the EDF scheduler is fed to the XNG File Generator in order to prepare automatically the XNG hypervisor configuration files. These files are used to build the hypervisor image that is deployed to the target platform. The execution on the target platform can be used to verify at the physical layer that the time critical functions of an application meet their deadlines.

This paper is structured as follows: the methods used are described in Sect. 2. More specifically, the Pluto code optimization method is described in Sect. 2.1, the HEFT runnable scheduler in Sect. 2.2, the SWC scheduling based on EDF in Sect. 2.3 and the XNG File Generator in Sect. 2.4.

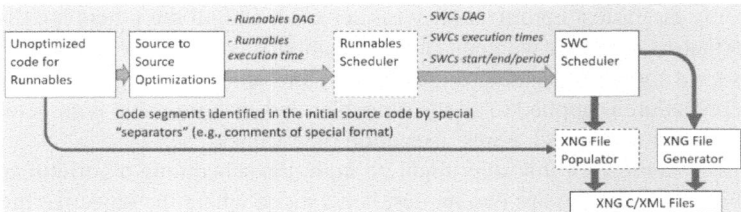

Fig. 1. The XbC backend of the XANDAR project.

2 XbC Backend Toolchain

2.1 Source to Source Optimizations

Code optimizations can be applied either manually by the developer, or automatically by the compiler (or other tools), or by using a semi-automatic optimization approach, where the work is split between the programmer and the compiler. In the latter case, the code optimizations (and their parameters) are specified at a high level by the programmer, leaving the implementation task to the compiler, which executes the process fully automatically. To this end, several source-to-source trans-formation tools exist, such as Pluto [6], which is used in this project. It is important to note that Pluto automatically checks the correctness of a transformation, so that incorrect transformations are not carried out.

The XANDAR toolchain operates by taking annotated source code as input from the user. It then identifies and applies the appropriate optimizations and their parameters based on the input patterns. Specifically, the user is required to supply a consistent annotation at the start and end of each runnable. These annotations are necessary for the Pluto tool to perform loop transformations.

The loop transformations supported are register blocking (also known as unroll and jam), loop tiling, loop merge, loop distribution, loop parallelization and vectorization (vectorization is supported only for icc compiler). For register blocking, three different register blocking factors are used as well as the case where no blocking is applied (4 different parameters which are specified by the user). For loop tiling, six different tile sizes are used here as well as the case where no tiling is applied (7 different parameters). Regarding loop parallelization, each loop kernel can be broken down into $m = [1, cores]$ different threads, where cores is the number of physical CPU cores. An analytical model for loop tiling has been developed in [9, 10] but it has not yet integrated to the toolchain. Regarding loop merge/distribution, either loop merge (maxfuse) or loop distribution (nofuse) is enabled, so there are only two options here. In vectorization there are no input parameters; vectorization is carried out by Pluto. So, in overall, $(56 \times cores)$ optimization sets are selected for each runnable; the optimization parameters are specified by the user. Note that the tool is configurable, and the user can change the number of parameters evaluated. The solutions that do not meet the Logical Execution Time (LET) constraint are discarded.

All the $(56 \times cores)$ optimization sets are carried out by Pluto and their source code is first generated, then compiled, and then run on the target hardware platform so as to measure the execution time of each optimization set. For each m value (number of threads), only the fastest optimization set is selected, and all the others are discarded. It is important to note that we keep m optimization sets and not one, as the number of threads used for each runnable is specified by the scheduling algorithm in the next step. This procedure is applied to all the runnables and each runnable is associated with 'cores' optimization sets and 'cores' execution time values.

Since the overhead of this step might be high, the scheduling algorithm (which is explained in the next step) has two modes, i.e., a mode where the objective function is just the minimum scheduling length, and a mode where the objective function is both scheduling length and scheduling time (the time needed to obtain the output schedule). In the latter case, the number of optimization sets being propagated is not 56 x cores, but lower; this is achieved by merging these two steps into one and using an iterative scheduling approach.

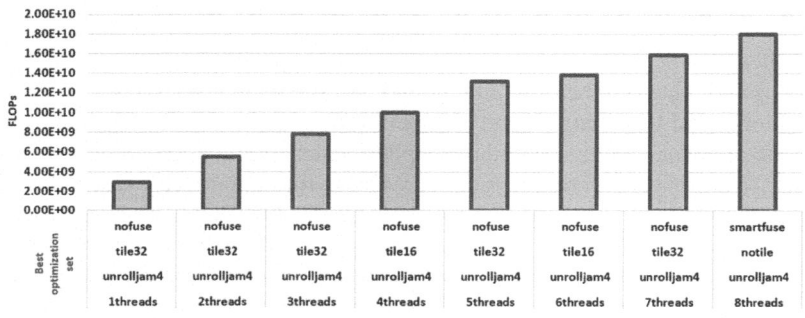

Fig. 2. Evaluation of the proposed framework (Sect. 2.1 only) using the 3 mm benchmark.

2.1.1 Source to Source Optimizations – Experimental Results

To analyse the studied transformations, we relied on the Polybench [11] suite, where we used 19 linear algebra kernels (2mm, 3mm atax, bicg, cholesky, doitgen, durbin, gemm, gemver, gesummv, gramschmidt, lu, ludcmp, mvt, symm, syr2k, syrk, trisolv, trmm). These kernels include both memory-intensive and computationally-intensive kernels, making them ideal for benchmark characterization and profiling. All the benchmarks compiled with the LARGE DATASET [11]. Since the page size is limited only Fig. 2 is shown here (3mm benchmark).

The hardware platform used was a PC with Intel(R) Xeon(R) Silver 4114 CPU 2.20GHz and 64 GB memory. The operating system was Ubuntu 18.04.6 LTS. As can be observed in Fig. 2, different optimization sets give best performance for different number of threads. Furthermore, different optimization sets give the best execution time for different input sizes too (this is not shown here). Also, performance aligns with the number of threads used as this benchmark is data parallel.

2.2 Runnables Scheduler

Efficient application scheduling is critical for achieving high performance in parallel computing systems. This problem has proved to be NP-complete [12], heading research efforts in obtaining low complexity heuristics that produce good quality schedules. Such an example is HEFT [7] (which is used in this project), one of the most efficient list scheduling heuristics in terms of makespan and robustness.

The reason we built upon low complexity heuristics is that stochastic search algorithms, like Integer Linear Programming and Constraint Programming, entail lengthy scheduling times. Consequently, they are impractical for this project, as the scheduling process needs to be applied many times. This is because the scheduling process a) needs to be applied for each SWC separately, b) needs to be applied once for each m value (number of threads). Thus, in the scenario where there are 8 different CPU cores and 1000 SWCs, the scheduling algorithm needs to be applied 8000 times, and a stochastic search algorithm might be impractical in this case.

The XANDAR mapper generates the number of threads that each runnable uses as well as the order that the runnables are executed. The XANDAR mapper generates the output schedule but it does not produce the entire output source code(this step is not automated); therefore, the user needs to appropriately annotate the source code, e.g., specify in the code the number of threads used in each runnable.

2.2.1 Problem Formulation

Resource Model: In this project the target hardware platform consists of a single multicore CPU. The CPU is treated as an m-core device, where m = [1, cores] and cores is the number of the physical CPU cores. As noted, although the target hardware platform to be used in this project is homogeneous, our solution is applicable to heterogeneous hardware platforms too.

Workflow Model: A workflow application is modeled as a Directed Acyclic Graph (DAG), G = (V, E), where V is the set of u nodes and each node u ∈ V represents a runnable, which includes instructions that must be executed on the same CPU core. E is the set of e communication edges between the runnables; each e(i, j) ∈ E represents the runnables-dependence constraint such that runnable t_i should complete its execution before runnable t_j is started [13, 14]. The n × cores computation cost matrix W stores the computation costs of the runnables (their execution time), where n is the number of the runnables and cores is the number of the physical CPU cores; each element $w_{t,j}$ ∈ W refers to the estimated time to execute runnable t on [1,cores] CPU cores. The W values can be found by simulation, emulation or by running the runnables on the HW; for the rest of this document, we will use the word simulation. The execution of any runnable is considered non-preemptive. For the rest of this paper, we will be using the words runnable and task interchangeably.

Each edge e(i, j) ∈ E is associated with a non-negative weight value $d_{i,j}$ that represents the amount of data to be transmitted from runnable t_i to runnable t_j. The data transfer rate between any two processors on the network is assumed to be fixed and constant [14]. The communication cost of an edge (t_i, t_j) equals to the amount of data transmitted from task t_i to task t_j, or $d_{i,j}$, divided by the data transfer rate of the network. Since the data transfer rate of the intra-processor bus is much higher than the data transfer rate of the interprocessor network, the communication cost between two runnables scheduled on the same processor is taken as zero. These model simplifications are common in this scheduling problem [13, 14].

Problem Definition: This problem is the static scheduling of a single application, in a set of heterogeneous devices, consisting of a set of n moldable tasks, whose computation cost matrix W is unknown, in such a way that both the scheduling length and the scheduling time (to deliver the output schedule), are minimized. It is important to note that the scheduling time highly depends on the time needed to simulate the runnables and get their computation costs. Although our method is applicable to heterogeneous computing systems, for the rest of this document we will assume a homogeneous system.

The application tasks are assumed moldable [15] (a single runnable can be executed by more than one CPU cores); moldable tasks are the runnables being allocated to a fixed number of CPU cores before execution and stay unchanged afterwards. Thus, given a multi-core CPU with 'cores' physical CPUs, we consider every task as an m-threaded implementation, where m = [1, cores]. The CPU core utilization factor is defined as, $factor_{t,m} = w_{t,1}/w_{t,m}$.

2.2.2 Proposed Method

To improve the scheduling length of HEFT, we propose low complexity heuristics to find which tasks are going to be implemented as single-threaded (ST) implementations, which as multi-threaded (MT) implementations, as well as the number of threads used. It is important to note that by scheduling all the tasks as MT implementations, fewer processing elements are available but with higher computation capability, while by scheduling all the tasks as ST implementations, more processing elements are available but with lower computation capability. Using ST implementations is more efficient for some DAGs, while MT implementations is more efficient for other DAGs.

The default HEFT [7] algorithm assumes rigid (non-moldable) tasks, and thus HEFT does not support multi-threaded tasks. Therefore, to better evaluate and compare our method, we have implemented HEFT using either ST CPU implementations (SHEFT) only or max-threaded CPU implementations (MHEFT) only.

In Fig. 3, we show the scheduling length (makespan) of these three methods for 81 different DAGs (see Sect. 2.2.3 for more information about the DAGs used). As it can be observed in the first 27 DAGs, MHEFT performs better than SHEFT, while SHEFT performs better than MHEFT for the remaining DAGs, e.g., in tall and skinny DAGs where the tasks cannot be executed in parallel, it is more efficient to allocate all the CPU cores into the tasks, since the remaining CPU cores will be idle. The third method, which is the method to be used in this project, is either more efficient than both SHEFT and MHEFT, or follows the trend of the best of the two.

The Algorithm which enhances HEFT to support multi-threaded tasks can be found in [2] and introduces the following key points:

1. MT implementations are more efficient when the task parallelism is low.
2. When the task parallelism is high, ST/MT implementations are more efficient when the range of the execution time values among different tasks, is low/high, respectively.

3. ST implementations are more efficient for tasks with high Communication to Computation Ratio (CCR) values.

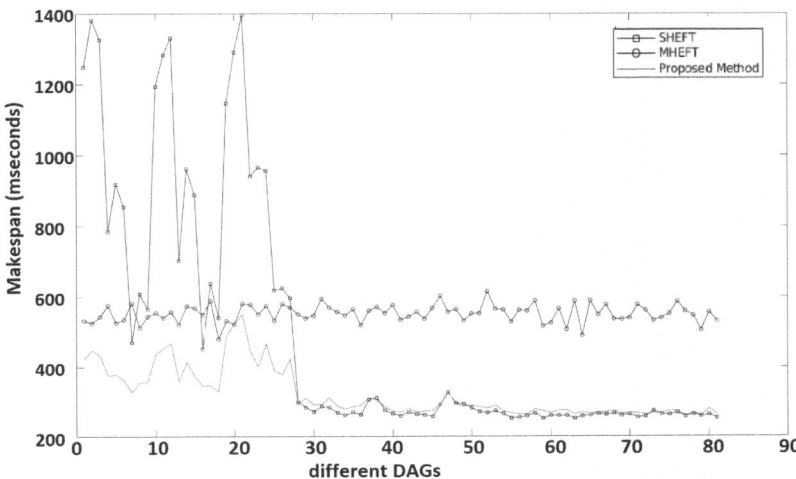

Fig. 3. Makespan evaluation of the three proposed methods for 81 different DAGs and 8 CPU cores.

It is important to note that the above method is developed to address the general case where more than one processor is supported, e.g., AI coprocessor. In this project the problem is simplified as there is only one processor.

The proposed method also reduces the scheduling time of HEFT when the computation costs are unknown. This is achieved by reducing the number of computation costs required by HEFT and therefore, the number of simulations re-quired/performed. Instead of simulating/running all tasks on all cores (to generate the DAG's computation costs) and then schedule the tasks (by using HEFT), we combine these two phases using an iterative approach; the generation of the DAG's computation costs and the scheduling of the tasks are applied together, in an iterative approach. First, the DAG is generated whose computation costs refer to one core of the reference processor only (ST implementation). Then, the MT implementations are simulated only when necessary and by using a limited number of cores only.

For the rest of this document, we will refer to the aforementioned methods as

Method A. Optimize the scheduling length only.

Method B. Optimize both the scheduling length and the scheduling time (the time needed to obtain the output schedule). Note that Method A achieves better scheduling lengths since the execution time values of all the MT implementations are known and thus processed.

2.2.3 Experimental Setup

The proposed method is evaluated by using 972 different synthetic DAGs. The comparison metric used for evaluating the schedule's length is speedup (Eq. 1) which is computed by dividing the sequential execution time by the parallel execution time (makespan). The sequential execution time is computed by executing all tasks as MT implementations that use all the CPU cores.

$$Speedup = \sum_{t_i \in V} w_{i,f} \qquad (1)$$

where f is the number of the physical CPU cores.

The simulation gain (Eq. 2) is given by dividing the overall number of simulations needed to generate matrix W by the number of simulations performed by our method (simulations).

$$Simulation.gain = \frac{CPU.cores \times tasks}{simulations} \qquad (2)$$

To generate the DAGs, we used the synthetic DAG generation program Daggen [16] with five different parameters defining the DAG's shape:

- n: number of DAG nodes. Four different values are used n = (50, 100, 200, 300).
- fat: this parameter affects the height and the width of the DAG. The width of the DAG is the maximum number of tasks that can be executed concurrently. A small value will lead to a thin DAG with low task parallelism, whereas a large value induces a fat DAG with a high degree of parallelism. The following fat values are used fat = (0.2, 0.5, 0.8).
- density: determines the number of edges between two levels of the DAG, with a low value leading to few edges and a large value leading to many edges, density = (0.2, 0.5, 0.8).
- regularity: the regularity determines the uniformity of the number of tasks in each level. A low value indicates that levels contain dissimilar numbers of tasks, whereas a high value indicates that all levels contain similar numbers of tasks, regularity = (0.2, 0.5, 0.8).
- jump: indicates that an edge can go from level l to level l+jump, jump = (1, 2, 4).

To obtain the random computation and communication costs, the following parameters have been used β_w (range percentage of computation costs among different tasks): A high value implies wider computation costs among tasks while a low value implies narrower costs. β_w = (0.5, 1, 1.5). In Eq. 3, w is the average computation cost of the DAG and is selected randomly.

$$\overline{w} \times \left(1 - \frac{\beta_w}{2}\right) \leq w_{t,p_{ref},1} \leq \overline{w} \times \left(1 + \frac{\beta_w}{2}\right) \qquad (3)$$

The communication cost of the tasks is zero as all the tasks run on the same CPU. The runnables data are stored into the CPU's main memory (or cache) and thus the cost of sending/receiving data among runnables is assumed zero. All the above parameters give 972 DAGs.

2.2.4 Experimental Results

The results are illustrated by using boxplots in Matlab. On each box, the central red line indicates the median value, the displayed value shows the mean, and the bottom and top edges of the box indicate the 25th and 75th percentiles, respectively. The whiskers extend to the most extreme data points not considered outliers, and the outliers are plotted individually using the '+' symbol.

Results for Method A. The default HEFT algorithm assumes rigid (non-moldable) tasks, and thus, HEFT does not support multi-threaded tasks. Therefore, to better evaluate and compare the method to be used in this project, we have implemented HEFT using either ST CPU implementations (SHEFT) only or max-threaded CPU implementations (MHEFT) only.

The three methods are evaluated using 960 random DAGs and 8 CPU cores (Fig. 4). Although not shown here, the higher the number of CPU cores the better the MHEFT behaves over SHEFT, since in SHEFT more cores remain idle when the number of cores is high. SHEFT achieves better performance than MHEFT in most cases, but this depends on the shape of the DAG. The proposed method achieves significant makespan gains. Note that compared to SHEFT, the proposed method's smallest gain values are higher than one in most cases.

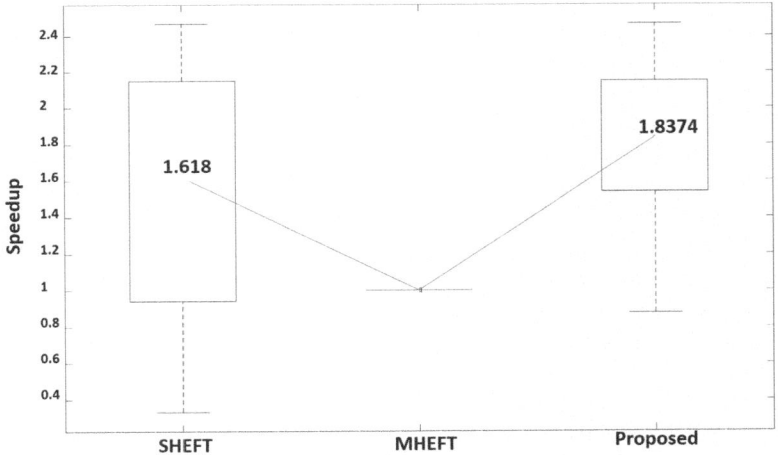

Fig. 4. Evaluation of Method A for 960 random DAGs (8 CPU cores).

Results for Method B. In Method B, the makespan gain is slightly lower compared to Method A (Fig. 5), as in Method A all the execution time values of the MT implementations are known and thus being used to find a better solution. However, in Method B, there are x7 fewer simulations (on average, only 1.14 binaries are run to find their execution times, per runnable). Although not shown here, as in Method A, the higher the number of the CPU cores, the higher the makespan gain over SHEFT and MHEFT.

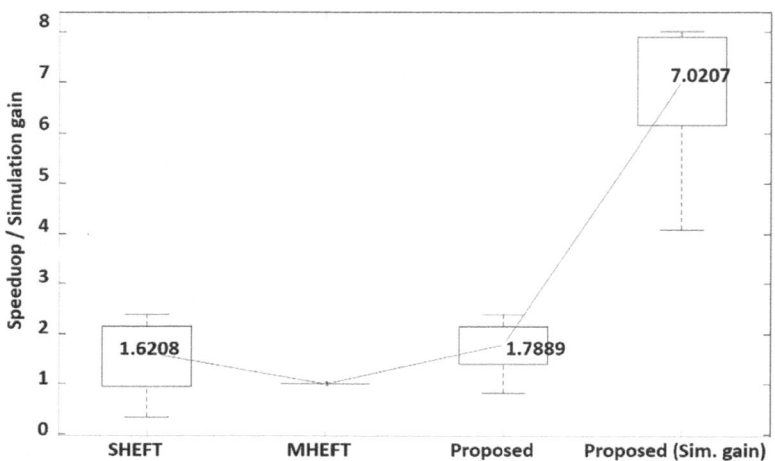

Fig. 5. Evaluation of Method B for 960 random DAGs (8 CPU cores).

2.3 SWC Scheduler

2.3.1 SWC Scheduler Problem Formulation

The HEFT Scheduler described in Sect. 2.2 was responsible for scheduling the runnables within the SWCs based on the number of processors employed and the cache configuration selected. In this way, alternative implementations are provided for each SWC based on these parameters. SWC Scheduling has to be performed according to the system specifications i.e., deadlines that have to be met. This level of scheduling depends heavily on the system resources (e.g., number of available processors) and the selected SWC implementation among the ones provided by the HEFT scheduler for each SWC. To schedule the SWCs, the popular Earliest Dead-line First (EDF) algorithm [17] is extended to support additional features. The classic EDF algorithm is optimal, provided the system has a single-core processor and task preemption is allowed. However, in XANDAR project, a) the hardware target platform consists of a multi-core processor, b) preemption of the SWCs is not allowed in order to avoid task switching overhead and c) the selection of the appropriate implementation for each SWC has also to be tackled efficiently at the input of the SWC Scheduler.

The resource model is the same as the one specified in Subsect. 2.2.1. The workflow model differs in a way where a) the graph is cyclic, b) each node is also associated with a period (each node is repeated periodically) and a deadline. This problem is the static scheduling of a number of periodic SWCs with deadlines on a homogenous multicore processor, where each SWC is assumed moldable (a SWC can be executed by different number of CPU cores).

2.3.2 Proposed SWC Scheduler Architecture

The EDF algorithm is extended (based on [18]) to support multiple CPU cores and additional features such as CPU affiliation and hypervisor partition sharing from multiple SWCs. The proposed EDF scheduler is responsible for scheduling the SWCs on a multi-core system and meeting their deadlines as they are determined by the application specifications. The HEFT scheduler of the SWC runnables generates the DAG graph description of the SWCs in a special text file format that will serve as input to the SWC EDF Scheduler. In this text file the worst execution and the release times and the deadline of each SWC is determined. Moreover, the hypervisor partition that will implement this SWC is also defined. Since each SWC can be implemented with a number of alternative implementations examined by the HEFT scheduler, the features (e.g., processors required, cache configuration, execution time, etc.) of these implementations are also listed within the text file that serves as input to the EDF Scheduler. Two SWCs may share the same partition if they have many common data structures that would introduce large communication overhead if they had to be transferred between different partitions. Implementing more than one SWC with the same partition implies that both of them have to be scheduled on the same processor core (CPU affiliation).

An example DAG graph with 6 SWCs, is shown in Fig. 6. In this figure only the release times and the deadlines of the SWCs appear at the bottom of each SWC. However, each SWC may have multiple alternative implementations requiring different number of processor and these implementations are defined at the stage of the HEFT scheduler. The SWC EDF scheduler also needs as input a map of the SWCs to implementations. SWC Scheduling results may be quite different according to the selected implementation of each SWC. The application developer is responsible of selecting the appropriate mapping of SWC to implementations. Let's assume that the list of SWC implementations is ordered in descending execution times. If there is some kind of cost associated to each implementation, then it makes sense to assume that the list of implementations is ordered e.g., in ascending cost. Otherwise there would be no reason to include in this list, implementations that are both most expensive and worse in terms of execution time. The cost of each implementation may have to do with cache complexity, number of required processors, power consumption, etc.

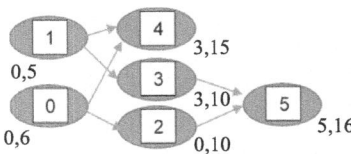

Fig. 6. Example SWC DAG graph with the release time and deadline of each SWC.

Mapping SWCs to appropriate implementations can be a trivial problem if the lower cost implementations are selected first to see if the deadlines are met. If they are not met then, some SWC implementations should be replaced with higher speed and cost SWCs. A trivial way to find the optimal solution, is the testing of all possible combinations but this may introduce a large overhead especially if the number of SWCs and their implementations is high. Another trivial way is to test the medians of the SWC implementation lists and if deadlines are still not met, then to use the faster and most expensive ones. Mapping SWCs to implementations is generally an optimization problem that can be solved fast using heuristics but this problem is out of the scope of this work. Other inputs of the SWC EDF Scheduler are the number of available processor cores and the overall DAG graph period P. The execution of SWCs in the DAG graphs is assumed to be repeated periodically every P, time units. Sporadic tasks can be modelled by switching to different DAG graphs and different scheduling plans.

Algorithm 1. Extended EDF Scheduling algorithm

1. Initialization:
    - Copy SWC implementations LET times to current execution time vector CEX
    - Current time t=0
2. Let S be the set of SWCs s_i that can be scheduled at time t (started in previous time frame, or have RT(s_i)≤t).
3. New frame F duration t_F=min(DL(S)). Update current time to the end of new frame t=t+t_F.
4. Assign frames already started in frame F-1 but not finished yet to their old CPUs
5. If available CPU cores f>0
    Select SWC_j not already assigned to a CPU with s_j=argmin{DL(S')}, where S' is S without the SWCs already assigned to CPUs
    Else goto 8
6. If CPUs required by s_j, f_j≤f
    assign s_j to f_j free CPUs.
    f=f-f_j
    else examine s_j scheduling in next time frame
7. Goto 5
8. Reduce CEX of s_j of the SWCs assigned in this current frame F by t_F:
    CEX(s_j)=CEX(s_j)-t_F.
    If CEX(s_j)==0 AND t>DL(s_j) then FAILURE to meet s_j deadline
9. If ∃ s_j, with CEX(sj)>0 goto 2

The scheduling algorithm does not determine the processor core where different time segments (as the ones defined in [18]) of a single SWC will be executed. Therefore, a CPU assignment takes place after the first EDF-based scheduling takes place. This step is the one that differentiates the developed SWC Scheduler from an ordinary non-preemptive EDF Scheduler. In this step, the following factors have to be taken into consideration: (a) SWCs already started should continue their execution on the same processor cores that were initially allocated, (b) SWCs belonging to the same partition with other SWCs already executed on a processor should also be executed on the same processor (CPU affiliation). Factors (a) and (b) should also be valid for multithread (multicore) SWCs. A more detailed description of the SWC Scheduler appears in Algorithm 1.

2.3.3 SWC Scheduler – Experimental Results

Using the example defined by the DAG graph of Fig. 6 with SWC execution times equal to 5, 3, 3, 4, 5, 1, respectively, two cases are tested with 2 and 4 processor cores. The scheduling is successful even with 2 processor cores. SWC 1 and 3 had been defined to share the same hyper-visor partition and therefore they are both executed on CPU0.

The second use case is a real Avionics application. The behavioral description of Fig. 7 is translated into the SWC EDF Scheduler input. The descriptive SWC component names are translated into SWC identities (SWC "cas" and "postprocessing" are implemented with 3 and 2 SWCs, respectively, sharing the same hypervisor partition). The higher complexity of this use case stems from the fact that all SWCs have multi-thread (and thus, multicore) alternative implementations. Moreover, many SWCs share the same partition as already mentioned. Non-zero release times also pose additional restrictions. A deadline of 200 time units is used as the DAG graph period P and f = 8 processors. If the slowest SWC implementations are selected for the SWCs and in this case the output scheduling plan is unacceptable since SWC 9 ends at time 201 > P (Fig. 8a). If the fastest SWC implementations are used, then we get the results of Fig. 8b which is an acceptable scheduling plan for this application. Moreover, all the restrictions in the number of processors and the partitions required for the implementation of each SWC are preserved. In both the two use cases examined, the developed SWC EDF Scheduler operates according to its specifications and leads to optimal scheduling plans.

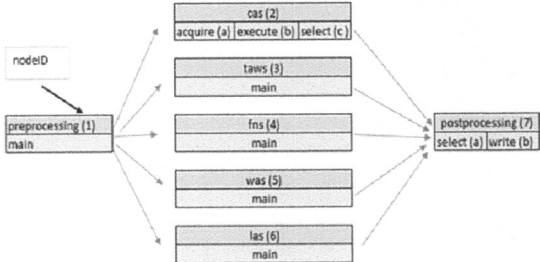

Fig. 7. Avionics use case and its description as SWC EDF Scheduler input with 10 nodes.

2.4 XNG Hypervisor File Generator

The realization of the EDF-based SWC scheduling described in the previous section can be performed on real hardware platforms with the aid of the Fentiss XNG hypervisor. All the scheduling parameters including starting/ending, execution times of the SWCs, number of CPU cores used per SWC, etc. are taken into consideration in order to schedule the SWCs on the right hardware resources and on the right time slots. In Fig. 9, the overall flow is depicted. Each SWC is implemented as a different XNG hypervisor partition (Chapter 5 of [4]). The duration of the Major Frame (MAF) can be selected equal to the DAG period P. A MAF is common to all physical CPUs but can be split to different partition windows in each thread. Partitions can be assigned to different Virtual CPUs on the same physical CPU.

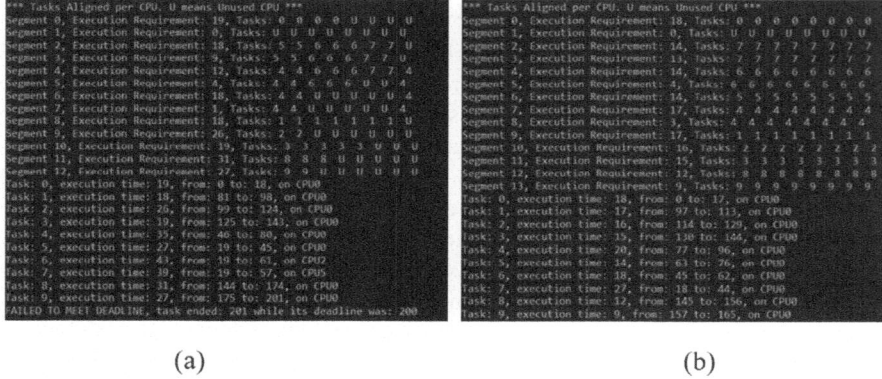

Fig. 8. SWC EDF scheduling results for SWC mapping to the slowest implementations (a) and the fastest implementations (b).

XNG requires a number of configuration XML and C files in order to generate an executable image that can be deployed on the target platform. For this reason, an XML configuration and C file generator is developed. The generated XML and C files are compiled and the image file: sys_img.elf is generated. This image file can be deployed on the target platform: Zedboard with Xilinx Zynq7000 two-core FPGA. More powerful FPGAs like ZynqMP Ultrascale (ZCU102 board) with 6 ARM cores can be supported with no major modifications on the side of the schedulers and the XNG hypervisor file generator.

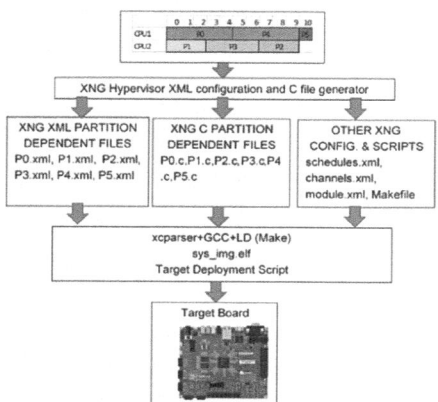

Fig. 9. XNG Hypervisor File Generator flow.

In the context of this work, the XNG Hypervisor File Generator was tested on a Zed-boad target with a restricted number of processors equal to 2. Deploying the SWC EDF scheduling plans on a target board can either be used to realize the full application if the functionality of the initial SWCs is copied in the template C and XML files generated by the XNG File Generator. Alternatively, the skeleton C/XML files can be directly compiled and deployed on the target board to evaluate a scheduling plan on a real environment and measure the deviations from the theoretical SWC start/end times estimated by the SWC EDF Scheduler. For the verification of these SWC start/end times, the XNG Hypervisor system time is queried at the begin and the end of each SWC. The timestamps retrieved can be printed through the Zedboard serial console. However, this poses a significant delay that in real applications can be comparable to the execution time and the deadline of a SWC. Moreover, when SWCs from different processors are trying to print their messages through the common serial port these messages are scrambled. Hence, large time units of 1 s have been used in order to make sure that the delay for printing messages will be much smaller than the SWC execution time and the possibility to get scrambled messages is small. In the examples tested on the target Zedboard platform there was an offset in the SWC start/end times slightly higher than 6ms. The scheduled SWC LET times had an average deviation of 2.5ms. Part of this time deviation is owed to the hypervisor calls needed to get the system time. However, they can be taken into consideration in order to develop robust applications with predictable behavior.

3 Conclusions

The goal of the XANDAR EU-funded project was to deliver a model-based toolchain following the X-by-Construction (XbC) paradigm targeting to reduce both cost and errors in the design of safety-critical systems. This article presents the XbC backend of the project that is responsible for performing the scheduling and mapping activities of the runnable and software components, the code-optimization and code parallelization techniques as well as the generation of the hypervisor configuration files that are customized for the target multicore platform. The developed XbC backend was shown capable of addressing the requirements posed by the use-cases of the project.

Acknowledgments. This study was funded by European Union's Horizon 2020 (grant number 957210).

References

1. XANDAR EU-funded project. https://xandar-project.eu/. Accessed 27 March 2024
2. XANDAR. Deliverable D1.5: Use Case Design and Development Report
3. Masing, L., Dörr, T., et al.: XANDAR: exploiting the X-by-Construction paradigm in model-based development of safety-critical systems. In: Proceedings of the Design, Automation & Test in Europe Conference & Exhibition, Virtual (2022)
4. FentISS. Software user manual, XNG hypervisor., Reference: 14–033.009.sum.08-r18617
5. FentISS. Software user manual, XNG ARMv7A-VMSA-TZ extension, Reference: 14–033.082.sum.04-r18615. Publication date: 25/05/2021
6. PLUTO - An automatic parallelizer and locality optimizer for affine loop nests. https://pluto-compiler.sourceforge.net/. Accessed 21 Feb 2024

7. Topcuouglu, H., Hariri, S., Wu, M-Y.: Performance-effective and low-complexity task scheduling for heterogeneous computing. IEEE Trans. Parallel Distrib. Syst. **13**(3), 260–274 (2002)
8. Saifullah, A., Ferry, D., Li, J., Agrawal, K., Lu, C., Gill, C.D.: Parallel real-time scheduling of DAGs. IEEE Trans. Parallel Distrib. Syst. **25**(12), 3242–3252 (2014). https://doi.org/10.1109/TPDS.2013.22979192014
9. Kelefouras, V., Djemame, K., Keramidas, G., Voros, N.: An analytical model for loop tiling transformation. embedded computer systems: architectures. In: Modeling, and Simulation Proceedings, pp. 95–107. Springer Nature. ISBN 9783031045790 2022 (2021)
10. Kelefouras, V., Djemame, K., Keramidas G., Voros, N.: A Methodology for Efficient Tile Size Selection for Affine Loop Kernels. International Journal of Parallel Programming, 50 (3–4). 405–432 (2022). ISSN 0091-7036
11. PolyBench/C the Polyhedral Benchmark suite. https://web.cse.ohio-state.edu/~pouchet.2/software/polybench/. Accessed 27 March 2024
12. Beaumont, O., Boudet, V., Rastello F., Robert, Y.: Matrix multiplication on heterogeneous platforms. IEEE Trans. Parallel Distrib. Syst. (2001)
13. Arabnejad, H., Barbosa, J.G.: List scheduling algorithm for heterogeneous systems by an optimistic cost table. IEEE Trans. Parallel Distrib. Syst. **25**(3), 682–694 (2014). https://doi.org/10.1109/TPDS.2013.57
14. Daoud, M.I., Kharma, N.: A high performance algorithm for static task scheduling in heterogeneous distributed computing systems. J. Parallel Distrib. Comput. **68**(4), 399–409 (2008). https://doi.org/10.1016/j.jpdc.2007.05.015
15. Bleuse, R., Hunold, S., Kedad-Sidhoum, S., Monna, F., Mounié, G., Trystram, D.: Scheduling independent moldable tasks on multi-cores with GPUs. IEEE Trans. Parallel Distrib. Syst. **28**(9), 2689–2702 (2017). https://doi.org/10.1109/tpds.2017.26758912017
16. Baskiyar, S., SaiRanga, P.: Scheduling directed a-cyclic task graphs on heterogeneous network of workstations to minimize schedule length. In: International Conference Parallel Processing Workshops, https://doi.org/10.1109/ICPPW.2003.1240359 (Nov 2003)
17. Kruk, Ł., Lehoczky, J., Ramanan, K., Shreve, S.: Heavy traffic analysis for EDF queues with reneging. Ann. Appl. Probab. **21**(2) (2011)
18. Short, M.: Improved task management techniques for enforcing EDF scheduling on recurring tasks. In 16th IEEE Real-Time and Embedded Technology and Applications Symposium Proceedings, pp. 56–65. https://doi.org/10.1109/RTAS.2010.22

Author Index

A
Adamopoulou, Evgenia II-179
Adhikary, Asmita II-139
Agosta, Giovanni II-231
Alexakis, Theodoros II-179
Ali Khan, Asif I-230
Ali, Muhammad II-59
Aliagha, Ensieh II-59
Almeeva, Liliia I-199
Altenberg, Jan II-47
Altmeyer, Sebastian I-1
Amerini, Irene II-231
Antache, Marius II-215
Antonescu, Mihai II-215
Apostolopoulos, Dimitris II-203
Armeniakos, Giorgos I-155
Avramopoulos, Hercules II-203
Axinte, Cristian-Tiberius II-215

B
Barenghi, Alessandro II-191
Baroni, Andrea I-199
Batina, Lejla II-139
Bereholschi, Leonard David I-230
Blume, Holger I-138, I-167
Bortoloti, Matheus I-183
Brandner, Florian I-18
Bringmann, Oliver I-59
Brokalakis, Andreas II-165
Buhan, Ileana II-139
Buiu, Octavian II-215
Burrello, Alessio I-46

C
C. Papadopoulos, Nikolaos II-119
Carro, Luigi I-216
Chen, Jian-Jia I-230
Chen, Kuan-Hsun I-230
Chen, Yizhi I-76, II-109
Christou, George II-152
Ciobanu, Cătălin Bogdan II-215

Collignon, Alexander Marc II-1
Costinescu, Simona II-215
Cristian Trusca, Petre II-215

D
Daghero, Francesco I-46
Daskalakis, Emmanouil II-179
de Moura, Rafael Fão I-216
Di Giamberardino, Mauro II-231
Ditu, Bogdan II-215
Drîmbărean, Alexandru II-215

E
Elnashar, Mahmoud II-59

F
Fawzi, Haitham S. I-34
Fernandez Salgado, Javier II-247
Fioravanti, Massimo II-231
Fornaciari, William II-231

G
Gallo, Luigi II-231
Gâlmeanu, Honorius II-215
Georgopoulos, Konstantinos II-165
Gesper, Sven I-167
Gheorghe, Cristian II-215
Giannoulis, Giannis II-203
Gietz, Jonathan I-59
Giuseppetti, Paolo II-231
Göhringer, Diana II-59, II-72
Gologanu, Mihai II-215
Grelck, Clemens I-1
Grosu, Daniel II-215
Güdemann, Matthias I-122

H
Hager-Clukas, Andreas I-108
Herkersdorf, Andreas I-34, I-93
Holzinger, Philipp II-72

Author Index

Homann, Jasper I-167
Hübner, Michael II-72

I
Iliadis, Thrasyvoulos II-119
Ioannidis, Sotiris II-152, II-165
Iskandar, Veronia II-72

J
Jackson, Carl Alexander II-1
Jahić, Jasmin I-183
Jahier Pagliari, Daniele I-46
Jalier, Camille I-93
Jordan, Michael I-216
Jouvelot, Pierre I-18
Jung, Alexander Louis-Ferdinand I-59
Jung, Andreas II-247
Jung, Matthias II-32, II-72

K
Kelefouras, V. II-261
Keramidas, G. II-261
Knödtel, Johannes I-199
Koci, Kejsi II-215
Köhler, Daniel I-138, I-167
Kosmidis, Leonidas II-127, II-247
Krahl, Markus I-122
Krstić, Miloš I-199
Krumke, Sven O. II-32
Kumar, Akash II-99
Kyriakakis, Thomas II-165
Kyriazi, Evrydiki II-203

L
Lenke, Oliver I-34
Lentaris, George I-155, II-203
Lobe, Elisabeth II-32
López Castillón, Pau II-247
Lu, Zhonghai I-76, II-109
Lübeck, Konstantin I-59

M
Macii, Enrico I-46
Madsen, Jan II-1, II-17
Maiano, Luca II-231
Manca, Federico II-85
Maria Trompouki, Matina II-247
Mauerer, Wolfgang II-32
Maurer, Florian I-34

Mavropoulos, M. II-261
Meidinger, Michael I-34
Meinl, Frank I-138, I-167
Memmi, Gérard I-18
Miedema, Lukas I-1
Miteloudi, Konstantina II-139
Moisă, Cosmin II-215
Moise, Vasile-Mădălin II-215
Morianos, Ioannis II-165
Muñoz Hernandez, Hector Gerardo II-72
Munteanu, Mihai II-215

N
Nemeti, Csaba II-215
Nikas, Kostantinos II-119
Nolte, Lars I-93
Novobilsky, Petr I-1

P
P. Katsikas, Georgios II-203
Palumbo, Francesca II-85
Papa, Lorenzo II-231
Papalamprou, Ilias I-155, II-203
Payá-Vayá, Guillermo I-167, I-246
Pedol, Mario II-231
Pedrajas Pérez, Josué II-127
Pelosi, Gerardo II-191
Peppes, Nikolaos II-179
Pernigotto, Manuel II-231
Petrellis, N. II-261
Pezzarossa, Luca II-1, II-17
Pimentel, Andy D. I-1
Pnevmatikatos, Dionisios II-119
Poncino, Massimo I-46
Popovici, Alexandru-Tudor II-215
Pro, Francesco II-231
Puşcaşu, Alexandru II-215

R
Radonjic, K. II-261
Ratto, Francesco II-85
Reichenbach, Marc I-199, II-72
Reiser, Daniel I-199
Rotar, Dănuţ II-215
Rufart Blasco, Eric II-247

S
Sachian, Mari-Anais II-215
Sapra, Dolly I-1

Satta, Paolo II-231
Schaffner, Tobias II-47
Schröter, Jonathan I-108
Schroth, Christof II-32
Seidlitz, Germain I-246
Serbu, Vlad-Gabriel II-215
Servadei, Lorenzo II-99
Shi, Jiyuan I-93
Solé Bonet, Marc II-127
Solinas, Alessandro II-231
Soudris, Dimitrios I-155, II-203
Sponner, Max II-99
Stan, Andrei II-215
Steiner, Lukas II-72
Steinmetz, Jannik I-59
Stratakos, Ioannis I-155, II-203
Suciu, George II-215
Surhonne, Anmol I-34
Svendsen, Winnie Edith II-17

T
Tanev, Georgi II-17
Thieu, Gia Bao I-167
Toumasis, Panagiotis II-203
Trompouki, Matina Maria II-127
Trovini, Giovanni II-231
Tudor, Cristina II-215
Twardzik, Tim I-93

U
Uleru, George-Iulian II-215

V
Vaddina, Kameswar Rao I-18
Valadasis, Alexandros II-203
van Drueten, Niels II-139
Vasiliadis, Giorgos II-152
Vest Madsen, Joel August II-1
Voros, N. II-261

W
Wallentowitz, Stefan I-108, I-122, II-47
Waschneck, Bernd II-99
Wehn, Norbert II-72
Weißbrich, Moritz I-246
Wen, Jianan I-199
Wild, Thomas I-34, I-93
Wille, Robert II-99

Y
Yayla, Mikail I-230

Z
Zarras, Apostolis II-152
Zhu, Wenyao I-76, II-109

The manufacturer's authorised representative in the EU is Springer Nature Customer Service Centre GmbH, Europaplatz 3, 69115 Heidelberg, Germany. If you have any concerns regarding our products, please contact ProductSafety@springernature.com

Printed and bound by CPI Group (UK) Ltd, Croydon, CR0 4YY

26/03/2026

02078968-0005